9th Workshop on Slavic Natural Language Processing (SlavicNLP 2023)

Dubrovnik, Croatia
6 May 2023

ISBN: 978-1-7138-7379-2

Printed from e-media with permission by:

Curran Associates, Inc.
57 Morehouse Lane
Red Hook, NY 12571

Some format issues inherent in the e-media version may also appear in this print version.

Printed with permission by Curran Associates, Inc. (2023)

Association for Computational Linguistics
209 N. Eighth Street
Stroudsburg, Pennsylvania 18360

Phone: 1-570-476-8006
Fax: 1-570-476-0860

acl@aclweb.org

Additional copies of this publication are available from:

Curran Associates, Inc.
57 Morehouse Lane
Red Hook, NY 12571 USA
Phone: 845-758-0400
Fax: 845-758-2633
Email: curran@proceedings.com
Web: www.proceedings.com

EACL 2023

The 9th Workshop on Slavic Natural Language Processing 2023

Proceedings of the Workshop (SlavicNLP 2023)

May 6, 2023

Introduction

This volume contains the papers presented at SlavNLP 2023: the 9th Workshop on Natural Language Processing (NLP) for Slavic Languages. The workshop is organized by ACL SIGSLAV, the Special Interest Group of the Association for Computational Linguistics on NLP for Slavic Languages.

The SlavNLP / BSNLP workshops have been convening for over fifteen years, with a clear vision and purpose. On one hand, the languages from the Slavic group play an important role due to their widespread use and diverse cultural heritage. These languages are spoken by about one-third of all speakers of the official languages of the European Union, and by over 400 million speakers worldwide.

The current political and economic developments in Central and Eastern Europe—the foremost of which is the invasion of Ukraine by Russia—place the societies where Slavic languages are spoken at the center of events of global importance. Rapid technological advancement is urgently needed to help societies deal with massive flows of information—including counteracting the impact of disinformation, propaganda, etc.

On the other hand, despite the rapid growth of European consumer markets, research on theoretical and applied NLP in these languages still lags behind the "major" languages. In comparison to English, which has dominated the digital world since the advent of the Internet, many of these languages still lack resources, processing tools and applications—especially those with smaller communities of speakers.

The Slavic languages pose a wealth of fascinating scientific challenges. The linguistic phenomena specific to the Slavic languages—complex morphology and free word order—present non-trivial problems for the construction of NLP tools, and require rich morphological and syntactic resources.

The SlavNLP workshop brings together researchers in NLP for Slavic languages from academia and industry. We aim to stimulate research, foster the creation of tools and the dissemination of new results. The workshop serves as a forum for the exchange of ideas and experience and for discussing shared problems. One fascinating aspect of Slavic languages is their structural similarity, as well as an easily recognizable lexical and inflectional inventory spanning the entire group, which—despite the lack of mutual intelligibility—creates a special environment in which researchers can fully appreciate the shared problems and solutions.

In order to stimulate research and collaboration further, we have organized the fourth SIGSLAV Challenge: a Shared Task on multilingual named entity recognition (NER). Due to rich inflection, free word order, derivation, and other phenomena present in the Slavic languages, work on named entities is a challenging task.

Fostering research and development on the problems of named entities—detecting mentions of names, lemmatization (normalization), classification, and cross-lingual matching—is crucial for cross-lingual information access and for the wider use of NLP in Slavic languages. This edition of the challenge covers three languages: Czech, Polish, and Russian, building on the data from the second and the third editions of the shared task, which covered six languages: Bulgarian, Czech, Polish, Russian, Slovene, and Ukrainian. It covers five types of named entities: persons, locations, organizations, events, and products.

This year the workshop received 26 regular submissions, of which we selected 9 for oral presentation and 9 for poster presentation. Two additional presentations were based on ACL Findings papers, published by EACL separately. These papers cover a wide range of topics in NLP for various Slavic languages. Seven teams registered to participate in the NER Challenge, of which three submitted results, and two submitted additional papers with descriptions of their NER systems. These papers are also included in this volume, and their work is discussed in the special session dedicated to the NER Challenge.

This workshop's presentation—the regular Workshop papers and the Shared Task Challenge—cover at least ten Slavic languages: Bosnian, Bulgarian, Croatian, Czech, Montenegrin, Polish, Russian, Serbian, Slovene, and Ukrainian.

This workshop continues the proud tradition established by the earlier BSNLP workshops, which were held in conjunction with the following venues:

- ACL 2007 Conference in Prague, Czech Republic.

- IIS 2009: Intelligent Information Systems, in Kraków, Poland.
- TSD 2011: 14th International Conference on Text, Speech and Dialogue in Plzeň, Czech Republic.
- ACL 2013 Conference in Sofia, Bulgaria.
- RANLP 2015 Conference in Hissar, Bulgaria.
- EACL 2017 Conference in Valencia, Spain.
- ACL 2019 Conference in Florence, Italy.
- EACL 2021 Conference in Kyiv, Ukraine.

We hope that this work will help stimulate further growth of our rich and exciting field.

The SlavNLP Organizers: Michał Marcińczuk, Preslav Nakov, Maciej Ogrodniczuk, Jakub Piskorski, Senja Pollak, Pavel Přibáň, Piotr Rybak, Josef Steinberger, Roman Yangarber

Organizing Committee

Workshop Organizer

Jakub Piskorski, Polish Academy of Sciences
Michał Marcińczuk, Wroclaw University of Science and Technology, Samurai Labs
Preslav Nakov, Mohamed bin Zayed University of Artificial Intelligence
Maciej Ogrodniczuk, Polish Academy of Sciences
Senja Pollak, Jožef Stefan Institute
Pavel Přibáň, University of West Bohemia
Piotr Rybak, Polish Academy of Sciences
Josef Steinberger, University of West Bohemia
Roman Yangarber, University of Helsinki

Program Committee

Program Committee

Željko Agić, Unity Technologies
Bogdan Babych, Heidelberg University
Radovan Garabík, Ľ. Štúr Institute of Linguistics, Slovak Academy of Sciences
Milos Jakubicek, Lexical Computing
Olha Kanishcheva, University of Jena
Anisia Katinskaia, University of Helsinki
Cvetana Krstev, University of Belgrade, Faculty of Philology
Vladislav Kubon, Charles University
Petya Osenova, Sofia University St. Kl. Ohridskiand IICT-BAS
Alexander Panchenko, Skolkovo Institue of Science and Technology
Maciej Piasecki, Wroclaw University of Science and Technology
Lidia Pivovarova, University of Helsinki
Pavel Přibáň, University of West Bohemia, Faculty of Applied Sciences
Marko Robnik-šikonja, University of Ljubljana, Faculty of Computer and Information Science
Alexandr Rosen, Charles University, Prague
Agata Savary, Paris-Saclay University
Serge Sharoff, University of Leeds
Josef Steinberger, University of West Bohemia
Marko Tadić, University of Zagreb, Faculty of Humanities and Social Sciences
Marcin Woliński, Institute of Computer Science, Polish Academy of Sciences

Table of Contents

Named Entity Recognition for Low-Resource Languages - Profiting from Language Families

Sunna Torge[*†], **Andrei Politov**[*], **Christoph Lehmann**[*], **Bochra Saffar** and **Ziyan Tao**
TU Dresden, Center for Information Services and High Performance Computing (ZIH), Germany
Center for Scalable Data Analytics and Artificial Intelligence (ScaDS.AI) Dresden/Leipzig, Germany
{sunna.torge,andrei.politov,christoph.lehmann}@tu-dresden.de

Abstract

Machine learning drives forward the development in many areas of Natural Language Processing (NLP). Until now, many NLP systems and research are focusing on high-resource languages, i.e. languages for which many data resources exist. Recently, so-called low-resource languages increasingly come into focus. In this context, multi-lingual language models, which are trained on related languages to a target low-resource language, may enable NLP tasks on this low-resource language. In this work, we investigate the use of multi-lingual models for Named Entity Recognition (NER) for low-resource languages. We consider the West Slavic language family and the low-resource languages Upper Sorbian and Kashubian. Three RoBERTa models were trained from scratch, two mono-lingual models for Czech and Polish, and one bi-lingual model for Czech and Polish. These models were evaluated on the NER downstream task for Czech, Polish, Upper Sorbian, and Kashubian, and compared to existing state-of-the-art models such as RobeCzech, HerBERT, and XLM-R. The results indicate that the mono-lingual models perform better on the language they were trained on, and both the mono-lingual and language family models outperform the large multi-lingual model in downstream tasks. Overall, the study shows that low-resource West Slavic languages can benefit from closely related languages and their models.

1 Introduction

The success of recent large language models such as the GPTX-family (Brown et al., 2020) is due to a vast amount of training data and the availability of appropriate compute resources which allow to train these models. However, the availability of training data varies extremely between the languages of the world. High-resource languages such as English allow to train language models, performing impressively well on a variety of NLP tasks (Liu et al., 2019), whereas for the majority of the languages these large corpora are not available and thus, the same training concept does not necessarily yield well performing language models. This imbalance is addressed by multi-lingual models and transfer learning approaches.

Large multi-lingual language models such as XLM-R (Conneau et al., 2020) are trained on text data in 100 different languages and show good results on a variety of NLP downstream tasks in different languages, like e.g. Named Entity Recognition (NER) in German. However, there are many low-resource languages in the world, which are still not covered by these commonly available language models due to the lack of a reasonable amount of training data. This problem is addressed by different transfer learning approaches. One approach considers language families and the transfer based on the similarities of the languages of the same family (de Vries et al., 2021). In this case, the small amount of training data can partly be compensated by the similarities of the languages within the family. While training multi-lingual language models on languages from the same family, the training process profits from a larger amount of training data and from structural similarities of the languages at the same time.

In contrast to the training of multi-lingual language models, Ostendorff and Rehm (2023) consider the transfer from large language models for high-resource languages to large language models for lower-resource languages based on the overlapping vocabulary. In this approach, a large language model for a high-resource language (HRL) is used together with a small language model for a lower-resource language (LRL) in order to initiate the training of a large language model for LRL. This approach yields promising results and extensions to other language pairs which need to be investi-

[*] These authors contributed equally.
[†] Corresponding author.

Proceedings of the 9th Workshop on Slavic Natural Language Processing 2023 (SlavicNLP 2023), pages 1–10
May 6, 2023

gated. However, as this approach is based on an overlapping vocabulary, language families are of special interest.

In this paper, we present investigations on the West Slavic language family. The aim of this work was to assess the possibilities for low-resource languages like Upper Sorbian (Howson, 2017) and Kashubian (Nomachi, 2019) to profit from language models from the same language family. For this reason, we trained mono-lingual and multi-lingual language models from the same language familiy and evaluated them on the downstream task NER. Since there are several publicly available mono-lingual language models for slavic languages (Tikhonov et al., 2022), for comparison we evaluated some of them on the same downstream task.

Our contributions are as follows. We consider the languages Czech (cs), Polish (pl), Upper Sorbian (hsb), and Kashubian (csb), all being members of the West Slavic language family (Sussex and Cubberley, 2006). We trained three RoBERTa models (Liu et al., 2019) from scratch, two mono-lingual models for Czech and Polish respectively and one bi-lingual model for Czech and Polish, based on the Czech and Polish subset of the OSCAR data set (Abadji et al., 2022). For model evaluation, we used the downstream task, Named Entity Recognition (NER), as described in (Rahimi et al., 2019) and the corresponding wikiann dataset. We evaluated the three RoBERTa models on Czech and Polish NER and on Upper Sorbian and Kashubian NER. For comparison, we also considered existing SOTA mono- and multi-lingual models, namely the Czech RoBERTa model RobeCzech[1] (Straka et al., 2021), the Polish BERT model HerBERT[2] (Mroczkowski et al., 2021), and the multi-lingual RoBERTa model XLM-R[3] (Conneau et al., 2020), and evaluated them on Czech and Polish NER and on Upper Sorbian and Kashubian NER.

2 Related work

In de Vries et al. (2021), the impact of language families on low-resource languages was investigated. The authors used mono-lingual BERT models (source languages English, German, Dutch) and the multi-lingual mBERT to show, that linguistic structure can be transferred for the low-resource languages Gronings and West Frisian, which are closely related to the source languages.

A different approach is taken in Ogueji et al. (2021), where a transformer-based model is trained on 11 low-resource African languages belonging to a single language family. This expands the training data corpus by utilizing data within one language family. In contrast, we are interested in detecting those language combinations, which best support dedicated low-resource languages.

There is a variety of Czech and Polish language models available, as shown in Tikhonov et al. (2022). In Straka et al. (2021) RobeCzech, a Czech RoBERTa Model is presented and evaluated on several downstream tasks, including NER using two datasets (Ševčíková et al., 2007; Konkol and Konopík, 2013). A Polish RoBERTa model is described in (Dadas et al., 2020) and evaluated on NER, using the NKJP dataset (Przepiórkowski, 2011). In Mroczkowski et al. (2021) HerBert, a Polish BERT model is presented, trained on six different Polish datasets and evaluated on the NKJP dataset. For several reasons we decided to train models from scratch as baseline models. First, we wanted to compare mono-lingual and multi-lingual language models, which are trained on a subset of the languages of a language family, based on the same training corpora. Our particular focus was on the Sorbian language, which is spoken in a region of Germany adjacent to both Poland and the Czech Republic. As in practice geographic distances between countries, syntactic similarity and syntactic overlap play an important role for transfer learning (de Vries and Nissim, 2021), we wanted to train a czech-polish model. However, for comparison, we considered existing Czech and Polish language models in addition. Secondly, we were interested in performance analysis of distributed model training on our HPC infrastructure. These results are beyond the scope of this paper. Evaluating language models on NER is very common. Especially for balto-slavic languages there is a series of work, addressing the shared tasks of the Balto-Slavic NLP workshop series, e.g. (Suppa and Jariabka, 2021; Ljubešić and Lauc, 2021). In Piskorski et al. (2021) results of the last workshop are presented. As a starting point however, we restricted our investigations to NER for only three entites, namely Person, Organisation, and Location.

[1]https://huggingface.co/ufal/robeczech-base
[2]https://huggingface.co/allegro/herbert-base-cased
[3]https://huggingface.co/xlm-roberta-base

	N_D	low_LBP_D	RED_D	Meta_S
pl	443	209	607	10,121
cs	127	98	339	6,689

Table 1: Number of deleted documents and sentences (in thousands) after pre-processing

3 Training of Baseline Models

This investigation considers publicly available pre-trained language models such as RobeCzech, HerBERT and XLM-RoBERTa as well as models trained from scratch. In this section, the setup for training language models from scratch is described, which comprises training data, model architecture, tokenizer and the concrete training process.

3.1 Training Data

For the training of all models, the OSCAR (Open Super-large Crawled ALMAnaCH coRpus) dataset (version 22.01) (Ortiz Suárez et al., 2020; Abadji et al., 2022) was used. The Czech partition of the OSCAR dataset has a size of 58.6 GB, which comprises of 10,381,916 documents, and consists of 5,452,724,456 words. The Polish partition of the OSCAR dataset has a size of 139.0 GB, it comprises of 19,301,137 documents, and consists of 12,584,498,906 words. Before training a language model, we performed some preprocessing steps. Noisy documents, i.e. with high number of punctuation, were deleted. Documents were filtered, based on a low language-belonging probability (LBP) to the Czech and Polish languages respectively. The LBP is part of the meta data of the OSCAR dataset. We set the upper threshold for deletion to 0.6. A de-duplication step was performed in order to get rid of redundant documents. Sentences with less than 30 characters were deleted, as they have a high probability to be the meta data of web pages such as cookies, copy rights, urls etc. Table 1 depicts the deleted information, namely the number of noisy documents (N_D), documents with a low language-belonging probability (low_LBP_D), the redundant documents (RED_D), and the number of meta data sentences (Meta_S).

3.2 Model Architecture and Tokenizer

We used the RoBERTa architecture, a transformer-based architecture (Liu et al., 2019) with 125M parameters, 12 layers, 12 self-attention heads, and 768 hidden size for each of the models, we trained. As usual, models were trained on the masked language model objective. We trained three tokenizers, one each for Czech, Polish, and Czech and Polish, which are based on the Byte-Pair Encoding (BPE) tokenizer (Sennrich et al., 2016). The vocabulary size was set to 52K for each tokenizer, i.e. also for the multi-lingual tokenizer since the languages, both members of the West Slavic language family, are similar, especially in their lexical part. Given the same vocabulary size for each tokenizer, we also chose the same architecture for all models.

Overall, we trained two mono-lingual and one multi-lingual Roberta language models. The used models were trained using the official code released in the huggingface library[4], version 4.18.0. For training the multi-lingual model, the concatenation of the Czech and the Polish subset of the OSCAR dataset was used.

3.3 Training from Scratch of Mono- and Multi-Lingual Language Models

Within the concrete training process, all model weights were randomly initialized. The maximum sequence length was set to 512 tokens. All three models were trained with the same hyperparameters, which are presented in Table 2. We used the AdamW (Loshchilov and Hutter, 2017) optimizer for optimising the cross-entropy loss. The training

	Czech	Polish	Czech-Polish
Optimizer	AdamW		
Grad. acc.	10		
Warmup steps	55,700	75,000	117,000
Steps	1,160,200	1,563,900	2,434,100
Batch size	128		
Epochs	10		
Learning rate	4e-4		
Weight decay	0.01		
Adam β_1	0.9		
Adam β_2	0.98		

Table 2: Hyperparameter setting during training from scratch.

of models was done in a distributed manner on a node equipped with 2x AMD EPYC CPU 7352 (24 cores, multi-threading capable), 1 TB of RAM and 8x NVIDIA A100-SXM4 GPUs (40 GB HBM2 vRAM), in a fully connected intra-node topology (8x8 links, 3rd generation NVLink). We used PyTorch 1.11.0. While training, the data parallelism strategy of PyTorch DistributedDataParallel (DDP) was utilized. The training time for a mono-lingual model was approx. 48 hours. The training time for the multi-lingual model was approx. 100 hours.

[4] https://huggingface.co/roberta-base

During training of the three language models, the loss shows a strong decrease within the first 10% of the calculation steps and afterwards it decreases slowly. This structure remains the same for all three models. Figure 1 depicts the decrease of the cross-entropy loss during the training of the multi-lingual RoBERTa model. The loss is logged every 600 steps, and with gradient accumulation steps set to 10, this results in ≈ 400 data points. The warmup steps and the regularization term (weight decay) prevent the model from overfitting. The

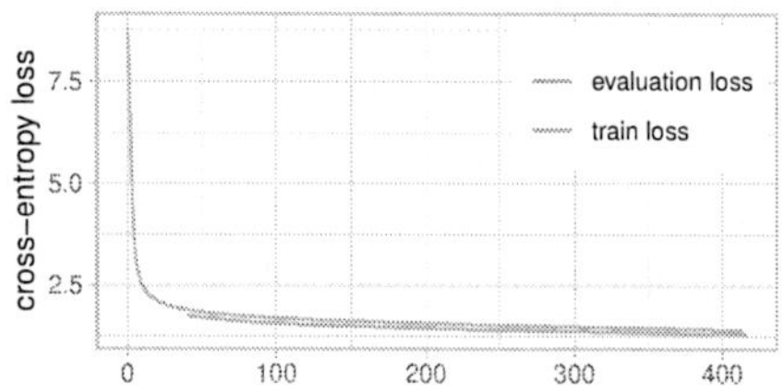

Figure 1: Cross-entropy loss on training (orange) and evaluation data (blue) during training of Czech-Polish LM

cross-entropy loss we obtained after training and evaluation, is shown in Table 3 for each of the trained language models. After this preparation

	Czech	Polish	Czech-Polish
Train loss	1.6	1.46	1.4
Evaluation loss	1.5	1.34	1.3

Table 3: Cross-Entropy Loss after training from scratch for each language model.

phase there are three models available that were trained from scratch.

4 Model Evaluation Results

Throughout the experiments, the main goal is to investigate whether the low-resource languages, Upper Sorbian and Kashubian, can benefit from language models that are trained for closely related higher-resource languages (here: Czech and Polish). Thereby, the experiment is twofold: First, the self-trained (from scratch) mono-lingual models and the multi-lingual language model are evaluated on the downstream task NER wrt the low-resource-languages of interest. Second, there is a further comparison with publicly available pre-trained mono- and multi-lingual language models such as e.g. RobeCzech or XLM-RoBERTa.

	cs	pl	hsb	csb
Train	20,000	20,000	150	150
Test	10,000	10,000	150	150
Size (MB)	9.860	9.764	0.073	0.088

Table 4: Number of sentences in training and test data for each language, Size of each data set (Bytes)

4.1 Evaluation Data

All of our evaluation experiments are based on the WikiANN dataset, which is a multi-lingual NER dataset consisting of Wikipedia articles annotated with LOC (location), PER (person), and ORG (organisation) tags in the IOB2 format. We used the subsets for Czech (cs), Polish (pl), Upper Sorbian (hsb), and Kashubian (csb) of the version (Rahimi et al., 2019). Table 4 depicts the number of sentences for each language and the size of each subset and clearly showing Upper Sorbian (hsb), and Kashubian (csb) as low-resource languages. Exemplary for the Czech language, in Table 5 the class distribution of the Czech wikiann subset is listed, which shows a sufficiently balanced dataset.

Class label	**Number of sentences**
Location	20,956
Organisation	17,938
Person	18,523

Table 5: Class distribution for the Czech wikiann subset.

4.2 Evaluation Setup on NER

In this section the evaluation setup of used models in connection with the wikiann data set is presented.

The following RoBERTa models which were trained from scratch are considered: 1. the mono-lingual models (Czech, Polish) and 2. the multi-lingual language model (Czech-Polish). Furthermore, three existing pretrained models are used, namely: 1. Czech RoBERTa (RobeCzech) (Straka et al., 2021), 2. Polish BERT model (HerBERT) (Mroczkowski et al., 2021), 3. the multi-lingual RoBERTa model (XLM-RoBERTa) (Conneau et al., 2020), for each using the official code released in the Huggingface library[5].

All models from above are evaluated on the downstream task NER based on the wikiann data set (see section 4.1) for the following languages:

[5] https://huggingface.co/ufal/robeczech-base, https://huggingface.co/allegro/herbert-base-cased, https://huggingface.co/xlm-roberta-base

Model	Evaluation NER (wikiann)			
Czech RoBERTa	cs	pl	hsb	csb
Polish RoBERTa	cs	pl	hsb	csb
Czech-Polish RoBERTa	cs	pl	hsb	csb
RobeCzech	cs	pl	hsb	csb
HerBERT	cs	pl	hsb	csb
XLM-R	cs	pl	hsb	csb

Table 6: Evaluation: Models and Languages

i) Czech (cs), ii) Polish (pl), iii) Upper Sorbian (hsb), and iv) Kashubian (csb). For the evaluation, which comprises of fine-tuning on training data and evaluation on the validation data, we used a stratified train - validation split; 80% for training and 20% for validation, keeping the same distribution of the entities in both splits. In the case of the low-resource languages hsb and csb, only 150 examples are available for fine-tuning. The hyperparameters for a full run of the fine-tuning process were chosen as follows: batch size 24, epochs 15. Based on different seeds a total of 20 runs was performed, whereby the integer seeds from $123, 124, \ldots, 142$ were used to control the data shuffling within the fine-tuning process. For each combination of language model and language data set, we chose the same 20 seeds in order to allow a reproducible comparison of the different models. An overview of all combinations within the evaluation is given in Table 6. Each of the trained language models is evaluated on NER for each of the languages under consideration.

4.3 Evaluation on Czech and Polish NER

We evaluated the language models on the downstream task NER on the languages cs, pl, hsb and csb as depicted in Table 6. In Figure 2 and Figure 3 we show the F1-score and accuracy, respectively, for all models we evaluated on the NER downstream task. The language, depicted in the header of each box plot is used for fine-tuning the corresponding model for the downstream task NER.

In this section we discuss our results concerning the languages cs and pl. First, we consider the models, trained from scratch, named Czech, Polish, and Czech-Polish. It can be seen that both of the mono-lingual models show a better accuracy on the language, they were trained on, in comparison with the Czech-Polish model. This is in line with the investigations on fine-tuning for NER on the majority of eight different languages (Rust et al., 2021). However, the decrease in performance is different in the two cases. This is possibly due to the training data size, since the Polish dataset (139.0 GB) is more than twice the size of the Czech (58.6 GB) (see section 3.1). Regarding the F1-score, in case of the Polish language, the Czech-Polish model performs slightly better than the Polish model.

We now compare our models with some existing models. In case of the Czech downstream task, it turns out that the Czech as well as the Czech-Polish models show a better F1-score than RobeCzech and XLM-R. Concerning the accuracy, RobeCzech performs comparable (slightly better) to our models, however the variance is more balanced. In case of the Polish downstream task, considering the F1-Score our Czech-Polish model performs slightly better than our Polish model and HerBERT. In contrast, concerning the accuracy our Polish model performs the best with a larger distance to our Czech-Polish model and HerBERT. The HerBERT model, we evaluated, was trained on a small, but high-quality data set. For the F1-score, the coverage is more important, which could explain this distance. For both downstream tasks, Czech and Polish, the mono-lingual model for the respective language and the language family model (Czech-Polish) perform better than the large multi-lingual model.

For a more detailed analysis, we consider the single entities. Exemplary, we compare the Czech model with the Czech-Polish model based on the Czech downstream task. The respective confusion matrices are shown in Table 7 and Table 8. The values in the confusion matrices are the mean values over 20 runs based on seeds of the corresponding combination of language model and language data set. Both matrices report quite similar results. In the referred tables, the discussed cells are highlighted. The Czech-Polish-LM identifies slightly more concrete entities for "I-ORG" and "B-LOC" (see main diagonal in confusion matrices Table 7 and 8, e.g. Czech-Polish-LM: approx. 85 entities classified as "I-ORG" vs. Czech-LM: approx. 80). The reverse holds for "O" entities. On the other hand, "B-ORG" and "B-LOC" as well as "I-ORG" and "I-LOC" are mixed up more often. Thereby, I-LOC is more often misclassified as I-ORG over the models than vice versa. The pairs of entities including "PER" are classified properly as shown in the confusion matrices.

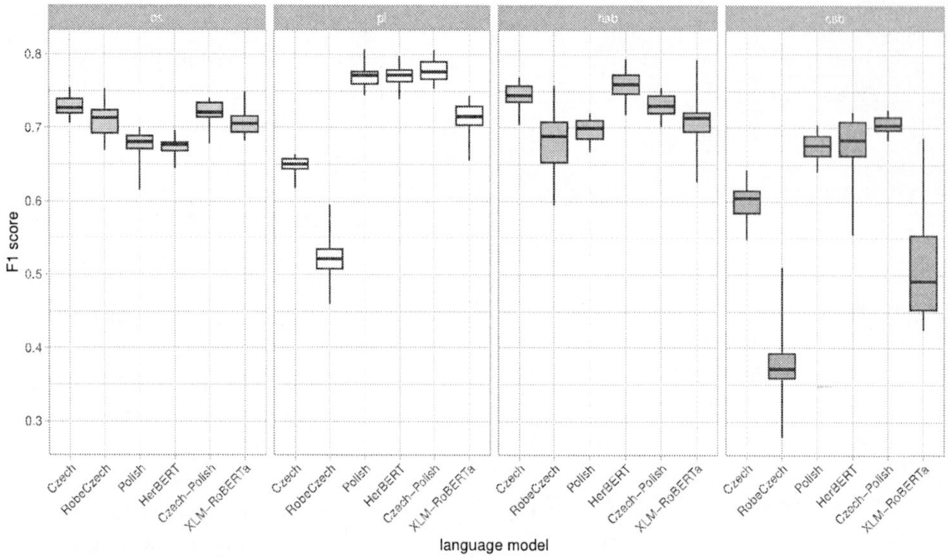

Figure 2: Boxplots of F1-score (20 runs) for all models and languages cs, pl, hsb, csb. The same set of seeds is used over all combinations.

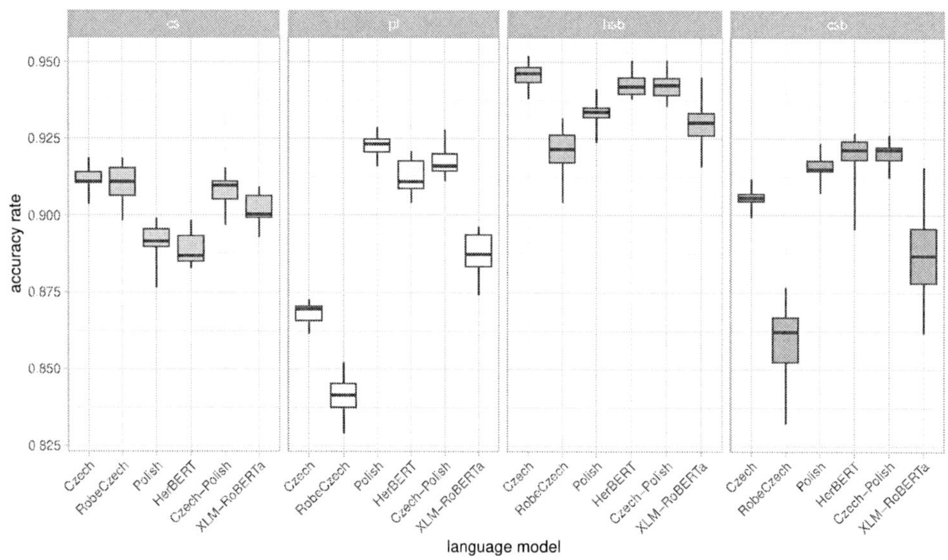

Figure 3: Boxplots of accuracy (20 runs) for all models and languages cs, pl, hsb, csb. The same set of seeds is used over all combinations.

	predicted label						
true label	O	B-PER	I-PER	B-ORG	I-ORG	B-LOC	I-LOC
O	788.40	1.20	2.25	2.40	3.60	4.50	5.65
B-PER	0.00	65.85	0.00	2.15	0.00	0.00	0.00
I-PER	6.95	0.00	82.60	0.10	4.30	0.95	1.10
B-ORG	2.10	3.35	1.05	45.90	0.00	9.60	0.00
I-ORG	7.65	2.05	6.85	3.20	80.10	2.80	6.35
B-LOC	2.80	1.15	0.00	7.55	2.00	58.50	1.00
I-LOC	1.00	0.00	1.75	0.00	15.25	0.90	45.10

Table 7: Mean values for confusion matrix (20 runs): Czech language model applied evaluated on cs data set. Highlighted cells refer to the discussion in the text.

	predicted label						
true label	O	B-PER	I-PER	B-ORG	I-ORG	B-LOC	I-LOC
O	775.85	1.30	2.30	4.90	7.65	9.30	6.70
B-PER	0.65	64.70	0.00	2.65	0.00	0.00	0.00
I-PER	6.50	0.80	82.95	0.00	2.85	2.00	0.90
B-ORG	2.35	2.10	1.00	46.95	0.10	9.50	0.00
I-ORG	3.90	1.45	5.95	3.45	84.70	1.45	8.10
B-LOC	1.50	0.80	0.00	7.95	1.65	61.05	0.05
I-LOC	1.95	0.00	0.70	0.00	14.55	0.30	46.50

Table 8: Mean values for confusion matrix (20 runs): Czech-Polish language model evaluated on cs data set. Highlighted cells refer to the discussion in the text.

4.4 Model Adaptation for Low-Resource Languages

The main goal of our work was to investigate, how language families may support low-resource languages within their family. For this purpose, we adapted the Czech, Polish, and Czech-Polish language models for the Upper Sorbian (hsb) and the Kashubian (csb) language. For each of the languages, the training data for fine-tuning for the NER downstream task comprises only 150 examples. The same holds for the evaluation data set.

In Figures 2 and 3, the F1-score and the accuracy is also presented for hsb and csb, comparing all considered models. For the downstream task NER in Upper Sorbian, the HerBERT model shows the best F1-score, which is surprising as the Upper Sorbian language is related more closely to Czech than to Polish (Howson, 2017). However, this might be caused by the high quality training data of the HerBERT model. Considering the accuracy, our Czech model performs the best, followed by our Czech-Polish model. The XLM-R model does perform worse than our Czech-Polish model, however the distance is not as large as in the case of the Polish language. The confusion matrices for our Czech model and the HerBERT model, evaluated on Upper Sorbian are shown in Table 9 and 10 resp. In general, the numbers are comparable, however, the HerBERT model does mix up less entities and identifies more "B-LOC" correctly, whereas our Czech model identifies more "I-ORG" entities.

For the downstream task NER in Kashubian, our Czech-Polish model shows the best F1-score, however the HerBERT model shows a similar accuracy, but a more balanced distribution. The interpretation of these results require a more thorough linguistic investigation, which is beyond the scope of this paper.

In Table 11, we summarize our results, presenting the mean F1-score and mean accuracy over 20 runs for all experiments.

We conclude, that language models, trained on languages within the same language family may improve downstream tasks for low-resource languages. This seems to be the case, if the language is not clearly related to a single language as in the case of Kashubian. However, mono-lingual models, trained on high-quality data may even outperform language family models, as it is the case with the Upper Sorbian language and the HerBERT model and our models, which were trained on a lower quality data set.

5 Conclusion and Future Work

In our paper, we investigated the West Slavic language family to evaluate the potential of language models for low-resource languages like Upper Sorbian and Kashubian. We trained three RoBERTa models from scratch, two mono-lingual models for both Czech and Polish respectively, and one multilingual model for Czech and Polish. These models were evaluated on the NER task for Czech, Polish, Upper Sorbian, and Kashubian. We also compared the performance of our models with existing SOTA mono- and multi-lingual models, namely RobeCzech, HerBERT, and XLM-R.

It can be seen that both mono-lingual models show better accuracy on the language they were trained on in comparison with the Czech-Polish model. The Czech and Czech-Polish models show a better F1-score than RobeCzech and XLM-R in the Czech downstream task. For both downstream tasks, the mono-lingual model for the respective language and the language family model (Czech-Polish) perform better than a large multi-lingual model. The adaptation of the language models for the Upper Sorbian and the Kashubian language was investigated. The HerBERT model shows the best F1-score for NER in Upper Sorbian. Our own

	predicted label						
true label	O	B-PER	I-PER	B-ORG	I-ORG	B-LOC	I-LOC
O	841.00	0.90	0.10	0.35	1.10	3.25	3.30
B-PER	0.30	46.15	0.05	0.60	0.00	1.45	0.45
I-PER	3.00	0.20	93.50	0.65	1.00	0.20	1.45
B-ORG	3.85	0.00	0.00	37.30	0.00	9.85	0.00
I-ORG	3.30	0.00	0.00	0.40	84.80	0.35	6.15
B-LOC	6.00	0.55	0.00	7.85	0.80	65.10	0.70
I-LOC	0.00	0.00	0.10	0.00	8.70	2.45	37.75

Table 9: Mean values confusion matrix (20 runs): Czech language model evaluated on hsb data set.

	predicted label						
true label	O	B-PER	I-PER	B-ORG	I-ORG	B-LOC	I-LOC
O	839.05	0.80	0.50	1.40	1.75	4.35	2.15
B-PER	0.60	45.55	0.25	1.20	0.00	1.35	0.05
I-PER	3.10	0.00	93.25	0.00	1.35	0.00	2.30
B-ORG	1.95	0.00	0.05	35.50	0.00	13.45	0.05
I-ORG	5.50	0.00	0.05	2.10	79.70	1.50	6.15
B-LOC	2.35	3.15	0.00	3.95	0.00	71.45	0.10
I-LOC	2.20	0.00	5.55	0.00	2.95	0.75	37.55

Table 10: Mean values confusion matrix (20 runs): HerBERT language model evaluated on hsb data set.

language_model	F1.cs	Acc.cs	F1.pl	Acc.pl	F1.hsb	Acc.hsb	F1.csb	Acc.csb
Czech	**0.729**	**0.911**	0.648	0.868	0.744	**0.946**	0.599	0.906
RobeCzech	0.710	**0.911**	0.521	0.841	0.679	0.921	0.377	0.860
Polish	0.676	0.892	0.769	**0.923**	0.697	0.933	0.677	0.916
HerBERT	0.674	0.888	0.771	0.912	**0.760**	0.943	0.676	0.920
Czech-Polish	0.720	0.908	**0.776**	0.918	0.730	0.942	**0.706**	**0.921**
XLM-RoBERTa	0.708	0.902	0.714	0.887	0.707	0.930	0.507	0.888

Table 11: Summary Results: Mean values of F1-score and accuracy over all 20 runs for all combinations of language model and language data set. Columnwise maximum values are bold.

Czech model performs the best for accuracy in Upper Sorbian. Our own Polish-Czech model shows the best F1-score for NER in Kashubian, while the HerBERT model shows similar accuracy.

Overall, the contribution has shown, that low-resource West Slavic languages such as Upper Sorbian or Kashubian can profit from closely related languages and their belonging models. But the crucial point seems to be the fundamental understanding of relatedness between low-resource languages and potentially promising high-resource languages. This requires a close collaboration with linguists, to successfully infer, where to profit from common training data and/or models. There is still a lot of potential to investigate more languages within a family and compare them with larger high-quality data sets (e.g. CNEC (Ševčíková et al., 2007), NKJP (Przepiórkowski, 2011)) and evaluate the models on modified NER tasks as described in Piskorski et al. (2021).

Furthermore, an interesting approach could be a cross-lingual and progressive transfer learning approach (Ostendorff and Rehm, 2023), where training of language models for low-resource languages starts with a large language model for a high-resource language and includes overlapping vocabulary. This method has yielded promising results for creating large models, but it refers to language families and not single languages.

Another development direction could be in building large corpora from existing parallel corpora. This would allow for the creation of high-quality training data for multi-lingual models and enable the training of models for low-resource languages that may not have sufficient training data available.

Acknowledgements

This work was supported by the German Federal Ministry of Education and Research (BMBF, SCADS22B) and the Saxon State Ministry for Science, Culture and Tourism (SMWK) by funding the competence center for Big Data and AI "ScaDS.AI Dresden/Leipzig“. The authors gratefully acknowledge the GWK support for funding this project by providing computing time through the Center for Information Services and HPC (ZIH) at TU

Dresden. The authors thank Alexander Fraser for helpful suggestions at the very beginning of this project, and the anonymous reviewers for supportive comments.

References

Julien Abadji, Pedro Ortiz Suarez, Laurent Romary, and Benoît Sagot. 2022. Towards a cleaner document-oriented multilingual crawled corpus. In *Proceedings of the Thirteenth Language Resources and Evaluation Conference*, pages 4344–4355, Marseille, France. European Language Resources Association.

Tom Brown, Benjamin Mann, Nick Ryder, Melanie Subbiah, Jared D Kaplan, Prafulla Dhariwal, Arvind Neelakantan, Pranav Shyam, Girish Sastry, Amanda Askell, Sandhini Agarwal, Ariel Herbert-Voss, Gretchen Krueger, Tom Henighan, Rewon Child, Aditya Ramesh, Daniel Ziegler, Jeffrey Wu, Clemens Winter, Chris Hesse, Mark Chen, Eric Sigler, Mateusz Litwin, Scott Gray, Benjamin Chess, Jack Clark, Christopher Berner, Sam McCandlish, Alec Radford, Ilya Sutskever, and Dario Amodei. 2020. Language models are few-shot learners. In *Advances in Neural Information Processing Systems*, volume 33, pages 1877–1901. Curran Associates, Inc.

Alexis Conneau, Kartikay Khandelwal, Naman Goyal, Vishrav Chaudhary, Guillaume Wenzek, Francisco Guzmán, Edouard Grave, Myle Ott, Luke Zettlemoyer, and Veselin Stoyanov. 2020. Unsupervised cross-lingual representation learning at scale. In *Proceedings of the 58th Annual Meeting of the Association for Computational Linguistics*, pages 8440–8451, Online. Association for Computational Linguistics.

Sławomir Dadas, Michał Perełkiewicz, and Rafał Poundefinedwiata. 2020. Pre-training polish transformer-based language models at scale. In *Artificial Intelligence and Soft Computing: 19th International Conference, ICAISC 2020, Zakopane, Poland, October 12-14, 2020, Proceedings, Part II*, page 301–314, Berlin, Heidelberg. Springer-Verlag.

Wietse de Vries, Martijn Bartelds, Malvina Nissim, and Martijn Wieling. 2021. Adapting monolingual models: Data can be scarce when language similarity is high. In *Findings of the Association for Computational Linguistics: ACL-IJCNLP 2021*, pages 4901–4907, Online. Association for Computational Linguistics.

Wietse de Vries and Malvina Nissim. 2021. As good as new. how to successfully recycle English GPT-2 to make models for other languages. In *Findings of the Association for Computational Linguistics: ACL-IJCNLP 2021*, pages 836–846, Online. Association for Computational Linguistics.

Phil Howson. 2017. Upper sorbian. *Journal of the International Phonetic Association*, 47(3):359–367.

Michal Konkol and Miloslav Konopík. 2013. Crf-based czech named entity recognizer and consolidation of czech ner research. In *Text, Speech, and Dialogue*, pages 153–160, Berlin, Heidelberg. Springer Berlin Heidelberg.

Yinhan Liu, Myle Ott, Naman Goyal, Jingfei Du, Mandar Joshi, Danqi Chen, Omer Levy, Mike Lewis, Luke Zettlemoyer, and Veselin Stoyanov. 2019. Roberta: A robustly optimized BERT pretraining approach. *CoRR*, abs/1907.11692.

Nikola Ljubešić and Davor Lauc. 2021. BERTić - the transformer language model for Bosnian, Croatian, Montenegrin and Serbian. In *Proceedings of the 8th Workshop on Balto-Slavic Natural Language Processing*, pages 37–42, Kiyv, Ukraine. Association for Computational Linguistics.

Ilya Loshchilov and Frank Hutter. 2017. Decoupled weight decay regularization.

Robert Mroczkowski, Piotr Rybak, Alina Wróblewska, and Ireneusz Gawlik. 2021. HerBERT: Efficiently pretrained transformer-based language model for Polish. In *Proceedings of the 8th Workshop on Balto-Slavic Natural Language Processing*, pages 1–10, Kiyv, Ukraine. Association for Computational Linguistics.

Motoki Nomachi. 2019. *14. Placing Kashubian on the language map of Europe*, pages 453–490. De Gruyter Mouton, Berlin, Boston.

Kelechi Ogueji, Yuxin Zhu, and Jimmy Lin. 2021. Small data? no problem! exploring the viability of pretrained multilingual language models for low-resourced languages. In *Proceedings of the 1st Workshop on Multilingual Representation Learning*, pages 116–126, Punta Cana, Dominican Republic. Association for Computational Linguistics.

Pedro Javier Ortiz Suárez, Laurent Romary, and Benoît Sagot. 2020. A monolingual approach to contextualized word embeddings for mid-resource languages. In *Proceedings of the 58th Annual Meeting of the Association for Computational Linguistics*, pages 1703–1714, Online. Association for Computational Linguistics.

Malte Ostendorff and Georg Rehm. 2023. Efficient language model training through cross-lingual and progressive transfer learning.

Jakub Piskorski, Bogdan Babych, Zara Kancheva, Olga Kanishcheva, Maria Lebedeva, Michał Marcińczuk, Preslav Nakov, Petya Osenova, Lidia Pivovarova, Senja Pollak, Pavel Přibáň, Ivaylo Radev, Marko Robnik-Sikonja, Vasyl Starko, Josef Steinberger, and Roman Yangarber. 2021. Slav-NER: the 3rd cross-lingual challenge on recognition, normalization, classification, and linking of named entities across Slavic languages. In *Proceedings of the 8th Workshop on Balto-Slavic Natural Language Processing*, pages 122–133, Kiyv, Ukraine. Association for Computational Linguistics.

Adam Przepiórkowski. 2011. National corpus of polish. LINDAT/CLARIAH-CZ digital library at the Institute of Formal and Applied Linguistics (ÚFAL), Faculty of Mathematics and Physics, Charles University.

Afshin Rahimi, Yuan Li, and Trevor Cohn. 2019. Massively multilingual transfer for NER. In *Proceedings of the 57th Annual Meeting of the Association for Computational Linguistics*, pages 151–164, Florence, Italy. Association for Computational Linguistics.

Phillip Rust, Jonas Pfeiffer, Ivan Vulić, Sebastian Ruder, and Iryna Gurevych. 2021. How good is your tokenizer? on the monolingual performance of multilingual language models. In *Proceedings of the 59th Annual Meeting of the Association for Computational Linguistics and the 11th International Joint Conference on Natural Language Processing (Volume 1: Long Papers)*, pages 3118–3135, Online. Association for Computational Linguistics.

Rico Sennrich, Barry Haddow, and Alexandra Birch. 2016. Neural machine translation of rare words with subword units. In *Proceedings of the 54th Annual Meeting of the Association for Computational Linguistics (Volume 1: Long Papers)*, pages 1715–1725, Berlin, Germany. Association for Computational Linguistics.

Magda Ševčíková, Zdeněk Žabokrtský, and Oldřich Krůza. 2007. Named entities in czech: Annotating data and developing ne tagger. In *Text, Speech and Dialogue*, pages 188–195, Berlin, Heidelberg. Springer Berlin Heidelberg.

Milan Straka, Jakub Náplava, Jana Straková, and David Samuel. 2021. Robeczech: Czech roberta, a monolingual contextualized language representation model. In *Text, Speech, and Dialogue*, pages 197–209, Cham. Springer International Publishing.

Marek Suppa and Ondrej Jariabka. 2021. Benchmarking pre-trained language models for multilingual NER: TraSpaS at the BSNLP2021 shared task. In *Proceedings of the 8th Workshop on Balto-Slavic Natural Language Processing*, pages 105–114, Kiyv, Ukraine. Association for Computational Linguistics.

Roland Sussex and Paul Cubberley. 2006. *The Slavic Languages*. Cambridge Language Surveys. Cambridge University Press.

Alexey Tikhonov, Alex Malkhasov, Andrey Manoshin, George-Andrei Dima, Réka Cserháti, Md.Sadek Hossain Asif, and Matt Sárdi. 2022. EENLP: Cross-lingual Eastern European NLP index. In *Proceedings of the Thirteenth Language Resources and Evaluation Conference*, pages 2050–2057, Marseille, France. European Language Resources Association.

MAUPQA: Massive Automatically-created Polish Question Answering Dataset

Piotr Rybak

Institute of Computer Science,
Polish Academy of Sciences
piotr.cezary.rybak@gmail.com

Abstract

Recently, open-domain question answering systems have begun to rely heavily on annotated datasets to train neural passage retrievers. However, manually annotating such datasets is both difficult and time-consuming, which limits their availability for less popular languages. In this work, we experiment with several methods for automatically collecting weakly labeled datasets and show how they affect the performance of the neural passage retrieval models. As a result of our work, we publish the MAUPQA dataset, consisting of nearly 400,000 question-passage pairs for Polish, as well as the HerBERT-QA neural retriever.

1 Introduction

Open-domain question answering (OpenQA) systems aim to provide answers to questions from a variety of topics, using a large collection of passages as a knowledge base. Recently, the development of such systems has been accelerated by the release of several large-scale question-passage datasets, such as MS MARCO (Nguyen et al., 2016), TriviaQA (Joshi et al., 2017), and Natural Questions (Kwiatkowski et al., 2019, NQ). These datasets enabled the training of neural passage retrieval models (e.g. Dense Passage Retrieval, Karpukhin et al., 2020), which can select passages from a knowledge base that are the most likely to contain the answer to the question.

However, the annotation of such datasets is a time-consuming and expensive process, which limits their availability for less popular languages (Rogers et al., 2022). Another limiting factor is the availability of real questions. Datasets like MS MARCO or Natural Question consist of real questions asked by search engine users. For less popular languages (like Polish), such a source of questions is not available. This leads to two alternatives: either to train a system on a small dataset (which might not be sufficient for the model to reach its full potential) or to create a dataset automatically. The first approach was recently described by Rybak et al. (2022) who published the PolQA dataset which consists of 7,000 trivia questions and 87,525 manually annotated passages.

In this work, we experiment with the latter approach and show how different methods for automatic data collection can impact the performance of the neural passage retrieval models. Our contributions can be summarized as follows:

1. We experiment with several methods for automatically collecting weakly-labeled question-passage pairs, and show their impact on the performance of the retrieval models.
2. We publish the MAUPQA dataset consisting of almost 400,000 question-passage pairs for Polish.[1]
3. We release the HerBERT-QA neural retriever, which achieves the best results on the PolQA dataset.[2]

2 Related Work

Weakly-labeled datasets Over the years, many techniques were developed for the automatic creation of weakly-labeled datasets. One general idea is to use a weak model to automatically label the unlabeled dataset (Lee, 2013). In the case of OpenQA, either simple lexical models like BM-25 (Robertson and Zaragoza, 2009) or more powerful neural models are used to retrieve relevant passages for given questions. To further improve the accuracy of retrieved examples the passages can be filtered out using cross-encoders (Ren et al., 2021) or answers (if available, Karpukhin et al., 2020).

However, the above method can only be used if the source of questions is available. If that is

[1] https://hf.co/datasets/ipipan/maupqa
[2] https://hf.co/ipipan/herbert-base-qa-v1

Proceedings of the 9th Workshop on Slavic Natural Language Processing 2023 (SlavicNLP 2023), pages 11–16
May 6, 2023

Dataset	Questions	Passages	Answers	Correct	Unambiguous	Relevant	Overall
PolQA	4,591	57,921	5,634	99%	99%	92%	90%
CzyWiesz-v2	29,078	29,078	-	100%	92%	73%	70%
GenGPT3	10,146	10,177	10,146	92%	44%	89%	33%
MKQA	4,036	4,036	4,036	73%	73%	21%	15%
MTNQ	135,781	142,008	-	60%	78%	80%	41%
MFAQ	172,768	178,937	-	81%	84%	55%	43%
Templates	15,993	15,993	14,520	88%	100%	89%	78%
WikiDef	18,093	18,093	18,093	95%	77%	88%	65%
All	385,895	398,322	46,795	76%	82%	69%	46%

Table 1: Basic statistics for all used datasets. *All* represents the concatenation of all MAUPQA datasets (i.e. without PolQA). *PolQA* refers to the training part of the PolQA dataset. *PolQA* dataset has more answers than questions since it might contain multiple answer variants for a single question (e.g. *7* and *seven*). Some datasets don't have any answers due to the way they were created.

not the case, then questions can be automatically created. Either using templates (Fabbri et al., 2020) or trained models (Lewis et al., 2021).

Another line of work takes advantage of existing datasets and translates them automatically to other languages (Lewis et al., 2020). The quality of the machine translation model directly impacts the quality of the created dataset (Bonifacio et al., 2021).

Polish OpenQA datasets Few datasets exist for Polish OpenQA. The first published dataset for passage retrieval was the *Czy wiesz?* dataset (Marcińczuk et al., 2013). It is a collection of 4,721 questions from the *Did you know?* section on Polish Wikipedia out of which only 250 questions were manually labeled with a relevant passage. Rybak et al. (2020) later annotated an additional 1,070 questions with relevant passages.

The PolQA dataset (Rybak et al., 2022) is a recently introduced dataset for Polish OpenQA. It consists of 7,000 trivia questions and 87,525 manually annotated passages (both positive and hard-negative). Even though the number of question-passage pairs is impressive for a less popular language like Polish, the number of unique questions is still rather limited.

3 MAUPQA Dataset

The MAUPQA dataset consists of seven parts. Four of them are created from scratch (Czy wiesz?, GenGPT3, Templates, WikiDef), and the other three are based on existing resources (MKQA, MTNQ, MFAQ).

3.1 Quality Assessment

To assess the quality of MAUPQA datasets, we sample and manually annotate 100 question-passage pairs for each dataset. Our manual verification consists of three aspects:

Correct We check if the question is a valid, grammatically correct question written in Polish.

Unambiguous We define that the question is ambiguous if it cannot be answered without providing additional information. For example, the question "Where is the headquarter of the company?" is ambiguous because it doesn't specify the name of the company and thus makes it impossible to answer the question.

Relevant The final aspect is the relevance of the passage to the question, i.e. whether the passage contains the answer to the question.

We also calculate the **overall** correctness of the example as the proportion of examples that satisfy all three of the above aspects. We show the results of the quality evaluation in the Table 1 together with the sizes of each dataset.

3.2 Datasets

Below, we describe each of the seven MAUPQA datasets:

CzyWiesz-v2 Similarly to the original *Czywiesz?* dataset, we first gather all questions from the *Did you know?* section on Polish Wikipedia together with a link to the relevant Wikipedia article. To select the relevant passage, we score all passages within this article using a multilingual cross-encoder (Bonifacio et al., 2021)[3] and choose the one with the highest score. We use a few simple heuristics to filter out questions regarding images (e.g. "Who is the famous general *in the photo*?"). Additionally, we remove questions from the KLEJ benchmark test set (Rybak et al., 2020).

The final dataset consists of 29,078 questions. They are grammatically correct, mostly unambiguous, and have a high rate of relevant passages (73%, see Table 1). Manual inspection shows that irrelevant passages are the result of the cross-encoder errors. In most cases, the relevant passage exists in the matching article but it was not selected.

GenGPT3 In the GenGPT3 dataset, we explore the application of the *text-davinci-003* model (Ouyang et al.) for generating question-answer pairs based on a given passage. To obtain passages, we use the Polish subset of CCNet (Wenzek et al., 2020). These passages turned out to be very diverse, covering domains such as news, legal, technical, etc. To guide the model in generating relevant questions, we use the prompt: *Napisz pytanie i odpowiedź do poniższego paragrafu. Pytanie musi mieć przynajmniej pięć słów. Odpowiedź może mieć najwyżej pięć słów* (Write a question and answer for the following passage. The question must be at least five words. The answer can be up to five words). In addition, we provide two examples within the prompt to help the model learn to generate appropriate question-answer pairs.

Through our experiments, we observe that the generated questions are grammatically correct in 92% of the cases and highly relevant (89% of the cases). However, we also find that the questions are often ambiguous, with 56% of them requiring a contextual understanding of the passage to answer.

MKQA The MKQA (Longpre et al., 2021) dataset consists of 10,000 questions sampled from the NQ dataset and manually translated into 25 languages (including Polish). We clean MKQA dataset by removing questions without answers, requiring long answers (*Why?* and *How?* questions), and ambiguous ones ("Who is the *current* president?"). We end up with 4,036 questions.

Since the original dataset doesn't include matching passages, we use the BM-25 algorithm (Robertson and Zaragoza, 2009) to select the top 100 candidate passages which we re-rank using a multilingual cross-encoder. In either case, we append the answer to the query to increase the performance of the passage retrieval. However, it still proved to be difficult to retrieve relevant passages and only 21% of them are correct.

MTNQ To create the machine-translated NQ dataset (MTNQ) we select all questions with relevant passages from the NQ dataset and split those passages into sentences. Then, we translate both questions and sentences into Polish using Allegro[4] machine translation model.

Even though the translation model is high quality (similar to Google Translate), the translations still contain many errors. Two main reasons are incorrectly translating named entities (e.g. movie titles) and very noisy input (NQ questions are Google search phrases). It is worth noting that MKQA, which is a manually translated subset of NQ, also has a high ratio of ungrammatical questions.

MFAQ The MFAQ dataset (De Bruyn et al., 2021) contains 234 million multilingual (4 million Polish) questions scraped from FAQ websites. However, many of them are artificially created, e.g. "What is the best hotel in *city*?" for hundreds of different *cities*. To clean the data, we cluster lexically similar questions and passages and remove clusters with over 5 questions. Additionally, some of the questions are not in Polish. We filter them using the fasttext language-id model (Joulin et al., 2017, 2016).

After filtering, the dataset contains 178,937 passages, i.e. less than 5% of the original dataset. This shows the risk of using questions extracted directly from crawled websites. The cleaned dataset has rather high quality, in terms of grammatical correctness, unambiguity, and relevance of passages. The MFAQ is much more diverse than other datasets (except for *GenGPT3*) and contains questions from a wide range of domains (customer support, lifestyle, technical, etc.).

Templates We take advantage of the Wikipedia structure to generate questions using predefined

[3] `https://hf.co/unicamp-dl/mMiniLM-L6-v2-mmarco-v2`

[4] `https://ml.allegro.tech/`

templates. For example, list pages group together similar entities (e.g. "Writers born in Poland") which allows generating questions like "Where was Zbigniew Herbert born?". We also use tables (e.g. "What is the capital of Poland?") and chronologies (e.g. "In which year World War 2 started?"). In total, we use 33 templates to generate questions. Since each question has a link to the relevant Wikipedia article, we use the same method as in the *CzyWiesz-v2* dataset to select the most relevant passage from the relevant article.

Overall, we created 15,993 questions from templates. They are high quality but the process of creating templates was surprisingly time-consuming and took a few hours per template.

WikiDef We use Wiktionary[5] to generate questions based on word definitions. Some definitions have links to Wikipedia articles which we use to create the question-passage pairs. For example, the definition of "Monday" is "the first day of the week". Based on it, we generate the question "What is the name of *the first day of the week*?". Then, we select the first passage from the linked Wikipedia article as the relevant passage. We remove short definitions (less than 5 words) containing names of 23 predefined "categories" (e.g. city) to avoid ambiguous questions (e.g. "What is the name of *a city in Poland*?").

We end up with 18,093 questions asking for word definitions. This is the least diverse dataset of all as all questions follow the same template. Even though we tried to filter unambiguous questions there are still 23% of them in the final dataset.

4 Evaluation

We use the Tevatron library (Gao et al., 2022) to train the neural retriever. For each dataset, we fine-tune the HerBERT Base model (Mroczkowski et al., 2021) for 2,000 steps, with batch size 128 and learning rate 10^{-5}. Otherwise, we use default parameters. We experimented with training models for 5,000 steps but it didn't increase the performance. We use a single hard-negative per question when training on PolQA dataset. For other datasets, we only use in-batch random negatives as they don't contain hard-negatives.

For evaluation, we use Accuracy@10 (i.e. is there at least one relevant passage within the top 10 retrieved passages) and NDCG@10 (i.e. score of each relevant passage within the top 10 retrieved passages depends descending on its position, Järvelin and Kekäläinen (2002)). Each model is evaluated on the PolQA development dataset. We use provided Polish Wikipedia dump as a knowledge base.

[5] https://www.wiktionary.org/

5 Results

The baseline retriever trained using manually annotated PolQA dataset achieves 60.8% accuracy@10 (see Table 2). Individually, none of the automatically created datasets has a comparable score.

As expected, the best model is *MTNQ* with an accuracy of 58.5%. It is the second largest dataset, similarly to PolQA it contains mostly trivia questions, and is based on manually labeled question-passage pairs. Comparably large *MFAQ* dataset obtains much lower performance (38.7%), probably due to domain mismatch as otherwise, its quality is higher than *MTNQ*.

The *MKQA*, which is a manually translated subset of *NQ* dataset achieves surprisingly good results (51.5%). It is unexpected considering that only 21% of its passages are actually relevant.

The second best result (54.2%) is achieved by the *GenGPT3* dataset. Despite the diverse nature of the questions from different domains, and the relatively modest size of the dataset, it exhibits a remarkable level of quality that allows it to serve as a reliable source for training a passage retriever.

The third best result (54.1%) is scored by *CzyWiesz-v2* dataset. The other two datasets created based on Wikipedia perform much worse, *Templates* obtains accuracy of 45.9% and *WikiDef* only 19.9%. It is also the lowest result of all datasets, probably due to its low diversity.

None of the datasets is perfect and each of them has its own disadvantages. However, the retriever trained on all of them results in better performance than the manually annotated dataset (61.2% vs 60.8%). If we further fine-tune the retriever pre-trained on MAUPQA, we obtain the state-of-the-art result for Polish passage retrieval of 62.7%. We name this retriever HerBERT-QA and release it alongside the created datasets.

6 Conclusion

In this work, we present MAUPQA, the largest Polish QA dataset with almost 400k question-passage pairs. Even though the dataset is created automatically it achieves competitive results on the Polish

Dataset	Acc@10	NDCG@10
PolQA	60.8%	26.9%
CzyWiesz-v2	54.1%	22.0%
GenGPT3	54.2%	22.1%
MKQA	51.5%	21.6%
MTNQ	58.5%	24.1%
MFAQ	38.7%	14.0%
Templates	45.9%	16.9%
WikiDef	19.9%	7.7%
All	61.2%	25.2%
All → PolQA	**62.7%**	**27.4%**

Table 2: Passage retriever performance trained on different datasets. We use top-10 accuracy and NDCG@10 on the PolQA development set. *All* represents the concatenation of all MAUPQA datasets (i.e. without PolQA). *All → PolQA* is a model first trained on the MAUPQA dataset and then fine-tuned on the PolQA dataset.

passage retrieval task and after fine-tuning on the PolQA dataset sets a new state-of-the-art performance.

Each of the seven datasets which make up MAUPQA has different properties and results in the vastly different performance of passage retrievers. Thanks to recent advancements of machine translation models, we recommend translating existing English datasets as the best way to cheaply obtain competitive QA datasets. Otherwise, generating questions using GPT-3 model proves to work well and can be applied to multiple different domains (for which there might not be an English dataset). If a set of questions already exists for a given language, then using pseudo-labeling also results in a surprisingly good dataset. However, to get the best performance, it is useful to combine multiple different datasets.

We believe our work will benefit the Polish NLP community, both by publishing a MAUPQA dataset, as well as the state-of-the-art passage retrieval model. Our study also lays a path for other languages on how to construct similar datasets.

Limitations

The MAUPQA dataset focuses only on the Polish language and the drawn conclusions might not hold for other languages. For example, the format of sentences in the *Did you know?* section of Polish Wikipedia makes it very easy to transform them into questions. This is not the case for other languages. Some of them don't even have the *Did you know?* section.

Except for choosing the number of training steps (2,000 or 5,000), we didn't perform any additional hyper-parameter search and used the default Tevatron values. We also tested only one encoder architecture (HerBERT Base). The results for other setups might be different.

Except for GenGPT3 and MFAQ, all datasets (including the evaluation dataset) use Wikipedia as a knowledge base. This might negatively impact the perceived performance of the retrievers trained on GenGPT3 and MFAQ. We suspect that those retrievers might generalize better to other domains but there are no Polish QA datasets on which we could have tested it.

7 Acknowledgments

We thank the Allegro.com Machine Learning Research team for giving us access to their machine translating model.

References

Luiz Henrique Bonifacio, Vitor Jeronymo, Hugo Queiroz Abonizio, Israel Campiotti, Marzieh Fadaee, , Roberto Lotufo, and Rodrigo Nogueira. 2021. mMARCO: A multilingual version of MS MARCO passage ranking dataset.

Maxime De Bruyn, Ehsan Lotfi, Jeska Buhmann, and Walter Daelemans. 2021. MFAQ: a multilingual FAQ dataset. In *Proceedings of the 3rd Workshop on Machine Reading for Question Answering*, pages 1–13, Punta Cana, Dominican Republic. Association for Computational Linguistics.

Alexander Fabbri, Patrick Ng, Zhiguo Wang, Ramesh Nallapati, and Bing Xiang. 2020. Template-based question generation from retrieved sentences for improved unsupervised question answering. In *Proceedings of the 58th Annual Meeting of the Association for Computational Linguistics*, pages 4508–4513, Online. Association for Computational Linguistics.

Luyu Gao, Xueguang Ma, Jimmy J. Lin, and Jamie Callan. 2022. Tevatron: An efficient and flexible toolkit for dense retrieval.

Mandar Joshi, Eunsol Choi, Daniel Weld, and Luke Zettlemoyer. 2017. TriviaQA: A large scale distantly supervised challenge dataset for reading comprehension. In *Proceedings of the 55th Annual Meeting of the Association for Computational Linguistics (Volume 1: Long Papers)*, pages 1601–1611, Vancouver, Canada. Association for Computational Linguistics.

Armand Joulin, Edouard Grave, Piotr Bojanowski, Matthijs Douze, Hérve Jégou, and Tomas Mikolov. 2016. FastText.zip: Compressing text classification models.

Armand Joulin, Edouard Grave, Piotr Bojanowski, and Tomas Mikolov. 2017. Bag of tricks for efficient text classification. In *Proceedings of the 15th Conference of the European Chapter of the Association for Computational Linguistics: Volume 2, Short Papers*, pages 427–431, Valencia, Spain. Association for Computational Linguistics.

Kalervo Järvelin and Jaana Kekäläinen. 2002. Cumulated gain-based evaluation of ir techniques. *ACM Trans. Inf. Syst.*, 20:422–446.

Vladimir Karpukhin, Barlas Oguz, Sewon Min, Patrick Lewis, Ledell Wu, Sergey Edunov, Danqi Chen, and Wen-tau Yih. 2020. Dense passage retrieval for open-domain question answering. In *Proceedings of the 2020 Conference on Empirical Methods in Natural Language Processing (EMNLP)*, pages 6769–6781, Online. Association for Computational Linguistics.

Tom Kwiatkowski, Jennimaria Palomaki, Olivia Redfield, Michael Collins, Ankur Parikh, Chris Alberti, Danielle Epstein, Illia Polosukhin, Jacob Devlin, Kenton Lee, Kristina Toutanova, Llion Jones, Matthew Kelcey, Ming-Wei Chang, Andrew M. Dai, Jakob Uszkoreit, Quoc Le, and Slav Petrov. 2019. Natural questions: A benchmark for question answering research. *Transactions of the Association for Computational Linguistics*, 7:452–466.

Dong-Hyun Lee. 2013. Pseudo-label : The simple and efficient semi-supervised learning method for deep neural networks.

Patrick Lewis, Barlas Oguz, Ruty Rinott, Sebastian Riedel, and Holger Schwenk. 2020. MLQA: Evaluating cross-lingual extractive question answering. In *Proceedings of the 58th Annual Meeting of the Association for Computational Linguistics*, pages 7315–7330, Online. Association for Computational Linguistics.

Patrick Lewis, Yuxiang Wu, Linqing Liu, Pasquale Minervini, Heinrich Küttler, Aleksandra Piktus, Pontus Stenetorp, and Sebastian Riedel. 2021. PAQ: 65 million probably-asked questions and what you can do with them. *Transactions of the Association for Computational Linguistics*, 9:1098–1115.

Shayne Longpre, Yi Lu, and Joachim Daiber. 2021. MKQA: A linguistically diverse benchmark for multilingual open domain question answering. *Transactions of the Association for Computational Linguistics*, 9:1389–1406.

Michał Marcińczuk, Adam Radziszewski, Maciej Piasecki, Dominik Piasecki, and Marcin Ptak. 2013. Evaluation of baseline information retrieval for Polish open-domain question answering system. In *Proceedings of the International Conference Recent Advances in Natural Language Processing RANLP 2013*, pages 428–435, Hissar, Bulgaria. INCOMA Ltd. Shoumen, BULGARIA.

Robert Mroczkowski, Piotr Rybak, Alina Wróblewska, and Ireneusz Gawlik. 2021. HerBERT: Efficiently pretrained transformer-based language model for Polish. In *Proceedings of the 8th Workshop on Balto-Slavic Natural Language Processing*, pages 1–10, Kiyv, Ukraine. Association for Computational Linguistics.

Tri Nguyen, Mir Rosenberg, Xia Song, Jianfeng Gao, Saurabh Tiwary, Rangan Majumder, and Li Deng. 2016. MS MARCO: A Human Generated MAchine Reading COmprehension Dataset.

Long Ouyang, Jeffrey Wu, Xu Jiang, Diogo Almeida, Carroll Wainwright, Pamela Mishkin, Chong Zhang, Sandhini Agarwal, Katarina Slama, Alex Gray, et al. Training language models to follow instructions with human feedback. In *Advances in Neural Information Processing Systems*.

Ruiyang Ren, Yingqi Qu, Jing Liu, Wayne Xin Zhao, QiaoQiao She, Hua Wu, Haifeng Wang, and Ji-Rong Wen. 2021. RocketQAv2: A joint training method for dense passage retrieval and passage re-ranking. In *Proceedings of the 2021 Conference on Empirical Methods in Natural Language Processing*, pages 2825–2835, Online and Punta Cana, Dominican Republic. Association for Computational Linguistics.

Stephen E. Robertson and Hugo Zaragoza. 2009. The probabilistic relevance framework: BM25 and beyond. *Found. Trends Inf. Retr.*, 3:333–389.

Anna Rogers, Matt Gardner, and Isabelle Augenstein. 2022. QA dataset explosion: A taxonomy of nlp resources for question answering and reading comprehension. *ACM Comput. Surv.*

Piotr Rybak, Robert Mroczkowski, Janusz Tracz, and Ireneusz Gawlik. 2020. KLEJ: Comprehensive benchmark for Polish language understanding. In *Proceedings of the 58th Annual Meeting of the Association for Computational Linguistics*, pages 1191–1201, Online. Association for Computational Linguistics.

Piotr Rybak, Piotr Przybyła, and Maciej Ogrodniczuk. 2022. Improving question answering performance through manual annotation: Costs, benefits and strategies.

Guillaume Wenzek, Marie-Anne Lachaux, Alexis Conneau, Vishrav Chaudhary, Francisco Guzmán, Armand Joulin, and Edouard Grave. 2020. CCNet: Extracting high quality monolingual datasets from web crawl data. In *Proceedings of the 12th Language Resources and Evaluation Conference*, pages 4003–4012, Marseille, France. European Language Resources Association.

TrelBERT: A pre-trained encoder for Polish Twitter

Wojciech Szmyd, Alicja Kotyla, Michał Zobniów
Piotr Falkiewicz, Jakub Bartczuk, Artur Zygadło
deepsense.ai
research@deepsense.ai

Abstract

Pre-trained Transformer-based models have become immensely popular amongst NLP practitioners. We present TrelBERT – the first Polish language model suited for application in the social media domain. TrelBERT is based on an existing general-domain model and adapted to the language of social media by pre-training it further on a large collection of Twitter data. We demonstrate its usefulness by evaluating it in the downstream task of cyberbullying detection, in which it achieves state-of-the-art results, outperforming larger monolingual models trained on general-domain corpora, as well as multilingual in-domain models, by a large margin. We make the model publicly available. We also release a new dataset for the problem of harmful speech detection.

1 Introduction

Pre-trained language models based on the Transformer architecture (Vaswani et al., 2017) have dominated the field of NLP. The models vary in size, with the largest ones reaching hundreds of billions of parameters, and are trained with different objectives, such as causal language modeling (Radford et al., 2019; Brown et al., 2020) or masked language modeling (Devlin et al., 2019; Liu et al., 2019). By processing large amounts of text, they learn to capture general knowledge about the language and can then be fine-tuned to perform domain-specific tasks.

Regardless of the neural network architecture design choices, an important factor is the domain of the training data. For years, research in the field of NLP was mostly focused on the English language, but models and resources for many other languages have also been published recently. Multilingual models have also been developed (Conneau et al., 2020; Xue et al., 2021) which are capable of understanding more than 100 languages at once. The corpora used for pre-training are typically mixtures of general-domain data sources, such as crawled websites, books or Wikipedia articles.

The language can vary significantly across domains, not only in terms of the vocabulary, but also syntax, semantics and pragmatics. While the language of the aforementioned general-domain sources conforms to the linguistic norms, there is a large and important domain where the language is distinctly different and rapidly changing, namely social media. Apart from the obvious differences, such as the occurrence of hashtags or emojis, people have figured out how to shout using capital letters, or that ending a message with a period might be perceived as sarcastic. In order to properly represent such characteristics in the language models, it is necessary for them to be exposed to domain-specific texts not only during the supervised fine-tuning, but also in the pre-training phase.

In this work, we introduce TrelBERT, an encoder-only language model initialized with existing general-domain weights and adapted to the social media domain by pre-training it on over 40 million Polish tweets with the masked language modeling objective. TrelBERT proves to be well-suited for application of NLP in social media, achieving state-of-the-art results for downstream tasks operating on Polish Twitter data. We make the model publicly available[1].

The main contribution of our research is the introduction of the first Polish language representation model pre-trained on Twitter data. Our model achieves state-of-the-art results in the cyberbullying detection task (part of the Polish NLP benchmark), outperforming all existing solutions, including larger general-domain Polish models, as well as multilingual in-domain models. We also release a dataset of 1000 tweet IDs labeled for the problem of harmful speech detection which is a less biased (randomly sampled using the streaming API) and more up-to-date alternative to the existing one.

[1] https://huggingface.co/deepsense-ai/trelbert

Proceedings of the 9th Workshop on Slavic Natural Language Processing 2023 (SlavicNLP 2023), pages 17–24
May 6, 2023 ©2023 Association for Computational Linguistics

2 Related work

In this section, we review the current state of Polish NLP and provide an overview of language models trained in the social media domain.

2.1 NLP for Polish language

Polish is a language spoken by over 40 million people who constitute a large population of potential beneficiaries of high-quality NLP systems. In early 2020, according to the six-level taxonomy proposed by (Joshi et al., 2020), Polish was considered one of the "Underdogs" – languages that "have a large amount of unlabeled data [...] and are only challenged by lesser amount of labeled data". In the following years, taking advantage of self-supervised learning, several Transformer-based models for Polish have been released, including encoder-only models such as PolBERT (Kłeczek, 2020), Polish RoBERTa (Dadas et al., 2020) and HerBERT (Mroczkowski et al., 2021), as well as decoder-only papuGaPT2 (Wojczulis and Kłeczek, 2021) and encoder-decoder plT5 (Chrabrowa et al., 2022). All of these were trained on general-domain corpora, i.e. collections of texts extracted from sources such as Wikipedia, books, newspapers, crawled websites or movie subtitles.

To compare the performance of Polish language models across a set of downstream tasks, (Rybak et al., 2020) have designed the KLEJ benchmark. It consists of 9 datasets for classification and regression, with data sources ranging from customer reviews to news summaries to Twitter messages. In KLEJ, the current state-of-the-art results (averaged across 9 tasks) are those of (Mroczkowski et al., 2021), whose HerBERT-large ranks first in the leaderboard[2], and HerBERT-base is the best performing among the base models.

Recently, (Augustyniak et al., 2022) have proposed a newer benchmark, called LEPISZCZE[3], in which they decided to keep 5 datasets from KLEJ and introduce 8 new ones, including corpora of transcribed call center conversations, legal documents and political tweets.

2.2 Language models for social media

In recent years, language models trained specifically on Twitter data have been a topic of interest for many NLP researchers, motivated by their applicability in tasks such as sentiment analysis, hate speech detection, or named entity recognition. As confirmation of this statement, 4 out of 12 tasks in the *SemEval 2023* competition[4] were based on Twitter data. Monolingual models have been trained on tweets in languages such as English (Nguyen et al., 2020), Arabic (Antoun et al., 2020; Abdelali et al., 2021), French (Guo et al., 2021), Hebrew (Seker et al., 2022), Indonesian (Koto et al., 2021), Italian (Polignano et al., 2019) and Spanish (González et al., 2021; Pérez et al., 2022). Some of them were initialized with weights of existing general-domain models and adapted to Twitter data by continued pre-training, while others were trained on Twitter data from scratch.

Recently, following the success of multilingual models such as XLM-R (Conneau et al., 2020), analogous Twitter-specific models have also been released. XLM-T (Barbieri et al., 2022) is initialized with XLM-R weights and pre-trained on 198M tweets (1.7B tokens) reflecting the distribution of over 30 languages in Twitter data, including around 1M tweets in Polish. TwHIN-BERT (Zhang et al., 2022) is trained from scratch on 7B tweets covering over 100 languages (around 100M tweets in Polish), with a contrastive social objective in addition to masked language modeling. Both XLM-T and TwHIN-BERT use the XLM-R tokenizer. The authors of Bernice (DeLucia et al., 2022), on the other hand, create a Twitter-specific tokenizer, and use it to train a masked language model on 2.5B tweets (56B tokens) in 66 languages (including more than 10M tweets in Polish) from scratch.

3 TrelBERT

We introduce a language model trained on Polish tweets which we call TrelBERT[5]. It is a Transformer encoder model trained with the masked language modeling objective. Rather than training TrelBERT from scratch, we take advantage of existing weights and adapt them to the social media domain.

As our starting point, we use HerBERT-base (Mroczkowski et al., 2021), the best performing one among Polish *base* models[6]. HerBERT was initialized with weights from XLM-R (Conneau et al., 2020) and further pre-trained on a mixture of general-domain Polish corpora with 8.6B tokens in total. Its tokenizer is a variant of Byte-Pair Encod-

[2] https://klejbenchmark.com/leaderboard

[3] https://lepiszcze.ml

[4] https://semeval.github.io/SemEval2023/tasks

[5] *trel* is the Polish word for *trill*, as a reference to *tweet*

[6] we did not consider training *large* models in this work

ing (BPE-Dropout; Provilkov et al., 2019) and has a vocabulary of 50k tokens.

3.1 Training data

We collected a random sample of 90 million tweets in Polish using the official Twitter API. The language of tweets was determined based on information provided in Twitter metadata. Only tweets created between November 2017 (when the limit of 280 characters per tweet was introduced) and July 2022 were taken into consideration.

Similar to (Nguyen et al., 2020), we preprocessed the tweets by replacing all user mentions and URLs with special tokens: *@anonymized_account* and *@URL*. We also merged multiple user mentions at the beginning of tweets into a single token as we discovered they are not part of the tweet text content but only reflect who the user is replying to in a discussion thread. We did not preprocess hashtags or emojis.

We used the pre-computed HerBERT tokenizer extended with the two additional tokens mentioned above. To best align our model with the maximum tweet length limit, we set *max_length* for truncation of tokenized tweets to 128. We filtered out tweets that have fewer than 5 tokens after tokenization from the dataset. The resulting corpus consisted of 90M tweets (2B tokens) with an average of 23 and a median of 18 tokens per tweet.

3.2 Model pre-training

We initialized our model with HerBERT-base and trained it using AdamW optimizer with a linear learning rate schedule (peak value 5e-5, warm-up for 6% steps) and the masked language modeling objective. During our experiments, we set the batch size to 2184. We trained TrelBERT for 41,208 steps (1 epoch). As we later evaluated the predictions of several model checkpoints, we noticed a visible degradation in performance on non-Twitter downstream tasks as pre-training progressed. The publicly available TrelBERT checkpoint is one that we obtained after 20k training steps, i.e. after being trained on around 44M tweets.

4 Evaluation

To compare the performance of TrelBERT with other Polish language models and Twitter-specific multilingual models, we used the KLEJ benchmark (Rybak et al., 2020) and the Political Advertising Detection task (Augustyniak et al., 2020).

4.1 KLEJ – fine-tuning

We fine-tuned the models on KLEJ tasks using Polish RoBERTa scripts[7] which we adapted to the *transformers* library. All models were trained for 10 epochs, except for models fine-tuned on the cyberbullying detection task, which were trained for 1 epoch. We used AdamW optimizer with the following hyperparameters: $\epsilon = 10^{-6}, \beta_1 = 0.9, \beta_2 = 0.98$ and a polynomial decay learning rate schedule with a peak value of 1e-5. The batch size was set to 16. The warm-up stage was set to the first 6% of the training steps.

4.2 KLEJ – cyberbullying detection

Among the tasks available in KLEJ, the one which is most relevant to our research is called cyberbullying detection (**CBD**) (Ptaszynski et al., 2019), formulated as a binary classification of harmful Twitter messages. It was originally introduced as part of the *PolEval2019* competition[8], and then included in KLEJ.

The dataset consists of 10,041 training and 1000 test examples. It is highly imbalanced, with only 851 positive class examples in the training set and 134 examples in the test set. The F1 score is used to measure the performance of models in this task.

We repeated the fine-tuning of several pretrained models to the CBD dataset five times and evaluated them on the test set. The scores reported in Table 1 are the mean values of the five finetuning runs. Additionally, the score for Polbert-CB (Ptaszynski et al., 2022), the Polish BERT trained for Automatic Cyberbullying Detection, is given.

The tweets included in the CBD dataset were created in late 2018 and obtained by processing answers to tweets posted by the most popular accounts, followed by further data selection and filtering according to the procedure provided in (Ptaszynski et al., 2019). To measure how our solution generalizes to the broader Twitter data distribution, we also checked the results on another test dataset which we prepared, entitled `harmful_tweets_1k`[9]. It consists of 1000 tweets in Polish randomly sampled from the years 2019 to 2022, which were then labeled by the three of us following annotation guidelines used during the creation of cyberbullying detection task (Ptaszynski et al., 2019), achieving a Fleiss' kappa value of

[7]https://github.com/sdadas/polish-roberta

[8]http://2019.poleval.pl/index.php/tasks/task6

[9]https://github.com/deepsense-ai/trelbert

Model	F1 score	Accuracy	Recall	Precision
		CBD test dataset		
HerBERT base	66.0	90.5	68.6	63.6
HerBERT large	71.4	92.3	71.6	**71.4**
Polbert-CB	67.2	91.5	64.9	69.6
TrelBERT (ours)	**74.5**	**92.7**	**79.1**	70.4
XLM-T	66.5	90.8	68.1	65.4
TwHIN-BERT base	66.2	90.6	68.5	64.1
TwHIN-BERT large	68.8	91.8	68.3	70.1
Bernice	69.1	92.7	68.5	69.8
		`harmful_tweets_1k` dataset		
HerBERT base	58.3	90.6	62.3	55.1
HerBERT large	62.8	92.0	64.2	62.0
Polbert-CB	56.5	91.7	50.9	63.5
TrelBERT (ours)	**66.3**	**92.3**	**68.9**	64.1
XLM-T	53.1	87.6	66.2	44.5
TwHIN-BERT base	49.3	89.4	48.8	50.2
TwHIN-BERT large	59.9	92.0	56.6	**64.5**
Bernice	60.7	91.8	59.2	62.2

Table 1: Results on the cyberbullying detection task.

$\kappa = 0.74$. By doing so, we obtained the test dataset, 10.6% of which were harmful Twitter messages.

TrelBERT achieves the best average results for both datasets, significantly outperforming all existing models for Polish, as well as multilingual models trained on Twitter data. In particular, it performs much better not only than HerBERT-base (which it was initialized with), but also than the *large* models. The difference between TrelBERT and all other models is especially visible in the recall value, with precision remaining more or less on par with other best-performing models. The results indicate that, if applied in a real-world scenario, TrelBERT would be able to capture more harmful content than its competitors. For one of the fine-tuned checkpoints, we submitted the predictions to the KLEJ leaderboard, officially setting the new state-of-the-art in the CBD task (F1 score = 76.1).

4.3 KLEJ – other tasks

Apart from cyberbullying detection, the KLEJ benchmark consists of 8 other tasks:

- **CDSC-E** – natural language inference; the task is to determine the logical relationship between a pair of sentences as one of entailment, contradiction or neutral
- **CDSC-R** – a semantic relatedness task, the goal of which is to predict the relatedness (ranging from 0 to 5) between a pair of sentences
- **AR** – prediction of ratings (range 1-5) for product reviews from an e-commerce platform
- **PolEmo2.0** – sentiment analysis of online consumer reviews; the training dataset consists of reviews from two domains: medicine and hotels; in **PolEmo2.0-IN** the test set consists of reviews from the same domains, while in **PolEmo2.0-OUT** the test set comes from the product and school domains
- **DYK** – a binary classification task devised based on a question-answer dataset "Did you know" (Marcińczuk et al., 2013)
- **PSC** – a text similarity task formulated as binary classification of news article-summary pairs
- **NKJP-NER** – a named entity classification task, the goal of which is to predict the presence and type of a named entity from six categories: `persName`, `orgName`, `geogName`, `placeName`, `date` and `time`

We measured how TrelBERT and other Twitter-specific models perform in these out-of-domain tasks. In this set of experiments, we fine-tuned each model once. The scores reported in Table 2

Model	NKJP	CDSC-E	CDSC-R	PE2-I	PE2-O	DYK	PSC	AR
TwHIN-BERT base	87.0	92.0	90.8	86.0	69.4	51.3	84.8	84.4
TwHIN-BERT large	89.4	92.2	91.4	88.8	75.3	52.8	82.0	85.7
Bernice	89.0	92.2	91.1	84.8	68.2	44.9	88.2	85.1
XLM-T	90.9	93.9	91.8	86.0	76.3	41.1	82.4	85.5
TrelBERT (ours)	94.4	93.9	93.6	89.3	78.1	67.4	95.7	86.1
HerBERT base	94.5	**94.5**	94.0	90.9	80.4	68.1	**98.9**	87.7
HerBERT large	**96.4**	94.1	**94.9**	**92.2**	**81.8**	**75.8**	**98.9**	**89.1**

Table 2: Results on the KLEJ benchmark (excluding CBD). For DYK and PSC tasks, the F1 score is reported. In AR, the micro-average of the mean-absolute error per class (wMAE) is used to measure performance. In CDSC-R, Spearman correlation is applied for evaluation. For the remaining tasks, accuracy is reported.

are mostly obtained by uploading predictions to the KLEJ benchmark page without publishing the results. The scores for HerBERT-base, HerBERT-large and TrelBERT are taken directly from the leaderboard. Unsurprisingly, due to being adapted towards the language of social media, TrelBERT achieves slightly worse results than HerBERT-base on all 8 tasks operating on data out of its domain. As expected, the Twitter-specific multilingual models perform worse than Polish-only ones, although the differences for some of the tasks are not vast. The discrepancy in performance metrics between Twitter-only based models and general-domain models in general-domain tasks (particularly noticeable in tasks DYK, PSC and PE2-O) shows how the language of social media is different from linguistic norms. This might also suggest that general knowledge about the world and language (which a model can learn from general-domain corpora) is relevant to domain-specific tasks such as harmful speech detection.

4.4 Political advertising detection

We also conducted experiments on another Twitter-based downstream task, Political Advertising Detection, proposed in (Augustyniak et al., 2020). The related dataset consists of 1701 human-annotated tweets (1020 for training, 340 for validation and 341 in the test set) collected by searching for specific hashtags and keywords related to the Polish presidential elections in 2020. The goal of the task is to perform token-level sequence labeling with 9 categories (healthcare, welfare, defense, legal, education, infrastructure, society, foreign policy and immigration) with an imbalanced number of examples. The task is included in the LEPISZCZE benchmark (Augustyniak et al., 2022).

The results reported in Table 3 are macro F1 scores achieved by selected models averaged over 5 fine-tuning runs. The fine-tuning process was similar to that described in 4.1, the only difference being the learning rate which we set to 1e-5. All the evaluated Polish-only models perform better than multilingual Twitter-specific ones, but there is no significant difference between TrelBERT and the two HerBERT variants. However, taking into account the rather small size of the dataset (for a sequence labeling problem with 9 categories, some of them with very few examples) and its collection and annotation procedures (bias towards certain keywords), we do not draw any general conclusions about the capabilities of the model.

Model	Macro F1
Bernice	62.62 ± 4.28
XLM-T	64.42 ± 0.90
TwHIN-BERT large	67.20 ± 1.60
TwHIN-BERT base	67.63 ± 1.54
HerBERT base	69.23 ± 1.87
TrelBERT (ours)	70.08 ± 0.50
HerBERT large	71.32 ± 1.38

Table 3: Results on the Political Advertising Detection test set for selected models.

5 Conclusion

In this paper, we have introduced TrelBERT, the first Polish language representation model pretrained on Twitter data. It achieves state-of-the-art results in a cyberbullying detection task, outperforming all existing solutions, including larger general-domain Polish models, as well as multilingual in-domain models. Additionally, we contribute by releasing a harmful speech dataset with labeled tweet IDs which could be used as an alternative test set for cyberbullying detection.

Limitations

By taking the characteristics of the language used by the social media community into consideration, we are aware that applying a general-purpose tokenizer has some major limitations. Emojis, emoticons, user mentions, hashtags, and URLs are inseparable elements of Twitter language and their existence should not be unnoticed or treated as noise in a good-quality corpus. Emojis and emoticons could be interpreted as digital gestures or face expressions. By replacing all user mentions and URLs with *@anonymized_account* and *@URL* tokens, we lose the meaning they convey. On the other hand, doing so was necessary for ethical (user mentions) or pragmatic reasons (preprocessing and tokenizing URLs would be difficult).

Also, measuring the performance of the model on just two downstream tasks with data from Twitter does not seem to be a sufficiently fair benchmark to prove the superiority of our model. Unfortunately, the vast majority of languages (including Polish) suffer from a lack of high-quality labeled datasets.

Last but not least, the language of social media is changing rapidly. TrelBERT outperforms other models in the cyberbullying detection task, but we expect it to degrade performance on future data. Thus, updating the weights of the model by means of further pre-training on latest tweets is necessary to keep the model effective.

Ethics Statement

Due to the nature of our data, there were several ethical issues to consider. First, we anonymized all the usernames mentioned in tweets by replacing them with *@anonymized_account* token. Despite the fact that the data is publicly available, we decided to prevent the model from learning sentiment about specific users based on what the community writes about them. We did not want the model to produce harmful output tokens for specific users.

Secondly, there is a great deal of harmful content in social media, which we could possibly try to remove from the training corpus as part of data preprocessing to prevent the model from learning this kind of language. However, if we are to use such models to detect hate speech or cyberbullying, they need to know it. We believe that exposing a model to harmful content only during the fine-tuning stage may not be enough.

References

Ahmed Abdelali, Sabit Hassan, Hamdy Mubarak, Kareem Darwish, and Younes Samih. 2021. Pre-training BERT on Arabic Tweets: Practical considerations. *ArXiv*, abs/2102.10684.

Wissam Antoun, Fady Baly, and Hazem Hajj. 2020. AraBERT: Transformer-based model for Arabic language understanding. In *Proceedings of the 4th Workshop on Open-Source Arabic Corpora and Processing Tools, with a Shared Task on Offensive Language Detection*, pages 9–15, Marseille, France. European Language Resource Association.

Lukasz Augustyniak, Krzysztof Rajda, Tomasz Kajdanowicz, and Michał Bernaczyk. 2020. Political advertising dataset: the use case of the Polish 2020 presidential elections. In *Proceedings of the The Fourth Widening Natural Language Processing Workshop*, pages 110–114, Seattle, USA. Association for Computational Linguistics.

Łukasz Augustyniak, Kamil Tagowski, Albert Sawczyn, Denis Janiak, Roman Bartusiak, Adrian Szymczak, Marcin Wątroba, Arkadiusz Janz, Piotr Szymański, Mikołaj Morzy, Tomasz Kajdanowicz, and Maciej Piasecki. 2022. This is the way: designing and compiling LEPISZCZE, a comprehensive NLP benchmark for Polish.

Francesco Barbieri, Luis Espinosa Anke, and Jose Camacho-Collados. 2022. XLM-T: Multilingual language models in Twitter for sentiment analysis and beyond. In *Proceedings of the Thirteenth Language Resources and Evaluation Conference*, pages 258–266, Marseille, France. European Language Resources Association.

Tom Brown, Benjamin Mann, Nick Ryder, Melanie Subbiah, Jared D Kaplan, Prafulla Dhariwal, Arvind Neelakantan, Pranav Shyam, Girish Sastry, Amanda Askell, Sandhini Agarwal, Ariel Herbert-Voss, Gretchen Krueger, Tom Henighan, Rewon Child, Aditya Ramesh, Daniel Ziegler, Jeffrey Wu, Clemens Winter, Chris Hesse, Mark Chen, Eric Sigler, Mateusz Litwin, Scott Gray, Benjamin Chess, Jack Clark, Christopher Berner, Sam McCandlish, Alec Radford, Ilya Sutskever, and Dario Amodei. 2020. Language models are few-shot learners. In *Advances in Neural Information Processing Systems*, volume 33, pages 1877–1901. Curran Associates, Inc.

Aleksandra Chrabrowa, Łukasz Dragan, Karol Grzegorczyk, Dariusz Kajtoch, Mikołaj Koszowski, Robert Mroczkowski, and Piotr Rybak. 2022. Evaluation of transfer learning for Polish with a text-to-text model. In *Proceedings of the Thirteenth Language Resources and Evaluation Conference*, pages 4374–4394, Marseille, France. European Language Resources Association.

Alexis Conneau, Kartikay Khandelwal, Naman Goyal, Vishrav Chaudhary, Guillaume Wenzek, Francisco

Guzmán, Edouard Grave, Myle Ott, Luke Zettlemoyer, and Veselin Stoyanov. 2020. Unsupervised cross-lingual representation learning at scale. In *Proceedings of the 58th Annual Meeting of the Association for Computational Linguistics*, pages 8440–8451, Online. Association for Computational Linguistics.

Sławomir Dadas, Michał Perełkiewicz, and Rafał Poświata. 2020. Pre-training Polish Transformer-based language models at scale. In *Artificial Intelligence and Soft Computing: 19th International Conference, ICAISC 2020, Zakopane, Poland, October 12-14, 2020, Proceedings, Part II*, page 301–314, Berlin, Heidelberg. Springer-Verlag.

Alexandra DeLucia, Shijie Wu, Aaron Mueller, Carlos Aguirre, Philip Resnik, and Mark Dredze. 2022. Bernice: A multilingual pre-trained encoder for Twitter. In *Proceedings of the 2022 Conference on Empirical Methods in Natural Language Processing*, pages 6191–6205, Abu Dhabi, United Arab Emirates. Association for Computational Linguistics.

Jacob Devlin, Ming-Wei Chang, Kenton Lee, and Kristina Toutanova. 2019. BERT: Pre-training of deep bidirectional transformers for language understanding. In *Proceedings of the 2019 Conference of the North American Chapter of the Association for Computational Linguistics: Human Language Technologies, Volume 1 (Long and Short Papers)*, pages 4171–4186, Minneapolis, Minnesota. Association for Computational Linguistics.

José Ángel González, Lluís-F. Hurtado, and Ferran Pla. 2021. TWilBert: Pre-trained deep bidirectional transformers for spanish twitter. *Neurocomputing*, 426:58–69.

Yanzhu Guo, Virgile Rennard, Christos Xypolopoulos, and Michalis Vazirgiannis. 2021. BERTweetFR : Domain adaptation of pre-trained language models for French tweets. In *Proceedings of the Seventh Workshop on Noisy User-generated Text (W-NUT 2021)*, pages 445–450, Online. Association for Computational Linguistics.

Pratik Joshi, Sebastin Santy, Amar Budhiraja, Kalika Bali, and Monojit Choudhury. 2020. The state and fate of linguistic diversity and inclusion in the NLP world. In *Proceedings of the 58th Annual Meeting of the Association for Computational Linguistics*, pages 6282–6293, Online. Association for Computational Linguistics.

Fajri Koto, Jey Han Lau, and Timothy Baldwin. 2021. IndoBERTweet: A pretrained language model for Indonesian Twitter with effective domain-specific vocabulary initialization. In *Proceedings of the 2021 Conference on Empirical Methods in Natural Language Processing*, pages 10660–10668, Online and Punta Cana, Dominican Republic. Association for Computational Linguistics.

Dariusz Kłeczek. 2020. Polbert: Attacking Polish NLP Tasks with Transformers. In *Proceedings of the PolEval 2020 Workshop*. Institute of Computer Science, Polish Academy of Sciences.

Yinhan Liu, Myle Ott, Naman Goyal, Jingfei Du, Mandar Joshi, Danqi Chen, Omer Levy, Mike Lewis, Luke Zettlemoyer, and Veselin Stoyanov. 2019. Roberta: A robustly optimized bert pretraining approach. *ArXiv*, abs/1907.11692.

Michał Marcińczuk, Marcin Ptak, Adam Radziszewski, and Maciej Piasecki. 2013. Open Dataset for Development of Polish Question Answering Systems. In *Proceedings of Human Language Technologies as a Challenge for Computer Science and Linguistics'13*, pages 479–483, Poznań. Fundacja UAM.

Robert Mroczkowski, Piotr Rybak, Alina Wróblewska, and Ireneusz Gawlik. 2021. HerBERT: Efficiently pretrained transformer-based language model for Polish. In *Proceedings of the 8th Workshop on Balto-Slavic Natural Language Processing*, pages 1–10, Kiyv, Ukraine. Association for Computational Linguistics.

Dat Quoc Nguyen, Thanh Vu, and Anh Tuan Nguyen. 2020. BERTweet: A pre-trained language model for English tweets. In *Proceedings of the 2020 Conference on Empirical Methods in Natural Language Processing: System Demonstrations*, pages 9–14, Online. Association for Computational Linguistics.

Juan Manuel Pérez, Damián Ariel Furman, Laura Alonso Alemany, and Franco M. Luque. 2022. RoBERTuito: a pre-trained language model for social media text in Spanish. In *Proceedings of the Thirteenth Language Resources and Evaluation Conference*, pages 7235–7243, Marseille, France. European Language Resources Association.

Marco Polignano, Valerio Basile, Pierpaolo Basile, Marco de Gemmis, and Giovanni Semeraro. 2019. AlBERTo: Modeling Italian social media language with bert. *Italian Journal of Computational Linguistics*, 5:11–31.

Ivan Provilkov, Dmitrii Emelianenko, and Elena Voita. 2019. Bpe-dropout: Simple and effective subword regularization. *arXiv preprint arXiv:1910.13267*.

Michal Ptaszynski, Agata Pieciukiewicz, and Paweł Dybała. 2019. Results of the poleval 2019 shared task 6: First dataset and open shared task for automatic cyberbullying detection in polish twitter.

Michal Ptaszynski, Agata Pieciukiewicz, Pawel Dybala, Pawel Skrzek, Kamil Soliwoda, Marcin Fortuna, Gniewosz Leliwa, and Michal Wroczynski. 2022. Polish bert trained for automatic cyberbullying detection.

Alec Radford, Jeff Wu, Rewon Child, David Luan, Dario Amodei, and Ilya Sutskever. 2019. Language models are unsupervised multitask learners.

Piotr Rybak, Robert Mroczkowski, Janusz Tracz, and Ireneusz Gawlik. 2020. KLEJ: Comprehensive benchmark for Polish language understanding. In *Proceedings of the 58th Annual Meeting of the Association for Computational Linguistics*, pages 1191–1201, Online. Association for Computational Linguistics.

Amit Seker, Elron Bandel, Dan Bareket, Idan Brusilovsky, Refael Greenfeld, and Reut Tsarfaty. 2022. AlephBERT: Language model pre-training and evaluation from sub-word to sentence level. In *Proceedings of the 60th Annual Meeting of the Association for Computational Linguistics (Volume 1: Long Papers)*, pages 46–56, Dublin, Ireland. Association for Computational Linguistics.

Ashish Vaswani, Noam Shazeer, Niki Parmar, Jakob Uszkoreit, Llion Jones, Aidan N Gomez, Ł ukasz Kaiser, and Illia Polosukhin. 2017. Attention is all you need. In *Advances in Neural Information Processing Systems*, volume 30. Curran Associates, Inc.

Michał Wojczulis and Dariusz Kłeczek. 2021. papugapt2 - polish gpt2 language model.

Linting Xue, Noah Constant, Adam Roberts, Mihir Kale, Rami Al-Rfou, Aditya Siddhant, Aditya Barua, and Colin Raffel. 2021. mT5: A massively multilingual pre-trained text-to-text transformer. In *Proceedings of the 2021 Conference of the North American Chapter of the Association for Computational Linguistics: Human Language Technologies*, pages 483–498, Online. Association for Computational Linguistics.

Xinyang Zhang, Yury Malkov, Omar Florez, Serim Park, Brian McWilliams, Jiawei Han, and Ahmed El-Kishky. 2022. TwHIN-BERT: A socially-enriched pre-trained language model for multilingual tweet representations. *arXiv preprint arXiv:2209.07562*.

Croatian Film Review Dataset (Cro-FiReDa): A Sentiment Annotated Dataset of Film Reviews

Gaurish Thakkar and **Nives Mikelić Preradović** and **Marko Tadić**
Faculty of Humanities and Social Sciences, University of Zagreb, Zagreb 10000, Croatia
gthakkar@m.ffzg.hr, nmikelic@ffzg.hr,marko.tadic@ffzg.hr

Abstract

This paper introduces Cro-FiReDa, a sentiment-annotated dataset for Croatian in the domain of movie reviews. The dataset, which contains over 10,000 sentences, has been annotated at the sentence level. In addition to presenting the overall annotation process, we also present benchmark results based on the transformer-based fine-tuning approach.

1 Introduction

The goal of sentiment analysis is to classify the polarity of text (*e.g.*, positive, negative, neutral, or mixed). In this paper, we describe the process of annotating a sentiment analysis dataset in Croatian. As shown in the example below, the label indicates the sentiment polarity of the text.

Hr "I bio sam zadivljen i tijekom finalne borbene scene ."

En "And I was also amazed during the final battle scene."

- **Label** : positive

Croatian is a low-resource language in terms of sentiment analysis resources. There is currently no Croatian dataset for the domain of movie reviews. The dataset presented here is the first sentiment movie review dataset. The texts for the annotation campaign are taken from the Croatian movie review website and cover multiple genres, namely adventure, series (serija), and sci-fi. In addition to the other metadata described below, the website includes a summary of the entire text of the author's review. The dataset, annotation guidelines, trained models, and associated code will be made available to the public. In this work, we describe our entire workflow for creating the resource. We also present the experimental scores for the sentiment analysis task using pre-trained transformer models.

The rest of the paper is structured as follows: In Section 2, we review the related work on the dataset with regard to its annotation as well as modelling. In Section 3, we describe the annotation process in detail. In Section 4, we present the statistics of the annotated dataset before presenting the baseline scores in Section 5. We complete the paper with the conclusion, discussion, and future work in Section 6.

2 Related Work

In this section, we will highlight the related work on resources and models for sentiment analysis. Sentiment analysis is a well-researched field, and there are a number of resources for various languages, such as English (Maas et al., 2011; Pang and Lee, 2005; Keung et al., 2020), German (Cieliebak et al., 2017; Sänger et al., 2016; Clematide et al., 2012), French (Apidianaki et al., 2016), and Italian (Basile and Nissim, 2013). There are few resources available for Croatian sentiment analysis. The stance (and sentiment) annotated dataset (Bošnjak and Karan, 2019) contains comments submitted by users for online news articles. Pelicon et al. (2020) created a dataset for sentiment analysis of Croatian news articles and performed zero-shot classification using Slovene resources. Zhou et al. (2015) performed multiple levels of sentiment analysis on multilingual Wikipedia articles using machine translation. Öhman et al. (2020) compiled a parallel dataset for sentiment and emotion analysis based on movie subtitles. The dataset was created by manually annotating 25K Finnish and 30K English sentences, which were then projected onto 30 other languages, including Croatian. Agić et al. (2010) presented rule-based annotated Croatian news articles in the finance domain that captured the general sentiment of the text. Rotim and Šnajder (2017) compiled a dataset of gaming review text spans in Croatian that were tagged with positive and negative labels. There are also a few

Proceedings of the 9th Workshop on Slavic Natural Language Processing 2023 (SlavicNLP 2023), pages 25–31

Croatian sentiment lexicons, such as those developed by Ljubešić et al. (2020); Glavaš et al. (2012). The ParlaSent-BCS (Mochtak et al., 2022) dataset is another resource that has Croatian sentences in parliamentary debates tagged with sentiment polarity. Tikhonov et al. (2022) provide an overview of existing resources for East European languages, including Croatian.

3 Text and Annotations

In this section, we describe our annotation procedure in greater depth. First, we describe the backgrounds of the annotators. Second, the guidelines and methodology for annotation are explained. Third, the statistical aspects of the dataset are discussed.

3.1 Annotation Procedure

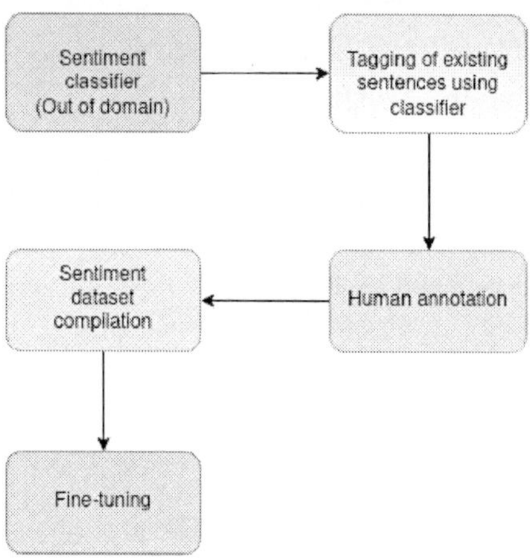

Figure 1: The dataset creation process.

The task is defined as a sentence-level sentiment task in which each sentence in the training set is annotated with a single label. The dataset consists of professional reviews from the Croatian movie review website[1]. The adventure, TV series, and science fiction (sci-fi) genres were chosen as subcategories. Each review instance is accompanied by the following data fields:

1. **Review**: the text written by the professional reviewer.

2. **First impression**: short summary of the overall review.

3. **Overall assessment**: the score assigned by the reviewer. The reviewers rate the film on different scales, the scores range from (0-10) to (1-5) stars.

4. **Date**: date of the review.

In addition, the review text has formatted information about the title, IMDB rating, producers, actors, directors, genres, and date of release. The dataset contains a total of 216 adventure-related reviews, 114 sci-fi reviews, and 76 series reviews. We framed the sentiment annotation task as a sentence-level label correction task. The overall methodology is presented in Figure 1. Each review has undergone sentence segmentation, in which the entire review has been broken down into individual sentences. All reviews were sorted by sentence length and divided into groups so that each annotator received an equal amount of sentences, but at the same time, no annotator received partial review text. This was done to make sure that no student received a partial review. An empirical method was used to determine the N=23 groups. A minimum of three (and a maximum of five) annotators have annotated a single sentence. Each review was pre-annotated using the deep-learning sentiment classification model (Thakkar et al., 2021). The classification model was trained using the SentiNews dataset, which is composed of Croatian and Slovenian news articles in a multitask setup, and has reported an F1-score of 63.86. This step has sped up the annotation process, as annotators are no longer required to tag the sentence from scratch, but only correct the tag if it is incorrect. A total of 82 students participated in the study. All the annotators were undergraduate students of linguistics and informatics between the ages of 22 and 24. All the annotators were native Croatian speakers. The final label for a sentence is chosen by a majority vote.

3.2 Annotation Scheme

The guidelines for the annotation were largely adopted from Mohammad (2016). Learners were presented with five categories of sentiment: 1—negative, 2—neutral, 3—positive, 4—mixed, and 5—other/sarcasm. Evidently, the negative review is labelled as negative, while the positive review is labelled "positive". The release date and genre of the film are categorised as neutral facts. Sentences that have both positive and negative connotations are classified as "mixed". If figurative language exists, it is labelled as "other/sarcasm".

[1] https://www.recenzijefilmova.com/

The annotation guidelines describe each instance of the label with multiple examples.

3.3 Web Interface

All of our annotation tasks used the online tool INCEpTION (Klie et al., 2018) because it enables simple semantic annotations. The platform simplifies the administration of annotation projects involving many annotators. Because we did not want participants to see each other's work, each group of students was assigned a separate project. Each user was subsequently able to view only the files assigned to him or her after logging into the system with his or her credentials. Before moving on to the next document, each user would perform the annotation process and lock the document. The locking mechanism signified the document's completion and allowed us to monitor its completion status and overall work status. Each student has averaged four hours on the assignment.

3.4 Inter-annotator agreement

Using Fleiss Kappa, we have measured the inter-annotator agreement of the dataset across multiple groups. The scores suggest moderate (0.41-0.60) to substantial (0.61-0.80) levels of annotator agreement. Table 1 lists the agreement for every label. During the phase of judging, the annotators were required to report any uncertainties. The majority of queries pertained to metadata present in the review text, such as the title. There were 843 disagreements in which there was no clear majority winner. These sentences were characterised by conditionals or mixed sentiments and were filtered out as they were not additionally annotated by anyone and will be taken up for future work.

Hr "Za one koji vole ovu vrstu filma , trebali biste biti u mogućnosti uživati , ali za lojalnog ljubitelja izvornog filma , ovaj se može vidjeti kao još jedan od najljepših ili najmanje omiljenih ."

En "For those who like this type of film, you should be able to enjoy it, but for a loyal fan of the original film, this one can be seen as another of the best or least favorite."

3.5 Corpus Statistics

Table 1 shows the statistics for the final sentiment annotated dataset. Out of 10,464 sentences, we have 59 percent neutral statements. This is clear because the majority of the text contains factual information about the movie/series. There are a total of 875 reviews that have text summaries associated with the main text. The mean number of space-separated tokens for review text and summary is 731 and 47, respectively.

Label	# of instances	agreement
neutral	6205	0.51
positive	2031	0.53
negative	1290	0.42
mixed	862	0.30
sarcasm	76	0.04
total	10464	

Table 1: Statistics of the sentiment dataset. Numbers represent sentences. Kappa statistics for each label

3.6 Dataset Analysis

Out of 10,388 samples, around 2,257 instances retained their original classification tag. The remaining 8,131, which constitute around 78 percent of the final dataset, were modified by the annotators. In these modifications, more than 50 percent of the changes (4,813 instances) were from negative label to neutral, followed by a positive to neutral annotation change (1,053 instances). The sentences that changed from non-neutral to neutral were mostly informative, similar to title sentences with polar words. We also sampled a few random reviews and checked the polarity of the individual sentences in the review, ignoring the neutral sentences. This number of positive and negative sentences does hint at the possibility of a relationship with the overall rating of the review given by the reviewer. For instance, if there were an equal number of positive and negative sentences, the movie would receive a 3/5 or 5/10 rating. On the other side, if the review contains more compliments, it will receive a rating higher than 3. Exactly 654 sentences in the groups received the same annotated class provided by the authors.

4 Experiments

4.1 Experimental Setup

We performed experiments for the task of sentiment analysis. To benchmark the dataset on sentiment classification, we use the fine-tuning approach proposed by Devlin et al. (2019). We used the CroSlo-Engual BERT (Ulčar and Robnik-Šikonja, 2020)

as our contextualised pre-trained language model and performed fine-tuning using a softmax classification head. CroSloEngual BERT was trained on corpora from Croatian, Slovenian, and English languages with a total of 5.9 billion tokens. For training, only the positive, negative, and neutral class instances were used. We divided the dataset into train tests in an 80:20 ratio and used 10% of the train set for development. We used a learning rate of 1e-05 and weight decay of 0.02 with early stopping on evaluation loss with patience of 4. A batch size of 16 was used during training. In addition, a hidden dropout and attention of 0.2 were used as regularization constants. Each of the experiments used a GPU with 24 GB of VRAM. Each epoch of sentiment training lasted longer than 20 minutes. In addition, we also present the results utilising the three strategies described in Pelicon et al. (2020). The reported approaches employ 10-fold cross-validation for training stage. A hidden layer (768,250), ReLU activation, and a softmax classification layer are used in the second and third methods (250, number of classes). The overlapped long texts used in the second technique are used to build an oversampled dataset. The third method averages all the vectors corresponding to the overlapping sentences, rather than oversampling them. The vectors are subsequently sent through a ReLU-equipped two-layered classification head.

5 Results

The scores for the sentiment task are reported using the F1, and accuracy (macro) metrics. In the case of fine-tuning setup, each experiment was performed five times with different random seeds, and the mean of all the scores is reported in Table 2. We also tested the XLM-RoBERTa (Conneau et al., 2019) and classla/bcms-bertic (Ljubešić and Lauc, 2021) language models, both of which were pretrained in Croatian, but the results were no better than the CroSloEngual BERT. All the scores are comparable, as the final scores are reported on the same test set that was held out during the training phase.

5.1 Error Analysis

A manual error analysis points to two major categories of errors. First, there are instances in the annotated set that have polar labels for metadata about the movie. Second, the trained model also has problems dealing with conditionals. Two instances are provided below.

1. **Hr** "Ako tražite nešto zbog čega razmišljate , a usredotočujete se dosta na odnos , onda bi vas ova serija trebala zabaviti."

   En "If you are looking for something to make you think and focus a lot on the relationship, then this series should entertain you."

2. **Hr** "Kad bi samo satovi znanosti u školi bili zabavni."

   En "If only science lessons at school were fun."

5.2 Discussion

All the annotators were presented with a questionnaire to be answered upon the completion of the task. The questionnaire included basic questions like how much time was required on average, good and bad experiences, as well as suggestions for future enhancements. Apart from the enhancement of the user interface for the annotation tool, one common request was to include neutral-positive and neutral-negative. These were mainly sentences that were objective in nature, but invoked sentiment. For example,

Hr "Ocjena na IMDb.com mu je 6,4 / 10 , a na Tomatoesima malih 36%."

En "The rating on IMDb.com is 6.4 out of 10, and on Tomatoes it is 36%."

This was one of the sentences in which two annotators had tagged it neutral, while the other two had tagged it with a negative label.

6 Conclusion and Future Work

With this paper, we have presented the sentiment annotated movie review dataset for Croatian. We performed experiments using curated datasets for the sentiment analysis task for the Croatian language. Out of 21 unique categories of film reviews, to name a few, we have processed only three categories (adventure, series (serija), and sci-fi). In the future, we would like to use the gold-annotated dataset in a distant-supervised learning regime to perform sentiment classification on all the non-annotated reviews. Another area of research would be to formally evaluate how pre-suggestions of the model before manual annotation could influence annotators' decisions. For example, a systematic

Configuration	F1	Accuracy
FT †	79.78 (0.008)	84.71 (0.006)
CV ◇	71.19 (0.007)	80.43 (0.003)
Sampling average ◇	70.84 (0.003)	80.13 (0.002)
CV sampling ◇	70.69 (0.005)	80.18 (0.002)

Table 2: Results of the experiments. †: Devlin et al. (2019). ◇: Methods reported in Pelicon et al. (2020)

comparison of labelling sentences from scratch versus allowing people to correct/retain automated labels could be conducted. In addition, we would like to experiment with mixed and sarcasm-tagged sentences. The dataset also contains metadata, such as genres and document-level sentiment ratings, which can be explored in the future.

Acknowledgement

The work presented in this paper has received funding from the European Union's Horizon 2020 research and innovation program under the Marie Skłodowska-Curie grant agreement no. 812997 and under the name CLEOPATRA (Cross-lingual Event-centric Open Analytics Research Academy)

Limitations

Although the current dataset mainly covers the genres of sci-fi, adventure, and series, there are other genres (games and books) that are missing from the dataset. The models were trained on a 24 GB GPU. Hence, we expect this could limit reproducibility. The downside of the presented approach is the decision to use an existing classifier to pre-annotate the texts. The suggestions could bias the students.

Ethics Statement

The annotated dataset reported in this paper involved manual effort. This is an output of the annotation campaign conducted with students of linguistics and informatics in order to aid in learning about sentiment analysis as part of their coursework. The students were compensated with course credits at the end of the campaign.

References

Željko Agić, Nikola Ljubešić, and Marko Tadić. 2010. Towards sentiment analysis of financial texts in Croatian. In *Proceedings of the Seventh International Conference on Language Resources and Evaluation (LREC'10)*, Valletta, Malta. European Language Resources Association (ELRA).

Marianna Apidianaki, Xavier Tannier, and Cécile Richart. 2016. Datasets for Aspect-Based Sentiment Analysis in French. In *International Conference on Language Resources and Evaluation*, Portoro, Slovenia.

Valerio Basile and Malvina Nissim. 2013. Sentiment analysis on Italian tweets. In *Proceedings of the 4th Workshop on Computational Approaches to Subjectivity, Sentiment and Social Media Analysis*, pages 100–107, Atlanta, Georgia. Association for Computational Linguistics.

Mihaela Bošnjak and Mladen Karan. 2019. Data set for stance and sentiment analysis from user comments on Croatian news. In *Proceedings of the 7th Workshop on Balto-Slavic Natural Language Processing*, pages 50–55, Florence, Italy. Association for Computational Linguistics.

Mark Cieliebak, Jan Milan Deriu, Dominic Egger, and Fatih Uzdilli. 2017. A Twitter corpus and benchmark resources for German sentiment analysis. In *Proceedings of the Fifth International Workshop on Natural Language Processing for Social Media*, pages 45–51, Valencia, Spain. Association for Computational Linguistics.

Simon Clematide, Stefan Gindl, Manfred Klenner, Stefanos Petrakis, Robert Remus, Josef Ruppenhofer, Ulli Waltinger, and Michael Wiegand. 2012. MLSA — a multi-layered reference corpus for German sentiment analysis. In *Proceedings of the Eighth International Conference on Language Resources and Evaluation (LREC'12)*, pages 3551–3556, Istanbul, Turkey. European Language Resources Association (ELRA).

Alexis Conneau, Kartikay Khandelwal, Naman Goyal, Vishrav Chaudhary, Guillaume Wenzek, Francisco Guzmán, Edouard Grave, Myle Ott, Luke Zettlemoyer, and Veselin Stoyanov. 2019. Unsupervised cross-lingual representation learning at scale. *CoRR*, abs/1911.02116.

Jacob Devlin, Ming-Wei Chang, Kenton Lee, and Kristina Toutanova. 2019. BERT: Pre-training of deep bidirectional transformers for language understanding. In *Proceedings of the 2019 Conference of the North American Chapter of the Association for Computational Linguistics: Human Language Technologies, Volume 1 (Long and Short Papers)*, pages 4171–4186, Minneapolis, Minnesota. Association for Computational Linguistics.

Goran Glavaš, Jan Šnajder, and Bojana Dalbelo Bašić. 2012. Experiments on hybrid corpus-based sentiment lexicon acquisition. In *Proceedings of the Workshop on Innovative Hybrid Approaches to the Processing of Textual Data*, pages 1–9, Avignon, France. Association for Computational Linguistics.

Phillip Keung, Yichao Lu, György Szarvas, and Noah A. Smith. 2020. The multilingual amazon reviews corpus. In *Proceedings of the 2020 Conference on Empirical Methods in Natural Language Processing*.

Jan-Christoph Klie, Michael Bugert, Beto Boullosa, Richard Eckart de Castilho, and Iryna Gurevych. 2018. The inception platform: Machine-assisted and knowledge-oriented interactive annotation. In *Proceedings of the 27th International Conference on Computational Linguistics: System Demonstrations*, pages 5–9. Association for Computational Linguistics. Event Title: The 27th International Conference on Computational Linguistics (COLING 2018).

Nikola Ljubešić and Davor Lauc. 2021. BERTić - the transformer language model for Bosnian, Croatian, Montenegrin and Serbian. In *Proceedings of the 8th Workshop on Balto-Slavic Natural Language Processing*, pages 37–42, Kiyv, Ukraine. Association for Computational Linguistics.

Nikola Ljubešić, Ilia Markov, Darja Fišer, and Walter Daelemans. 2020. The LiLaH emotion lexicon of Croatian, Dutch and Slovene. In *Proceedings of the Third Workshop on Computational Modeling of People's Opinions, Personality, and Emotion's in Social Media*, pages 153–157, Barcelona, Spain (Online). Association for Computational Linguistics.

Andrew L. Maas, Raymond E. Daly, Peter T. Pham, Dan Huang, Andrew Y. Ng, and Christopher Potts. 2011. Learning word vectors for sentiment analysis. In *Proceedings of the 49th Annual Meeting of the Association for Computational Linguistics: Human Language Technologies*, pages 142–150, Portland, Oregon, USA. Association for Computational Linguistics.

Michal Mochtak, Peter Rupnik, and Nikola Ljubešić. 2022. The sentiment corpus of parliamentary debates ParlaSent-BCS v1.0. Slovenian language resource repository CLARIN.SI.

Saif Mohammad. 2016. A practical guide to sentiment annotation: Challenges and solutions. In *Proceedings of the 7th Workshop on Computational Approaches to Subjectivity, Sentiment and Social Media Analysis*, pages 174–179, San Diego, California. Association for Computational Linguistics.

Emily Öhman, Marc Pàmies, Kaisla Kajava, and Jörg Tiedemann. 2020. XED: A multilingual dataset for sentiment analysis and emotion detection. In *Proceedings of the 28th International Conference on Computational Linguistics*, pages 6542–6552, Barcelona, Spain (Online). International Committee on Computational Linguistics.

Bo Pang and Lillian Lee. 2005. Seeing stars: Exploiting class relationships for sentiment categorization with respect to rating scales. In *Proceedings of the ACL*.

Andraž Pelicon, Marko Pranjić, Dragana Miljković, Blaž Škrlj, and Senja Pollak. 2020. Zero-shot learning for cross-lingual news sentiment classification. *Applied Sciences*, 10(17).

Leon Rotim and Jan Šnajder. 2017. Comparison of short-text sentiment analysis methods for Croatian. In *Proceedings of the 6th Workshop on Balto-Slavic Natural Language Processing*, pages 69–75, Valencia, Spain. Association for Computational Linguistics.

Mario Sänger, Ulf Leser, Steffen Kemmerer, Peter Adolphs, and Roman Klinger. 2016. SCARE — the sentiment corpus of app reviews with fine-grained annotations in German. In *Proceedings of the Tenth International Conference on Language Resources and Evaluation (LREC'16)*, pages 1114–1121, Portorož, Slovenia. European Language Resources Association (ELRA).

Gaurish Thakkar, Nives Mikelić Preradović, and Marko Tadić. 2021. Multi-task learning for cross-lingual sentiment analysis. In *Proceedings of the 2nd International Workshop on Cross-lingual Event-centric Open Analytics.*, pages 76–84, Ljubljana, Slovenija. CEUR Workshop Proceedings.

Alexey Tikhonov, Alex Malkhasov, Andrey Manoshin, George-Andrei Dima, Réka Cserháti, Md.Sadek Hossain Asif, and Matt Sárdi. 2022. EENLP: Cross-lingual Eastern European NLP index. In *Proceedings of the Thirteenth Language Resources and Evaluation Conference*, pages 2050–2057, Marseille, France. European Language Resources Association.

M. Ulčar and M. Robnik-Šikonja. 2020. FinEst BERT and CroSloEngual BERT: less is more in multilingual models. In *Text, Speech, and Dialogue TSD 2020*, volume 12284 of *Lecture Notes in Computer Science*. Springer.

Yiwei Zhou, Alexandra Cristea, and Zachary Roberts. 2015. Is Wikipedia really neutral? a sentiment perspective study of war-related Wikipedia articles since 1945. In *Proceedings of the 29th Pacific Asia Conference on Language, Information and Computation*, pages 160–168, Shanghai, China.

A Appendix

Task	Metric	Value
sentiment	learning rate	1e-5
	weight decay	0.02
	batch size	16
	epochs	10

Table 3: List of hyperparameters, model parameters and their values used during the experiments.

#	Category
1	adventure
2	new-films
3	biography
4	comedy
5	documentary
6	sci-fi
7	thriller
8	sport
9	war
10	western
11	mystery
12	crime
13	family
14	drama
15	music
16	history
17	action
18	romance
19	animation
20	fantasy
21	horror
22	series

Table 4: List of categories.

Too Many Cooks Spoil the Model: Are Bilingual Models for Slovene Better than a Large Multilingual Model?

Pranaydeep Singh, Aaron Maladry and **Els Lefever**
Ghent University / Groot-Brittanniëlaan 45, 9000 Gent
{pranaydeep.singh, aaron.maladry, els.lefever}@ugent.be

Abstract

This paper investigates whether adding data of typologically closer languages improves the performance of transformer-based models for three different downstream tasks, namely Part-of-Speech tagging, Named Entity Recognition, and Sentiment Analysis, compared to a monolingual and plain multilingual language model. For the presented pilot study, we performed experiments for the use case of Slovene, a low(er)-resourced language belonging to the Slavic language group. The experiments were carried out in a controlled setting, where a monolingual model for Slovene was compared to combined language models containing Slovene, trained with the same amount of Slovene data. The experimental results show that adding typologically closer languages indeed improves the performance of the Slovene language model, and even succeeds in outperforming the large multilingual XLM-RoBERTa model for NER and PoS-tagging. We also reveal that, contrary to intuition, distant or unrelated languages also combine admirably with Slovene, often outperforming XLM-R as well. All the bilingual models used in the experiments are publicly available.[1]

1 Introduction

The last decade has witnessed the increasing popularity of large language models, such as BERT (Devlin et al., 2019) and XLM-RoBERTa (Conneau et al., 2020). These transformer-based models have not only pushed the state-of-the-art for a wide range of NLP tasks, but have also shown to perform well in a multilingual setting. Despite their success, these models are also confronted with a number of challenges. First, questions arise regarding their sustainability, given the exponential rise in parameters, and deployability in practical applications. Second, although these models have been shown to achieve good performances for multilingual setups, research has shown that the performance of low(er)-resourced languages, when considering the amount of available Wikipedia data, is below baseline (Wu and Dredze, 2020).

In this research, we want to investigate (1) whether a low(er)-resourced language benefits more from adding data from a typologically closer language, than from more distant languages, and (2) how the performance of such a small dedicated "close family" language model relates to the performance obtained with a purely monolingual model, trained with the same amount of data, on the one hand, and a plain multilingual XLM-RoBERTa model trained with 105 different languages and a huge data set, on the other hand.

For these pilot experiments, we opted to train various transformer-based language models for Slovene, a low(er)-resourced Slavic language. The motivation to perform these "family language model" experiments for a Slavic language originates from the fact that the Slavic languages show a high structural similarity, with a similar inflectional system, and also share a common core vocabulary. As a result, we hypothesize that adding other Slavic languages will boost the performance of the Slovene language model. For each model, we evaluate the performance on three different NLP tasks, namely Part-of-Speech tagging, Named Entity Recognition and Sentiment Analysis.

2 Related research

Deep contextualised multilingual language models, such as mBERT and XLM-R, have shown to perform well for many NLP tasks and for a variety of languages, including low(er)-resourced languages. Nevertheless, previous research has revealed that more similar languages are more helpful for boosting the performance for low(er)-

[1] https://github.com/pranaydeeps/BLAIR

Proceedings of the 9th Workshop on Slavic Natural Language Processing 2023 (SlavicNLP 2023), pages 32–39

resourced languages. Pires et al. (2019) have investigated the degree to which the representations in Multilingual BERT (Devlin et al., 2019) generalise across languages, by fine-tuning the multilingual model on task-specific data from one language, and evaluating it on another language. Although the authors show that mBERT is able to perform cross-lingual generalization very well, the transfer works best for typologically similar languages, even suggesting that the model works best for languages with similar word orders (Pires et al., 2019). De Vries et al. (2022) performed an extensive transfer learning evaluation with 65 different source languages and 105 target languages, and have shown that, amongst other factors, matching language families, writing systems, word order systems, and lexical-phonetic distance significantly impact the cross-lingual performance.

Multilingual models, such as mBERT and XLM-RoBERTa, use a wide variety of languages from different genera, including the Slavic languages, as part of the same multilingual model. In contrast, other multilingual models have been trained on a smaller selection of languages, with a stronger focus on Slavic languages. The researchers of the DeepPavlov initiative, for example, developed a model for Bulgarian, Czech, Polish and Russian (Arkhipov et al., 2019). While this model was initialised from the multilingual BERT model and then fine-tuned on the task-specific data in the different languages, the CroSloEngual model was pre-trained from scratch for Croatian, Slovene and English and fine-tuned for task-specific data for all languages (Ulčar and Robnik-Šikonja, 2020). This model was built with the intention to apply it for multi- and cross-lingual training, making use of existing data sets for the same task in multiple languages. By doing so, the amount of task-specific data significantly increases, resulting in increased performance of the tasks of NER, POS-tagging and Dependency Parsing. Although this shows that multilingual training causes an increase in performance, the main motivation for the multilingual aspect of the model is the data-hungry nature of the transformer architecture. This same motivation has also led to a transformer model that exclusively uses languages of the Slavic genus. The BERTić language model (Ljubešić and Lauc, 2021) was trained from scratch for Bosnian, Croatian, Montenegrin and Serbian. Whereas the CroSloEngual model uses more distant languages, BERTić selected these languages because they are very closely related, are mutually intelligible and because they are considered part of the same Serbo-Croatian macro language (according to the ISO 639-3 Macrolanguage Mappings). As such, BERTić could be considered not a monolingual or multilingual but rather a macrolingual model. While these languages are exceptionally closely related, this setup does invite the following questions: "How important is the similarity of languages in a combined multilingual language model?" and "Is it preferable to include more closely related languages over distant languages when building a multilingual model?".

To compare language model performance for similar languages, researchers have often used the World Atlas of Language Structures (WALS) to group typologically similar languages (Yu et al., 2021). WALS (Dryer and Haspelmath, 2013) is a large database of structural (phonological, grammatical, lexical) properties of languages gathered from descriptive sources such as reference grammars. These linguistic features allow for comparison through qualitative features. This means that they can show in what ways languages are similar and in what ways they differ. However, beside counting the number of shared features, this does not allow for a quantitative comparison. One metric that does allow for a quantitative comparison, i.e. measure *how similar* the languages are, is LDND (Levenshtein Distance Normalized Divided)(Wichmann et al., 2010). This metric was also used by de Vries et al. (2022) in the context of cross-lingual training (training on data from other languages for the same task). Their work has shown that "languages with low LDND distances between source and target language (i.e. when two languages share cognates) are indeed associated with high accuracy, whereas high LDND distances (very dissimilar languages) seem less informative".

3 System Description

In this research, we want to investigate whether adding data from typologically closer languages improves the performance of a RoBERTa-based language model for three downstream tasks, namely Part-of-Speech tagging, Named Entity Recognition and Sentiment Analysis. To this

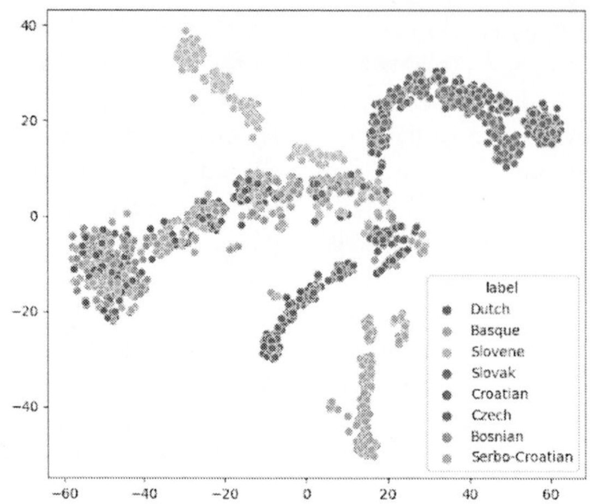

Figure 1: Clustered embeddings from the first layer of XLM-RoBERTa for data from each of the experimental languages visualized with t-SNE. Note that Slovene (in green) is the focal language of this research for which the distance to the other clusters matters most.

end, we performed experiments for the following RoBERTa-based language models including Slovene: (1) a Slovene monolingual model, (2) a Slovene combined with Serbo-Croatian model, (3) a Slovene combined with Slovak model, and (4) a Slovene combined with Czech model. We also performed experiments with two typologically distant languages, Dutch and Basque, for comparison. The motivation for combining specifically these languages with Slovene originates from the LDND measures but can also be linguistically supported. As shown in Table 1, the LDND scores[2] show that Croatian and Serbian are the two closest languages to Slovene. This is in accordance with the fact that these three languages are part of the same sub-group i.e. South-Slavic languages. Croatian is also a neighbouring language. Although Czech (the third-closest language) is not a geographical neighbour and belongs to the West-Slavic sub-group, the areas where Slovene and Czech are spoken share a long (Central European) cultural history (being strongly influenced by developments in the Holy Roman Empire and later the Austro-Hungarian Empire). Therefore, Czech and Slovene can be considered cultural neighbours. Although Slovak has a quite high LDND, the language is mutually intelligible with Czech and shares the same German-dominated cultural history. Therefore, we also included it as one of the languages for our experiments. To evaluate the hypothesis that closely-related languages are more useful for training a multilingual language model than unrelated languages, we also selected two control languages with a high LDND. For this purpose, we found that Basque and Dutch would be good candidates, as their LDND distance is more than twice the distance compared to the Slavic languages[3]. Basque is a completely unrelated language and a prime example of an isolated language that should be sub-optimal for multilingual applications in combination with Slovene. Dutch is part of the same larger Indo-European language family as Slovene, which makes them somewhat, albeit relatively distantly, related. Dutch, therefore, serves as a bridge between related and unrelated languages. These typological distances are also empirically evident in pre-trained multilingual models like mBERT and XLM-RoBERTa. Figure 1 demonstrates the embeddings from the first layer of XLM-R in different languages, visualised using t-SNE (van der Maaten and Hinton, 2008), a dimensionality reduction technique often used for visualising high-dimensional embeddings in 2-dimensions. Similar inferences to the LDND distances can be made using these clusters. Slovak and Czech prove to be quite close. Similarly, Serbo-Croatian, Croatian, and Bosnian also appear to be nearly indistinguishable. Both

[2] Calculated and presented by de Vries et al. (2022).

[3] We only selected languages with Latin script because the difference in the script could potentially increase the difficulty of modeling two languages simultaneously. For our experiments, Serbian data in Latin script was considered as 'Serbo-Croatian', meaning that this data does not include Serbian data written in the Cyrillic script.

Language	Distance
Croatian	28.36
Serbian	34.19
Czech	35.68
Bulgarian	40.24
Slovak	44.25
Polish	46.38
Russian	51.63
Ukrainian	52.49
Belarusian	53.85
Basque	100.12
Dutch	90.84

Table 1: LDND distance between Slovene and closely related (Slavic) languages as well as two more distant languages sharing the same Latin script (Basque and Dutch).

	Wiki Data	OSCAR Data
Slovene	276 MB	1 GB
Slovak	300 MB	6 GB
Czech	1 GB	33 GB
Bosnian*	143 MB	165 KB
Croatian*	302 MB	169 MB
Serbo-Croatian*	435 MB	9 MB
Dutch	1.7 GB	47 GB
Basque*	279 MB	503 MB

Table 2: Data sizes of the monolingual corpora used for pre-training the monolingual Slovene baseline and bilingual models. Languages marked with an * have smaller data sizes than Slovene.

the Serbian-Croatian-Bosnian cluster, as well as the Czech-Slovak cluster, are quite close to the Slovene cluster. Dutch and Basque are distantly clustered, with Basque being the farthest of all the visualised languages.

3.1 Experimental setup

As explained, we train bilingual models for Slovene with closely related Slavic languages (Serbo-Croatian, Czech, and Slovak) and with more distant and unrelated languages (Basque and Dutch). To construct monolingual data sources for each of these languages, we use OSCAR 2.0[4] and the latest Wikipedia data dumps[5]. An overview of these sources is summarised in Table 2. Slovene, having a total of 1.276 GB of data serves as the focal point of all the experiments, and therefore data for all the other languages was restricted to the same amount. This allows us to focus the evaluation on the effect of each added language individually and removes data size as a potential variable impacting the performance.

Because of the limited available data and the low LDND distance between Croatian and Serbian (only 19.4), the fact that they are mutually intelligible and considered to be part of the same macro language, we combine the data for Serbian, Croatian and Bosnian to a total data size of 1.06 GB to train a macro-lingual model like BERTić. The data for Basque was also slightly lesser with a combined data size of 782 MB, which might account for some slight disparities. By running the experiments in a controlled setting, viz. evaluating language models built with a very limited data set of similar size, we ensure that the data size is not a variable when drawing inferences from the experiments.

To construct each bilingual model, we combine the data for Slovene (1.276 GB) with the same amount (1.276 GB in size) of randomly selected monolingual data from a second test language, except for Basque (782 MB) and Serbo-Croatian (1.06 GB). After shuffling the combined data, we construct a BPE Tokenizer with 64,000 sub-words and train for the Masked Language Modelling (MLM) objective, using a standard RoBERTa-base architecture, with a max sequence length of 512, starting learning rate of $6e-4$, 3000 warm-up steps and a weight decay of 0.01. We use 32 Nvidia A100 (40 GB) GPUs, with a batch size of 32 per device, and gradient accumulation for 8 steps, thus adding up to an effective batch size of 8192. The AdamW optimizer was used for optimisation with an epsilon of $1e-6$, a β_1 value of 0.9, and a β_2 value of 0.98. All the bilingual models were trained for 30 epochs, or approximately 60,000 steps, which took approximately 40 hrs per model.

Finally, we also train a monolingual Slovene model with only the base 1.276 GB of Slovene data, with identical hyper-parameters, except restricting the vocabulary to 32,000 to account for only having a single language. The monolingual model is intended to serve as a benchmark to quantify the potential improvements obtained by adding the secondary test language in combination with Slovene.

[4]https://huggingface.co/datasets/oscar-corpus/OSCAR-2109

[5]https://dumps.wikimedia.org/backup-index.html

4 Evaluation and Discussion

We evaluated the various versions of the RoBERTa language model on three different downstream tasks: one semantic task, being Sentiment Analysis, one syntactic task, being Part-of-Speech (POS) Tagging, and one task requiring both syntactic and semantic understanding, namely Named Entity Recognition (NER). For Sentiment Analysis, we use the SentiNews dataset (Bučar et al., 2018), which consists of news documents annotated with three sentiment labels (neutral, positive, and negative). We use the sentence-level sentiment setup with approximately 169,000 sentences, distributed into 80:10:10 for training, validation, and testing, respectively. For NER we, use the WikiANN (Rahimi et al., 2019) dataset with 15,000 train samples, and 10,000 samples each for validation and testing. Finally, for POS Tagging, the SSJ Treebank part of the Universal Dependencies[6] project is used, consisting of 13,000 annotated sentences, split into an 80:10:10 setup for training, validation and testing as well. For all downstream tasks, the respective RoBERTa models were fine-tuned for 10 epochs, with a learning rate of $5e-5$ with 500 warmup steps followed by a linear weight decay of 0.01. The results are summarised in Table 3.

Firstly, the Monolingual Slovene model seems to perform comparably to XLM-Roberta on all tasks, while only performing slightly worse than the Upper-Bound (UB) SloBERTa[7] model, which was trained on significantly (21 times) more data. This indicates that the presence of the additional 99 languages does not have a significant impact on Slovene performance. The bilingual model with Slovene+Serbo-Croatian seems to perform the best for NER, even outperforming the state-of-the-art SloBERTa (UB), while the Slovene+Czech model seems to be the best for POS Tagging, and only 0.06% worse than the UB, while the Slovene-Slovak model works best for Sentiment Analysis. For all three tasks, the best models come from the typologically closely related languages, however, the models with distant languages, Slovene+Dutch and Slovene+Basque, do not perform as badly as hypothesized. Both models outperform the monolingual baseline, while sometimes also competing with the closely related languages in some settings. This is an interesting and rather counter-intuitive finding, since it suggests that the addition of data, irrespective of the language, is helpful for a given target language. Even Basque, with an LDND distance of more than 100, is able to influence the Slovene performance in a positive sense. This incites the following question: If all languages are indeed useful, irrespective of their differences, why is XLM-RoBERTa the worst performing model then, with the highest amount of combined data? A logical inference would then be that after a certain amount of languages, the representation power of the RoBERTa-base setup is not sufficient to model all 104 languages simultaneously, resulting in degradation for the poorly represented languages in the data, as would be the case for Slovene. These observations might still indicate, however, that a multilingual model with 3 or more languages might show further improvements to our bilingual setup.

In general, one can observe a downward trend as we move further away from Slovene in terms of typological similarity or LDND distance. This trend can be seen more clearly in Figure 2 for POS and NER, while the trend is not as explicit for Sentiment Analysis, with a few anomalies. We dive further into the potential reasons for the inconsistencies with Sentiment Analysis performance in the next section.

5 Manual evaluation for Sentiment Analysis

As the results for the sentiment analysis task do not align with our hypothesis and do not follow the tendencies we noticed for the other tasks, we decided to have a look at the predicted labels to find an explanation for these deviant results.

A closer look at the evaluation data revealed a couple of reasons for the unexpected results. The evaluation data was selected from curated economic and political news corpora, characterised by a more neutral writing style. As a result, the sentiment is often implicit or ambiguous and requires world knowledge and human experience to be interpreted correctly. This is also confirmed by the modest inter-annotator agreement reported by Bučar et al. (2018), with F1-scores below 65% for their 3-way classification models.

As shown in Example 1, a rather neutral statement can also carry an implicit (negative) sentiment although it was annotated as neutral in the data set.

[6] https://universaldependencies.org/

[7] https://huggingface.co/EMBEDDIA/sloberta

	UB	SL-SBC	SL-CS	SL+SK	SL+NL	SL+EU	Monolingual	XLM
NER	0.9410	**0.9441**	0.9422	0.9425	0.9396	0.9406	0.9396	0.9409
POS	0.9902	0.9892	**0.9896**	0.9887	0.9892	0.9889	0.9878	0.9865
Sentiment	0.6835	0.6633	0.6660	**0.6757**	0.6657	0.6628	0.5925	0.6664

Table 3: F1-scores for the tasks of NER, POS-tagging, and Sentiment Analysis. The Upper-Bound (UB) is the monolingual SloBERTa model, trained with 21 times more monolingual data compared to our monolingual Slovene RoBERTa baseline model).

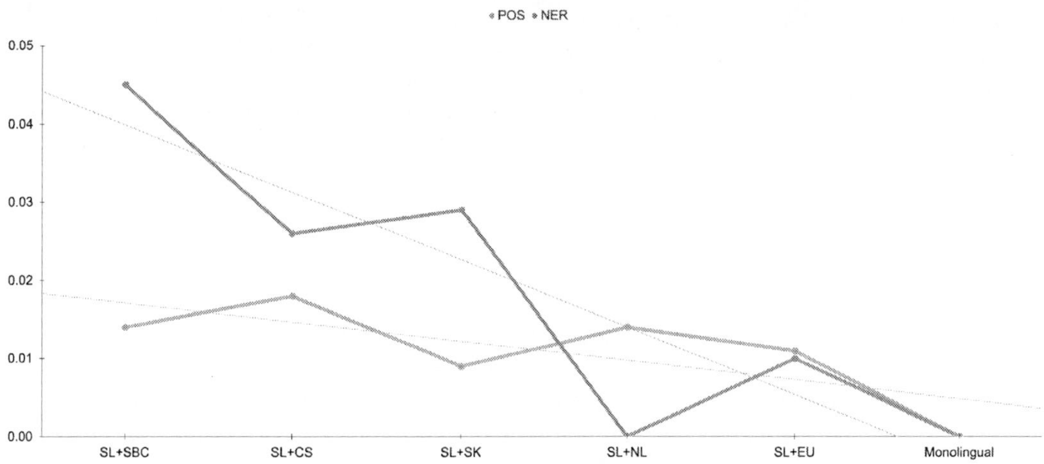

Figure 2: Differences in F1-score of all evaluated models compared to the monolingual baseline. The models are listed on the X-axis in ascending order of linguistic distance of the second language (in relation to Slovene). The monolingual baseline is included for completeness.

Example 1

Več kot milijon Parižanov se je ***moralo*** *v službo odpraviti kar peš ali s kolesom*

(translation: More than a million Parisians ***had to go*** *to work on foot or by bicycle)*

A second cause for errors is that the annotators also took the context into account for labeling the sentiment of individual sentences. This can cause a contextual sentiment to seep into the label of a rather neutral sentence. In Example 2, a neutral sentence was tagged as "positive", although this cannot be inferred from the sentence itself.

Example 2

SI*: Vsak bo tako prispeval polovico zneska.*

(translation: Each will thus contribute half of the amount.)

In some cases, the erroneous sentence splitting of news articles resulted in single-word sentences (named entities and numbers), as shown by the following examples:

Example 3

Lukea Koper

Intereuropa

Gorenje

KRKA

1,75%

While these single-word sentences should be neutral, they were still annotated with a positive or negative sentiment (most likely due to the context again).

In order to get a general idea of how the bilingual models compare to the monolingual Slovene model, we performed a shallow evaluation of the results. Considering the complexity of the task, we focused on samples that were not predicted or annotated as neutral. This way, we get an indication of the performance on more explicit sentiments. This evaluation has underlined the improvement of both the Dutch+Slovene and Serbo-Croatian+Slovene models over the monolingual model (which, in turn, generally outperforms the multilingual model). In Examples 4, 5, and 6, both bilingual models with Dutch and Serbo-Croatian predict a correct sentiment, whereas the monolingual model fails.

Example 4

Nižji dobiček ameriških podjetij

(translation: Lower profits for US companies)

Example 5

Najbolj je padla prodaja oblačil in tehničnega blaga.

(translation: Sales of clothing and technical goods fell the most)

Example 6

Ko ugotoviš, da si pogumna oseba, lahko premagaš strah in neuspeh.

(translation: When you realize that you are a brave person, you can overcome fear and failure.)

When comparing non-neutral sentences where these two bilingual models disagree, it becomes a lot harder to find tendencies. In some cases where the sentiment is more explicit, the Serbo-Croatian+Slovene model provides a more intuitive prediction, as shown in Example 7, 8, 9. However, more analysis and further statistical evidence is needed to support this hypothesis.

Example 7

Najprej nekaj besed o Jožetu Pučniku: voditelj demokratične opozicije Slovenije je na svoji koži izkusil surovost prejšnjega režima, sedem let je bil v zaporu zaradi "subverzivne dejavnosti".

(translation: First, a few words about Jože Pučnik: the leader of Slovenia's democratic opposition experienced the cruelty of the previous regime firsthand, he was in prison for seven years for "subversive activity".)

Bilingual Dutch prediction: Positive

Bilingual Serbo-Croatian Prediction: Negative

Example 8

Sama sebe sem bodrila, res mi je odleglo.

(translation: I cheered myself up, I was really relieved.)

Bilingual Dutch prediction: Negative

Bilingual Serbo-Croatian Prediction: Positive

Example 9

Tudi Petrol je cenejši za skoraj tri odstotke.

(translation: Petrol is also cheaper by almost three percent.)

Bilingual Dutch prediction: Negative

Bilingual Serbo-Croatian Prediction: Positive

6 Conclusion

This paper presents a pilot study to investigate whether adding data from typologically close languages improves the performance of a monolingual model for a low-resourced language, Slovene in this case. To summarise the results, our experiments showed that adding data from a second language always helps, even if this language is more distant. In addition, the trained bilingual models outperform the very large multilingual model in almost all cases. Finally, the bilingual Slavic models outperform the bilingual models with more distant languages for the task of Named Entity Recognition and POS Tagging barring a few anomalies, whereas this is not confirmed for the task of Sentiment Analysis. As the results for Sentiment Analysis were somewhat counter-intuitive and not in line with the findings of the other tasks, we decided to also perform a small manual analysis where we outlined a number of issues with the complexity and subjectivity of the sentiment analysis task, including modest inter-annotator agreement and a number of ambiguous instances.

In future research, we will perform validation experiments for additional combinations and downstream tasks, especially because the deviant scores for Sentiment Analysis might be partly due to the nature of the evaluation set used. Additionally, it would also be worthwhile to check whether adding additional data for a second language (like Croatian) would have a stronger positive impact on the evaluation of Slovene compared to adding the same amount of data for a third language (Czech). Finally, we will also investigate simultaneously adding more than two languages to the training setup, to find the optimal inflection point for multilingual setups, after which some performance degradation is likely.

References

Mikhail Arkhipov, Maria Trofimova, Yuri Kuratov, and Alexey Sorokin. 2019. Tuning multilingual transformers for language-specific named entity recognition. In *Proceedings of the 7th Workshop on Balto-Slavic Natural Language Processing*, pages 89–93, Florence, Italy. Association for Computational Linguistics.

Jože Bučar, Martin Žnidaršič, and Janez Povh. 2018. Annotated news corpora and a lexicon for sentiment analysis in slovene. *Language Resources and Evaluation*, 52:895–919.

Alexis Conneau, Kartikay Khandelwal, Naman Goyal, Vishrav Chaudhary, Guillaume Wenzek, Francisco Guzmán, Edouard Grave, Myle Ott, Luke Zettlemoyer, and Veselin Stoyanov. 2020. Unsupervised cross-lingual representation learning at scale. In *Proceedings of the 58th Annual Meeting of the Association for Computational Linguistics*, pages 8440–8451, Online. Association for Computational Linguistics.

Wietse de Vries, Martijn Wieling, and Malvina Nissim. 2022. Make the best of cross-lingual transfer: Evidence from POS tagging with over 100 languages. In *Proceedings of the 60th Annual Meeting of the Association for Computational Linguistics (Volume 1: Long Papers), ACL 2022, Dublin, Ireland, May 22-27, 2022*, pages 7676–7685. Association for Computational Linguistics.

J. Devlin, M.-W. Chang, K. Lee, and K. Toutanova. 2019. BERT: Pre-training of deep bidirectional transformers for language understanding. In *Proceedings of the 2019 Conference of the North American Chapter of the Association for Computational Linguistics: Human Language Technologies, Volume 1 (Long and Short Papers)*, pages 4171–4186, Minneapolis, Minnesota. Association for Computational Linguistics.

Matthew S. Dryer and Martin Haspelmath, editors. 2013. *WALS Online (v2020.3)*. Zenodo.

Nikola Ljubešić and Davor Lauc. 2021. Berti\'c– the transformer language model for bosnian, croatian, montenegrin and serbian. *arXiv preprint arXiv:2104.09243*.

Telmo Pires, Eva Schlinger, and Dan Garrette. 2019. How multilingual is multilingual BERT? In *Proceedings of the 57th Annual Meeting of the Association for Computational Linguistics*, pages 4996–5001, Florence, Italy. Association for Computational Linguistics.

Afshin Rahimi, Yuan Li, and Trevor Cohn. 2019. Massively multilingual transfer for NER. In *Proceedings of the 57th Annual Meeting of the Association for Computational Linguistics*, pages 151–164, Florence, Italy. Association for Computational Linguistics.

Matej Ulčar and Marko Robnik-Šikonja. 2020. Finest bert and crosloengual bert: less is more in multilingual models. In *Text, Speech, and Dialogue: 23rd International Conference, TSD 2020, Brno, Czech Republic, September 8–11, 2020, Proceedings 23*, pages 104–111. Springer.

Laurens van der Maaten and Geoffrey Hinton. 2008. Visualizing data using t-sne. *Journal of Machine Learning Research*, 9(86):2579–2605.

Søren Wichmann, Eric W Holman, Dik Bakker, and Cecil H Brown. 2010. Evaluating linguistic distance measures. *Physica A: Statistical Mechanics and its Applications*, 389(17):3632–3639.

Shijie Wu and Mark Dredze. 2020. Are all languages created equal in multilingual bert? *CoRR*, abs/2005.09093.

Dian Yu, Taiqi He, and Kenji Sagae. 2021. Language embeddings for typology and cross-lingual transfer learning. In *Proceedings of the 59th Annual Meeting of the Association for Computational Linguistics and the 11th International Joint Conference on Natural Language Processing (Volume 1: Long Papers)*, pages 7210–7225, Online. Association for Computational Linguistics.

7 Limitations

The primary limitation of this work is that the hypothesis can be validated for more languages, tasks, and typological families. However, it takes a lot of computational resources (1280 GPU hours on Tesla A100 GPUs) and training time, to train and validate each model, thus having quite a large carbon footprint (approximately 85kg of CO_2 emission per model). The results are also not consistent for the task of Sentiment Analysis but this can be accounted for by the issues mentioned in Section 5. The tasks, while being varied (in a semantic and syntactic sense), might not cover general language understanding as well as comprehensive benchmarks like GLUE. However, since we attempt to validate the hypothesis for under-resourced languages, large benchmarks are often hard to come by.

Machine-Translated Texts from English to Polish Show a Potential for Typological Explanations in Source Language Identification

Damiaan J. W. Reijnaers
University of Amsterdam
info@damiaanreijnaers.nl

Elize Herrewijnen
Utrecht University
National Police Lab AI
e.herrewijnen@uu.nl

Abstract

This work examines a case study that investigates (1) the achievability of extracting typological features from Polish texts, and (2) their contrastive power to discriminate between machine-translated texts from English. The findings indicate potential for a proposed method that deals with the explainable prediction of the source language of translated texts.

1 Introduction

In the modern-day world of global interconnectedness, *the act of translation* has evolved into an indispensable part of daily life as a result of the growing availability of ever more advanced translation engines (Vieira et al., 2021, pp. 1515–16). This trend has been further amplified by the increasing accessibility of such tools; *e.g.*, through their integration into messaging services or social media platforms (Xinxing (2023); Turovsky (2016)). The recently acquired prominent position of translation tools in human society brings attention to the value of comparatively un(der)explored areas in machine translation (MT) that are more ethical in nature.

Found within this space is the task of determining the source language of a machine-translated text, also referred to as Source Language Identification[1] (SLI). This task may not only contribute to the qualitative improvement of translation engines, it further has a practical application in the field of forensics—bad actors use translation tools too.

The viability of SLI relies on the premise that, despite considerable progress in MT as a result of 'the transformer revolution' (Zhang and Zong, 2020, p. 2229), machine translations may still be imperfect or *unnatural*: they may contain artifacts that indicate that a text originated in a different language, even when being grammatically and semantically sound. Nida and Taber (1969) coined the term 'translationese' to refer to this phenomenon that is now widely recognised in the literature. Translationese may arise from various causes, with the characteristics of the *source language* (*i.e.*, source language interference) playing a prominent role (Rabinovich et al., 2017). An understanding of the features leading to such perceived linguistic unnaturalness might therefore allow the source language to be identified from translated text alone. We propose a methodology that exploits these *symptoms of translationese* to approach the task of SLI.

Although research on translationese has mostly concerned *human* translation, an emerging line of work specifically focuses on MT, with the majority of effort in this area dealing with evaluating MT models (*e.g.*, Graham et al. (2020); Kurokawa et al. (2009)). While some authors presuppose that translationese across humans and machines is similar (Riley et al., 2020, p. 7738), empirical evidence suggests that *structural* properties of the source language (*i.e.*, grammar) 'shine through' more overtly in text translated by machines (Bizzoni et al., 2020, p. 288). As MT is ultimately trained on human translation, of particular interest is therefore how structural features of human translationese can be identified. A common strategy for this involves training a classifier to leverage *surface features* indicative of structural translationese: surface features comprise easily observable attributes of texts, such as parts of speech (PoS). Particularly the latter have demonstrated encouraging performance in the form of n-grams (Baroni and Bernardini (2005, p. 268); Rabinovich et al. (2017, p. 534), Pylypenko et al. (2021, p. 8603)). Drawing on these results, we employ such features in our method.

While SLI remains largely unexplored, many have studied its equivalent in (human) second-language acquisition: *Native* Language Identification (NLI[2]). This field was initially researched

[1] To our knowledge, the task was mentioned only once in a recent paper by La Morgia et al. (2023), coincidentally aligning with our own formulation of the novel task.

[2] Not to be confused with Natural Language Inference,

Proceedings of the 9th Workshop on Slavic Natural Language Processing 2023 (SlavicNLP 2023), pages 40–46

by Koppel et al. (2005) and gained momentum through a shared task (Tetreault et al., 2013). The inherent reliance of both NLI and SLI on leveraging features of language interference makes the former a highly relevant field. A shortcoming of many NLI approaches is their lack of explainability (Berti et al., 2022, p. 8); a quality that is naturally demanded by the field of forensics (Cheng, 2013, pp. 547–49), and a quality that could provide useful insight into the limitations of current approaches in MT. As we exploit the structural properties of a source language that hint at the origin through its artifacts, correspondingly, explanations ought to be in terms of the *structural differences* between the source and target language of a translated text. We aim to achieve this by reformulating SLI as a typological feature prediction task. Such features are the products of the field of linguistic typology and serve to *distinguish between the structural properties* of languages (Daniel, 2010, pp. 1–2). Consequently, they have the capacity to provide human-interpretable explanations that are linguistically grounded. Berzak et al. (2014) show that the typology of native languages are predictable within the context of NLI, providing further ground to our approach. In a paper published in the field of law, Kredens et al. (2020) similarly advocate the need for typology-based explanations in SLI-like contexts, indicating a convergence of ideas. Our paper contributes by presenting a practical implementation, while also adding to its theoretical foundation.

To further underline the potential of a typological approach to achieve explainable SLI, we present a case study that examined the feasibility of extracting typological features from Polish texts, and their capacity to discriminate between translated texts from English. The Slavic language family poses an interesting testbed for such analyses, as it exhibits unique features in contrast to English (§2.1), while still being in relative linguistic proximity. Our preliminary experiments indicate that structural features reminiscent of the origin language display significant promise for typology prediction to warrant further research that implements the methodology proposed in this work. We are currently examining the effectiveness of our method in practice.

In the following section, we provide the aforementioned experiments. The paper then proceeds by explicating our proposed methodology. It concludes by discussing the findings and limitations.

which is also commonly abbreviated as NLI in the literature.

2 Experimenting with Polish and English

To gauge the exploitability of features specific to the Polish language, we conducted two experiments. The first experiment analyses Polish word order to gain an intuition on the practical utility of the features. Experiment 2 then compares the applicability of *all* features listed in the following subsection. All code relating to the experiments and the scraping of the data can be found on GitHub.[3]

2.1 Language-specific features of Polish

Word order Polish is a strongly inflected language and therefore exhibits a relatively flexible word order (Kuh, 1990). This manifests at the level of the constituent, *i.e.*, '**S**ubject–**O**bject–**V**erb order' (Kubon et al., 2016, p. 16), but also at the level of parts of speech (PoS); *e.g.*, adjectives may be placed both before *and* after a noun (Bielec (2012, p. 211); Siewierska and Uhlířová (1998, pp. 109, 168, 134–37)). These differences may lead to errors in machine-translated texts to and from English (Popović and Arčan, 2015, p. 98, 100).

Verbal aspect Polish explicitly marks verbal aspect, which may be a source of error (Kupsc (2003, p. 17); Zangenfeind and Sonnenhauser (2014)).

Negation The Slavic double negation may cause error in translations from English (Hossain et al. (2020); Popović and Arčan (2015, p. 101)).

Cases Polish morphologically marks words by seven cases. English translations may show unnatural case distributions (Wolk and Marasek, 2019).

2.2 Dataset and preprocessing

The data was scraped from Vinted (a marketplace platform tailored towards second-hand clothing) in two locales: Polish (.pl) and English (.co.uk). Samples were translated via Google Translate.[4] Each language (pair) forms a category, resulting in 4 categories of 7,500 samples. Texts are typically short in length and 'in nature' (*e.g.*, skipping conventional words: *"Brand new boxed excellent condition"*), and are often ungrammatical, presenting an additional challenge. This allows for a realistic assessment, as it accommodates real-world use cases. Surface features were assigned using `SpaCy`.[5]

[3] `https://github.com/damiaanr/xai-srclangid`

[4] API endpoint of *Google Dictionary*. This endpoint is less accurate than the live version on translate.google.com.

[5] The `en_core_web_trf` and `pl_core_news_lg` models were used for English and Polish respectively: spacy.io.

Table 1: Entropy of conditional probability distributions of relevant PoS tags. The → symbol denotes translation. A number closer to one means a higher level of 'uncertainty', *i.e.*, a more flexible word order.

unigram	**EN**	**PL**	**PL→EN**	**EN→PL**
t =PROPN	.70	.78	.63	.62
t =NOUN	.77	.82	.69	.69
t =ADJ	.56	.67	.49	.60
t =DET	.41	.51	.33	.45
t =PRON	.72	.77	.59	.82
t =AUX	.68	.71	.70	.66
t =PART	.55	.78	.51	.76
t =X (oth.)	.56	.68	.50	.59
t =SCONJ	.60	.76	.56	.78

2.3 Experiment 1: Word order freedom

A measure for 'word order freedom' is computed for all four categories of samples in the dataset. Similarly to Kubon et al. (2016, p. 15) and Nikolaev et al. (2020), the scores are calculated by measuring the entropy H, here for PoS bigrams given their unigrams (*i.e.*, the entropy of the next PoS tag given a current tag; see Equation 1, where $\mathcal{T}$ is the set of all tags). The results are reported in Table 1. Tags with higher entropy in English than in Polish are excluded as these are deemed irrelevant in light of this experiment. SPACE and SYM were also omitted.

$$H(t \in \mathcal{T}) = -\sum_{t' \in \mathcal{T}} \Big(P(t, t'|t) \cdot \log_{|\mathcal{T}|} P(t, t'|t) \Big) \quad (1)$$

As expected, the results show a relative freedom of word order in Polish, while all translations seem to be less free than original texts. A plausible explanation for this phenomenon is that MT models tend to stick to fixed constructions 'that it learned to be valid,' therefore indirectly allowing less variance in word order (Bizzoni et al., 2020, p. 280). As Polish allows for a high degree of variation in word order, the translations from English are not necessarily invalid; they might just be *unnatural*—precisely what it means for a model to 'suffer' from translationese.

2.4 Experiment 2: Detecting translation

We now put forward an array of hand-crafted features, designed to capture characteristics of Polish, to train a vanilla SVM to discriminate between original and translated Polish texts. Each feature corresponds to a set of classes (listed below), the frequency counts of which are concatenated into a single vector for every sample (except for PoS-entropy classes, which are qualitative values). Each test set comprised 1,500 samples (train 6,000). The following categories of classes were considered:

Table 2: Accuracy of a linear SVM trained on features extracted from 12K Polish texts from the Vinted platform, half of them translated from English. Tested on a balanced set of 3K samples vs. a random baseline of $\frac{1}{2}$.

feature	**acc.**	**Δ baseline**	**# classes**
constit. order	.553	+.053	10
verbal aspect	.597	+.097	2
negations	.519	+.019	1
cases	.556	+.056	7
A–N order	.636	+.136	2
PoS entropy	.645	+.145	14

1. **Constituent order** Two- or three-component orderings (*e.g.*, SVO, or SV). 10 of 12 occurred.
2. **Verbal aspect** Imperfective or perfective.
3. **Negations** Contains only the word *nie*.
4. **Cases** Seven grammatical cases (*e.g.*, dative).
5. **Adjective–Noun order** Either A–N or N–A.
6. **PoS entropy** §2.3. No SYM, PUNCT, X, SPACE.

The results for each independent set of features are reported in Table 2. In part, features that may grasp more subtle 'unnaturalities' (*i.e.*, translationese) appear to outperform those that seem effective at capturing errors (*i.e.*, large semantic shifts or ungrammatical forms), indicating that translations have fewer of the latter (*e.g.*, incorrect case markers or wrong negations). This is not surprising—as MT train sets contain human translation, they inevitably exhibit translationese (Riley et al., 2020, pp. 7337–38), while presumably having few 'plain errors.'

Given the nature of the dataset and the sparse number of employed features, we judge the performance to be surprisingly well above a random baseline. A closer look at ADJ–NOUN orderings (Figure 1) shows that observations align with expectations.

3 A methodology for explainable SLI

We now put forth a two-part methodology that places an intermediary map to typological features in between the definitional map of SLI from translated text to source language. This effectively elevates the problem of SLI to a 'typology prediction-like' task that is unique in that it aims not to grasp

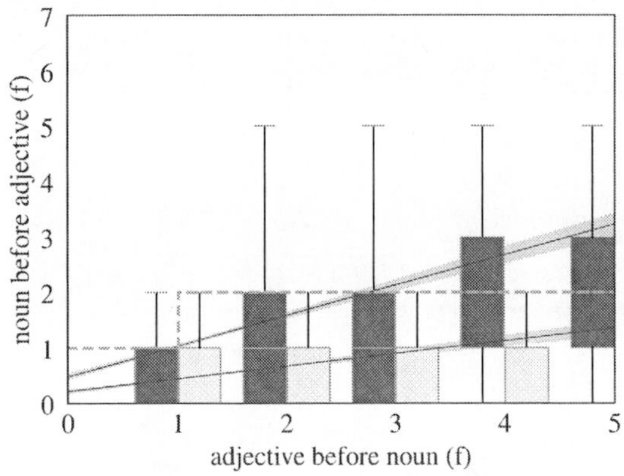

Figure 1: Density comparison of ADJ–NOUN vs. NOUN–ADJ usage in orig. Polish (dark) and translated from English (light). Samples below the discriminator (dashed red) were classified as translations. Regressors in blue.

the typology of the language in which a translated text is given, but rather to identify the typological features of the origin language of the text. The first mapping, from translated text to a prediction of the typological features of its source language, may be realised by an appeal to surface features. These lend themselves well for verifying whether the model exploiting these surface features has truly 'learned' to identify the artifacts of the typology characteristic to the source language. Moreover, surface features show promise for typology prediction in the first place, as established in the previous sections. The incentive to identify source *features* instead of source *languages* is motivated by the fact that the second mapping, from predicted typological features to a set of possible languages carrying these features, subsequently becomes a more trivial component in the pipeline that can be addressed by traditionally interpretable models, such as SVMs. The typological features then become the 'building blocks' of the explanations for predictions.

As brought up in the introduction, the choice for typological features is justified by their tendency to capture the structural elements of a source language, which are especially pronounced in machine translationese. As an additional consequence, they tend to be more robust than, *e.g.*, lexical features, for language change manifests slowest in the core structural elements of a language (Trudgill, 2020, p. 1)—precisely those grasped by high-level typological descriptions. For example, word order features are "diachronically stable" (Ponti et al., 2019, p. 579). We therefore hypothesise that SLI approaches based in typology perform more consistently across MT models, linguistic (sub)communities, and genres. Moreover, typological features naturally reflect phylogenetic relationships between languages (Berzak et al., 2014); this paves the way for 'fuzzy' classifications that align with the historical development of languages along geographical lines, as predictions may not necessarily be restricted to a single source language, but (branches of) a language family instead. They have the additional capacity to *transcend* these genealogical boundaries where overlapping typology challenges traditional linguistic classification, as is, *e.g.*, the case with Ukrainian in relation to Russian and Polish (Shevelov, 1980). This and the previous implication may especially prove beneficial in forensic contexts. Lastly, an approach that is rooted in a robust body of linguistic research offers a ground for verification of the internal reasoning of a resulting model. It moreover keeps open a dialogue between linguistics and AI: developments in linguistic typology may inform work in SLI, and possibly vice-versa.

The World Atlas of Language Structures online (WALS) appears to be a natural fit as a basis from which to draw the reasoning underlying the prediction of source languages and the corresponding explanations; it is a rich, freely available resource of typological features in a table-like format for over 2,000 languages (Dryer and Haspelmath, 2013).

A diagram of the method is given in Figure 2.

4 Discussion and conclusion

Discussion A perceived limitation of the method stems from the presumption that typology prediction is more challenging than SLI, as this could harm the performance of a model that implements the suggested methodology. However, we argue that this is only of secondary concern to a work that primarily focuses on explainability. An aim for *trustworthy* explanations requires the internal reasoning of a model to align with the reasoning conveyed in *explanations* for the model's behaviour. Our method thus needs to incorporate human-understandable concepts (*e.g.*, typological features) that are potentially less sophisticated than those developed by more 'naive', 'black-box' methods. Furthermore, although introducing typology likely complicates the task in the general case, the complexity may be reduced in a multilingual setting, for the ability to predict a fixed set of typological features provides access to a wide prediction

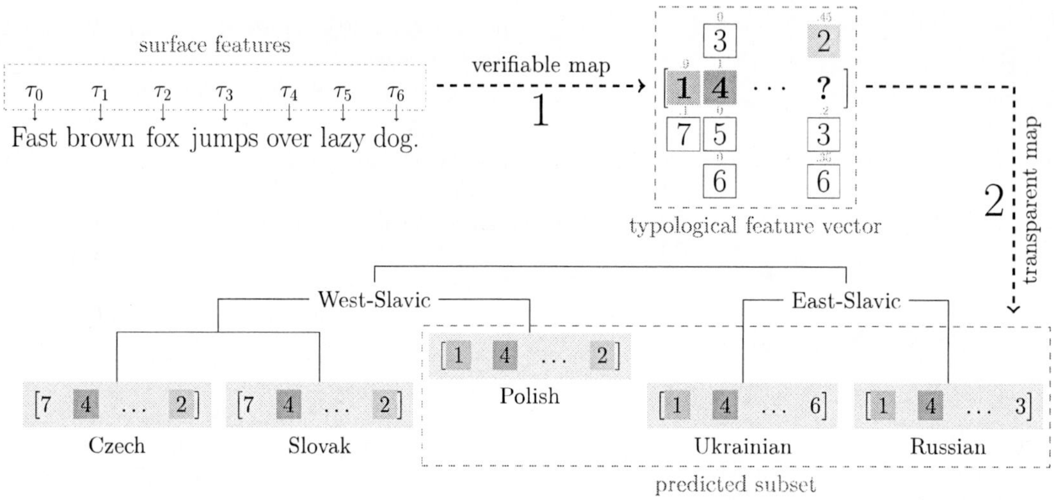

Figure 2: Intuitive diagram of a two-segment pipeline that (1) maps from surface features of a translated text to a typological feature vector w.r.t. the source language of the translated text, to (2) a (subset of) source language(s). Every element in the typological feature vector is predicted independently, resulting in a probability distribution over classes *per feature*. In this example, the source is Polish: *"Szybki brazowy lis przeskakuje nad leniwym psem."*

range of languages (namely, all that have these features set). Moreover, surface features are required only for the target language—this is assumed to always hold, as the availability of a language in MT usually means that tools to assign surface features are also available. The latter points actually testify to the assumed strengths of the method.

The experimental results in section 2 indicate that features specifically designed to accommodate *known* differences within a certain language pair may be fruitfully used for the methodology proposed in section 3. However, the method is likely to be limited by its reliance on WALS, which contains much more generally described features than those introduced in our case study (Ponti et al., 2019, p. 571). For example, Polish is classified as an 'ADJ–NOUN language' (feature 87A), placing English and Polish in the same category, while, clearly, the latter language is more permitting in its word order for adjectives and nouns, as was also observed in our case study. The broad nature of WALS may limit the ability of the method to exploit surface features in the way that was manually done in experiment 2. Moreover, it may pose an additional challenge to define a subset of WALS features that is relevant for pointing to the source language of (small) texts in the first place. Kredens et al. (2020, pp. 17–19) come to a similar conclusion about the usefulness of WALS for this task. Their 2020 paper puts forward a framework for providing different types of explanations for SLI-like tasks, with those informed by typology comprising only one tier among the multiple levels elaborated on by the authors, which ultimately lessens the effect of this issue on the overall picture, in which our methodology takes on only a part of the solution.

In conclusion, while it is impossible to make hard assertions, the experimental findings indicate promising potential for further development of the proposed methodology. A natural progression of this work is to implement the method and to qualitatively analyse its performance by evaluating it on language pairs including Slavic languages. Especially in light of the latter, future approaches may additionally consider more fine-grained differences between Slavic languages, such as tendencies for nominal or verbal constructions between Ukrainian, Polish, and Russian (Pchelintseva, 2022, p. 168).

5 Limitations

The present work was limited in that it did not assess to what extent other sources of translationese (*e.g.*, the translation model) impact the feasibility of the suggested SLI approach. The study further lacked a comparative analysis of different translation engines to test the robustness of the considered features. Moreover, although the work posits the Slavic family as a tool for evaluating explainable SLI, it did not consider in detail the appropriate procedure for conducting such evaluation.

References

Marco Baroni and Silvia Bernardini. 2005. A New Approach to the Study of Translationese: Machine-learning the Difference between Original and Translated Text. *Literary and Linguistic Computing*, 21(3):259–274.

Barbara Berti, Andrea Esuli, and Fabrizio Sebastiani. 2022. Unravelling interlanguage facts via explainable machine learning.

Yevgeni Berzak, Roi Reichart, and Boris Katz. 2014. Reconstructing native language typology from foreign language usage. In *Proceedings of the Eighteenth Conference on Computational Natural Language Learning*, pages 21–29, Ann Arbor, Michigan. Association for Computational Linguistics.

Dana Bielec. 2012. *Polish: An Essential Grammar*, 2nd edition. Routledge, Oxfordshire.

Yuri Bizzoni, Tom S Juzek, Cristina España-Bonet, Koel Dutta Chowdhury, Josef van Genabith, and Elke Teich. 2020. How human is machine translationese? comparing human and machine translations of text and speech. In *Proceedings of the 17th International Conference on Spoken Language Translation*, pages 280–290, Online. Association for Computational Linguistics.

Edward K. Cheng. 2013. Being pragmatic about forensic linguistics. *Journal of Law and Policy*, 21(2):541–550.

Michael Daniel. 2010. 43 Linguistic Typology and the Study of Language. In *The Oxford Handbook of Linguistic Typology*. Oxford University Press.

Matthew S. Dryer and Martin Haspelmath, editors. 2013. *WALS Online (v2020.3)*. Zenodo.

Yvette Graham, Barry Haddow, and Philipp Koehn. 2020. Statistical power and translationese in machine translation evaluation. In *Proceedings of the 2020 Conference on Empirical Methods in Natural Language Processing (EMNLP)*, pages 72–81, Online. Association for Computational Linguistics.

Md Mosharaf Hossain, Antonios Anastasopoulos, Eduardo Blanco, and Alexis Palmer. 2020. It's not a non-issue: Negation as a source of error in machine translation. In *Findings of the Association for Computational Linguistics: EMNLP 2020*, pages 3869–3885, Online. Association for Computational Linguistics.

Moshe Koppel, Jonathan Schler, and Kfir Zigdon. 2005. Automatically determining an anonymous author's native language. In *Intelligence and Security Informatics*, pages 209–217, Berlin, Heidelberg. Springer Berlin Heidelberg.

Krzysztof Kredens, Ria Perkins, and Tim Grant. 2020. Developing a framework for the explanation of interlingual features for native and other language infuence detection. *Language and Law/Linguagem e Direito*, 6(2):10–23.

Vladislav Kubon, Markéta Lopatková, and Tomás Hercig. 2016. Searching for a measure of word order freedom. In *Proceedings of the 16th ITAT: Slovensko-český NLP workshop (SloNLP 2016)*, volume 1649 of *CEUR Workshop Proceedings*, pages 11–17, Bratislava, Slovakia. Comenius University in Bratislava, Faculty of Mathematics, Physics and Informatics, CreateSpace Independent Publishing Platform.

Hakan Kuh. 1990. *Correlation between inflection and word order*. Ph.D. thesis, The Ohio State University.

Anna Kupsc. 2003. Two approaches to aspect assignment in an English-Polish machine translation system. In *Proceedings of the 7th International EAMT workshop on MT and other language technology tools, Improving MT through other language technology tools, Resource and tools for building MT at EACL 2003*.

David Kurokawa, Cyril Goutte, and Pierre Isabelle. 2009. Automatic detection of translated text and its impact on machine translation. In *Proceedings of Machine Translation Summit XII: Papers*, Ottawa, Canada.

Massimo La Morgia, Alessandro Mei, Eugenio Nerio, and Francesco Sassi. 2023. Translated texts under the lens: From machine translation detection to source language identification. In *Proceedings of the symposium on Intelligent Data Analysis (forthcoming)*.

Eugene A. Nida and Charles R. Taber. 1969. *The theory and practice of translation*. Helps for translators. E. J. Brill, Leiden.

Dmitry Nikolaev, Taelin Karidi, Neta Kenneth, Veronika Mitnik, Lilja Saeboe, and Omri Abend. 2020. Morphosyntactic predictability of translationese. *Linguistics Vanguard*, 6(1):20190077.

Olena Pchelintseva. 2022. Aspectual properties of ukrainian verbal action nouns. *Russian Linguistics*, 46(3):167–180.

Edoardo Maria Ponti, Helen O'Horan, Yevgeni Berzak, Ivan Vulić, Roi Reichart, Thierry Poibeau, Ekaterina Shutova, and Anna Korhonen. 2019. Modeling Language Variation and Universals: A Survey on Typological Linguistics for Natural Language Processing. *Computational Linguistics*, 45(3):559–601.

Maja Popović and Mihael Arčan. 2015. Identifying main obstacles for statistical machine translation of morphologically rich South Slavic languages. In *Proceedings of the 18th Annual Conference of the European Association for Machine Translation*, pages 97–104, Antalya, Turkey.

Daria Pylypenko, Kwabena Amponsah-Kaakyire, Koel Dutta Chowdhury, Josef van Genabith, and Cristina España-Bonet. 2021. Comparing feature-engineering and feature-learning approaches for multilingual translationese classification. In *Proceedings of the 2021 Conference on Empirical Methods in Natural

Language Processing, pages 8596–8611, Online and Punta Cana, Dominican Republic. Association for Computational Linguistics.

Ella Rabinovich, Noam Ordan, and Shuly Wintner. 2017. Found in translation: Reconstructing phylogenetic language trees from translations. In *Proceedings of the 55th Annual Meeting of the Association for Computational Linguistics (Volume 1: Long Papers)*, pages 530–540, Vancouver, Canada. Association for Computational Linguistics.

Parker Riley, Isaac Caswell, Markus Freitag, and David Grangier. 2020. Translationese as a language in "multilingual" NMT. In *Proceedings of the 58th Annual Meeting of the Association for Computational Linguistics*, pages 7737–7746, Online. Association for Computational Linguistics.

George Y. Shevelov. 1980. Ukrainian. In Alexander M. Schenker and Edward Stankiewicz, editors, *The Slavic Literary Languages: Formation and Development*. Yale Concilium on International and Area Studies, New Haven.

Anna Siewierska and Ludmila Uhlířová. 1998. *An overview of word order in Slavic languages*, pages 105–150. De Gruyter Mouton, Berlin, New York.

Joel Tetreault, Daniel Blanchard, and Aoife Cahill. 2013. A report on the first native language identification shared task. In *Proceedings of the Eighth Workshop on Innovative Use of NLP for Building Educational Applications*, pages 48–57, Atlanta, Georgia. Association for Computational Linguistics.

Peter Trudgill. 2020. Sociolinguistic typology and the speed of linguistic change. *Journal of Historical Sociolinguistics*, 6(2):20190015.

Barak Turovsky. 2016. Ten years of Google Translate. The Keyword. Accessed on March 3, 2023.

Lucas Nunes Vieira, Minako O'Hagan, and Carol O'Sullivan. 2021. Understanding the societal impacts of machine translation: a critical review of the literature on medical and legal use cases. *Information, Communication & Society*, 24(11):1515–1532.

Krzysztof Wolk and Krzysztof Marasek. 2019. Survey on neural machine translation into polish. In *Multimedia and Network Information Systems*, pages 260–272, Cham. Springer International Publishing.

Gu Xinxing. 2023. New features make Translate more accessible for its 1 billion users. The Keyword. Accessed on March 3, 2023.

Robert Zangenfeind and Barbara Sonnenhauser. 2014. Russian verbal aspect and machine translation. In *Dialog-21*, pages 743–752. s.n.

JiaJun Zhang and ChengQing Zong. 2020. Neural machine translation: Challenges, progress and future. *Science China Technological Sciences*, 63(10):2028–2050.

Comparing domain-specific and domain-general BERT variants for inferred real-world knowledge through rare grammatical features in Serbian

Sofia Lee
Vrije Universiteit Amsterdam
s.m.lee2@student.vu.nl

Jelke Bloem
University of Amsterdam
j.bloem@uva.nl

Abstract

Transfer learning is one of the prevailing approaches towards training language-specific BERT models. However, some languages have uncommon features that may prove to be challenging to more domain-general models but not domain-specific models. Comparing the performance of BERTić, a Bosnian-Croatian-Montenegrin-Serbian model, and Multilingual BERT on a Named-Entity Recognition (NER) task and Masked Language Modelling (MLM) task based around a rare phenomenon of indeclinable female foreign names in Serbian reveals how the different training approaches impacts their performance. Multilingual BERT is shown to perform better than BERTić in the NER task, but BERTić greatly exceeds in the MLM task. Thus, there are applications both for domain-general training and domain-specific training depending on the tasks at hand.

1 Introduction

The recent introduction of Transformer models (Vaswani et al., 2017) has precipitated a dramatic shift in the landscape of Natural Language Processing, bringing unprecedented gains in performance and accuracy. Of particular note is Bidirectional Encoder Representations for Transformers (BERT), a model which has become a baseline for NLP tasks (Devlin et al., 2018). As with other deep neural network models, however, it is largely unknown *how* BERT is able to achieve its performance. The bulk of NLP research focused on BERT, a sub-field that has come to be known as BERTology, has centred around probing underlying embeddings through various aptitude tests, comparing the performance of different BERT variants to each other as well as to human performance metrics. These tasks may consist of more traditional tasks such as the Cloze task, or more NLP-specific tasks such as named entity recognition or sentiment analysis. As English is the language of the original BERT models, these efforts have usually focused on investigating linguistic phenomena that exist in English. This leaves us with a knowledge gap of BERT's representation of linguistic typological features that are not shared with English but occur in other language families, such as the Slavic languages.

Due to the success of transformer models, many domain-specific derivatives of BERT have been produced. This includes topic-based domains such as scientific text model SciBERT (Beltagy et al., 2019), as well as domains of related languages such as the Finnish-Estonian model FinEstBERT (Ulčar and Robnik-Šikonja, 2020) and BERTić (Ljubešić and Lauc, 2021), a model for Bosnian, Croatian, Montenegrin and Serbian (BCMS). The introduction of domain-specific derivatives has sparked a debate within BERTology on how specific the dataset of the fine-tuning task should be. Should derivatives be trained on a more general dataset within a domain or should they be fine-tuned on a much more domain-restricted dataset?

We contribute to this debate by focusing on the case of closely related and under-resourced languages. We compare two variants of BERT: the domain-general Multilingual BERT (mBERT), and the language-specific model BERTić, trained from scratch on the BCMS languages. In particular, we explore how the two training approaches affect performance on rare grammatical phenomena in Serbian. Our case study is indeclinable nouns, a phenomenon typical of fusional languages where the same morphological form is used for all grammatical functions of a noun. This is a challenging phenomenon to model as it is typically infrequent and the usual morphological cues of the language aren't expressed. We create adapted versions of the common probing tasks of Masked Language Modeling and Named Entity Recognition specifically targeting this phenomenon.

We contend that such phenomena that do not occur in English pose unique challenges to language modelling, particularly in under-resourced

Proceedings of the 9th Workshop on Slavic Natural Language Processing 2023 (SlavicNLP 2023), pages 47–60
May 6, 2023

languages, and can reveal some of the overlooked underlying representations learned by BERT derivatives. We aim to show areas in which transformer-based language model training can improve, as well as emphasize the importance of analysing the linguistic capabilities of non-English BERT variants.

2 Background

Typically, BERT makes use of mixed-domain transfer learning. The first stage of training uses general-domain data, such as base BERT's training on Wikipedia and BookCorpus, followed by a fine-tuning domain-specific stage. Domain-specific pre-training has been proposed to be more effective. Beltagy et al. (2019) compare the results of a more general scientific domain BERT variant SciBERT with that of biomedical-specific BioBERT (Lee et al., 2019). SciBERT outperformed BioBERT in biomedical text tasks. Gu et al. (2021) contend that SciBERT's higher performance stems from its from-scratch training on scientific domain text.

Non-English language modelling provides distinct challenges compared to domain-specific training. Human languages differ in ways that exceed that of domains of the same language. While related languages may share vocabulary and grammatical features, they often differ vastly in information structure and syntax. Languages may also have varying amounts of quality data available. High resource languages such as English or German can be trained on monolingual text, while under-resourced languages may have no options but transfer learning. Transfer learning is the predominant approach to building language-specific variants of BERT. On top of base BERT, Multilingual BERT (mBERT) is additionally trained on the text of 104 language-specific Wikipedias without any cross-lingual alignment. mBERT achieved impressive cross-lingual performance and itself is used as a base for countless language-specific BERT derivatives, taking a mixed-domain training approach (Wu and Dredze, 2019).

However, several studies have shown that language-specific BERT models trained on a dataset consisting of only one language still perform better than mBERT-based models, especially in the case of under-resourced languages (Wu and Dredze, 2020). Bhattacharjee et al. (2021) show that a Bangla-specific variant, BanglaBERT, outperforms both mBERT and a Bangla-English bilingual variant. Tanvir et al. (2021) similarly show that an Estonian-specific BERT outperforms multilingual variants in five out of seven tasks. Likewise, Martin et al. (2022) find that a BERT variant trained ground-up on a Swahili dataset outperforms multilingual models. BERTić, a variant trained on Bosnian, Croatian, Montenegrin and Serbian, also outperforms both mBERT and a trilingual Croatian, Slovene and English BERT in nearly every task (Ljubešić and Lauc, 2021).

2.1 Grammatical embedding and indeclinable nouns

BERT shows a surprising ability to perform grammatical generalisation. Madabushi et al. (2022) find that BERT even outperforms human subjects in a task predicting article use (e.g. *a/an, the*) in English and tends to agree with annotators when annotators agree with each other. Multilingual models have also demonstrated that synthetic transfer can occur between languages (Guarasci et al., 2022). Meanwhile, Haley (2020) show that BERT can perform the Wug test, a standard grammatical generalisation test (Berko Gleason, 1958), significantly better than chance in English, French, Spanish and Dutch.

However, there are still many gaps in this research. Firstly, high-resource languages are used for these studies, where a model will have more evidence to generalize over grammatical patterns. Although some patterns may be transferred to under-resourced languages, these languages may present a diverse range of unique or rare typological features. Secondly, few if any of the languages studied are fusional languages, meaning its inflectional endings encode several pieces of information at the same time (Bender, 2019). The nature of word paradigms in these languages provides significant challenges for generalisation and statistical modelling due to the multitude of forms for each word.

One phenomenon common to many fusional languages is that of the indeclinable noun. Indeclinable nouns are nouns which exhibit an extreme form of case syncretism in which the same form is used for all grammatical functions. In many cases, such nouns form some sort of semantic class, such as being loanwords or abbreviations. As an example, although English is not a highly inflected language, it does have indeclinable nouns which violate the usual *-s* suffix in forming the plural, such as 'moose'. This word retains the same form in the singular and plural, and this is said to be the case due to its being a loanword from Eastern Algonquian. Fusional languages that have indeclinable nouns include Russian (Nedomová, 2013), Czech (Naughton, 2006), Upper Sorbian (Corbett, 1987), Lithuanian (Mathiassen, 1996), Latvian (Kalnača and Lokmane, 2021), Latin (Schmitz, 2004), and both modern and ancient Greek. Indeclinable nouns serve as a fitting rare phenomenon to probe because they are present in a variety of under-resourced languages, appear relatively infrequently in corpora, and often require some kind of intuition from a speaker in order to correctly identify and use. To date, no studies that focus specifically on indeclinable nouns and language modelling exist, although indeclinable nouns are shown to cause low performance in NER tasks in a Greek edition of BERT (Singh et al., 2021).

2.2 Serbian as a subject for BERTology

Serbian is one of four mutually intelligible varieties of a pluricentric language referred to collectively as Bosnian-Croatian-Montenegrin-Serbian (BCMS). It is a highly inflected language, inflecting for case, number and gender in nouns, adjectives and some verb participles. Serbian is also a fusional language, as the same endings may encode different features. Serbian also has indeclinable nouns.

As with many other highly inflected languages, nouns in Serbian fall under a variety of paradigms with different numbers of unique forms. Masculine and neuter nouns exhibit one less form than feminine nouns, while some nouns, such as *ljubavi* 'love' only distinguish between three forms (four in some dialects). Indeclinable nouns in Serbian are a particularly restricted class. Whereas other languages may not place semantic restrictions on indeclinable loanwords, Serbian reserves indeclinability to two types of words: certain numbers, and loanwords or foreign names with a female referent that do not end in *-a* (Fidler et al., 2005). The latter are particularly infrequent in Serbian corpora as a whole but also grow in frequency daily due to an ever-increasing amount of global news and celebrity gossip written in the language.

Although Željko Bošković (2006) and Fidler et al. (2005) observe that indeclinable nouns are not allowed in sentences without an adjective that clarifies the case assignment, recent Serbian tabloids have simply used indeclinable names in case assigning roles as with any other name. Example 1, a lyric from 'In corpore sano' by Konstrakta, Serbia's entry in 2022 Eurovision, demonstrates how the indeclinability of female proper names may still be assigned cases even without a preposition.

(1) Koj-a li je
which-.F.SG.NOM Q be.3.SG.PRS
tajn-a zdrav-e
secret-.F.SG.NOM healthy-.F.SG.GEN
kos-e Megan
hair-.F.SG.GEN Meghan.F.SG.GEN
Markl?
Markle.F.SG.GEN
'Just what is the secret to the healthy hair of Meghan Markle?'

While indeclinable nouns function the same way in Bosnian and Croatian, Serbian requires all names to be written phonetically. Names are thus obfuscated from their native spelling, making them less likely to benefit from transfer learning. Indeclinable nouns in Serbian are thus especially suited as indicators of named entity recognition ability, semantic awareness, and real world knowledge.

2.3 Serbian as an under-resourced language

In comparison to high-resource languages such as English, research on Serbian NLP is sparse. Miletic (2018) provides a treebank for Serbian consisting of 81K tokens. A Python package by Ostrogonac et al. (2020), *nlpheart*, provides text processing tools for Serbian, although at the time of writing it remains unavailable. As a whole, NLP studies on Serbian are few, and tools tend to be defunct. The situation is not significantly improved even when factoring in the related Croatian, Bosnian or Montenegrin languages. Many tools are also grouped in with the related but not mutually intelligible Slovene. Ljubešić and Dobrovoljc (2019) provide a NLP pipeline for Slovene, Croatian and Serbian consisting of a part-of-speech tagger, a lemmatiser, a tokeniser, a dependency parser, and a named-entity recogniser.

Ulčar and Robnik-Šikonja (2020) provide a multilingual BERT model, CroSloEngual BERT or cseBERT, which although trained on Croatian and Slovene, has been shown to perform well on Serbian NLP tasks. Moving closer to Serbian, BERTić (Ljubešić and Lauc, 2021) is trained on the CLASSLA web corpus, based on Bosnian, Croatian, Montenegrin, and Serbian websites, the Riznica corpus of Croatian literature and newspapers (Ćavar and Brozović Rončević, 2012), and the cc100 corpus (Conneau et al., 2020). The corpora on which BERTić is trained are currently the largest for the BCMS languages. Ljubešić and Lauc

Meaning	'Jelena' (name)	'Marko' (name)	'hill'	'joy'	'Jean' (name)
Nominative	Jelen-a	Mark-o	brd-o	radost-Ø	Džin-Ø
Genitive	Jelen-e	Mark-a	brd-a	radost-i	Džin-Ø
Dative/Locative	Jelen-i	Mark-u	brd-u	radost-i	Džin-Ø
Accusative	Jelen-u	Mark-a	brd-o	radost-Ø	Džin-Ø
Vocative	Jelen-o	Mark-o	brd-o	radost-i	Džin-Ø
Instrumental	Jelen-om	Mark-om	brd-om	radost-i	Džin-Ø

Table 1: Common noun declension paradigms, including indeclinable names.

(2021) find that BERTić outperforms both mBERT and the Slovene-Croatian-English model CroSloEngual BERT (Ulčar and Robnik-Šikonja, 2020) in morphosyntactic tagging, named entity recognition, social media geolocation prediction, and commonsense casual reasoning. They also find that despite the lack of exposure to Serbian in cseBERT, there are no significant improvements in Serbian performance between cseBERT and BERTić, aside from one Serbian NER task. For this last reason, we use BERTić for this study.

3 Methodology

We compare BERTić and mBERT on two tasks: a feminine Named Entity Recognition (NER) task, targeting the name domain in which the indeclinable noun phenomenon occurs, and Masked Langauge Modelling (MLM), a more intrinsic evaluation task. BERTić is pretrained with the ELECTRA training objective, where instead of masking tokens, tokens are corrupted and a detection task is performed (Clark et al., 2020). MBERT uses the standard BERT MLM training objective. Other multilingual BERT-based models are available such as XLM-R (Conneau et al., 2020) and mT5 (Xue et al., 2021), but these all use the standard MLM objective rather than ELECTRA. Out of these, we chose to compare to mBERT as this comparison was also made by Ljubešić and Lauc (2021). Both models use WordPiece subword tokenization (Schuster and Nakajima, 2012).

For the feminine NER task, NER-fine-tuned variants of both BERTić and mBERT are used. The BERTić variant we use is the *bcms-bertic-ner* variant, which has been fine-tuned on the Croatian hr500k dataset, Serbian SETimes.SR dataset, and the ReLDI-hr and ReLDI-sr Internet (Twitter) datasets in Croatian and Serbian respectively. In total, the dataset consists of 768k tokens. Since a NER variant is not readily available for mBERT at the time of testing, we use *bert-base-multilingual-cased-ner-hrl* instead. This model is fine-tuned on Arabic, German, English, Spanish, French, Italian, Latvian, Dutch, Portuguese and Chinese NER. The training process is not well documented, but appears to consist mainly of newspapers from the early- to mid-2000s. This datedness ensures that mBERT does not have an extra advantage from being exposed to a wider selection of modern names. SpaCy[1] is used as a baseline for comparison. For the MLM task we only use the base BERTić and mBERT models. All tasks are performed using a Dell Optiplex 7010 with an Intel i7 processor and 12GB of RAM.

3.1 Named Entity Recognition

We sourced a list of names of popular female celebrities from nationality category lists in the Serbian Wikipedia. All names are converted from Serbian Wikipedia's default Serbian Cyrillic script to Serbian Latin script and edited for capitalisation errors. Details of which names we included and spelling variation and exceptional cases can be found in Appendix A. In total, 1323 names are included, of which 812 names are completely indeclinable, meaning the name does not include any declinable element. 511 contain at least one declinable element, of which 13 appear to be of Southern Slavic origin. 30 names are fully declinable.

We take the log_{10} frequency of each name across all three Serbian BERTić training corpora as a weighting score for that name to use in the evaluation. For example, *Madona* ('Madonna', a singer), appearing 5,060 times in the corpus, scores approximately 9.36. Unattested names, such as *Zelda Rubenstejn* ('Zelda Rubinstein', actress in 'the *Poltergeist* film series), are given a score of 0. There are 166 unattested names and 92 names with one attestation. The greatest number of attestations is 11602. Scores follow a Zipfian distribution.

[1] `https://spacy.io/`

We generated a feminine NER test corpus by filtering the three Serbian-specific corpora, on which BERTić was trained, for lines containing names from the list. This process generates 97,981 sentences, which is reduced by 6,619 or 6.75% when pruned for duplicates. Names are annotated with their name type, which could be either *indeclinable*, *Slavic*, *fully declinable*, or *declinable*. Names of any declinable type are also labelled by one of five cases: Nominative, Genitive, Dative/Locative, Accusative or Instrumental. Vocative, which is virtually unseen in the dataset, is ignored, and Dative and Locative are combined due to their identical forms. All input, including names, is tokenized by the model's tokenizer. In evaluation, models are awarded a point only for complete, unbroken names identified, with the B-PER token in the beginning of the name and the I-PER token at the end. Other categories are discarded and names not included in the name list are ignored.

3.2 Masked Language Modelling

In the Masked Language Modelling task, a set of 216 sentences for each name in the name list is automatically generated using templates, totalling 285,758 sentences. A mask was inserted at a predetermined spot for the models to fill in. Each sentence could be of one or two types: a low-context type, in which there is one sentence containing the name and mask with minimal context, and a high-context type, in which the declinability of the name is demonstrated by one of eleven sentences that involve case assignment. This distinction is made to differentiate between the use of information from the embedding itself (low-context condition) and from the grammatical inflections in the contextual sentence (high-context condition). By only providing the nominative form in the low-context sentences, no information about the gender of the name is available if it does not have a feminine form, i.e ends in *-a*. High-context sentences provide inflectional information that can indicate gender through feminine inflections, either by having no inflections or through the native inflections. All sentences are written to be as gender neutral as possible otherwise.

Low-context sentences consist of one completely open-ended sentence (e.g 'Laura Dern is [MASK]') and sentence types that elicit particular parts-of-speech that may encode information about gender in Serbian, such as an adjective (e.g. 'Laura Dern is very [MASK]'). The high-context condition involves a context sentence containing a name paired with a high-frequency other name — three male names and three female names. Each of the cases are represented. An example is 'Vladimir is afraid of Laura Dern (genitive)'. This is then followed by a sentence with a mask as in the low-context condition. The full set of sentence types with glossing can be seen in Appendix B.

All input, including names, is tokenized by the model's tokenizer. All sentences include a single mask, in which any element from a model's vocabulary can be predicted, including subtokens. The top five suggestions for each sentence by each model are counted, regardless of model confidence. Responses are manually scored and only deemed correct if the suggested word is a word in Bosnian, Croatian, Montenegrin or Serbian and fall into one of the following word types: 1) a noun referring to a woman, such as *političarka* 'politician (f.)'; 2) an adjective with a feminine ending, e.g. *srećna* 'happy (f.)'; 3) the possessive feminine adjective, *njen* or *njezin*; 4) a feminine past participle, e.g. *pročitala* 'read (f.)'; or 5) the feminine plural past participle of *biti* 'to be', *bile*. Nouns of feminine gender that do not refer to humans, such as *ulica* 'street' or *reka* 'river' are not counted as correct. Nouns that are grammatically feminine but not semantically, such as *osoba* 'person' were not counted. All proper names, even if feminine, are ignored. A single animal word, *mačka* 'cat' which also double as slang term for a woman, is included, while others, such as *zmija* 'snake' or *riba* 'fish' are excluded. Words that are feminine but not in the BCMS lexicon are not considered correct. Finally, subtokens (word segments), even if ungrammatical, are scored as correct as long as it indicates a feminine gender.

4 Results

4.1 Named Entity Recognition

mBERT scores the highest in the feminine Named Entity Recognition task (87.49%), outperforming both BERTić (57.79%) and the spaCy baseline (35.98%).[2] Figure 1 visualizes these results by the log frequency of each name in the corpus as operationalized in Section 3.1. Furthermore, mBERT and BERTić both performed slightly worse with

[2] A χ^2 test of independence shows that there is a statistically significant association between correctness and model type, $\chi^2 = 45238.63$ (2, N = 300348), $p < 0.00001$.

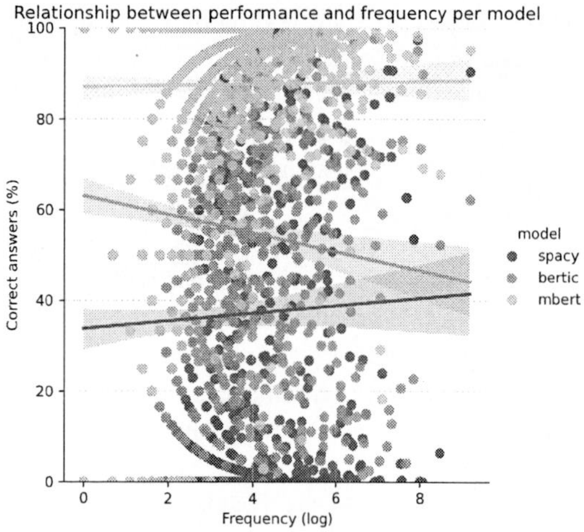

Figure 1: NER results

indeclinable names than the average (86.37% and 55% respectively) whereas spaCy saw a significant improvement with them (47.57%). Results with regression lines for each name type are shown in Figure 2 or in Appendix C for the spaCy baseline. BERTić shows a weak negative but significant correlation between performance and name frequency, r(1321) = -0.11, $p < 0.0005$. No such correlation is found for mBERT or spaCy.

4.2 Masked Language Modelling

BERTić provides feminine forms 49.16% of the time whereas mBERT only provides feminine forms 15.75% of the time.[3] Figure 3 visualizes these results by name frequency. Forms that are feminine but do not appear to be Serbian words were excluded.

BERTić shows higher performance (49.64%) in low-context sentences than high-context ones (44.15%) whereas mBERT performed worse in low-context sentences (15.08%) compared to high-context sentences (22.71%). For both BERTić and mBERT, declinable names of all types resulted in a feminine form more often than an indeclinable form. BERTić selects a feminine form 33.17% of the time with indeclinable names, 82.68% of the time with Slavic names, 75.67% of the time with fully declinable names, and 74.26% of the time with other declinable names (Figure 4a). mBERT only selects a feminine form 8.65% of the time with indeclinable names, 27.13% of the time with Slavic names, 27.45% of the time with fully declinable names, and 27.02% of the time with other declinable names (Figure 4b).

Since low-context sentences only use nominative case, we evaluate case performance only for high-context sentences. There is little variation between the performances per case of both BERTić (M = 50.26, SD = 2.38) and mBERT (M = 14.67, SD = 1.31). Cases rank from highest to lowest performance for BERTić are nominative (52.32%), accusative (51.56%), instrumental (51.46%), dative (50.27%) and genitive (45.66%), whereas for mBERT the order is dative (16.69%), genitive (15.25%), accusative (14.84%), instrumental (13.74%) and nominative (12.85%). We also compare the distribution of the feminine forms per name to the frequency of each name in the corpus. BERTić showed a very weak correlation between performance and frequency, r(1321) = .08, $p < 0.005$. Thus, BERTić is somewhat more likely to select a feminine form to complete a sentence when the sentence is focused on a more common the name in the corpus. This is especially the case when the sentence concerns an indeclinable name. No such correlation is found for mBERT.

5 Discussion

5.1 Named Entity Recognition

In contrast to the results of Ljubešić and Lauc's (2021) general NER task, BERTić trails significantly behind mBERT in our feminine NER task. In the general task both models reach near 90% accuracy, while in our task only mBERT did. Only when the name is fully declinable and in the accusative case both models perform similarly, but our dataset has only 30 of 1323 fully declinable names and indeclinable is the most common type (exact numbers are in Section 3.1).

An error analysis reveals that BERTić produces excessive span errors, exhibiting a tendency to over-segment all names. From the first 10000 lines of the srWAC celebrity sub-corpus, when looking at both male and female names, BERTić over-segments on 6348 lines a total of 12123 times, sometimes even twice in the same name. Understandably, the names in question, being uncommon, lack embeddings in BERTić and are thus tokenized into subtokens, but this does not explain why BERTić performs significantly worse than mBERT, which is even less likely to have full token embeddings for such a name. In many cases, BERTić and mBERT are tokenising

[3] A χ^2 test of independence shows that there is a statistically significant association between correctness and model type, χ^2 = 363597.04 (2, N = 2857670), $p < 0.00001$.

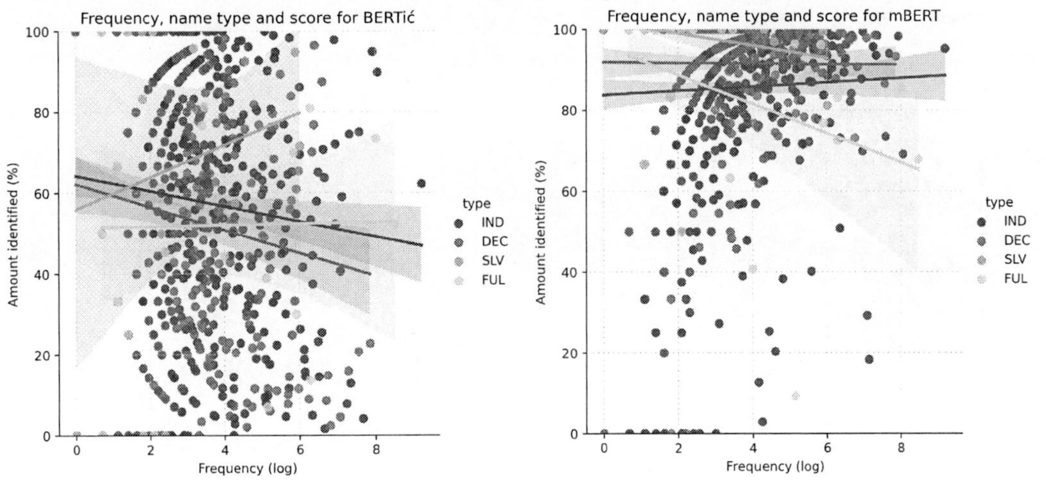

(a) BERTić NER results per name type

(b) mBERT NER results per name type

Figure 2: NER results for both models with regression lines for each name type, including indeclinable (IND), declinable (DEC), Slavic (SLV) or fully declinable (FUL).

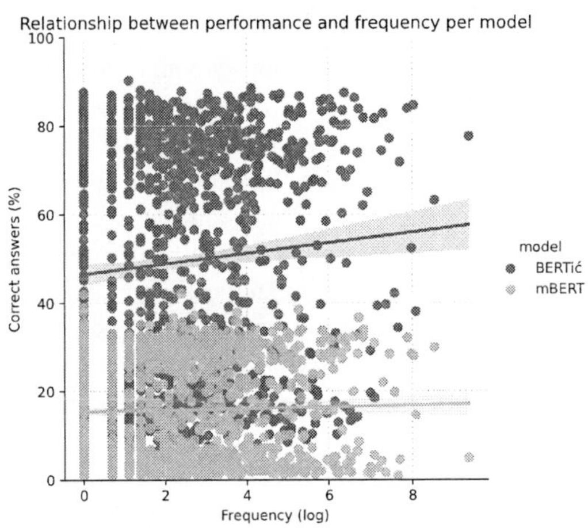

Figure 3: Overall MLM scores for BERTić and mBERT

names into similar subtokens, but only mBERT consistently labels the beginning of a name with the correct B-PER tag instead of I-PER (indicating a separate name). For mBERT, over-segmentation occurs 495 times in the same sample. Of this, 207 occur with a name containing the characters *ž*, *š* or *đ*. As mBERT is trained with all diacritics stripped out, this hints at an encoding error.

However, not all of BERTić's low scores can be attributed purely to low performance. In some cases, BERTić provides answers that demonstrate more advanced comprehension of context. Phrases such as *vlada Margaret Tačer* 'the government of Margaret Thatcher' are labelled as organisations by BERTić whereas only the name *Maragret Tačer* is tagged by mBERT. BERTić performance here has higher practical significance. Although Singh et al. (2021) suggest that indeclinable nouns pose particular challenges in the NER task, we only see minor differences. This could be attributed to the fact that most female foreign names are indeclinable, potentially causing models, particularly the language-specific BERTić, to struggle with the whole semantic class of female foreign names (i.e. our entire dataset), including declinable ones.

5.2 Masked Language Modelling

The MLM task shows that indeclinable names are particularly challenging to both mBERT and BERTić. Unlike in the NER task, both models clearly fare worse when facing sentences with indeclinable names. BERTić performs better when a name is more common, suggesting that higher representation in a dataset helps. Interestingly, BERTić scores lower in the high-context sentences compared to the low-context sentences, whereas mBERT scores higher in low-context sentences. While mBERT may need more context in order to identify the language being used, it is unclear why BERTić sees a performance loss when working with high-context sentences. The effect of the divergent vocabularies of the tokenizers should be limited on this task as we also scored subtokens.

mBERT and BERTić, to varying degrees, both show evidence that names of famous people are being discussed. *poznata* 'famous' (f.) is among the

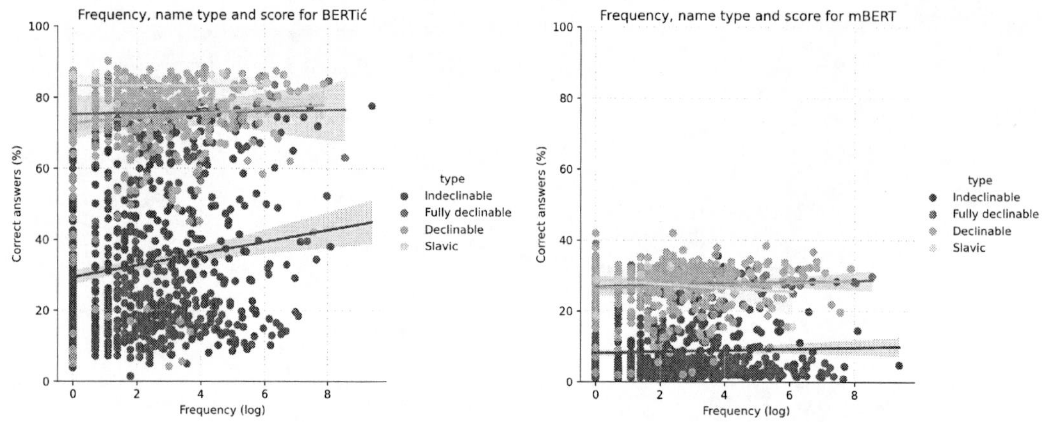

(a) MLM scores for BERTić

(b) MLM scores for mBERT

Figure 4: MLM scores for both models with regression lines for each name type.

top results for both mBERT and BERTić. However, BERTić shows a larger variety of words such as *zanimljiva* 'interesting' (f.) and *pametna* 'smart' (f.). In general, BERTić is able to produce 244 feminine words compared to mBERT's considerably smaller 62, a large amount of which are actually sub-words. BERTić, through its specialised training, appears able to produce more relevant descriptors.

5.2.1 Language identification

mBERT occasionally confuses the text with that of other Slavic languages, which is understandable given that it does not specialise in BCMS. The incredibly high occurrence of *v* ('in' in a considerable number of Slavic languages) suggests that mBERT is able to identify the text as being in some Slavic language, but not specifically Slovene, Czech, or Slovak. *v* however is not grammatical in any of the sentences given and has a low confidence score.

Slovene and Croatian in particular share a considerably large amount of vocabulary. Many of its top results (*za*, *dobra*, *velika*, *na*, *brzo* to name a few) are shared vocabulary with Slovene if not other Slavic languages, and some frequent responses with high scores, such as *objavil*, are most likely Slovene. Although such forms also exist in Kajkavian Croatian, this language variant is most likely unrepresented in mBERT's training set. This language confusion is probably a result of mBERT's domain-general training.

The issues that mBERT faces show one of the situations in which domain-general training may be ill-suited. These issues are exacerbated in low-context sentences. One of the ways that this may be rectified is through fine-tuning. A future study could explore how mBERT's performance could improve if fine-tuned for Serbian texts.

5.2.2 Language standards

Considering that the training set contains corpora in all variants of BCMS, BERTić mixes both Serbian standard spellings and spellings not considered standard Serbian in its responses. However, this occurs much less often than one would expect. BERTić shows a strong preference for Serbian forms for some words but uses non-standard or Bosnian, Croatian or Montenegrin forms for others. In some cases, the Serbian form of a word is not used at all. Table 2 shows some examples.

We also observe frequent output of Ijekavian spelling forms which are the standard in other BCMS regions, as opposed to Standard Serbian Ekavian spelling. This suggests that training a language model on a combined dataset of all language variants may induce negative transfer of a feature that is more common in other variants.

Twelve words in mBERT's result set are in Cyrillic, whereas BERTić has none. By not supporting Cyrillic, BERTić is effectively restricted to only Latin-using domains, ignoring the bi-alphabetism of Serbian. As the choice between the two alphabets is not arbitrary and can be tied to register, ideally a model would be trained on both Cyrillic and Latin text in their original scripts.

5.3 Implications for under-resourced languages

A known limitation of most large language models is that they reproduce social biases which are reflected in the training data (Mehrabi et al., 2019).

Lemma	Meaning	Serbian standard	Non-standard
lepa	'beautiful'	48512	20945
devojka	'girl'	10564	217
srećna	'happy, lucky'	0	3015
vredna	'valuable, worthwhile'	0	1528
volela	'love' (past participle)	0	68
pevačica	'singer' (f.)	0	50
poslednja	'last, final'	9	9
devojčica	'girl' (diminutive)	0	3

Table 2: Frequencies of Serbian standard and non-standard duplets in BERTić responses to the MLM task.

The effect of ethnic tensions in the Balkan region is well-known, and studied by sociolinguists, but less so in NLP. Considering that training on less data may amplify any biases within that data, BERTić or any other language model trained on corpora emerging from current or recent conflict will have a greater tendency to reproduce conflict discourse since the proportion of conflict-neutral training data is smaller. We observed evidence of this.

During the masked language modelling task, BERTić produces *Srbin* 'Serb' 8883 times and *Hrvat* 'Croat' 1115 times. In fact, *Srbin* is the 38th most common word in BERTić's answer set, while *Hrvat* is the 151th most common word. Additionally, BERTić also produces *musliman* ('a male follower of Islam', sometimes used to refer to Bosnians) 101 times. These forms largely surface in the most open-ended sentence in the MLM task. In contrast, mBERT does not produce any of these words once.

The fact that ethnic discourse is reproduced in BERTić has implications for other languages from conflict zones. Languages are not under-resourced simply because of neglect, but because of social, political and historical factors that create their present status. In the case of Serbian and its close relatives, political factors such as national language policies complicate the development of tools for each language standard. Both practical and political reasons impact the appropriateness of a BCMS-general model. Attempts to develop NLP tools for BCMS or any of the national standards must contend with the forces that continue to shape the identity of BCMS and its speakers.

6 Conclusion

We evaluated the performance of two BERT variants, multilingual BERT (mBERT) and BERTić, on Serbian indeclinable nouns, using a NER task and a MLM task. While in a general NER task, BERTić and mBERT show similar performance on Serbian (Ljubešić and Lauc, 2021), mBERT outperforms BERTić in our feminine NER task. In the MLM task, BERTić vastly outperforms mBERT and both models performed significantly worse on indeclinable names. BERTić produces a larger diversity of pragmatically correct responses overall. These results indicate that BERTić may encode information about gender and names, but whether the encoding can be considered a morphological feature of nouns or is specific to a semantic domain of names remains unclear. We only see that BERTić's performance is sensitive to name frequency. mBERT on the other hand produces feminine forms significantly less often, and produces responses from related languages such as Slovene and Czech.

The results from the NER task suggest that multilingual models perform better when the names are not native to the text language. On the other hand, language-specific tasks such as sentence completion will produce significantly more relevant results from models trained specifically for the language, as the embeddings contain a significantly larger amount of vocabulary for the target language.

Potential future directions include research on other typologically rare grammatical features, the behaviour of BERT with other kinds of fusional languages and probing how contextual real-world knowledge inferred from them may be encoded. The representation of bi-alphabetical languages in language modelling could be explored further, as well as the ways language-specific training compares to more general training when dealing with closely related variants. More broadly, we claim that research on closely related languages contributes to our knowledge of the conditions and factors that affect the choice between using a transfer learning or in-domain learning approach.

Acknowledgements

We would like to thank Lisa Bylinina for insightful comments on an earlier version of this work, as well as the workshop's anonymous reviewers for their helpful comments.

Limitations

Due to our starting point of studying existing resources, our study was limited to already existing models. It might have been possible to train or tune better-performing models for the Serbian language specifically by making our own model. The choice to use existing resources also comes with some methodological issues for the NER task - in particular, that there were most likely differences between the fine-tuning procedures on the NER task of both models. A controlled experiment in which both base models are tuned on the same NER data would exclude some possible sources of variation between the two approaches, but would have also cost significantly more training resources. Our choice also means we had no control over hyperparameters - perhaps a Serbian-specific tuning could improve performance.

Due to the limited resources available for Serbian, we had to use sentences from a corpus that BERTić was trained on for the NER evaluation. However, as this overlap is only with the pre-training dataset and the NER-specific tuned BERTić used different datasets we expect that this choice had limited consequences for NER performance on the evaluation set. We also did not have a proper NER gold standard available in which all names in text were annotated, so we were only able to report accuracy, not recall, on our own silver standard.

Our study is a case study of a specific phenomenon in a specific language, thus there is no way to ascertain that other rare grammatical phenomena in other under-resourced languages would also benefit from language-specific training on the basis of only our study.

References

Iz Beltagy, Kyle Lo, and Arman Cohan. 2019. SciBERT: A pretrained language model for scientific text. In *Proceedings of the 2019 Conference on Empirical Methods in Natural Language Processing and the 9th International Joint Conference on Natural Language Processing (EMNLP-IJCNLP)*, pages 3615–3620.

Emily Bender. 2019. The #benderrule: On naming the languages we study and why it matters. *The Gradient*.

Jean Berko Gleason. 1958. The child's learning of English morphology. *Word*, 14.

Abhik Bhattacharjee, Tahmid Hasan, Kazi Samin, M. Sohel Rahman, Anindya Iqbal, and Rifat Shahriyar. 2021. Banglabert: Combating embedding barrier for low-resource language understanding. *CoRR*, abs/2101.00204.

Damir Ćavar and Dunja Brozović Rončević. 2012. Riznica: The Croatian Language Corpus. *Prace filologiczne*, 63:51–65.

Kevin Clark, Minh-Thang Luong, Quoc V Le, and Christopher D Manning. 2020. Electra: Pre-training text encoders as discriminators rather than generators. *arXiv preprint arXiv:2003.10555*.

Alexis Conneau, Kartikay Khandelwal, Naman Goyal, Vishrav Chaudhary, Guillaume Wenzek, Francisco Guzmán, Edouard Grave, Myle Ott, Luke Zettlemoyer, and Veselin Stoyanov. 2020. Unsupervised cross-lingual representation learning at scale. In *Proceedings of the 58th Annual Meeting of the Association for Computational Linguistics*, pages 8440–8451, Online. Association for Computational Linguistics.

Greville G. Corbett. 1987. The morphology/syntax interface: Evidence from possessive adjectives in Slavonic. *Language*, 63(2):299–345.

Jacob Devlin, Ming-Wei Chang, Kenton Lee, and Kristina Toutanova. 2018. BERT: pre-training of deep bidirectional transformers for language understanding. *CoRR*, abs/1810.04805.

Masako Fidler, Stephen Wechsler, and Larisa Zlatić. 2005. The many faces of agreement. *The Slavic and East European Journal*, 49:170.

Yu Gu, Robert Tinn, Hao Cheng, Michael Lucas, Naoto Usuyama, Xiaodong Liu, Tristan Naumann, Jianfeng Gao, and Hoifung Poon. 2021. Domain-specific language model pretraining for biomedical natural language processing. *ACM Transactions on Computing for Healthcare (HEALTH)*, 3(1):1–23.

Raffaele Guarasci, Stefano Silvestri, Giuseppe De Pietro, Hamido Fujita, and Massimo Esposito. 2022. Bert syntactic transfer: A computational experiment on italian, french and english languages. *Computer Speech & Language*, 71:101261.

Coleman Haley. 2020. This is a BERT. now there are several of them. can they generalize to novel words? In *Proceedings of the Third BlackboxNLP Workshop on Analyzing and Interpreting Neural Networks for NLP*, pages 333–341, Online. Association for Computational Linguistics.

Andra Kalnača and Ilze Lokmane. 2021. *Latvian Grammar*.

Jinhyuk Lee, Wonjin Yoon, Sungdong Kim, Donghyeon Kim, Sunkyu Kim, Chan Ho So, and Jaewoo Kang. 2019. BioBERT: a pre-trained biomedical language representation model for biomedical text mining. *Bioinformatics*, 36(4):1234–1240.

Nikola Ljubešić and Kaja Dobrovoljc. 2019. What does neural bring? analysing improvements in morphosyntactic annotation and lemmatisation of Slovenian, Croatian and Serbian. In *Proceedings of the 7th Workshop on Balto-Slavic Natural Language Processing*, pages 29–34, Florence, Italy. Association for Computational Linguistics.

Nikola Ljubešić and Davor Lauc. 2021. BERTić - the transformer language model for Bosnian, Croatian, Montenegrin and Serbian. In *Proceedings of the 8th Workshop on Balto-Slavic Natural Language Processing*, pages 37–42, Kiyv, Ukraine. Association for Computational Linguistics.

Harish Tayyar Madabushi, Dagmar Divjak, and Petar Milin. 2022. Abstraction not memory: Bert and the english article system.

Gati Martin, Medard Edmund Mswahili, Young-Seob Jeong, and Jeong Young-Seob. 2022. SwahBERT: Language model of Swahili. In *Proceedings of the 2022 Conference of the North American Chapter of the Association for Computational Linguistics: Human Language Technologies*, pages 303–313, Seattle, United States. Association for Computational Linguistics.

T. Mathiassen. 1996. *A Short Grammar of Lithuanian*. Slavica Publishers.

Ninareh Mehrabi, Fred Morstatter, Nripsuta Saxena, Kristina Lerman, and Aram Galstyan. 2019. A survey on bias and fairness in machine learning. *CoRR*, abs/1908.09635.

Aleksandra Miletic. 2018. *Un treebank pour le Serbe: Constitution et exploitations*. Ph.D. thesis, Université de Toulouse - Jean Jaurès.

J. Naughton. 2006. *Czech: An Essential Grammar*. Routledge Essential Grammars. Taylor & Francis.

Zdeňka Nedomová. 2013. Paparazzi, matcho, guru, yeti - nesklonná životná apelativa v ruštině a češtině. *Studia Slavica*, 17(1):91–102.

Stevan Ostrogonac, Borko Rastovic, and Elizaveta Liliom. 2020. A python package for text processing for serbian: nlpheart. *Scientific Technical Review*, 70:41–45.

L. Schmitz. 2004. *Grammar of the Latin Language*. New Language Guides. Hippocrene Books.

Mike Schuster and Kaisuke Nakajima. 2012. Japanese and Korean voice search. In *2012 IEEE international conference on acoustics, speech and signal processing (ICASSP)*, pages 5149–5152. IEEE.

Pranaydeep Singh, Gorik Rutten, and Els Lefever. 2021. A pilot study for BERT language modelling and morphological analysis for ancient and medieval Greek. In *Proceedings of the 5th Joint SIGHUM Workshop on Computational Linguistics for Cultural Heritage, Social Sciences, Humanities and Literature*, pages 128–137, Punta Cana, Dominican Republic (online). Association for Computational Linguistics.

Hasan Tanvir, Claudia Kittask, Sandra Eiche, and Kairit Sirts. 2021. Estbert: A pretrained language-specific bert for estonian. In *Proceedings of the 23rd Nordic Conference on Computational Linguistics (NoDaLiDa)*, pages 11–19.

Matej Ulčar and Marko Robnik-Šikonja. 2020. FinEst BERT and CroSloEngual BERT: less is more in multilingual models. In *Text, Speech, and Dialogue: 23rd International Conference, TSD 2020, Brno, Czech Republic, September 8–11, 2020, Proceedings 23*, pages 104–111. Springer.

Ashish Vaswani, Noam Shazeer, Niki Parmar, Jakob Uszkoreit, Llion Jones, Aidan N. Gomez, Lukasz Kaiser, and Illia Polosukhin. 2017. Attention is all you need. *CoRR*, abs/1706.03762.

Shijie Wu and Mark Dredze. 2019. Beto, bentz, becas: The surprising cross-lingual effectiveness of BERT. In *Proceedings of the 2019 Conference on Empirical Methods in Natural Language Processing and the 9th International Joint Conference on Natural Language Processing (EMNLP-IJCNLP)*, pages 833–844, Hong Kong, China. Association for Computational Linguistics.

Shijie Wu and Mark Dredze. 2020. Are all languages created equal in multilingual BERT? In *Proceedings of the 5th Workshop on Representation Learning for NLP*, pages 120–130, Online. Association for Computational Linguistics.

Linting Xue, Noah Constant, Adam Roberts, Mihir Kale, Rami Al-Rfou, Aditya Siddhant, Aditya Barua, and Colin Raffel. 2021. mt5: A massively multilingual pre-trained text-to-text transformer. In *Proceedings of the 2021 Conference of the North American Chapter of the Association for Computational Linguistics: Human Language Technologies*, pages 483–498.

Željko Bošković. 2006. Case checking versus case assignment and the case of adverbial nps. *Linguistic Inquiry*, 37(3):522–533.

A Building the names list

This appendix contains the details of manually filtering the list of names of popular authors, singers, actresses, and other female celebrities that we sourced from nationality category lists in the Serbian edition of Wikipedia.

With the exception of *Rijana* ('Rihanna', a Barbadian singer), most names belong to American,

Canadian, British or Australian figures. Additionally, five names belonging to politicans and other personalities are added, these being *Hilari Klinton* 'Hilary Clinton', *Margaret Tačer* 'Margaret Thatcher', *Sara Pejlin* 'Sarah Palin', *Kondoliza Rajs* 'Condoleezza Rice' and *Monika Levinski* 'Monica Lewinsky'. All names are converted from Serbian Wikipedia's default Serbian Cyrillic script to Serbian Latin script using an online converter and then edited for capitalisation errors. In some rare cases, we added names that we found in the corpus scraping phase into the name list alongside the names found on Wikipedia. This includes some doublets such as *Šeril Sandberg* ('Sheryl Sandberg', former chief operating officer of Meta Platforms), whose name is also spelt *Šeril Sendberg*, and *Anđelina Džoli* ('Angelina Jolie', spelt in Wikipedia as *Andželina Džoli* but the former spelling is more commonly attested). These doublets are caused by ambiguities that arise when converting names to the Serbian phonetic system. Given that it is not possible to ensure that the models treat these doublets as the same name, they are treated as names of different people.

A few names are altered entirely from the Wikipedia titles. These names included the names of two rappers Saweetie and Megan Thee Stallion, whose names are replaced with their phonetic equivalents, *Saviti* and *Megan Di Stalion* respectively, as reflected by their spelling in Serbian tabloids. Conversely, two phonetic spellings of names, *Uma Terman* and *Vira Farmiga* are replaced with their corpus-attested spellings, *Uma Turman* and *Vera Farmiga* respectively, despite not reflecting the actual pronunciation of the names. One mononym, *Šeril* ('Cheryl', an English singer) is changed to *Šeril Kol* to avoid conflicts with other people named *Šeril*.

Finally, a number of names are pruned from the database. In cases where there are multiple people of the same name, duplicate entries are removed and treated as the same person. Some mononyms, are also removed for causing conflicts with common words. These names include *Niko*, the Serbian transliteration of American singer Nico, which is removed for being too similar to the common Serbian word *niko* 'no one'. *Keša* ('Ke$ha') is removed for being too similar to the genitive form of the slang word *keš*. Additionally, three mononyms are removed for being too similar to Balkan names: Selena, the mononym of singer Selena Pérez, is removed for being a very common Serbian name, *Monika*, a common Croatian name, and *Alija*, a Bosnian name. Three more mononyms, *Benks*, *Eš*, and *Pink*, are also removed for being too common. *Lenka* is removed for causing conflicts, as is *Sijera*. *Vivika A. Foks* is removed due to the middle initial consisting of just 'a', causing a conflict in some of the evaluation procedures. In total, 1323 names are included, of which 812 names are completely indeclinable, meaning the name does not include any declinable element. 511 contain at least one declinable element, of which 13 appear to be of Southern Slavic origin. 30 names are fully declinable.

B Sentence type templates

This appendix provides an overview of the templates that were used to generate the sentences for the Masked Language Modeling task.

B.1 Low-context sentences

B.1.1 Open-ended sentence

(1) [NAME] je [MASK] .
[NAME] be.3.SG.PRS [MASK]
'[NAME] is [MASK] .'

B.1.2 Adjective sentences

These sentences use adverbs to encourage an adjective to be produced.

(2) [NAME] je veoma [MASK] .
[NAME] be.3.SG.PRS very [MASK]
'[NAME] is very [MASK] .'

(3) [NAME] je takođe [MASK] .
[NAME] be.3.SG.PRS also [MASK]
'[NAME] is also [MASK] .'

(4) [NAME] je vrlo [MASK] .
[NAME] be.3.SG.PRS very [MASK]
'[NAME] is very [MASK] .'

(5) [NAME] je sada [MASK] .
[NAME] be.3.SG.PRS now [MASK]
'[NAME] is now [MASK] .'

(6) [NAME] je trenutno [MASK] .
[NAME] be.3.SG.PRS currently [MASK]
'[NAME] is currently [MASK] .'

(7) [NAME] je [MASK] širom svet-a.
[NAME] be.3.SG.PRS [MASK] throughout world-SG.GEN
'[NAME] is [MASK] throughout the world.'

B.1.3 Past participle sentences

These sentences are constructed to be filled with a past participle.

(8) [NAME] je [MASK] u
[NAME] AUX.3.SG.PRS [MASK] in
grad-Ø juče.
city-SG.ACC yesterday
'[NAME] was [MASK] in the city yesterday.'

(9) [NAME] je [MASK]
[NAME] AUX.3.SG.PRS [MASK]
knjig-u juče.
book-SG.ACC yesterday
'[NAME] was [MASK] a book yesterday.'

(10) [NAME] je [MASK] da
[NAME] AUX.3.SG.PRS [MASK] REL
ode.
leave-3.SG.PRS
'[NAME] [MASK] to leave.'

B.1.4 Possessive sentences

(11) [NAME] i [MASK] otac
[NAME] and [MASK] father-M.SG.NOM
razgovar-aju.
converse-3.PL.PRS
'[NAME] and [MASK] father are conversing.'

(12) [NAME] i [MASK] drugaric-a
[NAME] and [MASK] friend.F-F.SG.NOM
razgovar-aju.
converse-3.PL.PRS
'[NAME] and [MASK] friend-M.SG.NOM are conversing.'

(13) [NAME] i [MASK] pas
[NAME] and [MASK] father-M.SG.NOM
šet-aju se.
walk-3.PL.PRS REFL
'[NAME] and [MASK] dog are walking.'

B.1.5 Plural past participles sentences

These sentences explore how the models handle feminine plural past participles.

(14) [NAME] i jedn-a
[NAME] and one-F.SG.NOM
žen-a [MASK] su ovde
woman-F.SG.NOM AUX.3.PL.PRS here bit
malo ranije.
earlier
'[NAME] and some woman were here a bit earlier.'

(15) [NAME] i njen-a
[NAME] and her-F.SG.NOM
sestr-a [MASK] su ovde
woman-F.SG.NOM AUX.3.PL.PRS here bit
malo ranije.
earlier
'[NAME] and her sister were here a bit earlier.'

(16) [NAME] i [MASK] sestr-a
[NAME] and [MASK] sister-F.SG.NOM
bil-e su ovde malo
be-PTCP.F.PL AUX.3.PL.PRS here bit
ranije.
earlier
'[NAME] and [MASK] sister were here a bit earlier.'

B.1.6 Adjective embedded clauses

These sentences are constructed to be completed with an adjective inside an embedded clause.

(17) Veruj-e se da je
believe-3.SG.PRS REFL REL be.3.PL.PRS
[NAME] trenutno [MASK] .
[NAME] currently [MASK]
'It is believed that [NAME] is currently [MASK] .'

(18) Izjavil-o se da je
announce-PTCP.N.SG REFL REL be.3.PL.PRS
[NAME] trenutno [MASK] .
[NAME] currently [MASK]
'It was announced that [NAME] is currently [MASK] .'

B.2 High-context sentences

High-context sentences consists of two parts: a contextual sentence followed by one of three masked sentences.

B.2.1 Serbian names

These are the names used in the high-context sentences, taken from lists of most common Serbian names. Three are feminine, and three are masculine.

Feminine	Dragana, Jelena, Milica
Masculine	Marko, Ivan, Vladimir

B.2.2 Contextual sentence

Contextual sentences contain a common Serbian name [SN] as the subject or agent of a sentence, followed by one of the target names at the end in one of the cases.

Nominative

(19) [SN] je viši/viša nego [NAME]
[SN] be.3.PL.PRS taller than [NAME]
'[SN] is taller than [NAME]'

Genitive

(20) [SN] je velik-i
[SN] be.3.PL.PRS big-M.SG.NOM
fan-Ø [NAME]
fan-M.SG.NOM [NAME]
'[SN] is a big fan of [NAME]'

(21) [SN] se plaši [NAME]
[SN] REFL fear-3.SG.PRS [NAME]
'[SN] is afraid of [NAME]'

(22) [SN] stiže kod [NAME]
[SN] arrive-3.SG.PRS by [NAME]
'[SN] is arriving at [NAME]'s house'

Dative/Locative

(23) [SN] se divi [NAME]
[SN] REFL admire-3.SG.PRS [NAME]
'[SN] admires [NAME]'

(24) [SN] daj-e poklon [NAME]
[SN] give-3.SG.PRS gift-M.SG.NOM [NAME]
'[SN] gives a gift to [NAME]'

(25) [SN] čita članak o
[SN] read-3.SG.PRS article-M.SG.NOM about
[NAME]
[NAME]
'[SN] reads an article about [NAME]'

Accusative

(26) [SN] voli [NAME]
[SN] love-3.SG.PRS [NAME]
'[SN] loves [NAME]'

(27) [SN] ne zn-a za [NAME]
[SN] NEG know-3.SG.PRS for [NAME]
'[SN] do not know of [NAME]'

Instrumental

(28) [SN] se druž-i sa [NAME]
[SN] REFL socialise-3.SG.PRS with [NAME]
'[SN] is hanging out with [NAME]'

(29) [SN] id-e u centar-Ø
[SN] go-3.SG.PRS in centre-M.SG.NOM
grad-a sa [NAME]
city-M.SG.GEN with [NAME]
'[SN] is going downtown with [NAME]'

B.2.3 Masked sentences

Each contextual sentence is paired with one of three mask sentences.

(1) [NAME] je [MASK] .
[NAME] be.3.SG.PRS [MASK]
'[NAME] is [MASK] .'

(2) [NAME] je vrlo [MASK] .
[NAME] be.3.SG.PRS very [MASK]
'[NAME] is very [MASK] .'

(3) [NAME] je [MASK]
[NAME] AUX.3.SG.PRS [MASK]
knjig-u .
book-SG.ACC
'[NAME] was [MASK] a book yesterday.'

C NER results for spaCy baseline

This appendix shows the NER result visualizations for the spaCy baseline separated by name type, including indeclinable (IND), declinable (DEC), Slavic (SLV) or fully declinable (FUL).

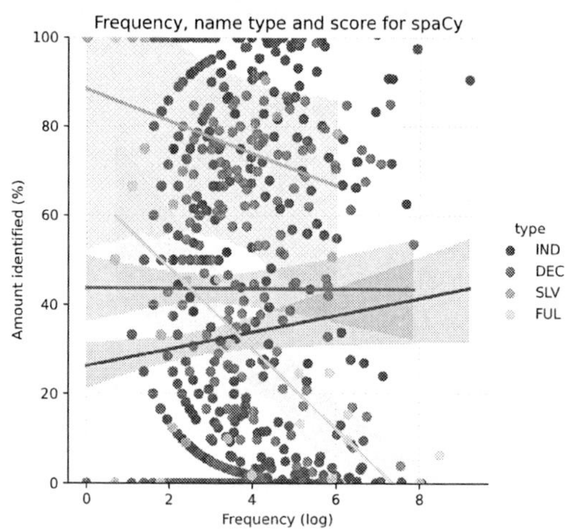

Figure 5: spaCy NER results per name type

Dispersing the *clouds of doubt*: can cosine similarity of word embeddings help identify relation-level metaphors in Slovene?

Mojca Brglez
Faculty of Arts, University of Ljubljana
mojca.brglez@ff.uni-lj.si

Abstract

Word embeddings and pre-trained language models have achieved great performance in many tasks due to their ability to capture both syntactic and semantic information in their representations. The vector space representations have also been used to identify figurative language shifts such as metaphors, however, the more recent contextualized models have mostly been evaluated via their performance on downstream tasks. In this article, we evaluate static and contextualized word embeddings in terms of their representation and unsupervised identification of relation-level (ADJ-NOUN, NOUN-NOUN) metaphors in Slovene on a set of 24 literal and 24 metaphorical phrases. Our experiments show very promising results for both embedding methods, however, the performance in contextual embeddings notably depends on the layer involved and the input provided to the model.

1 Introduction

In recent decades, metaphors have been recognized as a ubiquitous phenomenon in all types of discourse (Reijnierse et al., 2019; Cameron, 2003; Semino, 2008), and because of their central role in both language, thought and communication (Lakoff and Johnson, 1980; Steen, 2017; Burgers et al., 2016), they have been addressed by various fields and disciplines, from linguistics, neurolinguistics, psycholinguistics, cognitive linguistics, social science, and computer science. The main underlying mechanism of metaphor involves representing one domain in the terms of another (Lakoff and Johnson, 1980, 2003; Kövecses, 2020). The represented domain, usually more abstract, is called the target domain, and the domain it is represented by is called the source domain, which is usually more concrete and based on physical experience. For example, in the expression *political storm*, we represent the target domain of POLITICS in terms of the source domain of WEATHER.

For a metaphor to be apt (Tourangeau and Sternberg, 1981), the domains have to share certain features or relations, but otherwise be sufficiently different from one another. On the one hand, this semantic difference can be observed between the metaphorically used word and its context. Wilks (1978) put forward the idea of metaphors as "selectional preference violations", that is, the context of the metaphorically used word is not the context this word would normally select. On the other hand, metaphorically used expressions also exhibit some form of polysemy in themselves. The contextual meaning of the metaphorically used word is different from its most basic meaning which is expressed in literal contexts. The latter is also the defining factor of the most frequently used procedure for manual metaphor identification in texts (MIPVU, Steen, 2010).

These two facets of metaphors have often been used and explored in automatic metaphor identification approaches. Various methods have been proposed that model language and meaning on the basis of the distributional hypothesis (Harris, 1954), according to which similar words have similar contexts. In these models, the meanings of words are determined by their relationships to other words in that same space, and similar words tend to have similar vectors and similar neighbourhoods. Older approaches to metaphor modelling use distributional vectors created with the help of e.g. latent semantic analysis (Kintsch, 2000; Utsumi, 2011), while more recent ones use distributed word embeddings obtained through deep-learning (Mao et al., 2018; Su et al., 2017). An important distinction can also be drawn depending on the level of metaphor processing: word-level, relation-level, or sentence-level. On the word-level, the task is to determine the metaphoricity of a (or each) word. On the sentence-level, the whole sentence is classified for containing metaphor(s) or not. On the relation-level, which we are concerned with in this exper-

Proceedings of the 9th Workshop on Slavic Natural Language Processing 2023 (SlavicNLP 2023), pages 61–69
May 6, 2023

iment, the expressions under question are pairs of words that have a syntactic relation between a source and target term, for instance verb-object (***break** a promise*) or adjective-noun constructions (***deep** thought*). Related to and sometimes overlapping with relation-level metaphors is the wider class of multi-word expressions (MWEs), which include phraseological units such as idioms and proverbs, and other fixed expressions such as compounds and collocations (Gantar et al., 2018). Especially idioms can overlap with metaphoric expressions by their meaning non-compositionality by which the meaning of the whole cannot be directly derived from the meaning of its parts. Some idioms may in fact even stem from metaphorical conceptualizations, e.g. *to throw dust in someone's eyes*. Another shared characteristic can be lexicalization, that is, both MWEs and conventional metaphors can be included in dictionaries, for example *parent company*. However, MWEs mostly require some extent of syntactic fixedness, and, more importantly, they always require at least 2 constituent words, while metaphors can take form of a word, a phrase, or even a whole paragraph.

In Slovene, automatic figurative language processing is still in its early stages, with only a few semi-supervised (Brglez et al., 2021) and supervised automatic models proposed (Škvorc et al., 2022; Zwitter Vitez et al., 2022). The direct use of cosine similarity between the source and target word for metaphor identification in Slovene has not yet been explored and could possibly allow unsupervised extraction of metaphorical candidates from text, avoiding the need for manually annotated data.

The aim of the experiments presented here is two-fold: 1) to investigate the representation of metaphorical expressions in both static and dynamic embeddings and evaluate their use for metaphor identification, 2) to establish a baseline by which to distinguish between metaphor and non-metaphor.

2 Related Work

Metaphor identification has been approached from various perspectives, using or combining several tools and resources. State-of-the-art approaches for English and other more resourced languages use deep learning methods to train metaphor identification models on large annotated corpora in a supervised manner. Because the focus of our work is on unsupervised classification and evaluation of word embeddings for this purpose, here we only report on some previous work in this same direction.

One of the first unsupervised approaches is by (Shutova et al., 2010) to identify verbal metaphors in the BNC corpus. Starting with a seed set of 62 metaphorical verb-object and verb-subject pairs, they apply unsupervised noun and verb clustering on vectors obtained from corpus frequencies in order to extend the range of target and source concepts. Then, they search the BNC for metaphorical expressions using these two expanded lexicons and achieve a precision of 0.71.

Agres et al. (2016) evaluate both static Word2vec and distributional vectors on data from a behavioural study to test if they encapsulate metaphoricity, familiarity and meaningfulness. They test these features with a multiple regression analysis, to see if they are correlated with cosine similarity. For both vector types, their results show that low values of metaphoricity were predictors of high cosine similarity.

Su et al. (2017) also use word2vec embeddings trained on reference corpora for Chinese and English to investigate their use for the identification of nominal metaphors (X is Y). They devise a method that combines calculating the relatedness of words (X,Y) via cosine similarity with checking for hyper-/hyponymy relation in WordNet. If the similarity is lower than a predefined threshold and the concepts have no taxonomic relationship in WordNet, the candidate is classified as a metaphor. They establish the threshold value of cosine similarity as the best overlap (convergence) between literal recall, metaphor recall and accuracy, and determine it to be at 0.235 for English and 0.575 for Chinese. This also shows that the threshold varies greatly on the language involved and that language-specific baselines need to be determined.

Mao et al. (2018) use CBOW and SkipGram embeddings and WordNet to predict the metaphoricity of a verb in a sentence. For each target word, they find the best-fit synonym, hypernym or hyponym in WordNet that matches the context by having the highest cosine similarity to the context vector of the sentence. Then, they compute the cosine similarity between the best-fit word and the target word, and classify the target word as metaphor if the similarity is lower than a threshold of 0.6, which was pre-established on the basis of a development set.

Shutova et al. (2016) experiment with both visual and linguistic embeddings in predicting phrase-level metaphors. They obtain both individual word embedddings and joint phrase embeddings based on the SkipGram method, and investigate various combinations of measuring similarity via cosine distance. They obtain best results with their multimodal approach, while in linguistic embeddings-only setting, computing the similarity between the words in the phrase outperforms computing similarities of phrase embeddings.

In a semi-supervised manner, Zayed et al. (2018) use a seed set of verb-noun phrases to determine the metaphoricity of the candidate verbs on the phrase level. First, they find the most similar verb in the seed set using cosine distance and Word Mover's Distance, and compare the similarity of the candidate noun to the nouns associated with the most similar verbs in the seed set. They also compare GloVe and Word2Vec static embeddings methods, and achieve the best results using GloVE embeddings and cosine distance.

More recently, Pedinotti et al. (2021) tested the knowledge instilled in BERT models by applying the "landmark method" introduced in (Kintsch, 2000), which tries to determine which properties are transferred from the source to the target domain. Namely, metaphoricity relies on some common ground between the two domains which makes the comparison plausible. In their experiment, Pedinotti et al. check whether the representations of metaphors are closer to these common ground 'landmarks' or to the literal properties of source domain words that are not relevant to the metaphor mapping. They conclude that metaphorically used words are consistently more similar to literal landmarks in the first few layers of BERT embeddings. Moreover, they observe a difference comparing conventional and creative expressions: while models achieve steadily better accuracy (in terms of wrong answers) for conventional metaphors, the accuracy actually drops in the later layers for creative metaphors.

Among unsupervised approaches to MWEs, which are somewhat similar to relation-level metaphors, we can mention Cordeiro et al. (2019) and Garcia et al. (2021). Cordeiro et al. (2019) investigate English nominal compounds, where the head of the phrase is a noun (adjective-noun and noun-noun), and their syntactic counterparts in French and Portuguese. To distinguish compositional from non-compositional (idiomatic) MWEs, they measure the cosine similarity between the combined vectors of the parts and the vector of the compound. Moreover, they investigate the influence of various variables: different distributional models, preprocessing methods, dimension sizes, and context sizes. They find that the models can successfully capture idiomaticity, with word2vec as the best performing model for English, while for French and Portuguese, the PPMI-based models fared better. In addition, they find that models for the morphologically richer French and Portuguese benefit from preprocessing steps such as lemmatization and stopword removal. In a more recent approach, Garcia et al. (2021) investigate various contextual models for their representation of potentially idiomatic expressions, i.e. expressions that can be literal or idiomatic depending on the context, in English and Portuguese. They measure the cosine similarity of the embeddings of idiomatic compounds with 1) the embeddings of their meaning-preserving compounds and 2) literal synonyms of the components. Their experiments show the idiomatic phrases are closer to the literal synonyms than to their meaning-preserving paraphrases, leading to the conclusion that idiomaticity is not yet adequately captured by contextual models.

3 Methods

3.1 Dataset

To test our hypotheses, we create a small dataset consisting of metaphorical and non-metaphorical examples of use for 24 Slovene words (8 adjectives and 16 nouns). The examples include three types of constructions: adjective-noun with a potentially metaphorical adjective; adjective-noun with a potentially metaphorical noun; and noun-noun, where the first noun can be metaphorical. All the literal pairs are by default, in the absence of additional context to the contrary[1], considered literal. To provide a sentential context for later use with contextualized embeddings, we concordance one example sentence from the Slovenian reference corpus Gigafida 2.0 (Krek et al., 2019). For each metaphorical-literal pair, we take heed of acquiring syntactically equivalent pairs, thus matching in grammatical gender, case, and number in their

[1]It is possible to use a phrase considered literal on its own in a metaphorical manner. For instance, *dark clouds* is used literally in *The dark clouds spread over the city.*, and metaphorically in *I am plagued by the dark clouds of depression.*

Phrase type	Phrase	Frequency	Example sentence
$NOUN_m$– $NOUN_l$	**oblaki** dvoma ***[clouds** of doubt]*	11	*Politiki včasih izgubijo zaupanje, četudi se jim laganja izrecno ne dokaže; dovolj je že, da njihovo podobo zastrejo **oblaki dvoma**.* Politicians sometimes lose trust even if their lying is not explicitly proven; it suffices if their image is shrouded by **clouds of doubt.**
$NOUN_l$– $NOUN_l$	**oblaki** metana ***[clouds** of methane]*	9	*Temperatura na Titanu je ravno prava, da v spodnjih plasteh atmosfere nastajajo **oblaki metana**, iz katerih le ta občasno dežuje.* The temperature on Titan is just right for the **clouds of methane** to form in the lower layers of the atmosphere, where they occasionally rain.
ADJ_m – $NOUN_l$	**prežvečena** fraza ***[chewed-up** phrase]*	18	*Njegove besede so z dnevi postale **prežvečena fraza**, a so bile prispodoba vsega, kar se je sprehajalo skozi glave številnih, ki so lovili misli, da bi dojeli resničnost.* His words eventually became a **chewed-up phrase** but were a metaphor for everything that went through the heads of many who were hunting for thoughts to understand reality.
ADJ_l – $NOUN_l$	**prežvečena** hrana ***[chewed-up** food]*	39	*Neredko je vzrok za povečano dejavnost bakterij v črevesu tudi premalo **prežvečena hrana**.* Oftentimes the reason for the increased activity of gut bacteria is insufficiently **chewed-up food**.
ADJ_l – $NOUN_m$	moralni **steber** *[moral **pillar]***	12	*Na vasi učitelja dojemajo kot **moralni steber** in pričakujejo, da je vseh pogledih trden in pošten.* In the countryside, people perceive the teacher as a **moral pillar** and expect them to be firm and fair in all aspects.
ADJ_l – $NOUN_l$	sredinski **steber** *[central **pillar]***	9	*Ob **sredinski steber** vgradimo leseno pomično steno, s katero ohranimo krožni prehod med prostori, hkrati pa omogoča ločevanje kuhinjskega ali jedilnega dela od dnevne sobe.* By the **central pillar** we build a wooden sliding wall, which maintains the circular passage through the rooms while also allowing to separate the kitchen or dining area from the living room.

Table 1: Examples from the dataset: type of construction, phrase, frequency of the phrase in the reference corpus and an example sentence from the corpus. The subscripted letters $_l$ and $_m$ indicate literal or metaphorical use, respectively.

phrasal and sentential form. Moreover, in order to obtain comparable phrases and to alleviate the potential frequency bias in the embedding space, we avoid overly conventional, common phrases and only choose phrases with less than 65 occurrences in the corpus.

Examples of the three types of phrases are shown in Table 1. For example, for the word *oblak*[cloud], we find a literal word pair *oblaki metana*[clouds of methane] and a metaphorical word pair *oblaki dvoma*[clouds of doubt], and one sentence per pair where the phrases match in grammatical number, gender and case, while also having a similar (low) frequency in the corpus.

3.2 Word embedding models

We compare word embeddings obtained by two methods: static and dynamic. For static embeddings, we use the 100-dimensional CLARIN.SI-embed.sl fastText embeddings (Ljubešić and Erjavec, 2018). For dynamic/contextual embeddings, we obtain 768-dimensional embeddings from SloBERTa 2.0 (Ulčar and Robnik-Šikonja, 2021) a Slovene pre-trained RoBERTA model. Among the contextualized embedding models for Slovene, this architecture has performed best in most monolingual tasks (Ulčar et al., 2021).

In the static embeddings setting, we obtain the same FastText vector regardless of the context. To obtain contextual embeddings from SloBERTA, we test providing the model with different contexts:

- no-context (IND). The input to the model is just the individual word.
- phrase (PHR). The input to the model is the phrase only.
- sentence context (SENT). We present the model with the complete example sentence.

According to Wang and Zhang (2022) who explore word embedding similarity for word-sense disambiguation in different layers of contextual models, BERT-based models exhibit "first word position bias". In their experiments, the cosine similarity of two words that appeared at the start of the input sentences was considerably higher than the similarity of words that appeared in later positions. However, when simply prefixing and suffixing the input with quotation marks ("), the similarity dropped and lead to higher accuracy. For this reason, we also decide to prepend each of the inputs with a simple prompt *"Primer: "* ["Example: "]. Secondly, we experiment with embeddings obtained separately from each layer (input layer and all subsequent 12 layers). Ethayarajh (2019) has showed that BERT embeddings become increasingly more contextualized, i.e. context specific in the upper layers. Thus, we would expect to observe most relevant semantic differences between the constituent words of metaphorical phrases in the lower layers of the model.

3.3 Similarity metric

The first basic assumption driving our method is that because words participating in a metaphoric phrase originate in different conceptual / semantic domains, they should exhibit less similarity than words participating in a literal phrase that originate in the same or similar conceptual domain. This means the former should be represented further apart in the vector space than words participating in a literal phrase. To measure semantic similarity, we thus apply the frequently used cosine similarity metric that estimates the similarity of the words through the cosine of the angle between the words' vectors:

$$\cos(\theta) = \frac{A \cdot B}{\|A\| \, \|B\|}$$

For words that are split into subword tokens during tokenization with SloBERTa, we calculate the vector of the word from the element-wise mean of all its subword tokens. Secondly, from the perspective of word polysemy which is underscored in the MIPVU procedure, the contextual sense of a word that is used metaphorically is sufficiently different from its non-metaphorical, basic sense. Thus, in contextual word embedding models, we would we expect to observe a substantial self-dissimilarity of the word's embeddings if used metaphorically. However, we do not directly compare a word's embedding in a literal and a metaphorical sentence, because this would not enable unsupervised detection (one would always have to compare a metaphorical and a literal sentence). Instead, we compare the self-similarity of a candidate word between three contexts (individual word, phrase, or full sentence input to the model) outlined in the previous section. In other words, we hypothesise that without additional context, the model would retain and represent the most basic meaning if it sees the word individually, and, conversely, assign a more contextual, shifted meaning of the word in the context of a metaphorical phrase or a full sentence.

4 Results and discussion

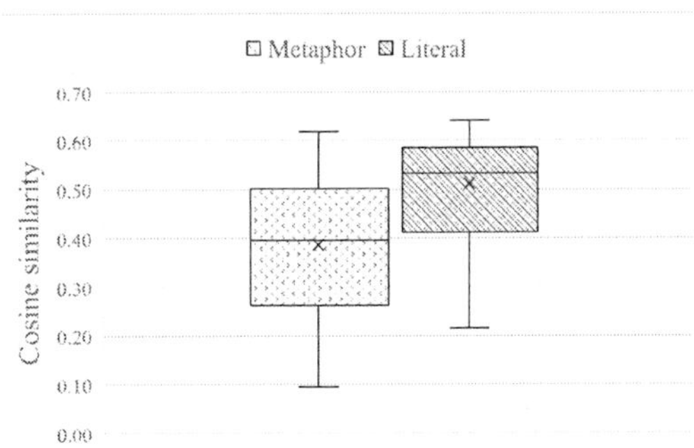

Figure 1: Average cosine similarity between fastText embeddings of words in literal and metaphorical phrases

Figure 1 shows that on average, words participating in metaphorical phrases tend to be more dissimilar than words in literal phrases, i.e. their cosine similarity is lower. This holds for most, but

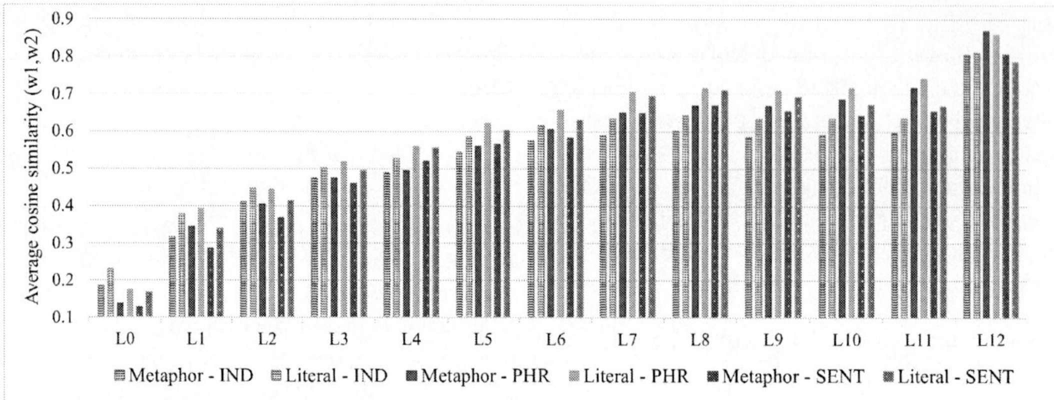

Figure 2: Average cosine similarity of words in metaphorical and literal phrases in different inputs (IND = individual word inputs, PHR = phrase input, SENT = full sentence input), by SloBERTa layer.

not all of the FastText embeddings (18 out of 24 pairs). As for contextualized SloBERTA embeddings (Figure 2), the same trend is observed for all three types of inputs (individual words, phrase inputs or sentences). Indicative are the differences between the blue (metaphorical) and the red (literal) column. The differences are larger in the first few layers, however, in the last layer, the metaphorical word pairs achieve even average higher cosine similarity than those in literal phrases. This would indicate that the initially present semantic distance is neutralized in the later layers of the model.

For the static embeddings, we first analyze the relationship and balance between recall and precision for the literal and metaphorical classes at different cosine similarity thresholds. As shown in Figure 3, the values converge and balance out with cosine similarity values between 0.42 and 0.49.

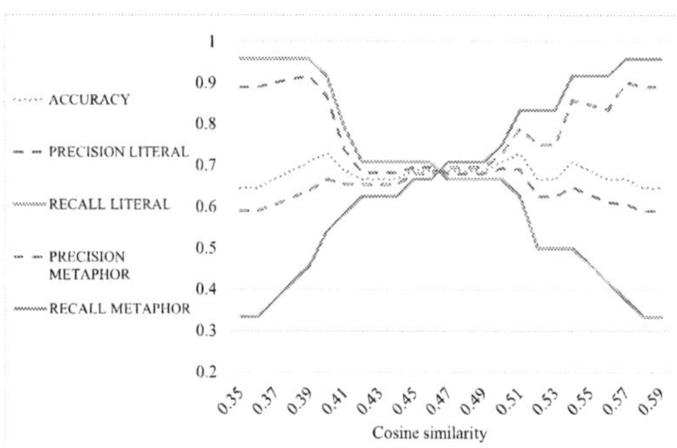

Figure 3: Balance of precision and recall in predicting metaphoricity by cosine similarity of fastText embeddings.

Then, for each of the scenarios (static, contextual, different layers of contextual embeddings, different inputs for contextualized embeddings, word similarity and self-similarity), we try to fit a linear regression model to the cosine similarity values to test the relevance for metaphor identification, and to determine the best threshold for unsupervised classification. The results in Table 2 show significance levels for cosine similarities between the first and second word in the phrase in different settings, and the cosine similarity threshold calculated with

Embedding	**Significance F**	**Cosine similarity threshold**
fastText	<**0.001**	0.4495
SloBERTA IND		
Layer 0	<**0.01**	0.2076
Layer 1, 4	<0.05	
Other layers	>0.05	
SloBERTA PHR		
Layer 0-4, 9	<0.05	
Layer 4-8	<**0.01**	(0.5267, 0.5905, 0.6309, 0.6777, 0.6924, 0.6887)
Other layers	>0.05	
SloBERTA SENT		
Layer 0-2	<**0.01**	(0.1473, 0.3119, 0.3914)
Layer 3, 6-9	<0.05	
Other layers	>0.05	

Table 2: Linear regression results for different embedding methods with cosine similarity as the predictor and metaphoricity as the dependent variable.

linear regression.

In the next step, we computed the self-similarity of the word in different contexts. We only focused on the words that are used both literally and metaphorically in our dataset. The average self-similarities are depicted in Figure 4. Not surprisingly, embeddings from the individual- and phrase-inputs are very similar throughout the model, as the context is practically identical. The least similar, as expected, are embeddings from the individual inputs compared to those from sentence inputs. There seem to be observable differences in the average word self-similarity, especially when comparing the individual word embedding to its sentence embedding and the word's embeddings in the phrase and sentence contexts. However, the linear regression and ANOVA tests show no significant relationship between the word's self-similarity in any of the layers and any of the settings: the absolute highest $R^2 = 0.2431$ ($f<0.1$) was achieved when comparing the embedding from the individual word to the embedding of the word in the sentence on the 4th layer. We assume that this is due to the design of contextualized models, which are intended to represent word meaning in wider contexts and fail to produce sensible representations when presented with narrower contexts.

Embedding	A	P	R	F1
FastText	0.69	0.70	0.67	0.68
SloBERTA IND				
Layer 0	0.69	**0.68**	0.71	0.69
SloBERTA PHR				
Layer 4	0.66	0.65	0.71	0.68
Layer 5	0.66	0.67	0.67	0.67
Layer 6	0.60	0.61	0.58	0.60
Layer 7	0.64	0.65	0.63	0.64
Layer 8	0.68	**0.68**	0.71	0.69
SloBERTA SENT				
Layer 0	**0.71**	0.68	**0.79**	**0.73**
Layer 1	0.69	**0.68**	0.71	0.69
Layer 2	0.58	0.59	0.54	0.57

Table 3: Prediction results in terms of accuracy (A), metaphor precision (P), metaphor recall (R), and F1 score.

To further evaluate cosine similarity as a predictor of metaphoricity, we classify our examples according to the thresholds obtained from linear regression models with significance levels $f<0.01$. We report the results in Table 3. The results are very comparable across models. The highest overall scores are achieved by predicting metaphoricity from the cosine similarities of words on the input layer (0) when the model receives the whole sentence as input. However, the differences in performance obtained from the embeddings from the 0th layer from different inputs must be purely incidental, as the embeddings there are not contextualized yet. The difference is only due to the additional positional embeddings that encode the position of the word in the sequence.

5 Conclusion

In this paper, we presented the first experiment on unsupervised identification of metaphors on the phrase level in Slovene with word embeddings. Based on a dataset of 24 comparable pairs of metaphorical and literal phrases, we investigated the use of cosine similarity in both static and contextual embeddings. The results show that both methods achieve comparable results in terms of precision, recall and accuracy when comparing cosine similarities between the phrase's constituent words. In line with previous research, we also intuit that lower layers exhibit less contextualized information and are generally more suited to the task. However, in our experiments with self-similarity, where we compared the candidate word's embeddings in different contexts, the results show no statistical significance and cannot be used to determine a metaphorical shift in meaning. In conclusion, this preliminary experiment showed promising results for unsupervised metaphor identification, but will have to be evaluated on more data which may contain less clear-cut examples of metaphorical and literal language. Future work includes testing the method on more examples and other embedding models. We also plan to investigate the use of psycholinguistic measures such as abstractness for relation-level metaphor identification, and evaluate the methods with respect to the syntactic type of construction used. Another interesting avenue for further research could be investigating other methods for combining subword embeddings, which could potentially provide a better word representation for the purposes of metaphor identification.

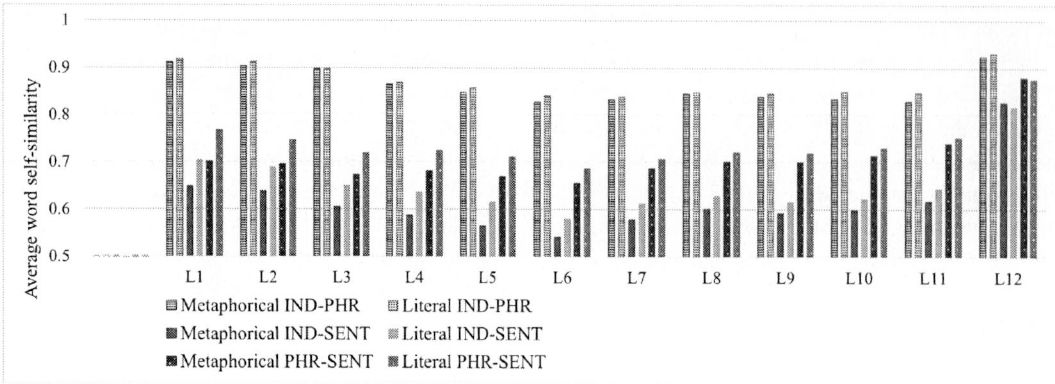

Figure 4: Average self-similarity of a candidate word in different inputs (IND=individual word, PHR=phrase input, SENT=full sentence input), by SloBERTa layer.

Limitations

Although the paper shows promising results, the findings can only be applied to the small set of data we used in our experiment. To validate them further, the approach would have to be tested on a much larger dataset containing less clear-cut examples. Secondly, our unsupervised metaphor identification approach was limited to adjective-noun and noun-noun phrases, meaning we cannot draw definite conclusions for the usefulness of this approach for identification of metaphors in other constructions. Thirdly, there is a plethora of language models available for Slovene. In this work, we only experimented with fastText and SloBERTa embeddings because of their good performance on other linguistic tasks. Other models, such as GPT, T5, BERT, or ELMo, could turn out to be more suitable for metaphor processing.

Acknowledgements

This project has received funding by the Slovenian Research Agency (ARRS) under the research core funding P6-0215.

References

Kat R. Agres, Stephen McGregor, Karolina Rataj, Matthew Purver, and Geraint A. Wiggins. 2016. Modeling metaphor perception with distributional semantics vector space models. In *Proceedings of the ESSLLI Workshop on Computational Creativity, Concept Invention, and General Intelligence (C3GI)*, page 1–14.

Mojca Brglez, Senja Pollak, and Špela Vintar. 2021. Simple discovery of COVID IS WAR metaphors using word embeddings. In *Odkrivanje znanja in podatkovna skladišča - SiKDD: 4 October 2021, Ljubljana, Slovenia*, page 37–40. Institut "Jožef Stefan".

Christian Burgers, Elly Konijn, and Gerard Steen. 2016. Figurative framing: Shaping public discourse through metaphor, hyperbole, and irony. *Communication Theory*, 26:410–430.

Lynne Cameron. 2003. *Metaphor in Educational Discourse*. Advances in Applied Linguistics. Bloomsbury Publishing.

Silvio Cordeiro, Aline Villavicencio, Marco Idiart, and Carlos Ramisch. 2019. Unsupervised compositionality prediction of nominal compounds. *Computational Linguistics*, 45(1):1–57.

Kawin Ethayarajh. 2019. How contextual are contextualized word representations? Comparing the geometry of BERT, ELMo, and GPT-2 embeddings. In *Proceedings of the 2019 Conference on Empirical Methods in Natural Language Processing and the 9th International Joint Conference on Natural Language Processing (EMNLP-IJCNLP)*, pages 55–65, Hong Kong, China. Association for Computational Linguistics.

Polona Gantar, Lut Colman, Carla Parra Escartín, and Héctor Martínez Alonso. 2018. Multiword Expressions: Between Lexicography and NLP. *International Journal of Lexicography*, 32(2):138–162.

Marcos Garcia, Tiago Kramer Vieira, Carolina Scarton, Marco Idiart, and Aline Villavicencio. 2021. Probing for idiomaticity in vector space models. In *Proceedings of the 16th Conference of the European Chapter of the Association for Computational Linguistics: Main Volume*, pages 3551–3564, Online. Association for Computational Linguistics.

Zellig S. Harris. 1954. Distributional structure. *WORD*, 10(2-3):146–162.

Walter Kintsch. 2000. Metaphor comprehension: A computational theory. *Psychonomic bulletin & review*, 7:257–66.

Zoltán Kövecses. 2020. *Extended Conceptual Metaphor Theory*. Cambridge University Press.

Simon Krek, Tomaž Erjavec, Andraž Repar, Jaka Čibej, Špela Arhar Holdt, Polona Gantar, Iztok Kosem, Marko Robnik-Šikonja, Nikola Ljubešić, Kaja Dobrovoljc, Cyprian Laskowski, Miha Grčar, Peter Holozan, Simon Šuster, Vojko Gorjanc, Marko Stabej, and Nataša Logar. 2019. Corpus of written standard Slovene Gigafida 2.0. Slovenian language resource repository CLARIN.SI.

George Lakoff and Mark Johnson. 1980. *Metaphors we Live by*. University of Chicago Press.

George Lakoff and Mark Johnson. 2003. *Metaphors we Live by*. University of Chicago Press.

Nikola Ljubešić and Tomaž Erjavec. 2018. Word embeddings CLARIN.SI-embed.sl 1.0. Slovenian language resource repository CLARIN.SI.

Rui Mao, Chenghua Lin, and Frank Guerin. 2018. Word embedding and WordNet based metaphor identification and interpretation. In *Proceedings of the 56th Annual Meeting of the Association for Computational Linguistics (Volume 1: Long Papers)*, pages 1222–1231, Melbourne, Australia. Association for Computational Linguistics.

Paolo Pedinotti, Eliana Di Palma, Ludovica Cerini, and Alessandro Lenci. 2021. A howling success or a working sea? testing what BERT knows about metaphors. In *Proceedings of the Fourth BlackboxNLP Workshop on Analyzing and Interpreting Neural Networks for NLP*, pages 192–204, Punta Cana, Dominican Republic. Association for Computational Linguistics.

Gudrun Reijnierse, Christian Burgers, Tina Krennmayr, and Gerard Steen. 2019. Metaphor in communication: the distribution of potentially deliberate metaphor across register and word class. *Corpora*, 14(3):301–326.

Elena Semino. 2008. *Metaphor in Discourse*. Cambridge University Press.

Ekaterina Shutova, Douwe Kiela, and Jean Maillard. 2016. Black holes and white rabbits: Metaphor identification with visual features. In *Proceedings of the 2016 Conference of the North American Chapter of the Association for Computational Linguistics: Human Language Technologies*, pages 160–170, San Diego, California. Association for Computational Linguistics.

Ekaterina Shutova, Lin Sun, and Anna Korhonen. 2010. Metaphor identification using verb and noun clustering. In *Proceedings of the 23rd International Conference on Computational Linguistics (Coling 2010)*, volume 2, pages 1002–1010.

Gerard Steen. 2010. *A Method for Linguistic Metaphor Identification: From MIP to MIPVU*. Converging evidence in language and communication research. John Benjamins Publishing Company.

Gerard Steen. 2017. Deliberate metaphor theory: Basic assumptions, main tenets, urgent issues. *Intercultural Pragmatics*, 14:1–24.

Chang Su, Shuman Huang, and Yijiang Chen. 2017. Automatic detection and interpretation of nominal metaphor based on the theory of meaning. *Neurocomputing*, 219:300–311.

Roger Tourangeau and Robert J. Sternberg. 1981. Aptness in metaphor. *Cognitive Psychology*, 13(1):27–55.

Matej Ulčar and Marko Robnik-Šikonja. 2021. Slovenian RoBERTa contextual embeddings model: SloBERTa 2.0. Slovenian language resource repository CLARIN.SI.

Matej Ulčar, Aleš Žagar, Carlos S. Armendariz, Andraž Repar, Senja Pollak, Matthew Purver, and Marko Robnik-Šikonja. 2021. Evaluation of contextual embeddings on less-resourced languages. *Computer Research Repository, https://arxiv.org/abs/2107.10614. Version 1.*

Akira Utsumi. 2011. Computational exploration of metaphor comprehension processes using a semantic space model. *Cognitive Science*, 35(2):251–296.

Yile Wang and Yue Zhang. 2022. Lost in context? on the sense-wise variance of contextualized word embeddings. *Computer Research Repository, https://arxiv.org/abs/2208.09669. Version 1.*

Yorick Wilks. 1978. Making preferences more active. *Artificial Intelligence*, 11(3):197–223.

Omnia Zayed, John Philip McCrae, and Paul Buitelaar. 2018. Phrase-level metaphor identification using distributed representations of word meaning. In *Proceedings of the Workshop on Figurative Language Processing*, pages 81–90, New Orleans, Louisiana. Association for Computational Linguistics.

Ana Zwitter Vitez, Mojca Brglez, Marko Robnik Šikonja, Tadej Škvorc, Andreja Vezovnik, and Senja Pollak. 2022. Extracting and analysing metaphors in migration media discourse: towards a metaphor annotation scheme. In *Proceedings of the Thirteenth Language Resources and Evaluation Conference*, pages 2430–2439, Marseille, France. European Language Resources Association.

Tadej Škvorc, Polona Gantar, and Marko Robnik-Šikonja. 2022. MICE: Mining idioms with contextual embeddings. *Knowledge-Based Systems*, 235:107606.

Automatic text simplification of Russian texts using control tokens

Anna Dmitrieva
University of Helsinki
Yliopistonkatu 4, 00100 Helsinki
anna.dmitrieva@helsinki.fi

Abstract

This paper describes the research on the possibilities to control automatic text simplification with special tokens that allow modifying the length, paraphrasing degree, syntactic complexity, and the CEFR (Common European Framework of Reference) grade level of the output texts, i.e. the level of language proficiency a non-native speaker would need to understand them. The project is focused on Russian texts and aims to continue and broaden the existing research on controlled Russian text simplification. It is done by exploring available datasets for monolingual Russian machine translation (paraphrasing and simplification), experimenting with various model architectures, and adding control tokens that have not been used on Russian texts previously.

1 Introduction and related work

Easy and Plain Language are tailored languages (Leskelä et al., 2022) often aimed at a specific audience, such as people with learning disabilities, children, or second language learners. Easy Language is even considered to be a rule-based variety that reverts to purposeful language planning and shows similarities with controlled languages (Maaß, 2020). Despite the growing number of tools for automatic text simplification, most simplified texts are still produced by experts who understand and cater to the needs of a particular group of readers. Because of that, it seems reasonable to concentrate on the task of controllable text simplification so that in the future, simplification tools can be tailored to specific target audiences.

At present, text simplification is often viewed as a monolingual text-to-text generation task borrowing ideas from statistical machine translation (Zhang and Lapata, 2017), and simplification models are trained in a similar fashion to translation models. The training requires large parallel datasets where the target sentences are simplified versions of the source sentences. There are multiple ways to control the output of text simplification tools. For example, editing operations can be directly controlled. Dong et al. (2019) presented a simplification model that could learn explicit editing operations such as additions, deletions, and keeping. Alva-Manchego et al. (2017) proposed a sequence labeling model to predict which simplification operations should be performed as a first step for a complete simplification pipeline. The model is built on a corpus with automatically labeled simplification operations, and the approach is proven to produce more straightforward texts than end-to-end models.

Other research shows that, apart from controlling editing operations, it is also possible to control specific dimensions of the output texts. Martin et al. (2020) identify four attributes related to the text simplification process: the amount of compression, paraphrasing, lexical and syntactic complexity – and use control tokens that are put in front of the source sentences to modify these attributes in output texts. This approach was later used in Martin et al. (2022) and in Anastasyev (2021). The latter was the winning solution for the RuSimpleSentEval (Sakhovskiy et al., 2021) shared task on Russian text simplification. This methodology is used in the present study as well. Other studies have shown that control tokens can be used for all kinds of linguistic attributes, including politeness and monotonicity (the closeness of the word order in the target sentence to the word order in the source sentence) (Schioppa et al., 2021). Some studies also demonstrate the successful usage of control tokens to generate texts for a given school grade level (Scarton and Specia, 2018; Nishihara et al., 2019).

In this project, we use various datasets for monolingual Russian machine translation tasks, namely paraphrasing and simplification, to build models for controllable text simplification. The data is

Proceedings of the 9th Workshop on Slavic Natural Language Processing 2023 (SlavicNLP 2023), pages 70–77
May 6, 2023 ©2023 Association for Computational Linguistics

described in Section 2. Section 3 talks about the control tokens used in this study, the process of choosing the optimal model architecture, and the results of the experiments. The final parts of the paper present the conclusions and discuss the limitations of this research.

2 Data

For this project, four different data sources were used:

- ParaPhraser Plus: a large automatically developed corpus for Russian paraphrase generation (Gudkov et al., 2020). Contains news headlines crawled from publicly available websites;
- Opusparcus: a paraphrase corpus for six European languages comprising subtitles from movies and TV shows (Creutz, 2018). Only the Russian part of the corpus was used;
- RuAdapt: a parallel Russian-Simple Russian dataset which consists of texts adapted for learners of Russian as a foreign language (Dmitrieva and Tiedemann, 2021). RuAdapt has three subcorpora: literary texts, encyclopedic entries, and fairytales. Sentence pairs in RuAdapt were aligned automatically and have cosine similarity scores provided by the aligner. Only sentences with cosine similarity above 0.31 but below 0.98 were used;
- The RuSimpleSentEval[1] datasets: development and public test set (Sakhovskiy et al., 2021). The original training set is currently unavailable. The public test set was not included in the general dataset; it was only used separately.

The size of the dataset can be seen in Table 1. 3398 sentence pairs from the RuSimpleSentEval public test set were held out for further testing.

The data only includes sentences with five tokens or longer. Furthermore, to avoid hallucinations in the output (incoherent texts possibly including facts not justified by the training data), the larger parts of the dataset, Paraphraser Plus and Opusparcus, were cleaned from sentence pairs where named entities do not match. The Natasha toolkit[2] was used to exclude sentence pairs where the target sentence has named entities absent in the source.

Dataset	Train	Dev	Test
Paraphraser Plus	338865	37652	7638
Opusparcus	103186	11465	2405
RSSE	2570	285	59
RA literature	8530	948	169
RA encyclopedic	2041	227	50
RA fairytales	135	15	4
Total	455327	50592	10325

Table 1: General dataset partition counts in sentence pairs. RA stands for RuAdapt, RSSE for RuSimpleSentEval. Held out RSSE public test set not included.

3 Experiments

3.1 Control tokens

Following Martin et al. (2022) and Martin et al. (2020), we chose four control tokens to represent four attributes related to the process of simplification mentioned above in Section 1:

- **NbChars**: the ratio between the lengths of source and target sentences in characters; represents the amount of compression. Same as in Martin et al. (2020);
- **LevSim**: the Levenshtein ratio between source and target sentences; represents the amount of paraphrasing. Same as in Martin et al. (2020);
- **DepTreeDepth**: the ratio between the syntactic tree depths of target and source sentences; represents the syntactic complexity. Similar to Martin et al. (2020). The dependency parsing is performed with the deeppavlov's[3] ru_syntagrus_joint_parsing model;
- **CEFRgrade**: the CEFR grade level of the target sentence; represents multiple simplification-related attributes. It is the only token not represented by ratio because it is easier to control the output's grade level directly rather than control how simplified the output will be compared to the source. The grade levels were calculated using code from the Textometr (Laposhina et al., 2018) API. Textometr's grade levels go from elementary A1 up to what can be described as C2+ (too

[1] https://github.com/dialogue-evaluation/RuSimpleSentEval

[2] https://github.com/natasha/natasha

[3] https://github.com/deeppavlov/DeepPavlov

complicated even for a native speaker) and can be transformed to a 0.0 to 10.0 scale. Only sentence pairs where the source's grade level was higher than or equal to the target's (which means that some pairs had to be reversed) and the target's CEFR level was not higher than C2 were kept in the dataset.

Here is what a source sentence with control tokens looks like before encoding and preprocessing with sentencepiece and fairseq (this sentence is from the ParaPhraser.ru corpus):

<CEFRgrade_0> <LevSim_0.4> <NbChars_1.15> Погода на завтра: преимущественно без осадков.

Weather for tomorrow: mostly without precipitation.

Previous research has shown that the NbChars and LevSim tokens work well for both English and Russian; therefore, they were chosen for the initial experiments, including experiments with choosing the model architecture. To the best of our knowledge, the DepTreeDepth token was never tried on Russian but has shown a slight performance increase for English (Martin et al., 2020), so it was included in later experiments. The reason for choosing CEFR grade level as one of the tokens was twofold. The first goal was to find a way to simplify texts for a particular grade level. Secondly, since the WordRank token used in Martin et al. (2020) did not work well for Russian (Anastasyev, 2021), it was necessary to find something else to represent the change in lexical (and other) complexity between sentences. Moreover, studies such as Scarton and Specia (2018) have shown that annotating the source sentences with information about the target grade level can positively affect the model's simplification performance. All tokens except CEFRgrade levels have 40 unique values from 0.05 to 2.

It should be noted that the studies that this paper is based on, namely Martin et al. (2022) and Anastasyev (2021), have different approaches to appending the control tokens to the model. In Martin et al. (2022), the tokens are appended to the beginning of the sentence. Then the sentence is encoded with sentencepiece, preprocessed with fairseq, and fed to the model. Therefore, no special embeddings just for the control tokens are added to the pretrained model, and the vectorization of control tokens happens as is. Anastasyev (2021) uses a different approach, in which he utilizes tokens from the mBART's dictionary that were not used in the training data to denote control tokens. To our understanding, all possible values of the control tokens receive their own embeddings from the pool of tokens known to the model but not utilized in the training data. During inference, if a control token with a certain value is not present in the training data, the closest possible value is found, and the model uses the embedding assigned to that value. Our study follows the Martin et al. (2022)'s approach for this project. It would be interesting to try and append new embeddings to the pretrained models for control tokens. For instance, in Schioppa et al. (2021), the authors introduce attribute control during fine-tuning by affecting a smaller subset of the original model parameters. However, not all frameworks currently have instruments for that.

3.2 Choosing the model architecture

The following versions of two transformer architectures, mBART (Liu et al., 2020) and T5 (Raffel et al., 2020), both proven very capable at monolingual translation tasks such as paraphrasing, were used in this project:

- mBART cc25, a model with 12 encoder and decoder layers trained on 25 languages' monolingual corpus[4]. The preprocessing, training, and inference process was identical to that of the RuSimpleSentEval competition baseline[5].
- a version of Google's multilingual T5 (Xue et al., 2021) with only Russian and some English embeddings left[6]. The training process was similar to the one used by David Dale for fine-tuning a T5 model for multiple tasks, including paraphrasing Russian texts (Dale, 2021). During inference, we used the number of beams of 3 and a no-repeat ngram size of 5.

The models' performance was evaluated with the SARI score (Xu et al., 2016) from the EASSE (Alva-Manchego et al., 2019) library. SARI compares **s**ystem output **a**gainst **r**eferences and against the **i**nput sentence, and correlates with

[4]https://github.com/facebookresearch/fairseq/blob/main/examples/mbart/README.md

[5]https://github.com/dialogue-evaluation/RuSimpleSentEval

[6]https://huggingface.co/cointegrated/rut5-base

Test set	mBART	T5
General	**44.3776**	40.781
RSSE	33.3876	**35.2519**

Table 2: Highest SARI scores for models with no control tokens.

Test set	mBART	T5
General test, true tokens	**53.9269**	38.9376
General test, $\text{NbChars}_{0.95}$, $\text{LevSim}_{0.4}$	**43.1563**	40.0487
RSSE, $\text{NbChars}_{0.95}$, $\text{LevSim}_{0.4}$	**38.9894**	34.6402
RSSE, $\text{NbChars}_{1.0}$, $\text{LevSim}_{1.0}$	15.944	**35.1672**

Table 3: Highest SARI scores for models with NbChars and LevSim control tokens. "True tokens" means tokens that represent the actual attribute values between source and target sentences.

human judgments of simplicity (Xu et al., 2016). It uses an arithmetic average of n-gram precisions and recalls of editing operations: addition, keeping, and deletions between the source, output, and references (ibid.). The models were evaluated on two test sets: a general test set from Table 1 and the public test set from RuSimpleSentEval. Before evaluation, sanity tests were conducted on the RSSE public test set: if the source file is used as the output file, the SARI score is 14.7, and if the target is used as output, the score is 100. During RuSimpleSentEval, the best system had a SARI score of 40.23 on the public test set.

As seen in Table 2, when trained without any control tokens, mBART has a much higher score on the general test set, but on the RSSE public test set, the scores are much lower, with T5 performing slightly better. However, adding two control tokens, NbChars and LevSim, improved the performance of mBART significantly on both test sets (see Table 3). T5, however, did not show a considerable performance gain. Moreover, when both tokens were set to 1.0, only mBART showed a SARI score similar to the SARI that can be obtained if the source sentences are passed as output (which means that the sentences were left unchanged as it is supposed to happen when these tokens are set to 1.0). It should be noted, however, that, despite high SARI scores, the output of mBART contained some incoherent sentences, similar to what Anastasyev (2021) reports (the models with highly rated performance still hallucinating in some cases).

To further investigate how the control tokens affect the model, we measured the actual values of the character length ratio and the Levenshtein similarity ratio between the model's output and the source sentences. Intuitively, suppose a model was asked to simplify sentences with NbChars set to 0.95. In that case, the average character length ratio between the system output and source sentences should be close to 0.95. As seen in Table 4, both models seem to learn the meaning of the tokens with further training, even though it does not necessarily mean SARI score improvement. Evidently, the mBART architecture was better at understanding the meaning of both control tokens, which is why it was chosen for further experiments. It should also be noted that the training process for mBART with fairseq was faster than training T5 with transformers, which influenced our choice of model.

3.3 Syntactic complexity

Training an mBART model with the same configuration as before on texts with just the DepTreeDepth token resulted in a considerable decrease in performance. After 5 initial epochs and additional 7 epochs after early stopping, the best SARI score on the general test set was 28.77 on epoch 7. Despite generally standard loss scores (not much different from previous experiments with and without control tokens), the models hallucinated quite a bit. The hallucinations made calculating the actual syntactic tree depth of the outputs impossible because there were too many word repetitions to create adequate syntactic trees. In conclusion, the tree depth ratio may not be an adequate enough metric to control syntactic complexity in Russian sentences. It should be noted that, as reported in Martin et al. (2020), the identical DepTreeDepth token also did not seem to control its attribute as well as the NbChars and LevSim tokens did in English texts, although it had the desired effect on the output.

3.4 CEFR grade levels

Firstly, we conducted multiple experiments to determine how many unique values should be allocated to this token. The starting range was from 0.7 to 8.5 with a step of 0.1 (the way the values come from Textometr). After a decrease in performance compared to models with no tokens (the highest SARI score obtained on the general test set was 35.84 on

Token	mBART				T5			
	4 epochs	3 epochs	2 epochs	1 epoch	800k	700k	600k	500k
$NbChars_{0.95}$	0,9119	0,9004	**0,9140**	0,8496	0,8976	0,8792	0,8684	0,7327
$LevSim_{0.4}$	**0,4812**	0,4814	0,5074	0,4980	0,5336	0,5648	0,6909	0,6666
$NbChars_{1.0}$	**0,9999**	0,9997	1,0002	0,9993	0,9914	0,9989	0,9315	0,8590
$LevSim_{1.0}$	0,9990	0,9989	**0,9993**	0,9987	0,8762	0,8442	0,7573	0,7085

Table 4: Mean attribute values calculated between the output and the source files (RSSE public test set). k (in 800k, 700k, etc.) = thousands of steps.

Control token CEFR level	SARI
0 (A1)	**46.4875**
1 (A2)	44.8701
2 (B1)	42.2034
3 (B2)	38.0583
Actual target CEFR level (best model)	38.9731

Table 5: SARI scores on the general test set for the model with a CEFR grade level control token: manually set values and actual values (CEFR grade levels of target sentences in the test set).

epoch 8/12), the number of unique values was lowered to 8, from 1 to 8. After that, the SARI scores increased up to 41 (epoch 4/7), but the model still hallucinated quite a lot. After that, the number of unique values was reduced to 6, corresponding to levels A1 (0) to C2 (5). This decreased the SARI scores slightly (highest SARI 38.97, epoch 8/10); however, the outputs became more coherent.

In order to test the influence of different token values on the output, during the inference, the token was set to lower grade levels, from A1 (0) to B2 (3). The testing has shown that the SARI score decreases when the CEFR grade level goes up (see Table 5). As expected, the lowest CEFR grade gives the highest SARI score. When studying this token's influence further, it became clear that, even though setting the token to a particular grade level leads to more sentences of that level in the output, the model still produces a lot of B1 and B2 (2 and 3) level sentences, as shown on Figure 1. The reason is likely because many sentences with these grade levels are in the training data.

Despite the model being able to learn the NbChars and LevSim control tokens together and the CEFRgrade separately, combining them in one model did not increase performance. On the contrary, there was no noticeable SARI increase across 18 epochs, and many outputs were incoherent with a lot of word repetitions. The reason for such be-

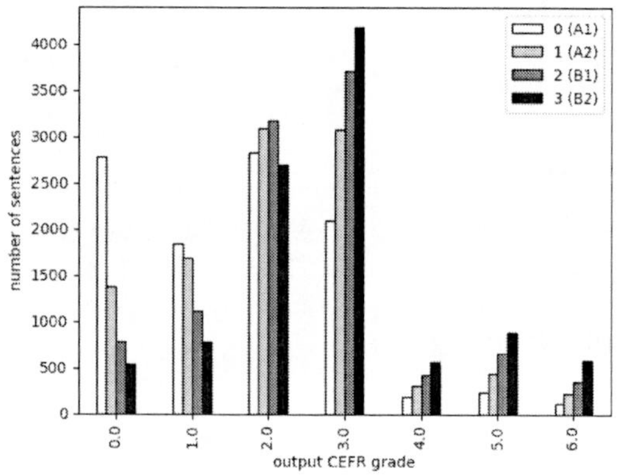

Figure 1: Influence of the CEFR grade level control token on the output. General test set. The numbers in the legend denote the control token values given to the model.

havior is unclear since in previous studies (see, for example, Martin et al., 2022, and Schioppa et al., 2021), different control tokens were successfully combined.

4 Conclusions

This paper continues and expands previous research on controlled text simplification. We studied the influence of control tokens on Russian texts using open-source datasets. Also, another transformer architecture was tested not previously used for these kinds of experiments. In the end, the choice fell on mBART, but the experiments have shown that T5 can also learn the meaning of control tokens. Two tokens were tested that have not been applied to Russian data before. The findings show that the DepTreeDepth token does not perform as well on Russian data as it did on English, according to previous research. The CEFRgrade token can influence the model's output in a desirable way, but according to the experiments' results, it cannot be combined with other tokens. Finally, it was confirmed that the other two tokens, NbChars and LevSim, work well on Russian data. Some examples of the models' outputs can be found in Appendix A. The best models' checkpoints and other supplementary materials can be found on GitHub: `https://github.com/annadmitrieva/controlled_simplification_ru`.

The findings show that some tokens are "harder" to learn for the models than others. Possible topics for future research include more in-depth studies of "difficult" tokens and finding methods for representing their attributes in more understandable ways to the models. Another possible topic is studying how to combine tokens more effectively and why some combinations do not work well.

Limitations

Data: the bigger portion of the dataset used in this study consists of paraphrases and not professionally done simplifications. There was an attempt to compensate for it by assigning CEFR grade levels to each sentence and reversing the pairs where the source was originally "easier" than the target. This is also partially why the distribution of target CEFR levels is so skewed towards B1 and B2: lower grade levels require more effort made by the author specifically towards simplification. A more balanced dataset would likely improve the models' performance and their ability to simplify sentences for any given grade level.

CEFR grade levels: it should be noted that Textometr, the software used for assigning the grade levels, is used primarily for texts, not single sentences, since CEFR grade levels are generally assigned to a text, and estimating an exact level of a single sentence can be difficult even for an expert. For some sentences, it is also challenging to lower the level below B: for example, when it contains mentions of phenomena that, in order to be understood by someone on level A, would need a detailed explanation, such as "Покров Пресвятой Богородицы" (*Intercession of the Theotokos*) or "Дом профсоюзов" (*Trade Unions Building*). On the other hand, some source sentences in the dataset are already quite simple, and modifying them to become more complex is out of the scope of the simplification task. The observations also show that in many cases, the model could not simplify a sentence to all possible grade levels: for example, sometimes, the model could only simplify a given sentence to levels 0 to 2 but not to 3. The model's behavior and limitations when it comes to controlling the grade level are in itself a separate topic for discussion.

Models: for the sake of time, the models' parameters were not changed during training or inference, and no search for more optimal parameters has been performed. It is likely that finding proper parameters could have improved the results of the experiments. However, the goal was not to increase the performance but to compare how models behave in different settings (with different tokens).

Acknowledgements

This work was partially supported by the Cultura foundation (Application 2021143).

References

Fernando Alva-Manchego, Joachim Bingel, Gustavo Paetzold, Carolina Scarton, and Lucia Specia. 2017. Learning how to simplify from explicit labeling of complex-simplified text pairs. In *Proceedings of the Eighth International Joint Conference on Natural Language Processing (Volume 1: Long Papers)*, pages 295–305, Taipei, Taiwan. Asian Federation of Natural Language Processing.

Fernando Alva-Manchego, Louis Martin, Carolina Scarton, and Lucia Specia. 2019. EASSE: Easier automatic sentence simplification evaluation. In *Proceedings of the 2019 Conference on Empirical Methods in Natural Language Processing and the 9th International Joint Conference on Natural Language Processing (EMNLP-IJCNLP): System Demonstrations*, pages 49–54, Hong Kong, China. Association for Computational Linguistics.

Daniil Anastasyev. 2021. RuSimpleSentEval. [Online; released 11-April-2021].

Mathias Creutz. 2018. Open subtitles paraphrase corpus for six languages. In *Proceedings of the Eleventh International Conference on Language Resources and Evaluation (LREC 2018)*, Miyazaki, Japan. European Language Resources Association (ELRA).

David Dale. 2021. Перефразирование русских текстов: корпуса, модели, метрики. [Online; posted 28-June-2021].

Anna Dmitrieva and Jörg Tiedemann. 2021. Creating an aligned Russian text simplification dataset from language learner data. In *Proceedings of the 8th Workshop on Balto-Slavic Natural Language Processing*, pages 73–79, Kiyv, Ukraine. Association for Computational Linguistics.

Yue Dong, Zichao Li, Mehdi Rezagholizadeh, and Jackie Chi Kit Cheung. 2019. EditNTS: An neural programmer-interpreter model for sentence simplification through explicit editing. In *Proceedings of the*

57th Annual Meeting of the Association for Computational Linguistics, pages 3393–3402, Florence, Italy. Association for Computational Linguistics.

Vadim Gudkov, Olga Mitrofanova, and Elizaveta Filippskikh. 2020. Automatically ranked Russian paraphrase corpus for text generation. In *Proceedings of the Fourth Workshop on Neural Generation and Translation*, pages 54–59, Online. Association for Computational Linguistics.

Antonina Laposhina, Tatyana Veselovskaya, Maria Lebedeva, and Olga Krivenko. 2018. Automated Text Readability Assessment For Russian Second Language Learners. In *Proceedings of the International Conference on Computational Linguistics and Intellectual Technologies "DIALOGUE"*, pages 396–406.

Leealaura Leskelä, Arto Mustajoki, and Aino Piehl. 2022. Easy and plain languages as special cases of linguistic tailoring and standard language varieties. *Nordic Journal of Linguistics*, 45(2):194–213.

Yinhan Liu, Jiatao Gu, Naman Goyal, Xian Li, Sergey Edunov, Marjan Ghazvininejad, Mike Lewis, and Luke Zettlemoyer. 2020. Multilingual Denoising Pre-training for Neural Machine Translation.

Christiane Maaß. 2020. *Easy Language – Plain Language – Easy Language Plus*, 1 edition, volume 3 of *Easy – Plain – Accessible*. Frank & Timme.

Louis Martin, Angela Fan, Éric Villemonte De La Clergerie, Antoine Bordes, and Benoît Sagot. 2022. MUSS: Multilingual Unsupervised Sentence Simplification by Mining Paraphrases. In *Proceedings of the Thirteenth Language Resources and Evaluation Conference*, pages 1651–1664.

Louis Martin, Éric Villemonte de La Clergerie, Benoît Sagot, and Antoine Bordes. 2020. Controllable Sentence Simplification. In *LREC 2020 - 12th Language Resources and Evaluation Conference*.

Daiki Nishihara, Tomoyuki Kajiwara, and Yuki Arase. 2019. Controllable text simplification with lexical constraint loss. In *Proceedings of the 57th Annual Meeting of the Association for Computational Linguistics: Student Research Workshop*, pages 260–266, Florence, Italy. Association for Computational Linguistics.

Colin Raffel, Noam Shazeer, Adam Roberts, Katherine Lee, Sharan Narang, Michael Matena, Yanqi Zhou, Wei Li, and Peter J. Liu. 2020. Exploring the Limits of Transfer Learning with a Unified Text-to-Text Transformer. *Journal of Machine Learning Research*, 21(140):1–67.

Andrey Sakhovskiy, Alexandra Izhevskaya, Alena Pestova, Elena Tutubalina, Valentin Malykh, Ivan Smurov, and Ekaterina Artemova. 2021. RuSimpleSentEval-2021 shared task: evaluating sentence simplification for Russian. In *Proceedings of the International Conference on Computational Linguistics and Intellectual Technologies "DIALOGUE"*, pages 607–617.

Carolina Scarton and Lucia Specia. 2018. Learning simplifications for specific target audiences. In *Proceedings of the 56th Annual Meeting of the Association for Computational Linguistics (Volume 2: Short Papers)*, pages 712–718, Melbourne, Australia. Association for Computational Linguistics.

Andrea Schioppa, David Vilar, Artem Sokolov, and Katja Filippova. 2021. Controlling machine translation for multiple attributes with additive interventions. In *Proceedings of the 2021 Conference on Empirical Methods in Natural Language Processing*, pages 6676–6696, Online and Punta Cana, Dominican Republic. Association for Computational Linguistics.

Wei Xu, Courtney Napoles, Ellie Pavlick, Quanze Chen, and Chris Callison-Burch. 2016. Optimizing Statistical Machine Translation for Text Simplification. *Transactions of the Association for Computational Linguistics*, 4(0):401–415.

Linting Xue, Noah Constant, Adam Roberts, Mihir Kale, Rami Al-Rfou, Aditya Siddhant, Aditya Barua, and Colin Raffel. 2021. mT5: A massively multilingual pre-trained text-to-text transformer. In *Proceedings of the 2021 Conference of the North American Chapter of the Association for Computational Linguistics: Human Language Technologies*, pages 483–498, Online. Association for Computational Linguistics.

Xingxing Zhang and Mirella Lapata. 2017. Sentence simplification with deep reinforcement learning. In *Proceedings of the 2017 Conference on Empirical Methods in Natural Language Processing*, pages 584–594, Copenhagen, Denmark. Association for Computational Linguistics.

A Example Appendix

Some examples of simplifications performed by the models can be found in Tables 6 and 7.

Partition	Text	Actual grade level
Source	Семья Березовского не дает согласия на закрытие уголовных дел против него *Berezovsky's family does not consent to the closure of criminal cases against him*	3
Target	Родственники Березовского не будут давать согласие на прекращение уголовных дел в отношении него *Berezovsky's relatives will not consent to the termination of criminal cases against [in relation to] him*	3
CEFRgrade_0	Семья Березовского не хочет закрывать дела *Berezovsky's family does not want to close cases*	0
CEFRgrade_1	Семья Березовского не хочет закрывать дела против него *Berezovsky's family does not want to close cases against him*	1
CEFRgrade_2	Семья Березовского не дает согласия на закрытие уголовных дел *Berezovsky's family does not consent to the closure of criminal cases*	2
CEFRgrade_3	Семья Березовского не согласна на закрытие уголовных дел против него *Berezovsky's family does not agree to the closure of criminal cases against him*	3

Table 6: Examples of simplifications with arbitrary CEFR grade levels. Original dataset: ParaPhraser.ru.

Partition	Text
Source	Андропов,военный атташе и водитель уцелели и пешком добрались до посольства. *Andropov, the military attache and the driver survived and reached the embassy on foot.*
Target	Андропов вместе с военным атташе и водителем уцелели, но пешком два часа по ночному городу пробирались в посольство. *Andropov, along with the military attache and the driver, survived, but they made their way to the embassy on foot for two hours through the night city.*
$\text{NbChars}_{1.0}$, $\text{LevSim}_{1.0}$	Андропов,военный атташе и водитель уцелели и пешком добрались до посольства. *Andropov, the military attache and the driver survived and reached the embassy on foot.*
$\text{NbChars}_{0.95}$, $\text{LevSim}_{0.4}$	До посольства добрались Андропов, атташе и водитель. *Andropov, the attache and the driver reached the embassy.*

Table 7: Examples of simplifications with arbitrary NbChars and LevSim parameters. Original dataset: RuSimple-SentEval public test.

Target Two Birds With One STONE: Entity-Level Sentiment and Tone Analysis in Croatian News Headlines

Ana Barić[1†] **Laura Majer**[1†] **David Dukić**[1†] **Marijana Grbeša**[2] **Jan Šnajder**[1]
[1]University of Zagreb, Faculty of Electrical Engineering and Computing, TakeLab
{ana.baric, laura.majer, david.dukic, jan.snajder}@fer.hr
[2]University of Zagreb, Faculty of Political Science
marijana.grbesa@fpzg.hr

Abstract

Sentiment analysis is often used to examine how different actors are portrayed in the media, and analysis of news headlines is of particular interest due to their attention-grabbing role. We address the task of entity-level sentiment analysis from Croatian news headlines. We frame the task as targeted sentiment analysis (TSA), explicitly differentiating between sentiment toward a named entity and the overall tone of the headline. We describe STONE, a new dataset for this task with sentiment and tone labels. We implement several neural benchmark models, utilizing single- and multi-task training, and show that TSA can benefit from tone information. Finally, we gauge the difficulty of this task by leveraging dataset cartography.

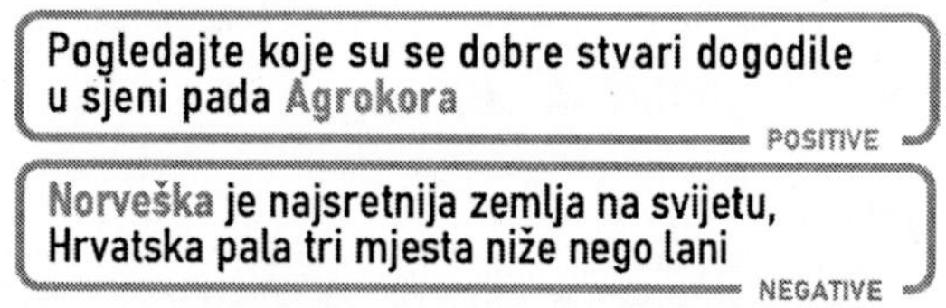

Figure 1: Examples of headlines from the STONE dataset with contrasting tone and entity-level sentiment (red: negative, green: positive).

1 Introduction

Sentiment analysis (SA) is a common method in media and communication studies used to examine how different topics, events, or actors are portrayed in the media. It has been used to address media bias, framing, agenda setting, priming, and negativity in the news; e.g., (Semetko and Valkenburg, 2000; Hopmann et al., 2010; Grbeša, 2012; Galpin and Trenz, 2019). While SA often involves entire news reports, news headlines emerge as a relevant unit of analysis as they play a central role in grabbing the attention of audiences in the digital environment (Kuiken et al., 2017; Scacco and Muddiman, 2020), optimize the relevance of the story for the headline scanning audience (Dor, 2003), and also act as a strong framing mechanism (De Vreese, 2005; Tankard Jr, 2001).

Although sentiment is often used interchangeably with tone, valence, affect, or polarity (cf. Boukes et al. (2020); Soroka et al. (2015)), here we consider sentiment and tone as distinct concepts. Sentiment is operationalized as a category that is always determined in relation to a particular entity, whereas tone is more general and captures the overall mood and polarity of the entire news story or another unit of analysis. This conceptualization draws on the distinction made by Lengauer et al. (2012) between the "actor-related dimension of negativity" and the "frame-related dimension of negativity". The former dimension corresponds to sentiment, while the latter corresponds to tone.

SA also has a long history in natural language processing (NLP) (Pang and Lee, 2008). The typical applications range from large-scale market research, product review analysis, and customer satisfaction estimation to voter profiling in political campaigns and media analysis. Typically, SA aims to determine the overall sentiment expressed in the text, thus corresponding to the "frame-related dimension of negativity". Often, this boils down to determining the sentiment *polarity* as either negative, neutral, or positive. In contrast, targeted sentiment analysis (TSA; Pei et al. (2019)) focuses on sentiment expressed toward specific targets. Specifically, entity-level sentiment analysis may be operationalized as TSA with the pre-extracted named entity (NE) mentions as targets, thus corresponding to the "actor-related dimension of negativity".

This paper addresses the TSA task for the Croatian language, more precisely, entity-level sentiment analysis from Croatian news headlines. To this end, we first propose a novel dataset for this task called STONE (Sentiment and TOne from NEws), with

[†]Equal contribution.

Proceedings of the 9th Workshop on Slavic Natural Language Processing 2023 (SlavicNLP 2023), pages 78–85
May 6, 2023

manually annotated entity-level sentiment and tone for news headlines. We investigate the relationship between targeted sentiment and tone, showing that there is a statistical dependence between the two. We then introduce and evaluate several neural benchmark models for this task. Building on our finding that targeted sentiment depends on the tone of a headline, we examine whether multitask modeling of TSA and tone can improve TSA prediction performance. Finally, to gauge the difficulty of the TSA on Croatian news headlines, we diagnose the dataset using the cartography technique of Swayamdipta et al. (2020), examining the relationship between annotator agreement and model correctness. The results show that, while TSA on Croatian news headlines is challenging for humans and state-of-the-art models, our benchmark models considerably outperform the baseline. We also show that using the tone signal in a multi-task setup can improve TSA performance further.

Our contribution is threefold: (1) a novel dataset for the task of entity-level sentiment and tone analysis in Croatian news headlines, which we make publicly available,[1] (2) neural benchmark models for this task in single- and multi-task setups, and (3) dataset diagnostics by means of dataset cartography. Our work brings valuable insights for TSA in the Slavic languages niche.

2 Related Work

The explicit emphasis on the target entity in TSA requires modeling the relationship between targets and their surrounding context. Previous work captured this target-context interaction by isolating the target entity with BIO tags and recurrent models (Hu et al., 2019; Li et al., 2019) or utilizing the attention mechanism (Zhang et al., 2016; Song et al., 2019). Another approach leveraged transformer-based models such as BERT for TSA tasks on user reviews (Gao et al., 2019; Rietzler et al., 2019) and Twitter data (Mutlu and Özgür, 2022) by focusing on target tokens for sentiment classification. In our work, we employ the target entity extraction method for the BERT-based model, but we simplify the extraction by using only target embeddings. Similar BERT-based approaches were adapted for the targeted sentiment analysis in the news domain on a sentence (Hamborg et al., 2021) and headline (Salgueiro et al., 2022) level for English and Spanish language, respectively.

In the realm of NLP for Slavic languages, our work is similar to that of (Pelicon et al., 2020), who annotated news articles for Slovene and Croatian language and performed sentiment classification of news articles on three levels of granularity (document, paragraph, and sentence level). However, they did not analyze sentiment toward specific named entities. Our work is most similar to (Baraniak and Sydow, 2021), who annotated and analyzed the dataset of news headlines for sentiment analysis toward target entities in English and Polish. We adopt a similar dataset design for annotating sentiment toward the target entity in news headlines for the Croatian language, but we also consider the general tone of the headline.

3 STONE Dataset

Our main contribution is STONE, a dataset containing headlines from Croatian news outlets labeled with sentiment towards NEs and the general tone of the headline. To compile the dataset, we first sampled the headlines from a database of news articles acquired by TakeLab Retriever,[2] a tool for analyzing Croatian online news media. To identify the NEs in the headlines, we ran the BERTić model fine-tuned for the task of NE recognition, which achieves an average F1-score of 89.21 on Croatian news hr500k dataset (Ljubešić and Lauc, 2021; Ljubešić et al., 2016). We retained only the headlines that contained at least one NE. If a headline contained several NEs, we randomly picked one as the target. Consequently, a headline may appear in our dataset several times with a different target.

We relied on a simple ternary annotation scheme, using the negative (NEG), neutral (NTR), and positive (POS) labels for both targeted sentiment and tone. While we considered more fine-grained schemes, such as the one proposed by Batanović et al. (2016), we decided to use the ternary one as it proved to be sufficient in preliminary annotation rounds. This aligns with our intuition that, as one of the primary purposes of news headlines is to draw attention and generate interest, sentiment and tone labels should capture the reader's immediate first impression rather than the result of a conscious and deliberate evaluation process.

The annotation was carried out by ten annotators using the Alanno tool for annotation management (Jukić et al., 2022). All annotators were native speakers of the Croatian language. The annota-

[1] https://takelab.fer.hr/retriever/stone.tar.gz

[2] https://retriever.takelab.fer.hr/

Tone	Sentiment NEG	NTR	POS
NEG	3231	3024	524
NTR	344	3541	689
POS	251	1699	3827

Table 1: Contingency table of tone and sentiment judgments for the ten annotators.

tors worked independently, with six annotators per instance to account for the highly subjective nature of the task. The data annotation process was completed within 14 person-hours. The text of the articles was not made available to the annotators, only the headline. For each instance, the annotators labeled both the tone and targeted sentiment but were advised first to determine the tone of the headline and then the targeted sentiment, assuming this order – going from general to more specific – would make annotating easier.

The annotators were instructed to judge the tone and the sentiment based on their immediate impression of the headline. The guidelines further instructed them to consider the presence of epithets portraying the target entity or entire headline in a certain light and the context providing information about the nature of the event described in the headline. If none of these features were relevant, the annotators were told to rely on background knowledge of the subject in question. The annotators were also instructed to report erroneously identified NEs, and these headlines were discarded.

The final dataset contains 2855 headlines. For targeted sentiment, 1486 headlines were labeled as negative, 653 as neutral, and 716 as positive. Regarding the tone, 1262 headlines were labeled as negative, 666 as neutral, and 927 as positive. Inter-annotator agreement with the Fleiss-kappa metric is $\kappa = 0.416$ and $\kappa = 0.493$ for targeted sentiment and tone, respectively, which is considered a moderate agreement (Landis and Koch, 1977). A moderate level of agreement is expected, considering the highly subjective nature of these tasks.

Table 1 shows the contingency table of unaggregated sentiment and tone labels. Unsurprisingly, and as exemplified by Figure 1, targeted sentiment and tone are not always aligned, although in most cases they are. We used a chi-squared test to test the statistical dependence of targeted sentiment and tone. The two variables are significantly associated, with $\chi^2 = 8550.77, p < .01$.

4 Benchmark Models

The backbone of all our experiments was the BERTić model (Ljubešić and Lauc, 2021), based on Electra (Clark et al., 2020). Pre-trained BERTić achieves state-of-the-art performance on many NLP tasks in Slavic languages, including Croatian. We use BERTIć to produce contextualized representations of NEs in the headline for TSA.[3]

Gold Dataset. We compiled the gold dataset for evaluating benchmark models by aggregating the labels of the ten annotators for both sentiment and tone using a majority vote. To sidestep the problem of adjudicating labels in cases with no majority agreement, we removed all instances where there are ties in either sentiment or tone annotations. We leave alternatives, including adjudication steps, more fine-grained schemes, or label distribution prediction for future work. The so-obtained gold set contains 2307 instances, of which 508 are negative, 1151 are neutral, and 648 are positive sentiment instances. For tone, there are 428 negative, 1060 neutral, and 819 positive instances. We randomly split the gold set into training, validation, and testing in a 70:10:20 ratio.

Single-task Setup. We implemented one rudimentary baseline and four deep-learning benchmarks in the single-task setup for the TSA task. We use the univariate Bayes as a baseline, with class likelihood parameters estimated by computing the labels' distribution for lemmatized NEs appearing in the training set. Entities were lemmatized using CLASSLA (Ljubešić and Dobrovoljc, 2019). The intuition was that the sentiment of some NEs will be predictable regardless of the context they appear in. For out-of-vocabulary NEs, the prediction was made by sampling a label from the training set distribution conditioned on the NE type.

We implemented four benchmark models. In the first model (*Target*), the entire headline is fed to the model, followed by the extraction of only the target NE embeddings span. The second model (*Masked*) is fed with a headline where the target entity is replaced by a special [MASK] token. This tests the assumption that the targeted sentiment depends only on the context independently of the concrete entity. We experimented with including the NE type as a feature concatenated to the averaged embedding of an NE span before feeding it to the classification layer for both target (*Target+Type*)

[3]`https://github.com/TakeLab/stone`

and masked (*Masked+Type*) models. We fed the averaged contextualized embeddings of the NE span to the classification layer in each model.

Multi-task Setup. Annotation analysis in Section 3 revealed that there is a statistical dependency between tone and sentiment labels. We hypothesize that this dependency can be leveraged to obtain more accurate TSA predictions. To investigate this, we combined TSA and tone classification tasks into a multi-task training design (Zhang et al., 2022). The multi-task setup was implemented on top of BERTić with one linear classification head for tone classification and the other for targeted sentiment classification (*Target* single-task model). We implemented three multi-task setups. The first, *Alternate Batch* setup mimics the suggested procedure for dataset annotation, where, for each instance, the tone is annotated first, and the entity-level sentiment is annotated second. Within each mini-batch, we first present the model with tone instances, calculate the loss, and update the parameters based on the derivatives of the tone loss gradients. We then do the same for same-batch instances but this time for sentiment labels. We alternate between the two tasks during each epoch. This is in contrast to the second setup we considered, *Alternate Epoch*, where we first update model parameters depending on all tone training instances and then update the parameters based on all sentiment training instances using the appropriate classification head. Task-wise updates are conducted in a mini-batch fashion. The third setup is *Average Batch*, where we calculate the loss on a mini-batch level for both tasks and then update the model parameters based on the derivatives of the averaged batch loss.

Experimental Results. All results were obtained by averaging over five independent runs with different random seeds. BERTić-based benchmarks were trained for 10 epochs with a batch size of 16. We minimized cross-entropy loss and clipped gradients to 1.0. We used the AdamW optimization algorithm (Reddi et al., 2019) with a learning rate of 1e-5. The learning rate was adjusted with a linear learning rate scheduler that used zero warmup steps. We report macro-F1 scores and per-class F1 scores. TSA results are shown in Table 2 (corresponding results for tone are in A.2).

All neural models outperformed the Bayes baseline by a large margin. In a single-task setup, the *Target* model performed best, with *Target+Type* being the close second. Masked experiment results show that not knowing what the exact entity is or knowing only its NE type is detrimental to overall model performance, except for determining the neutral sentiment. *Average Batch* and *Alternate Batch* multi-task setups beat all single-task variants in terms of macro-averaged F1-score, with *Average Batch* reaching the highest score. This suggests that tone, incorporated through multi-task training, is beneficial for TSA model performance. Overall best negative and positive sentiment results were also obtained in multi-task setups. The performance on the neutral label was consistent across setups, presumably because the neutral instances make up the majority of the dataset.

Single-task	AVG	NEG	NTR	POS
Univariate Bayes	.214	.079	.079	.266
Target	.752	.738	.782	.737
Target+Type	.749	.737	**.787**	.723
Masked	.506	.393	.702	.422
Masked+Type	.589	.500	.720	.548
Multi-task				
Alternate Batch	.751	**.748**	.784	.720
Alternate Epoch	.755	.747	.779	.740
Average Batch	**.757**	.742	.779	**.749**

Table 2: TSA macro-averaged and per-class F1-scores for single-task (baseline and four models) and multi-task *Target* model. The best results by setup are in **bold**.

5 Dataset Diagnostics

The dataset cartography method (Swayamdipta et al., 2020) makes it possible to analyze the characteristics of a dataset in relation to model performance. The method uses three metrics – *confidence*, *variability*, and *correctness* – to measure the model's performance on the individual instances over training epochs. Instances may then be grouped into three regions reflecting their difficulty: *easy-to-learn* instances are of high confidence and low variability, *hard-to-learn* instances are of both low confidence and low variability, while other instances are considered *ambiguous*.

Figure 2a shows the cartography of the STONE dataset for the *Average Batch* model. The dataset exhibits patterns already observed for other NLP datasets. This visualization is especially useful for identifying hard-to-learn instances with critically low correctness. However, as noted by Swayamdipta et al. (2020), poor model perfor-

Category		Title	Gold label	Model prediction	Majority
LOCALITIES	1	Kaos u **Portugalu**: Policajci su pucali na nogometnoj utakmici (*Chaos in* ***Portugal****: Policemen fired shots at a football game*)	NEG	NTR	.67
	2	**Italija** bilježi stalni porast broja zaraženih, ali ministar zdravstva očekuje početak pada potkraj proljeća (***Italy*** *is recording a constant rise of infected, but the minister of health is expecting a decline by the start of spring*)	NEG	NTR	.67
QUOTES	3	**Bandić**: Informatika se u škole uvodi da bi se izbacio vjeronauk (***Bandić****: Informatics is being introduced in schools to cancel religious studies*)	NEG	NTR	.83
	4	**Michael Phelps**: Sad mi je tek jasno da sam bio jednaki šupak od čovjeka kao Jordan (***Michael Phelps****: It is only now clear to me that I was just as big of an asshole as Jordan*)	NEG	NTR	.50
INFERENCE	5	Posrtali su tamo gdje nisu smjeli! Ovo su utakmice koje su **Hajduk** koštale osvajanja naslova prvaka (*They failed where they shouldn't have! These are the matches which cost* ***Hajduk*** *the championship title*)	NEG	NTR	.67
	6	Kraljica u seksi kombinezonu: U ovom se vojvotkinja **Catherine** nikad ne bi pojavila (*Queen in a sexy overall: Dutchess* ***Catherine*** *would never be seen wearing this*)	NEG	NTR/POZ	.83

Table 3: Instances with low model performance, grouped into categories. The target entities are in **bold**. All instances have a correctness value $\leq .1$, except example 3, which scored a correctness value of 1.

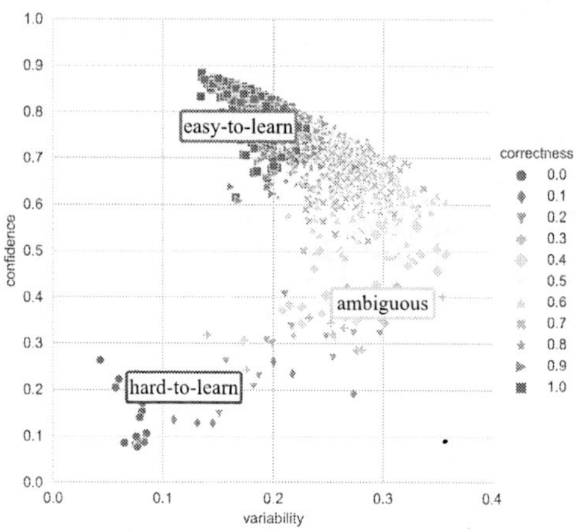

(a) Correctness

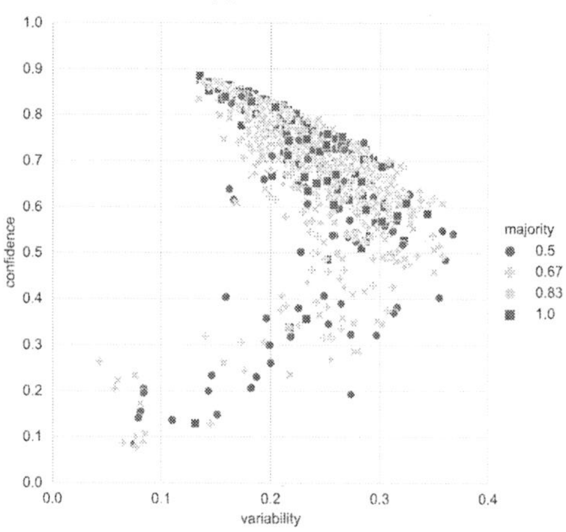

(b) Majority

Figure 2: STONE cartography with (a) correctness and (b) the majority metrics indicated with hue/shape.

mance may be due to ambiguity inherent to the instance rather than model limitations, and to distinguish between the two, it may be helpful to consider *human agreement* metric. We instead used the *majority* metric (the percentage of annotators that agreed on the gold label) to avoid the need to resolve ties for instances with no majority agreement stochastically. Figure 2b shows majority along with confidence and variability. Unlike in Figure 2a, one cannot identify prominent regions, suggesting there is no direct link between human consensus and the difficulty of an instance for the model.

Instead of looking at human consensus, to gain an insight into the phenomena the model seems to struggle with, we looked into instances with low correctness ($\leq .1$). Table 3 shows some examples. We preliminary identified three problematic categories of instances: (1) headlines with *localities* – the target entity refers to a location, and the sentiment is predominantly neutral, but in some cases the entity is a toponym that might be held responsible for the outcome. In this case, the negative evaluation may be transferred to the entity, which the model failed to infer; (2) headlines with *quotations* – the sentiment towards the speaker is usually neutral since no additional information is present, as shown in example 3. However, in example 4, the quote contains a negative observation about Phelps himself, which is atypical and failed to be recognized by the model; (3) evaluations based on *inference*, typical for headlines comprising multiple sentences. Instances such as examples 5 and 6 prove to be too difficult for the model while achieving sufficient consensus among the annotators.

6 Conclusion

We introduced a dataset for entity-level sentiment and tone analysis in Croatian news headlines. We tested neural benchmark models in a single- and multi-task setup, achieving the best results with representations of named entities and multi-task training. Dataset cartography identified several problematic cases for the model, which could be addressed in future work. Future work may also consider different framings of the TSA task.

Acknowledgments

This research was supported by the grant AIDWAS KK.01.2.1.02.0285. We acknowledge the insightful comments and suggestions provided by Irina Masnikosa, Nebojša Blanuša, and Mato Brautović.

References

Katarzyna Baraniak and Marcin Sydow. 2021. A dataset for sentiment analysis of entities in news headlines (SEN). *Procedia Computer Science*, 192:3627–3636.

Vuk Batanović, Boško Nikolić, and Milan Milosavljević. 2016. Reliable baselines for sentiment analysis in resource-limited languages: The Serbian movie review dataset. In *Proceedings of the Tenth International Conference on Language Resources and Evaluation (LREC'16)*, pages 2688–2696, Portorož, Slovenia. European Language Resources Association (ELRA).

Mark Boukes, Bob Van de Velde, Theo Araujo, and Rens Vliegenthart. 2020. What's the tone? Easy doesn't do it: Analyzing performance and agreement between off-the-shelf sentiment analysis tools. *Communication Methods and Measures*, 14(2):83–104.

Kevin Clark, Minh-Thang Luong, Quoc V Le, and Christopher D Manning. 2020. Electra: Pre-training text encoders as discriminators rather than generators. *arXiv preprint arXiv:2003.10555*.

Claes H De Vreese. 2005. News framing: Theory and typology. *Information design journal+ document design*, 13(1):51–62.

Daniel Dor. 2003. On newspaper headlines as relevance optimizers. *Journal of pragmatics*, 35(5):695–721.

Charlotte Galpin and Hans-Jörg Trenz. 2019. Converging towards Euroscepticism? Negativity in news coverage during the 2014 European Parliament elections in Germany and the UK. *European Politics and Society*, 20(3):260–276.

Zhengjie Gao, Ao Feng, Xinyu Song, and Xi Wu. 2019. Target-dependent sentiment classification with BERT. *IEEE Access*, pages 154290–154299.

Marijana Grbeša. 2012. Framing of the president: Newspaper coverage of Milan Bandić and Ivo Josipović in the presidential elections in Croatia in 2010. *Politička misao: časopis za politologiju*, 49(5):89–113.

Felix Hamborg, Karsten Donnay, and Bela Gipp. 2021. Towards target-dependent sentiment classification in news articles. In *Diversity, Divergence, Dialogue: 16th International Conference, iConference 2021, Beijing, China, March 17–31, 2021, Proceedings, Part II 16*, pages 156–166. Springer.

David Nicolas Hopmann, Rens Vliegenthart, Claes De Vreese, and Erik Albæk. 2010. Effects of election news coverage: How visibility and tone influence party choice. *Political communication*, 27(4):389–405.

Minghao Hu, Yuxing Peng, Zhen Huang, Dongsheng Li, and Yiwei Lv. 2019. Open-domain targeted sentiment analysis via span-based extraction and classification. In *Proceedings of the 57th Annual Meeting of the Association for Computational Linguistics*, pages 537–546, Florence, Italy. Association for Computational Linguistics.

Josip Jukić, Fran Jelenić, Miroslav Bićanić, and Jan Šnajder. 2022. Alanno: An active learning annotation system for mortals. *arXiv preprint arXiv:2211.06224*.

Jeffrey Kuiken, Anne Schuth, Martijn Spitters, and Maarten Marx. 2017. Effective headlines of newspaper articles in a digital environment. *Digital Journalism*, 5(10):1300–1314.

J. Richard Landis and Gary G. Koch. 1977. The measurement of observer agreement for categorical data. *Biometrics*, 33(1):159.

Günther Lengauer, Frank Esser, and Rosa Berganza. 2012. Negativity in political news: A review of concepts, operationalizations and key findings. *Journalism*, 13(2):179–202.

Xin Li, Lidong Bing, Piji Li, and Wai Lam. 2019. A unified model for opinion target extraction and target sentiment prediction. In *Proceedings of the AAAI conference on artificial intelligence*, volume 33, pages 6714–6721.

Nikola Ljubešić and Kaja Dobrovoljc. 2019. What does neural bring? analysing improvements in morphosyntactic annotation and lemmatisation of Slovenian, Croatian and Serbian. In *Proceedings of the 7th Workshop on Balto-Slavic Natural Language Processing*, pages 29–34, Florence, Italy. Association for Computational Linguistics.

Nikola Ljubešić, Filip Klubička, Željko Agić, and Ivo-Pavao Jazbec. 2016. New inflectional lexicons and training corpora for improved morphosyntactic annotation of Croatian and Serbian. In *Proceedings of the Tenth International Conference on Language Resources and Evaluation (LREC'16)*, pages 4264–4270, Portorož, Slovenia. European Language Resources Association (ELRA).

Nikola Ljubešić and Davor Lauc. 2021. BERTić - the transformer language model for Bosnian, Croatian, Montenegrin and Serbian. In *Proceedings of the 8th Workshop on Balto-Slavic Natural Language Processing*, pages 37–42, Kiyv, Ukraine. Association for Computational Linguistics.

Mustafa Melih Mutlu and Arzucan Özgür. 2022. A dataset and BERT-based models for targeted sentiment analysis on Turkish texts. In *Proceedings of the 60th Annual Meeting of the Association for Computational Linguistics: Student Research Workshop*, pages 467–472, Dublin, Ireland. Association for Computational Linguistics.

Bo Pang and Lillian Lee. 2008. Opinion mining and sentiment analysis. *Foundations and Trends in Information Retrieval*.

Jiaxin Pei, Aixin Sun, and Chenliang Li. 2019. Targeted sentiment analysis: A data-driven categorization. *arXiv preprint arXiv:1905.03423*.

Andraž Pelicon, Marko Pranjić, Dragana Miljković, Blaž Škrlj, and Senja Pollak. 2020. Zero-shot learning for cross-lingual news sentiment classification. *MDPI*.

Sashank J Reddi, Satyen Kale, and Sanjiv Kumar. 2019. On the convergence of Adam and beyond. *arXiv preprint arXiv:1904.09237*.

Alexander Rietzler, Sebastian Stabinger, Paul Opitz, and Stefan Engl. 2019. Adapt or get left behind: Domain adaptation through BERT language model finetuning for aspect-target sentiment classification. *arXiv preprint arXiv:1908.11860*.

Tomás Alves Salgueiro, Emilio Recart Zapata, Damián Furman, Juan Manuel Pérez, and Pablo Nicolás Fernández Larrosa. 2022. A Spanish dataset for targeted sentiment analysis of political headlines. *arXiv preprint arXiv:2208.13947*.

Joshua M Scacco and Ashley Muddiman. 2020. The curiosity effect: Information seeking in the contemporary news environment. *New Media & Society*, 22(3):429–448.

Holli A Semetko and Patti M Valkenburg. 2000. Framing European politics: A content analysis of press and television news. *Journal of communication*, 50(2):93–109.

Youwei Song, Jiahai Wang, Tao Jiang, Zhiyue Liu, and Yanghui Rao. 2019. Attentional encoder network for targeted sentiment classification. *arXiv preprint arXiv:1902.09314*.

Stuart Soroka, Lori Young, and Meital Balmas. 2015. Bad news or mad news? Sentiment scoring of negativity, fear, and anger in news content. *The ANNALS of the American Academy of Political and Social Science*, 659(1):108–121.

Swabha Swayamdipta, Roy Schwartz, Nicholas Lourie, Yizhong Wang, Hannaneh Hajishirzi, Noah A. Smith, and Yejin Choi. 2020. Dataset cartography: Mapping and diagnosing datasets with training dynamics. In *Proceedings of the 2020 Conference on Empirical Methods in Natural Language Processing (EMNLP)*, pages 9275–9293, Online. Association for Computational Linguistics.

James W Tankard Jr. 2001. The empirical approach to the study of media framing. In *Framing public life*, pages 111–121. Routledge.

Meishan Zhang, Yue Zhang, and Duy-Tin Vo. 2016. Gated neural networks for targeted sentiment analysis. *Guide Proceedings*.

Zhihan Zhang, Wenhao Yu, Mengxia Yu, Zhichun Guo, and Meng Jiang. 2022. A survey of multi-task learning in natural language processing: Regarding task relatedness and training methods. *arXiv preprint arXiv:2204.03508*.

A Appendix

A.1 Dataset

Dataset Sampling. News headlines were taken from a news article database obtained through TakeLab Retriever, a tool for analyzing Croatian online news media. We used a stratified sampling technique on news outlet and date published attributes. A total of 3000 news headlines were sampled from 29 diverse news outlets, covering the time period between January 2000 and August 2022.

Annotation Guidelines. Annotation guidelines were given to annotators in the Croatian language. The instructions included the definition of named entities, targeted sentiment and tone for news headlines as well as annotation labels. We provided multiple annotation examples grouped by observed headline patterns.

The general guideline for annotating tone was to consider the impression of the headline, whereas for sentiment, it was the intentional impression towards the target entity. Further guidelines included: (1) when a headline contains a combination of positive and negative attributes toward the target entity, the final impression should be considered; (2) when the target entity's action expressed in the headline can be considered intrinsically negative or positive, this is transferred to the sentiment; (3) when the target entity is a toponym, it is crucial to identify whether it strictly represents a location (which is inherently neutral) or a metonymy (which can represent any sentiment); (4) when the headline contains a quotation, two cases are possible. If the chosen target entity is the author of the quote, the sentiment is usually neutral since no additional information is present. Otherwise, the attitude expressed by the author towards the entity is transferred to the sentiment of the target.

A.2 Tone Classification Results

Single-task	AVG	NEG	NTR	POS
Vanilla	**.773**	**.881**	**.598**	.840
Multi-task	AVG	NEG	NTR	POS
Alternate Batch	.761	**.881**	.575	.827
Alternate Epoch	.768	.875	.581	**.847**
Average Batch	.748	.876	.532	.835

Table 4: Tone classification macro-averaged and per-class F1-scores for single- and multi-task setups. The best results by setup are in **bold**.

Table 4 shows single- and multi-task tone classification results. The vanilla single-task tone model used BERTić with a classification layer on top. Multi-task setups are equivalent to the ones reported for TSA in Table 2. Results were averaged over five independent runs, using the same seeds, hyperparameters, and training procedures as for the TSA experiments.

Is German secretly a Slavic language? What BERT probing can tell us about language groups

Aleksandra Mysiak and **Jacek Cyranka**
Faculty of Mathematics, Informatics, and Mechanics
University of Warsaw
an.mysiak@student.uw.edu.pl, jcyranka@gmail.com

Abstract

In the light of recent developments in NLP, the problem of understanding and interpreting large language models has gained a lot of urgency. Methods developed to study this area are subject to considerable scrutiny. In this work, we take a closer look at one such method, the structural probe introduced by Hewitt and Manning (2019). We run a series of experiments involving multiple languages, focusing principally on the group of Slavic languages. We show that probing results can be seen as a reflection of linguistic classification, and conclude that multilingual BERT learns facts about languages and their groups.

1 Introduction

Transformers (Vaswani et al., 2017) have revolutionised the area of natural language processing. State-of-the-art solutions for virtually all NLP problems – including machine translation, text summarization and generation – are nowadays transformer-based. In recent years models such as BERT (Devlin et al., 2019) and Generative Pre-trained Transformers (Radford et al., 2018) have shifted the public view of artificial intelligence. This is also true for Slavic languages – for example, the Polish language understanding benchmark KLEJ (Rybak et al., 2020) is dominated by models such as HerBERT (Mroczkowski et al., 2021) or Polish RoBERTa (Dadas et al., 2020).

This success has led to a significant interest in studying the interpretability of such models. Multiple probing techniques have been developed to assess the extent of linguistic knowledge learned in masked language modelling, especially by models based on BERT. Those methods typically feature a set of secondary tasks that are learned by a smaller model (the *probe*), using BERT's embeddings as inputs.

Using probing with multiple tasks, Tenney et al. (2019) and Jawahar et al. (2019) have found a surprisingly regular structure encoded in BERT's layers. Their results are supported by Hewitt and Manning (2019), where the authors use the task of dependency tree prediction in a method they call the *structural probe*. They use it to find evidence of syntax learning, especially exhibited by BERT's middle layers. Going a step further, authors of Chi et al. (2020) apply structural probing to a multilingual version of BERT (Devlin et al., 2019), and find a degree of universality in how the syntactic relations are encoded in a single embedding space for multiple languages.

On the other hand, the interpretability of probing results is the subject of much discussion. Although authors typically use a baseline to quantify what the probe actually learned, those results are still called into question. A parameter-free method of probing is introduced by Wu et al. (2020), although the results prove to be much more conservative.

The problem of whether probes extract knowledge from embeddings or learn new tasks is discussed in depth by Hewitt and Liang (2019), where they are shown to be able to learn randomly generated control tasks. In Niu et al. (2022), the authors find a strong argument against interpreting accuracy as a measure of information contained. They show that performance drops when more layers become accessible to the probe, which theoretically should provide it with more information.

In this work, we aim to investigate the usability of probing techniques – specifically the structural probe of Hewitt and Manning (2019) – by relating them to real-life ideas developed by theoretical linguists, such as the classification of languages into families and word order types. We take a closer look at the group of Slavic languages and the claim that they constitute a separate word order class, as proposed by Haider and Szucsich (2022).

Proceedings of the 9th Workshop on Slavic Natural Language Processing 2023 (SlavicNLP 2023), pages 86–93

1.1 Main Contributions

Inspired by Chi et al. (2020), we investigate probing in a multilingual context, focusing our attention on relations between syntax encoding for a group of Slavic languages. We show that probing results can be related to pre-existing linguistic knowledge, which suggests that, in spite of interpretability problems, this methodology can be used to discover quantitative relations between languages.

To highlight the role of mBERT pre-training in recovering grammatical relations differentiating between language families, we contrast our findings with the results of a randomised baseline. In Table 2, we show that an identical architecture with random parameters does not uncover similar patterns. This suggests that the pre-training task of masked language modeling constructs the embedding space in a way that allows meaningful investigation of relations between languages.

2 Methodology

Our methodology is based on the structural probing method introduced in Hewitt and Manning (2019) and applied to a multilingual setting in Chi et al. (2020).

In this method, the most important data form is the dependency tree, which is a formal way of representing a sentence's syntax. Each word in a sentence is represented by a node, with (directed and labeled) edges indicating syntactical relations between words they connect.

The authors' idea is to find the structure of dependency trees in BERT's embedding space. To recover the structure of a tree, they aim to find a metric in the embedding space that approximates the distance between words in dependency trees (expressed as the number of edges). They search for an appropriate geometry in the family of linear transformations of the embeddings. Our loss function (L) thus becomes

$$L(B) = \sum_{\ell} \frac{1}{\left|s^{\ell}\right|^2} \sum_{i,j} \left| d_{T^{\ell}}\left(w_i^{\ell}, w_j^{\ell}\right) - d_B\left(\mathbf{h}_i^{\ell}, \mathbf{h}_j^{\ell}\right) \right|$$

where

- $\{s^{\ell}\}$ is the set of training sentences,
- $\left|s^{\ell}\right|$ is the sentence length,
- w_i^{ℓ} is the i-th word of s^{ℓ},
- $d_{T^{\ell}}\left(w_i^{\ell}, w_j^{\ell}\right)$ is the number of edges between w_i^{ℓ} and w_j^{ℓ} in the sentence's dependency tree,
- $\mathbf{h}_i^{\ell}$ is the contextualized embedding of word w_i^{ℓ} in sentence s^{ℓ}, taken from a BERT layer with a fixed index,
- B is a real matrix of shape (probe rank, embedding dimension),
- d_B is the squared Euclidean distance between vectors transformed by B, that is

$$d_B\left(\mathbf{h}_i^{\ell}, \mathbf{h}_j^{\ell}\right) = \left\|B\mathbf{h}_i^{\ell} - B\mathbf{h}_j^{\ell}\right\|_2^2 .$$

We can thus see that the real probe here is the matrix B, which is found by minimizing the loss using gradient descent.

Evaluation We assess the probes based on their ability to predict the structures of unseen dependency trees. For that, we utilise two metrics defined in Hewitt and Manning (2019).

The first metric is Spearman's rank correlation coefficient between predicted and gold standard distances (originally named distance Spearman, or "DSpr."). The coefficient is designed to measure monotonicity of a relation between two variables. Here, it is calculated separately for each sentence, averaged across all sentences of a given length, and then over lengths between 5 and 50. The coefficient is expressed as

$$\rho(X,Y) = \frac{\mathrm{cov}(\mathrm{R}(X), \mathrm{R}(Y))}{\sigma_{\mathrm{R}(X)}\sigma_{\mathrm{R}(Y)}}$$

where R is a ranking function, cov is a standard covariance, and σ is standard deviation.

The second metric is the UUAS – undirected, unlabeled attachment score. It requires construction of predicted undirected trees, which is done in an iterative process, based on a ranking of predicted distances. In each step, two words for which the embeddings are predicted to be the closest are connected, unless that would violate the tree property (that is, only if a path between them does not yet exist). This procedure is conducted until a spanning tree of the sentence is constructed. It is then evaluated by calculating the percentage of correctly placed edges, which gives us a value from range $[0, 100]$.

To give a sense of scale here, in Hewitt and Manning (2019) a non-contextualised baseline reaches a score of 26.8, and a randomly contextualised one – 59.8, while the highest value reached on BERT is 82.5, indicating over 82% of correctly predicted edges.

We collected values of both UUAS and DSpr. Since we found that both metrics are highly correlated (Pearson's $r > 0.97$) and lead to identical qualitative conclusions, our reporting focuses on the UUAS, which is easily interpretable as a percentage of successses.

Datasets In our work, we selected two groups of languages: train and test languages, listed in Table 1. The test set is a subset of the group of Slavic languages, with some additional non-Slavic languages added in the train set. For each of the languages, we source our data – manually annotated dependency trees – from the Universal Dependencies project (Nivre et al., 2017).

Language	Size	Train	Test	Slavic
Belarusian	22852	✓	✓	✓
Chinese	3996	✓		
Croatian	6913	✓	✓	✓
Czech	68494	✓	✓	✓
English	12542	✓		
Finnish	12216	✓		
French	14448	✓		
German	13813	✓		
Indonesian	4481	✓		
Latvian	12520	✓		
Lithuanian	2340	✓		
Polish	17721	✓	✓	✓
Russian	69629	✓	✓	✓
Slovak	8482	✓	✓	✓
Slovene	10902	✓	✓	✓
Spanish	14286	✓		
Ukrainian	5495	✓	✓	✓

Table 1: All considered languages, with dataset sizes in number of sentences. Note that the set of test languages is a subset of the train set.

Experimental setup We conduct all experiments at layer 7 (out of 1 - 12) of mBERT base, with a fixed probe rank of 128. Since our goal is not to investigate the properties of mBERT itself, but the properties of probing methodology and relations between languages, we do not consider the whole set of hyperparameters used in Hewitt and Manning (2019). We choose hyperparameters that were found to be optimal in Chi et al. (2020).

To balance the differences in dataset sizes – see Table 1 – and investigate the impact of those differences, we introduce an additional hyperparameter of dataset size. We consider subsets of 100, 1k, 2.5k, 5k, 7.5k and 10k sentences (where available).

Baseline To differentiate between the impact of probe training and mBERT pre-training, we utilise the mBERTRand baseline as described in Chi et al. (2020). In this setup, we run experiments on an mBERT-like architecture with randomly initialized parameters and no pre-training. As such, this baseline should not carry any linguistic information, other than what is learned by the probe itself.

In our setup of the baseline, we only consider a single test language - Polish - since the results were deemed to prove satisfactorily that pretraining enhances linguistic knowlege – see Section 4. The list of train languages remains the same.

3 Experimental results

3.1 Dataset size study

In Figures 1 and 2, we present averaged UUAS scores for probes trained on several dataset sizes and languages, all tested on Polish. In both cases, we can see a saturation of the score for datasets of 10k sentences – the score curves flatten out.

We can also see that the ranking of languages stabilizes, with minor changes between size 7.5k and 10k. For both mBERT and the baseline, it becomes well established that the best train language for Polish is Polish – which is not the case for smaller sizes, especially for 1k sentences and less. In the case of Belarusian, the maximum considered size is necessary to separate it from non-Slavic languages.

Non-baseline results for other test languages were similar, so the plots were omitted here. All numerical results can be found in Table 2 and Appendix A.

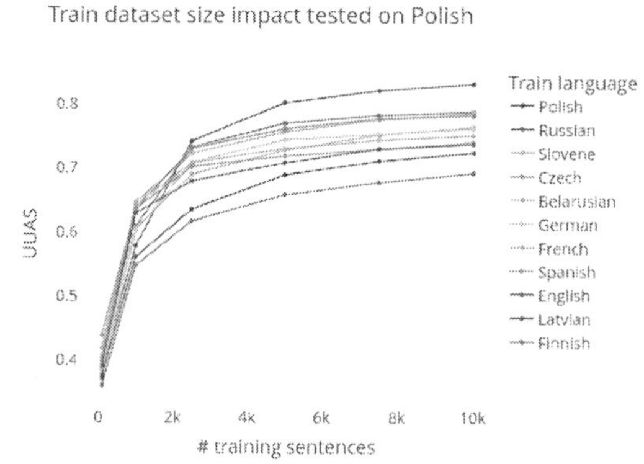

Figure 1: Plot of UUAS scores for probes trained on various languages and dataset sizes, tested on Polish, averaged across 3 independent runs. Higher values indicate better syntax recall.

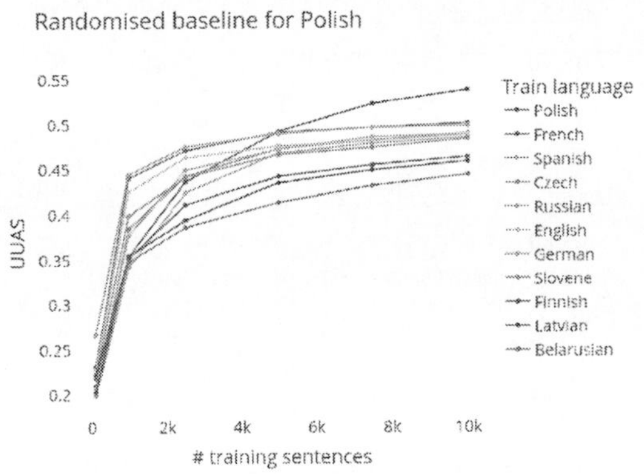

Figure 2: Plot of baseline UUAS scores for probes trained on various languages and dataset sizes, tested on Polish, averaged across 3 independent runs. Word embeddings here are randomly initialised, so the probe cannot access BERT's knowledge. Higher values indicate better syntax recall.

3.2 Relations between Slavic languages

Numerical results (averaged UUAS values) for training datasets of size 10k (the maximal considered) are shown in Table 2. The columns represent all test languages, with 2 additional columns for baseline results and an average across all test languages. The rows represent train languages, they are sorted by the Average column. Only the train languages with at least 10k sentences are shown. For additional languages with smaller sizes see Appendix A.

In non-baseline results, we can see a naturally emerging separation between Slavic and non-Slavic languages. There are significant (> 1 UUAS point in this context) score gaps in a couple of positions in the ranking: between Belarusian and other Slavic languages, between German and Belarusian, between German and other non-Slavic languages, and at the bottom of the ranking, between Finnish and other languages.

The baseline results are not statistically significantly correlated with non-baseline results tested on Polish, except for the visible dominance of Polish as the best train language. Excluding Polish from both rankings, we get $p = 0.38$, with $p = 0.04$ without the exclusion. We can see that the ranking here would be vastly different, with the top train languages being Polish, French, Spanish, and Czech. The bottom language is Belarusian, with a significantly worse result than any other language.

The experiments were executed using two RTX 2080 Ti GPU units (or equivalent). 2816 experiments were carried out in total, with an average experiment with 10k train sentences taking 16 minutes.

4 Discussion

The results for pre-trained mBERT described in the previous section and shown in Table 2 can be related to the following linguistic facts:

- For each test language, the set of top 5 train languages is exactly the same – it is the set of all Slavic languages present in train data for the given dataset size. The group of Slavic languages is recognised as inter-related.
- For each test language, the top-scoring non-Slavic train language is German. This can be related to a matter of discussion raised by Haider and Szucsich (2022) and referred to in Fuß (2022). Haider and Szucsich (2022) propose a new class of word order in languages, to which they postulate that all Slavic languages should belong. They also mention the fact that Germanic languages evolved from a grammar of the same type, which might explain the high scores of German as a predictor of Slavic languages' sentence structure.
- The Finnish language is the worst-scoring train language for all test languages. This can be related to the fact that it is the only language present in the train set that does not belong to the Indo-European family.

There is no such interpretation to be found for baseline results. As noted in the previous section, those results are not correlated with non-baseline results for Polish. In Figure 2 and Table 2, we can see Slavic languages mixed with non-Slavic languages, with no visible separation even for large dataset sizes. Except for the fact that Polish is the highest-scored train language, there is no clear relation between linguistic classification and the results of the baseline. We conclude that pre-training of mBERT plays a vital role in the ability of the probe to reproduce the well-known classification of Slavic languages.

Additionally, we can note that for main results, the scores achieved using the same train and test language differ between languages, ranging from 78.82 (Belarusian) to 83.19 (Polish). Although in

	Baseline	Slovene	Russian	Polish	Czech	Belarusian	Croatian	Slovak	Ukrainian	Average
					Slavic languages					
Slovene	48.39	81.43	76.16	78.52	**77.10**	75.19	**77.60**	82.26	77.08	**78.17**
Russian	48.95	75.35	81.32	**78.77**	76.75	**76.88**	76.08	80.54	**79.41**	78.14
Polish	53.87	75.64	**76.84**	83.19	77.07	75.91	75.03	81.20	77.74	77.83
Czech	48.96	**76.02**	76.37	78.20	80.47	74.96	75.90	**83.24**	77.45	77.83
Belarusian	44.44	72.88	75.54	76.38	73.94	78.82	73.36	77.97	76.99	75.73
					Non-Slavic languages					
German	48.56	**73.17**	**74.62**	**76.15**	**74.23**	**73.08**	**73.17**	**78.17**	**75.20**	**74.72**
English	48.86	70.34	73.08	73.75	71.42	70.40	72.03	75.79	73.36	72.52
French	50.14	70.20	72.22	75.07	71.10	70.93	71.84	74.57	73.01	72.37
Latvian	45.88	70.84	70.97	72.39	70.69	70.59	69.99	75.41	72.01	71.61
Spanish	49.86	69.64	71.12	73.99	70.20	69.70	70.57	72.55	71.66	71.18
Finnish	46.40	68.09	68.33	69.22	68.07	67.97	67.43	72.14	68.87	68.77

Table 2: Average UUAS scores for probes trained using 10k sentences. The test languages are in columns, and the train languages in rows. Higher values indicate better syntax recall and suggest syntactic similarity, with top results highlighted in each column. The results are averaged over three independent runs with different random seeds. Standard deviations of results are not reported, since values are below 1 UUAS point.

each case, the test language is also the best train language, the score values differ. This can be interpreted as a reflection of the fact that mBERT learns certain languages' representations more clearly, especially when coupled with results from Chi et al. (2020) and Alves et al. (2022). However, this could also be an artefact of dataset differences between languages – their quality, diversity and representativeness – which brings our attention back to the fact that interpretability remains an issue in probing.

5 Conclusions

Using Slavic languages as an example, we have shown that the method of structural probing can be used to achieve results that are clearly related to pre-existing linguistic knowledge. In spite of interpretability problems, we conclude that probing can be used to extract linguistic knowledge from transformer models. This can be used both to enhance our knowledge about language models, and about languages themselves. In this case, we show that mBERT implicitly learns facts about language groups during its simple pre-training tasks. We also conclude that the implication of Haider and Szucsich (2022) that German has a similar word order heritage as Slavic languages can be related to empirical data.

Limitations

The main limitation of this work is that it is concerned with a limited subset of languages. The only languages that have been investigated here are Slavic languages, and even then, some of them were omitted from experiments and results analysis – for example Slovak, Bulgarian or Ukrainian.

Another limitation explicitly stated in the work is the number of train sentences. In Subsection 3.1, we show that in order to draw meaningful conclusions, at least 5000 annotated sentences per language are needed. Coupled with the typical sizes of multilingual transfomer models, this leads to high computational and memory capacity being required to run experiments for multiple language groups.

References

Diego Alves, Marko Tadić, and Božo Bekavac. 2022. Multilingual comparative analysis of deep-learning dependency parsing results using parallel corpora. In *Proceedings of the BUCC Workshop within LREC 2022*, pages 33–42, Marseille, France. European Language Resources Association.

Ethan A. Chi, John Hewitt, and Christopher D. Manning. 2020. Finding universal grammatical relations in multilingual BERT. In *Proceedings of the 58th Annual Meeting of the Association for Computational Linguistics*, pages 5564–5577, Online. Association for Computational Linguistics.

Slawomir Dadas, Michal Perelkiewicz, and Rafal Poswiata. 2020. Pre-training polish transformer-based language models at scale. *CoRR*, abs/2006.04229.

Jacob Devlin, Ming-Wei Chang, Kenton Lee, and Kristina Toutanova. 2019. BERT: Pre-training of deep bidirectional transformers for language understanding. In *Proceedings of the 2019 Conference of the North American Chapter of the Association for Computational Linguistics: Human Language Technologies, Volume 1 (Long and Short Papers)*, pages 4171–4186, Minneapolis, Minnesota. Association for Computational Linguistics.

Eric Fuß. 2022. Early german = slavic? *Theoretical Linguistics*, 48(1-2):57–71.

Hubert Haider and Luka Szucsich. 2022. Slavic languages – "svo" languages without svo qualities? *Theoretical Linguistics*, 48(1-2):1–39.

John Hewitt and Percy Liang. 2019. Designing and interpreting probes with control tasks. In *Proceedings of the 2019 Conference on Empirical Methods in Natural Language Processing and the 9th International Joint Conference on Natural Language Processing (EMNLP-IJCNLP)*, pages 2733–2743, Hong Kong, China. Association for Computational Linguistics.

John Hewitt and Christopher D. Manning. 2019. A structural probe for finding syntax in word representations. In *Proceedings of the 2019 Conference of the North American Chapter of the Association for Computational Linguistics: Human Language Technologies, Volume 1 (Long and Short Papers)*, pages 4129–4138, Minneapolis, Minnesota. Association for Computational Linguistics.

Ganesh Jawahar, Benoît Sagot, and Djamé Seddah. 2019. What does BERT learn about the structure of language? In *Proceedings of the 57th Annual Meeting of the Association for Computational Linguistics*, pages 3651–3657, Florence, Italy. Association for Computational Linguistics.

Robert Mroczkowski, Piotr Rybak, Alina Wróblewska, and Ireneusz Gawlik. 2021. HerBERT: Efficiently pretrained transformer-based language model for Polish. In *Proceedings of the 8th Workshop on Balto-Slavic Natural Language Processing*, pages 1–10, Kiyv, Ukraine. Association for Computational Linguistics.

Jingcheng Niu, Wenjie Lu, and Gerald Penn. 2022. Does BERT rediscover a classical NLP pipeline? In *Proceedings of the 29th International Conference on Computational Linguistics*, pages 3143–3153, Gyeongju, Republic of Korea. International Committee on Computational Linguistics.

Joakim Nivre, Daniel Zeman, Filip Ginter, and Francis Tyers. 2017. Universal Dependencies. In *Proceedings of the 15th Conference of the European Chapter of the Association for Computational Linguistics: Tutorial Abstracts*, Valencia, Spain. Association for Computational Linguistics.

Alec Radford, Karthik Narasimhan, Tim Salimans, and Ilya Sutskever. 2018. Improving language understanding by generative pre-training.

Piotr Rybak, Robert Mroczkowski, Janusz Tracz, and Ireneusz Gawlik. 2020. KLEJ: comprehensive benchmark for polish language understanding. *CoRR*, abs/2005.00630.

Ian Tenney, Dipanjan Das, and Ellie Pavlick. 2019. BERT rediscovers the classical NLP pipeline. In *Proceedings of the 57th Annual Meeting of the Association for Computational Linguistics*, pages 4593–4601, Florence, Italy. Association for Computational Linguistics.

Ashish Vaswani, Noam Shazeer, Niki Parmar, Jakob Uszkoreit, Llion Jones, Aidan N Gomez, Ł ukasz Kaiser, and Illia Polosukhin. 2017. Attention is all you need. In *Advances in Neural Information Processing Systems*, volume 30. Curran Associates, Inc.

Zhiyong Wu, Yun Chen, Ben Kao, and Qun Liu. 2020. Perturbed masking: Parameter-free probing for analyzing and interpreting BERT. In *Proceedings of the 58th Annual Meeting of the Association for Computational Linguistics*, pages 4166–4176, Online. Association for Computational Linguistics.

A Results for all dataset sizes

This appendix shows result tables, similar to Table 2, for decreasing dataset sizes. The tables feature additional train languages (rows) for which 10k sentences were not available, sorted by UUAS scores averaged across all test languages.

The division into Slavic and non-Slavic sections has been dropped in cases where the two groups are not separated – we can see that this is true for all sizes below 7.5k. We can also see that scores in general decrease as the dataset size decreases, which is visible especially when comparing Table 7 with other tables.

As concluded in Subsection 3.1 and Section 4, smaller dataset sizes seem to provide less meaningful results. There is however a visible tendency in Tables 6 and 7 for a single train language to dominate the scores for all Slavic test languages – this might be a reflection of quality (e.g. diversity or representativeness of average sentence structure) of the randomly sampled train subsets.

The fact that Chinese is the bottom language in Tables 5 and 6 is also noticeable, and might suggest an impact of a different writing systems on results. Unfortunately, the sample sizes are not enough to draw any conclusions.

	Baseline	Slovene	Russian	Polish	Czech	Belarusian	Croatian	Slovak	Ukrainian	Average
				Slavic languages						
Russian	**48.61**	74.19	80.49	**78.27**	75.89	**76.37**	75.25	79.84	**78.55**	**77.36**
Slovene	47.42	80.08	75.06	77.54	**76.36**	74.07	**76.73**	81.01	76.20	77.13
Czech	48.24	**75.37**	75.47	77.72	79.69	74.06	74.87	**82.92**	76.64	77.09
Polish	52.30	74.39	**76.09**	82.11	75.97	75.30	74.33	79.90	76.76	76.86
Slovak	44.67	73.75	73.98	76.44	75.91	71.65	72.51	83.50	74.23	75.25
Belarusian	43.21	71.63	74.28	75.17	72.98	77.93	71.23	76.31	75.73	74.41
				Non-Slavic languages						
German	47.87	**72.62**	**74.01**	**75.32**	**73.70**	**72.92**	**72.36**	**77.41**	**74.62**	**74.12**
French	49.60	69.51	71.51	74.34	70.22	70.54	71.12	73.18	72.49	71.61
English	48.14	69.15	72.43	72.98	70.59	69.81	71.53	73.87	72.41	71.60
Latvian	44.93	69.17	69.95	71.11	69.31	68.80	67.53	74.04	70.02	69.99
Spanish	**49.64**	68.25	69.72	72.96	68.66	68.50	69.30	71.13	70.35	69.86
Finnish	45.49	66.51	66.83	67.77	66.55	67.14	66.05	69.92	67.52	67.29

Table 3: Average UUAS scores for probes trained using 7.5k sentences. The test languages are in columns, and the train languages in rows. Higher values indicate better syntax recally. The results are averaged over three independent runs with different random seeds. Standard deviations of results are not reported, since values are below 1 UUAS point.

	Baseline	Slovene	Russian	Polish	Czech	Belarusian	Croatian	Slovak	Ukrainian	Average
Croatian	47.29	**75.71**	73.64	75.84	**75.30**	73.12	78.84	79.02	75.81	**75.91**
Ukrainian	46.14	72.90	**76.22**	**77.23**	74.06	**75.65**	73.89	78.37	78.68	75.88
Czech	47.31	74.60	73.79	76.14	78.25	72.45	73.82	**81.48**	74.71	75.65
Russian	47.23	72.69	79.09	76.98	74.23	74.35	72.69	78.13	**76.93**	75.64
Slovene	46.64	78.97	73.19	75.66	74.42	72.21	**74.50**	79.09	74.40	75.30
Polish	49.20	71.87	73.59	80.17	73.03	72.35	71.31	78.13	74.08	74.32
Slovak	44.05	72.20	72.51	74.81	74.45	71.38	70.91	82.39	72.98	73.95
German	46.82	71.92	73.09	74.41	72.37	71.68	70.87	76.66	73.21	73.03
Belarusian	41.32	69.03	71.73	72.76	70.62	75.88	69.67	74.66	73.56	72.24
French	**49.12**	67.46	70.55	73.03	68.91	69.14	70.05	71.97	71.29	70.30
English	47.58	66.54	69.90	70.82	68.38	67.37	68.63	71.37	70.07	69.14
Spanish	48.96	67.57	69.04	71.88	68.14	67.54	68.45	70.81	69.48	69.11
Latvian	43.52	66.76	66.94	68.94	66.99	67.05	65.03	70.99	68.26	67.62
Finnish	44.25	64.52	65.04	65.84	63.78	64.44	63.69	67.95	65.22	65.06

Table 4: Average UUAS scores for probes trained using 5k sentences. The test languages are in columns, and the train languages in rows. Higher values indicate better syntax recally. The results are averaged over three independent runs with different random seeds. Standard deviations of results are not reported, since values are below 1 UUAS point.

	Baseline	Slovene	Russian	Polish	Czech	Belarusian	Croatian	Slovak	Ukrainian	Average
Slovene	44.17	75.27	70.12	72.23	**71.36**	69.30	**70.82**	75.73	70.80	**71.95**
Czech	44.26	**71.81**	69.14	73.01	74.40	70.47	70.24	**76.66**	69.79	71.94
Croatian	44.43	71.33	69.80	72.31	71.24	69.13	74.41	75.04	71.38	71.83
Russian	44.97	68.66	75.30	**73.22**	69.98	**71.30**	68.06	73.40	**73.02**	71.62
Ukrainian	43.18	68.37	**72.11**	72.80	69.55	71.23	68.51	73.57	73.40	71.19
Slovak	41.51	68.39	68.85	71.15	70.90	68.71	67.50	78.71	68.86	70.38
German	42.45	67.01	68.83	70.82	68.67	67.86	66.83	72.91	69.01	68.99
Polish	43.66	65.63	67.75	74.18	67.33	67.28	65.64	70.45	68.03	68.29
French	47.11	65.67	67.21	70.77	66.70	66.93	67.44	69.93	68.24	67.86
Belarusian	38.58	64.68	67.03	69.01	66.81	71.27	64.61	70.37	67.78	67.70
English	46.32	65.47	67.59	67.95	65.65	65.41	66.51	69.20	67.61	66.92
Spanish	**47.52**	64.25	66.79	70.20	65.51	65.33	65.17	68.63	67.26	66.64
Latvian	39.38	61.39	62.08	63.54	61.35	63.03	59.50	66.51	61.87	62.41
Indonesian	46.29	59.10	61.05	64.36	60.26	62.94	60.07	63.79	63.21	61.85
Finnish	41.09	60.94	60.31	61.70	59.68	60.08	59.41	64.04	60.49	60.83
Chinese	42.12	54.52	56.12	55.68	55.89	58.69	54.42	58.25	57.96	56.44

Table 5: Average UUAS scores for probes trained using 2.5k sentences. The test languages are in columns, and the train languages in rows. Higher values indicate better syntax recally. The results are averaged over three independent runs with different random seeds. Standard deviations of results are not reported, since values are below 1 UUAS point.

	Baseline	Slovene	Russian	Polish	Czech	Belarusian	Croatian	Slovak	Ukrainian	Average
Croatian	39.33	**64.04**	**63.10**	**65.33**	**63.81**	**63.89**	67.59	66.99	62.84	**64.70**
Slovene	39.90	66.04	62.39	64.69	63.48	63.52	**62.17**	**67.53**	**63.96**	64.22
Czech	38.46	59.71	60.39	63.56	64.71	61.49	60.12	66.76	62.84	62.45
Slovak	37.13	59.54	60.48	64.46	63.14	62.45	58.02	69.25	62.16	62.44
French	44.07	57.97	61.72	64.24	60.41	62.09	60.71	64.58	63.13	61.86
Ukrainian	36.96	59.42	61.24	63.38	59.82	63.01	57.96	63.81	64.16	61.60
Spanish	**44.47**	57.91	60.61	63.64	59.91	60.58	58.88	62.42	61.38	60.67
English	42.55	57.12	61.74	62.92	58.57	61.54	57.57	62.82	61.93	60.53
Belarusian	34.80	57.21	58.46	60.61	58.80	63.32	55.61	62.50	61.07	59.70
Russian	37.71	56.84	62.07	60.86	57.79	60.48	54.82	62.04	61.17	59.51
German	34.16	58.12	58.09	60.08	58.54	59.31	56.69	61.44	59.71	59.00
Indonesian	42.60	54.93	57.59	60.51	56.42	59.11	53.83	60.07	59.24	57.71
Lithuanian	36.82	53.85	54.51	57.00	54.05	57.00	52.85	59.97	55.96	55.65
Latvian	35.44	54.00	54.17	56.10	54.28	55.39	51.15	59.48	54.37	54.87
Finnish	35.24	52.42	53.47	54.76	52.48	54.64	50.86	55.99	53.49	53.51
Polish	35.38	49.85	52.59	57.84	50.06	55.03	49.22	54.27	52.77	52.70
Chinese	37.82	50.69	52.65	53.10	51.21	53.86	50.34	54.19	52.59	52.33

Table 6: Average UUAS scores for probes trained using 1k sentences. The test languages are in columns, and the train languages in rows. Higher values indicate better syntax recally. The results are averaged over three independent runs with different random seeds. Standard deviations of results are not reported, since values are below 1 UUAS point.

	Baseline	Slovene	Russian	Polish	Czech	Belarusian	Croatian	Slovak	Ukrainian	Average
Spanish	**26.62**	**37.49**	**42.61**	**43.93**	**41.23**	**43.83**	**37.26**	**44.33**	**42.11**	**41.60**
French	23.12	35.94	40.93	41.96	38.84	42.43	36.95	42.45	40.96	40.06
Slovene	22.10	34.23	38.29	40.61	38.13	41.03	35.81	42.88	38.19	38.65
Czech	20.20	35.26	38.26	39.94	36.60	41.19	35.41	41.89	38.61	38.39
Indonesian	22.66	33.74	37.95	39.79	37.05	41.07	34.60	41.10	38.48	37.97
Croatian	20.02	34.94	37.48	39.04	37.18	40.60	33.59	41.11	37.49	37.68
Ukrainian	22.31	34.03	37.02	39.45	36.91	40.34	33.73	40.79	36.83	37.39
Lithuanian	21.08	33.89	36.59	38.79	35.82	40.28	33.45	40.83	36.96	37.08
English	22.68	32.87	37.92	39.17	35.67	39.71	33.48	39.49	37.31	36.95
Polish	20.97	32.49	37.35	38.60	35.97	40.17	32.99	40.32	37.18	36.88
Chinese	23.30	33.48	36.68	37.88	36.17	40.11	33.99	40.41	35.90	36.83
Belarusian	21.82	33.30	36.12	37.92	36.15	40.24	32.26	39.63	36.19	36.48
German	19.89	32.68	36.73	38.22	35.49	39.57	33.07	39.49	36.41	36.46
Slovak	18.01	34.21	36.28	37.90	35.03	39.37	33.34	38.89	35.41	36.30
Latvian	22.21	33.59	35.78	37.58	35.60	39.35	32.48	39.79	35.86	36.25
Russian	20.71	32.35	35.06	37.24	35.60	38.33	32.33	39.55	35.58	35.76
Finnish	20.28	31.32	34.74	36.05	33.71	37.49	31.37	37.95	34.17	34.60

Table 7: Average UUAS scores for probes trained using 100 sentences. The test languages are in columns, and the train languages in rows. Higher values indicate better syntax recally. The results are averaged over three independent runs with different random seeds. Standard deviations of results are not reported, since values are below 1 UUAS point.

Resources and Few-shot Learners for In-context Learning in Slavic Languages

Michal Štefánik[◊] and **Marek Kaldčík**[◊] and **Piotr Gramacki**[♣] and **Petr Sojka**[◊]

[◊]Faculty of Informatics,
Masaryk University, Czechia

[♣]Department of Artificial Intelligence,
Wrocław University of Science and Technology, Poland

Abstract

Despite the rapid recent progress in creating accurate and compact in-context learners, most recent work focuses on in-context learning (ICL) for tasks in English. However, the ability to interact with users of languages outside English presents a great potential for broadening the applicability of language technologies to non-English speakers.

In this work, we collect the infrastructure necessary for training and evaluation of ICL in a selection of Slavic languages[1]: Czech, Polish, and Russian. We link a diverse set of datasets and cast these into a unified instructional format through a set of transformations and newly-crafted templates written purely in target languages. Using the newly-curated dataset, we evaluate a set of the most recent in-context learners and compare their results to the supervised baselines. Finally, we train, evaluate and publish a set of in-context learning models that we train on the collected resources and compare their performance to previous work.

We find that ICL models tuned on English are also able to learn some tasks from non-English contexts, but multilingual instruction fine-tuning consistently improves the ICL ability. We also find that the massive multitask training can be outperformed by single-task training in the target language, uncovering the potential for specializing in-context learners to the language(s) of their application.

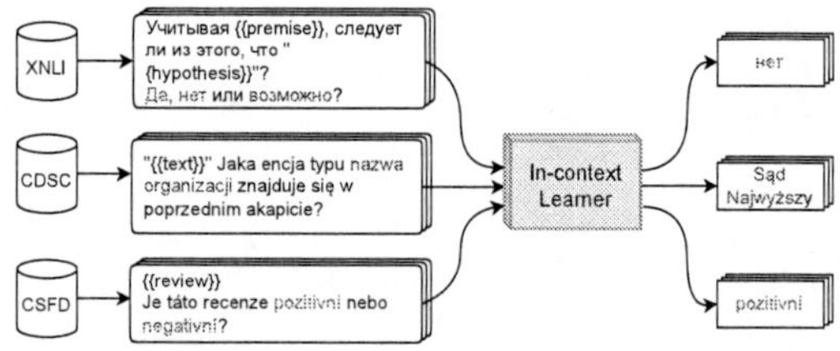

Figure 1: In this work, we transform Czech, Polish, and Russian datasets for diverse task types into a unified instructional format through a set of templates curated by the native speakers of target languages. The resulting collection enables an evaluation of existing in-context learners as well as the creation of new in-context learners interacting fully in the target language.

1 Introduction

The emergent ability of very large language models to understand unseen tasks from natural input text (Brown et al., 2020a), referred to as In-context Learning (ICL), recently motivated a large body of work focused specifically on creating more efficient models able to understand a new task from human instructions (Min et al., 2022; Sanh et al., 2022; Wei et al., 2022; Chung et al., 2022). The ICL models presented in these works reduce the number of parameters compared to the first in-context learners by orders of magnitude. In exchange, they assume that the generalization to new tasks emerges from a vast mixture of diverse training tasks seen in the training process.

The data volume and diversity requirements might also be the factor that substantially limits the application of current ICL models mainly to English. Acquiring a large and diverse set of tasks is relatively easy for English, which is in the spotlight of the NLP community. Unfortunately, there are fewer datasets in other languages, and the collection of new ones is costly. Previous work addresses this problem by automatic translation of some English datasets (Chandra et al., 2021), or by a cross-lingual training (Mishra et al., 2022) and evaluation (Conneau et al., 2018). However, such approaches do not resemble the use of instruction models by non-English speakers, expecting the models to interact *solely* in their native language.

This work evaluates the quality of in-context learning achievable in non-English languages to this date, specifically focusing on applicability in

[1]All our templates and models are available on `https://github.com/fewshot-goes-multilingual/slavic-incontext-learning`

Proceedings of the 9th Workshop on Slavic Natural Language Processing 2023 (SlavicNLP 2023), pages 94–105
May 6, 2023 ©2023 Association for Computational Linguistics

few-shot in-context learning for interaction in selected Slavic languages (Figure 1). Further, we assess the possibilities of further improvement under the assumption of limited data availability in the target language. We formulate these goals in two research questions:

RQ1: *How well can recent in-context few-shot learners* ***perform*** *in the interaction purely within our chosen, non-English languages?*

RQ2: *Can the improvements of in-context learning in a large-resource language* ***transfer*** *to lower resource, target languages?*

Given very limited previous work in in-context learning in our target languages, within our work, we first (i) survey and transfer a diverse set of datasets to instructional format through a set of transformations and newly-collected database of prompting templates with both the instructions and labels written in our target language(s). Our collected tasks include datasets for Named Entity Recognition, Sentiment Classification, Natural language Inference, and Question Answering in our target languages. After collecting the datasets of diverse tasks in the ICL-compatible format, we (ii) survey and evaluate in-context few-shot learners that can be applied to our target languages. Finally, we (iii) explore the possibility of further improving the in-context learners specific for our target languages along two axes: (a) by increasing models' exposure to target-language data and (b) by improving ICL ability in high-resource language, evaluating the cross-lingual transfer of such improvements.

This paper is structured as follows. Section 2 overviews the standard settings of in-context few-shot learning and surveys the previous work in this direction. Section 3 describes the evaluation datasets that we use and covers datasets' selection and unification process and templates database collection. Section 4 presents the settings used for training our in-context learners for Czech, Polish, and Russian. Finally, Section 5 presents the evaluation results, including existing and newly-trained in-context learners in the supervised baseline.

2 Background

In-context learners In-context learning from both human prompt and a set of input-output examples is initially observed as an emergent ability of GPT-3 (Brown et al., 2020b) trained on a vast collection of unlabelled texts for Causal language modeling (CLM) objective (Radford and Narasimhan, 2018). Subsequent work reproduces ICL ability and open-sources the resulting models, such as BLOOM (Scao et al., 2022) or OPT (Zhang et al., 2022). However, in-context learners trained in a solely unsupervised fashion are impractically large and hence, expensive for conventional use; In unsupervised settings, the ICL ability seems to emerge only when using far over 10 billion parameters (Brown et al., 2020b), thus requiring an extensive infrastructure to perform a single inference.

Computational overhead is addressed by a series of smaller models trained *specifically* for in-context learning. The smaller in-context learners are trained with a large mixture of tasks converted to a consistent sequence-to-sequence format via human-written *templates* (Bach et al., 2022) that define the input prompts for each task in the collection. A popular use of this framework includes prefixing the input sequence with natural-language *instructions*, such as the ones given to human annotators (Mishra et al., 2022). Large-scale instruction-based prompting in training over 1,600 tasks is also adopted in training TK-INSTRUCT (Wang et al., 2022) that we assess in our evaluations.

Recently, more attention has been dedicated to a selection of in-context training *tasks* under the assumption that some training tasks might be more beneficial for the emergence of in-context learning than others. In this direction, FLAN-T5 of Chung et al. (2022) further extends a database of tasks with the ones requiring multi-step reasoning in a *Chain-of-Thought* manner, where additionally to the correct prediction, the model is trained to predict a *sequence of steps* mapping the input to an output.

In-context Few-shot learning In-context learners are easily applicable in few-shot evaluation settings, where a small set of demonstrations for a given task exists. Given a dataset $\mathcal{D} : \{(x_1 \rightarrow Y_1), \dots, (x_i \rightarrow Y_i)\} \in \mathcal{D}$ containing pairs of *input* x_j with associated *label* Y_j, an *in-context few-shot learner* $\Theta(x) \rightarrow y$ aims to predict a correct $y_{k+1} \equiv Y_{k+1}$ given *input text* containing a sequence of k input-output *demonstrations*, and the predicted input x_{k+1} (Štefánik and Kadlčík, 2022; Gao et al., 2022):

$$\Theta([x_1 \rightarrow Y_1, \dots, x_k \rightarrow Y_k], x_{k+1}) \rightarrow y_{k+1} \quad (1)$$

	Name	Task	Size	Templates
cs	CNEC (Ševčíková et al., 2007)	NER	19k	3
	CSFD (this work)	Clf.	30k	3
	FBCom (Brychcín and Habernal, 2013)	Clf.	7k	3
	MALL (Brychcín and Habernal, 2013)	Clf.	30k	3
	SQAD (Medveď, 2022)	QA	8k	4
	CTKFacts (Ullrich et al., 2022)	NLI	5k	7
pl	PoliticAds (Augustyniak et al., 2020)	NER	1k	4
	KPWR (Broda et al., 2012)	NER	9k	4
	Polemo (Kocoń et al., 2019)	Clf.	8k	4
	CDSC (Wróblewska et al., 2017)	NLI	10k	4
ru	Polyglot (Al-Rfou et al., 2015)	NER	136k	3
	CEDR (Sboev et al., 2021)	Clf.	9k	3
	SberQuAD (Efimov et al., 2019)	QA	74k	4
	XNLI (Conneau et al., 2018)	NLI	399k	7

Table 1: Overview of datasets that we transform to a sequence-to-sequence format through manually-crafted templates in target languages.

Contrary to the standard supervised learning, in in-context learning, model Θ is *not* updated. Thus, it can rely solely on its ability to understand the task from input text.

Similarly to humans, the specific wording of input, i.e., *prompt* x_j, might play a large difference in the evaluation performance of the model. A prompt formulation optimal for one model type is likely not optimal for another (Lu et al., 2022). Therefore, in order to fairly compare different in-context learners, one should evaluate in-context learners on a larger set of diverse prompts (Bach et al., 2022). With this motivation, we also collect multiple prompts for each task, with a focus on their mutual diversity.

3 Datasets

The evaluation and training of new in-context learners for our target languages require (i) a collection of datasets for a representative range of tasks, and (ii) the transformation of these datasets into a unified, self-containing sequence-to-sequence form of inputs and outputs. Thus, one of our main contributions is the adaptation of the datasets for Czech, Polish, and Russian in a range of tasks: Named entity recognition, Sentiment classification, Natural language inference, and Question answering. The overview of the datasets for our target languages is shown in Table 1.

This section overviews the datasets in the target languages that we transformed, followed by a description of the process of constructing the templates for these datasets.

3.1 Data Collections in Target Languages

Contrary to English, labelled resources in our target languages for some tasks are relatively sparse, which conditions us to undertake some compromises in the diversity of the resources that we proceed with. The following text also covers the transformation that we had to perform with these datasets to cast them into a unified sequence-to-sequence format.

3.1.1 Czech Datasets

Contrary to Polish with a larger base of speakers, Czech datasets include all tasks that we aim to collect, including NER, Classification, QA, and NLI.

CNEC (Ševčíková et al., 2007) dataset for **NER** presents entities in the context of radio transcripts and news articles, featuring a relatively large collection of more than 10,000 original texts. We transform this dataset into sequence-to-sequence form by querying a specific type of entity, where we only use samples containing at most one occurrence of the requested entity to avoid ambiguity.

We note that all **classification** datasets that we find for evaluation are focused on a specific case of sentiment classification. Nevertheless, the volume, quality, and variance of sentiment classification datasets are relatively high; (i) **CSFD** presents a set of 30,000 public reviews from the movie critiques with diverse vocabulary and the challenging end task of predicting the corresponding star rating (0–5). The dataset is balanced, with each rating having a similar number of occurrences. To evaluate the models in a natural language, instead of predicting a specific numeric rating for each review, we transform the dataset labels to *positive/negative* classification, omitting samples with rating=3. (ii) **MALL** (Brychcín and Habernal, 2013) dataset is a semantically less complex collection of product reviews of online store products, and (iii) **FBCom** (Brychcín and Habernal, 2013) features a collection of scraped but verified Facebook comments presenting a sample of informal language. The latter two datasets come with three-class targets (positive/neutral/negative).

The only available Czech **QA** dataset, **SQAD** (Medveď, 2022), also builds a dataset on Wikipedia, containing the original articles in a full length, associated with manually-crafted questions and associated answer texts. To avoid the overhead of models' inference with full Wikipedia articles in a few-shot format, we synthesize the contexts containing answers by sequencing paragraphs containing the first answer occurrence. Thus, our curated context paragraphs resemble the format of the commonly-known English SQuAD dataset (Rajpurkar et al., 2016). We note that the original version of the dataset contains a strong statistical bias, with around half of the questions having the answer at the beginning of the article. To avoid exploiting this bias in evaluation, we randomly removed 90% of the questions whose answer starts in the first 50 characters.

Finally, **CTKFacts** (Ullrich et al., 2022) introduces a collection of **NLI** examples containing premises extracted from Wikipedia, with manually-crafted hypotheses to assess given the premises, in standard NLI settings.

3.1.2 Polish

The Polish datasets for our desired tasks are smaller than Czech, and contrary to Czech, to the date of writing, we find no publicly-available Polish QA dataset. However, we find two Polish **NER** datasets. **PoliticAds** (Augustyniak et al., 2020) presents input texts in a relatively unconventional domain of political advertising. A lot of entities are largely context-dependent, thus presenting adaptation challenges for general-domain models. Therefore, we complement this quite small and specific dataset with the **KPWR** (Broda et al., 2012) dataset. However, original KPWR has a very fine granularity of entities; thus, we transform the target entities to a second-level type (i.e. mapping entity *name-location-city* simply to *location*). After disambiguation analogical to CNEC, we obtain a sequence-to-sequence dataset with 9,000 inputs.

Consistently to Czech, we enrich the set with **Polemo** dataset (Kocoń et al., 2019) for sentiment **classification**, which contains a human-annotated set of consumer reviews from the domains of *medicine*, *hotels*, *products*, and *university*. Finally, we find **CDSC** dataset for **NLI** (Wróblewska et al., 2017), featuring a collection of premise-hypothesis pairs from a wide range of 46 thematic groups.

3.1.3 Russian

Being the language with a much larger speaker base, Russian is also the richest in resources. Thus, we pick the datasets for our tasks of interest that we assess as having the highest quality. **Polyglot** (Al-Rfou et al., 2015) is a large **NER** dataset curated from references to Wikipedia sites. We transform the datasets to per-entity-type prompt format, creating multiple prompts from each sample, resulting in more than 100 k input-output entity pairs. Consistently with other languages, we further include in the collection a **CEDR** dataset for sentiment **classification** originating in social media (Sboev et al., 2021). While its domain is not representative of many use cases, we assess the quality of annotations as superior to its alternatives and the number of labels (5) as practical for few-shot evaluation with reasonably long contexts.

SberQuAD (Efimov et al., 2019) is an extractive **QA** dataset comparable with English SQuAD in both the size and domain; Its 74,000 question-context-answer tuples are manually collected with the contexts originating in Wikipedia. Contrary to SQuAD, a small portion of questions has several different answers in the context, making the correct prediction ambiguous in some cases; We omit these cases in evaluations. Finally, we choose an **XNLI** dataset (Conneau et al., 2018) for evaluating **NLI** in Russian for its heterogeneity and size. However, other quality alternatives exist (see, e.g. Shavrina et al. (2020)), and our templates can be used with any other Russian NLI dataset as well.

3.2 Templates

For each of the referenced datasets, we write a new template mapping the samples of the dataset into a sequence-to-sequence format. To reinforce templates' heterogeneity, we start by reviewing existing templates of the analogical tasks in English, collected within BigScience's P3 project (Sanh et al., 2022). From existing templates, we pick a set of mutually most-distinct templates for each task and proceed to the writing phase. The resulting number of templates for each dataset was chosen subjectively to maintain a high level of heterogeneity among the templates of each dataset.

Inspired by the existing templates, we ask our target-language volunteer native speakers to write the templates in a form that they find "the most natural to ask for the solution for a given task from a human with a native understanding of their target language". We make sure that all the templates contain the exact-matching form of the expected response (i.e., *label*) so that the domain of possible answers is clearly enclosed by the prompt. The examples of some curated templates can be found in Table 2. A full list of the collected templates can be found in Appendix A.

Lang	Task	Template
cs	NER	{{text}} Jaká entita typu {{label_type}} se nachází v předchozím odstavci?
cs	Clf.	{{comment}} Je tato recenze {{"pozitivní, neutrální nebo negativní"}}?
cs	QA	{{context}} Q: {{question}} S odkazem na sekci výše je správná odpověď na danou otázku
cs	NLI	Za předpokladu, že {{evidence}} vyplývá, že {{claim}}? Ano, ne, nebo možná?
pl	clf.	"{{text}}" Ten tekst jest pozytywny, negatywny, neutralny czy dwuznaczny?
pl	NLI	Oceń czy poniższe zdania są zgodne ze sobą - tak, nie czy nie wiadomo? Zdanie A: {{premise}} Zdanie B: {{hypothesis}} Zgodność:
pl	NER	Jaka encja typu {{label_type_selected}} znajduje się w następującym tekście? "{{text}}"
ru	NER	{{text}} Какой объект типа {{label_type}} находится в предыдущем абзаце?
ru	NLI	Примите за истину следующее: {{premise}} Тогда следующее утверждение: "{{hypothesis}}" есть "правда", "ложь" или "неубедительно"?
ru	QA	Посмотрите на абзац ниже и ответьте на следующий вопрос: Абзац: {{context}} Вопрос: {{question}}
ru	Clf.	{{text}} Каково настроение этого обзора? радость, печаль, удивление, страх или гнев?

Table 2: Examples of instruction templates for each of the language + task pair that we collect in this work. A full list of templates collected in this work by our native speakers can be found in Appendix A Table 6.

We do not identify any instructional templates for the Named Entity Recognition task in the previous work. This is likely due to the complexity of fair evaluation of prediction containing a *sequence* of prediction, necessary for collecting *all* predictions for the prompted entity type; an evaluation of sequences is difficult by using the commonly-used generative measures. After consideration, we decided to reformulate the NER tasks in the form of information extraction, where we filter out samples where prompted entity type occurs more than once. This makes the task easier, but on the other hand, the evaluation is not biased by the models' ability to order predictions correctly. Based on that, we assume that such evaluation corresponds better to in-context learners' ability to identify entities.

4 Experiments

Making in-context learning in our target languages finally possible through the transformations described in the previous section, our first objective is to assess the current state-of-the-art of the recent in-context few-shot learners when used in the interaction *exclusively* in the target language (**RQ1**). We follow by outlining the perspectives in further enhancing the quality of target-language in-context few-shot learners by assessing the potential of cross-lingual transfer (**RQ2**).

4.1 In-context Few-shot Learning Evaluation

The overview of previous work on in-context learning covered in Section 2 shows a shifting interest from the over-parametrization to the scaling of diverse training tasks (Wang et al., 2022) and more explicit reasoning schemes, such as a Chain-of-Thought (Chung et al., 2022), where in addition to the final result, the model learns to predict the reasoning path that has led to the prediction. Our evaluation aims to assess how these aspects impact the quality of in-context few-shot learning in our target languages.

Multilingual fine-tuning To this date, we identify only one in-context learners' family that claims to support all our target languages: MTK-INSTRUCT (Wang et al., 2022). While its English counterpart (TK-INSTRUCT) fine-tunes T5 models (Raffel et al., 2020) on 1,616 tasks with English prompts, inputs, and targets, MTK-INSTRUCT is additionally fine-tuned on 576 tasks with inputs in 55 diverse languages, including Czech, Polish and Russian. Still, the instructional templates for these languages were written in English due to easier quality assurance. Thus, it remains an open question whether such-acquired in-context learning skills transfer to an interaction *solely* in the target language.

Hence, we assess the benefit of multilingual training by measuring and comparing the performance of English-only TK-INSTRUCT and multilingual TK-INSTRUCT of the same size (3 B parameters).

Fine-tuning strategy We evaluate the impact of a set of objectives of FLAN-T5 (Chung et al., 2022) complementary to a sole scaling of tasks of TK-INSTRUCT. Notably, these include (i) additional fine-tuning for a zero-shot setting, i.e. without presenting the model with demonstrations, (ii) fine-tuning for generating Chain-of-Thought, i.e. a sequence of steps leading the model to the answer, that is purposed to enhance the model's reasoning ability.

The evaluations of the impact of a fine-tuning strategy are also complemented by the assessment of our newly-trained in-context learners, trained on a single task type (QA), including the data in a target language; We detail our approach to train these models in Section 4.2.

Model size Finally, we evaluate both TK-INSTRUCT and FLAN-T5 in two different sizes: in a 700-million and in a four-times bigger, 3-billion-parameters variant. While it is perhaps not a surprising finding that the larger model would also perform better in the unseen language, the experiments in this axis assess the scale of improvement that can be expected by increasing computational costs for larger models, as compared to other adjustments.

4.2 Cross-lingual Transfer

In addition to the evaluation of existing in-context learners, we are interested in assessing how much the ICL in lower-resource languages can benefit from the improvements in a large-resource language (**RQ2**). This is particularly relevant given the fast pace of progress in general in-context learning focused primarily on English, naturally raising a question on how applicable these results are in languages for which data resources are sparser.

However, having no control over the specific data and training configuration of the existing models, we assess the scale of cross-lingual transfer by fine-tuning our own in-context learners that differ in the configuration in a large-resource language (English) while fixing the configuration in the target language. By also considering the choices of the previous work (Sanh et al., 2022), we pick the Question Answering as the one that we assume is crucial for obtaining in-context learning ability while also being available in our target languages.

Therefore, in our experiments, we *permute* only the English QA dataset and mix it in training with the QA dataset of the target language. We train in-context learners with three different configurations; (i) using *no* English QA dataset, (ii) using the standard SQuAD (Rajpurkar et al., 2016) containing more than 90,000 question-context-answer tuples, and (iii) using a lesser-known AdversarialQA (AQA) dataset (Bartolo et al., 2021) containing 30,000 more complex questions that *exploit* the flaws of QA models trained on SQuAD, making its samples complementary to SQuAD. Finally, we measure the impact of this change in Czech and Russian, for which the target-language QA datasets are available.

All our newly-trained in-context learners (further referred to as mTK-QA$_{SQuAD}$ and mTK-QA$_{AQA}$) are based on mT5 model (Xue et al., 2021) of 1.3-billion parameter size. We make our newly-trained in-context learners for both Czech[2] and Russian[3] publicly available for any use.

5 Results

Consistently with the previous work (Sanh et al., 2022; Wang et al., 2022), we jointly report the ROUGE-L score (Lin, 2004) over all the evaluation datasets (which we transform and create templates for (§3)) and all the evaluated in-context learners (§4.1), including the newly-trained ones introduced in this work (§4.2). To ease the readability, we split the reports by language, to the results on Czech datasets in Table 3, Russian datasets in Table 5, and Polish datasets in Table 4.

As a reference of the resulting ICL performance, for each dataset, we also train a **baseline model** that is also based on mT5 model (Xue et al., 2021), fine-tuned on the training split of the dataset transformed to a sequence-to-sequence format through a mixture of *all* the templates that we curated. Details on the training and evaluation configuration that we use can be found in Appendix B.

Multilingual training helps in most cases A comparison of mTK-INSTRUCT to TK-INSTRUCT of the same size through all languages (Tables 3, 5, 4) evaluates the significance of including the training data from the target language(s). Note that mT5, a base model for mTk-instruct, was pre-trained on mC4 balanced over languages, but mTk-instruct was finetuned on only 15 Polish, 5 Russian, and 2 Czech datasets making it about 1% of all data. Additionally, the training prompts for these datasets were English.

Still, we see that mTK-INSTRUCT is better than its English-finetuned counterpart in all evaluation datasets, except two Czech sentiment classification tasks. However, in some cases, the differences are relatively small; For instance, in the case of Polish CDSC, where English Tk-Instruct ends only 2.8 points behind the multilingual counterpart. The

[2] https://huggingface.co/fewshot-goes-multilingual/mTk-SQuAD_en-SQAD_cs-1B

[3] https://huggingface.co/fewshot-goes-multilingual/mTk-AdversarialQA_en-SberQuAD_ru-1B

Model \ Dataset + task	CNEC NER	CSFD Clf.	FBCom Clf.	MALL Clf.	SQAD QA	CTKFacts NLI
Supervised (mT5-1B)	67.9± 9.1	82.4±4.5	49.3±10.3	42.8±10.8	88.3±5.3	56.1±10.9
TK-Instruct (700M)	15.3± 6.7	14.1±7.1	25.2± 7.2	25.5± 8.4	5.6±4.8	**54.7**±8.2
TK-Instruct (3B)	32.8± 9.1	20.9±8.1	23.0± 7.4	25.1± 6.9	34.0±9.0	47.8±9.8
T5-FLAN (700M)	41.1±10.0	0.0± 0.0	0.0± 0.0	0.0± 0.0	46.5±8.4	30.3±9.3
T5-FLAN (3B)	49.6±10.4	0.0± 0.0	0.0± 0.0	0.1± 0.1	51.6±9.1	34.7±10.7
mTK-Instruct (3B)	62.5± 8.9	**90.2**±4.2	10.8±6.2	9.9±7.0	67.9±8.6	44.0±10.1
mTK-QA$_{none}$(1B)	72.0± 9.0	45.9±9.1	29.2±8.2	32.1±8.9	85.0±7.0*	35.4±10.5
mTK-QA$_{SQUAD}$(1B)	72.3± 9.1	72.9±6.6	**32.1**±9.0	**34.7**±9.2	**87.8**±5.3*	46.9±10.1
mTK-QA$_{AQA}$(1B)	**77.0**± 7.8	59.8±8.8	27.6±8.6	29.8±9.9	87.1±6.6*	42.7±10.7

Table 3: **In-context learners' performance in Czech:** ROUGE-L scores of selected in-context learners in Czech interaction using the listed datasets, for the best-performing template of each model. In-context learners were shown **three** demonstrations of each task. Included confidence intervals ($\alpha = 0.05$) are computed using bootstrapped evaluation (sample groups $n = 100$, repeats $r = 200$). Results marked with * denote cases where the held-out set of the listed dataset was used in training.

Model \ Dataset + task	PoliticAds NER	KPWR NER	Polemo Clf.	CDSC NLI
Supervised (mT5-1B)	5.9±5.1	63.3±10.3	51.9±9.9	75.5±8.5
TK-Instruct (700M)	5.6±4.3	8.6±5.4	28.3±8.6	52.3±8.2
TK-Instruct (3B)	17.6±8.1	54.6±11.2	19.5±8.4	67.8±8.8
T5-FLAN (700M)	6.8±5.5	33.8±9.8	24.3±8.6	10.0±6.4
T5-FLAN (3B)	18.4±7.3	60.5±7.8	**43.0**±9.0	**71.5**±9.0
mTK-Instruct (3B)	**32.1**±9.6	**67.6**±8.4	25.4±8.6	70.6±8.2

Table 4: **In-context learners' performance in Polish:** ROUGE-L scores of selected in-context learners in Polish interaction using the listed datasets. Configuration of evaluation is identical to Table 3.

Model \ Dataset + task	Polyglot NER	CEDR Clf.	SberQAD QA	XNLI NLI
Supervised (mT5-1B)	54.3±10.8	48.6±9.6	86.4±6.5	51.5±11.5
TK-Instruct (700M)	0.1±0.5	12.2±6.8	0.6±1.1	12.9± 6.9
TK-Instruct (3B)	3.6±3.9	17.7±8.3	8.1±4.1	22.2± 8.2
T5-FLAN (700M)	1.0±1.6	15.1±6.1	11.4±4.8	13.8± 6.2
T5-FLAN (3B)	2.0±2.5	24.4±7.4	19.6±5.6	26.0± 9.0
mTK-Instruct (3B)	57.6±11.2	**33.0**±9.9	73.7±6.7	**35.3**±10.3
mTK-QA$_{none}$(1B)	53.3±8.4	17.9±8.1	**89.1**±5.2*	19.6± 7.5
mTK-QA$_{SQUAD}$(1B)	50.3±9.3	7.5±4.5	84.6±6.0*	23.8± 8.8
mTK-QA$_{AQA}$(1B)	**66.3**±10.9	27.0±9.9	86.0±5.6*	32.3± 8.3

Table 5: **In-context learners' performance in Russian:** ROUGE-L scores of selected in-context learners in Russian interaction using the listed datasets. Configuration of evaluation is identical to Table 3.

error analysis of mTk-Instruct on two flawing classification tasks (FBCom and MALL) has shown that despite purely Czech prompts, the model generates English responses. This could be explained by a semantic similarity of our tasks to some of the model's fine-tuning datasets, but in our evaluation, we consider the divergence from the prompted language of interaction a valid failure.

Inconsistent benefits of CoT training Comparing the performance of T5-FLAN models with Tk-instruct models of the corresponding size, we find that T5-FLAN is superior in 17 out of 28 cases. However, the differences are often relatively small, and the performance of both in-context learners in these cases remains below the usable level nevertheless. Therefore, while it seems that fine-tuning to a Chain-of-Thought reasoning allows the modeling of features that are applicable also in some multilingual settings, these do not generalize over all in-context learning scenarios. Notably, T5-FLAN perhaps surprisingly fails on classification in Czech, where it shows an inability to understand the task even from the given demonstrations. On the other hand, we note that in two of four evaluation cases in Polish, the larger T5-FLAN performs superiorly to even multilingual mTk-Instruct of the same size.

Model size matters The comparisons of T5-FLAN and Tk-Instruct in their two size variants show the superiority of the larger model with the exceptions in 3 out of 28 cases, suggesting that model size can be an even more important condition of accurate in-context learning ability than utilization of target-language data in training.

It is also worth noticing that the difference in performance between two *sizes* of T5-FLAN are often very large; For instance, note the difference between Polish CDSC or Russian NLI. This suggests that the different sizes of T5-FLAN might, in fact, be very distinct in their representations.

Cross-lingual transfer A comparison of mTK-QA models that we train with and without the high-resource QA dataset (§4.2) outlines the potential for improvement of ICL in lower-resource languages with adjustments in the high-resource language. We see that including a complementary QA dataset in other-than-evaluated language can help in in-context learning of *all* new tasks, with improvements over 60% in Czech CSFD, or Russian XNLI.

Additionally, using a higher-quality AdversarialQA can also significantly, though not consistently, improve ICL ability for some tasks. For instance, note the difference of 12.9 points in sentiment classification of the Czech CSFD dataset or of 16 in Russian NER. This relatively large sensitivity to the data configuration in a high-resource language, from which we aim to transfer the ICL ability, suggests that recent and future improvements in models' ICL measured in English might also be directly applicable to other languages.

In-context learners trained on a single task are comparable to multi-task learners While outperforming the in-context learners trained on a much larger scale of tasks was not our initial objective, we note that at least one of our in-context learners trained using a single (QA) task *out-performs* mTk-Instruct in 6 out of 10 Czech and Russian evaluations. In *all* other cases, a QA model performs within the confidence interval of mTk-Instruct. Additionally, in 4 out of 10 cases, at least one of our QA models performs comparably or better than the supervised baseline. Hence, rather than a weak performance of mTk-Instruct, this result underlines the efficiency of Question answering as a proxy task for generalizing to the unseen tasks. We also find this result encouraging for creating in-context learners specialized to other target languages, with a perspective to outperform generic state-of-the-art learners in a similar methodology.

6 Conclusion

This paper documents our work in creating the evaluation benchmark for in-context learning for Czech, Polish, and Russian. We transform selected datasets into a compatible format, and with the aid of volunteer native speakers, we create templates for these datasets exclusively in the evaluated language. However, our templates can be applied to any other dataset of the supported types (NER, Classification, QA, and NLI).

In the interaction that is purely in the language(s) of our interest, we evaluate a set of recent in-context learners that we consider state-of-the-art in this area. We find that even in-context learners trained dominantly on English data might perform considerably well and even outperform a fully supervised baseline in some cases. However, on average, massive multilingual pre-training and instruction-based fine-tuning still largely improve the ICL ability.

Finally, we train a set of in-context learners specifically for our target languages by mixing the large QA datasets in English with smaller QA datasets in our target languages; In both Czech and Russian, such-created learners perform better or comparably to mTk-Instruct trained on a vastly larger collection of over 2,000 tasks from 55 languages. We believe that this finding will motivate future work in creating specialized but more accurate in-context learners also for other languages outside English.

We publicly release all data transformations, templates, and the newly-created in-context learners for any use.

Limitations

Templates While the templates that we curate with the help of native speakers were picked to maximize their mutual diversity, we acknowledge that the volumes of templates that we create for some datasets do not cover the full variance of possible prompts of our tasks. Therefore, our templates might not be optimal for our evaluated in-context learners.

Models In-context learners fine-tuned specifically for in-context instruction learning, including our introduced ones, are orders of magnitude smaller than the original language models acquired from sole pre-training like 175-billion-parameter GPT-3 (Brown et al., 2020b), but still remain compute-demanding for widespread deployment; We notice the inference time of a single sample for our 1B models to range between 3 and 10 seconds on a four-core CPU typical for middle-level personal computers to this date.

Analogically, also the application of our methodology (§4.2) to other languages with similar size of the base model (1.3 B) constrains the users to use dedicated GPU hardware with a minimum of

30 GB memory. We train our assessed in-context learners using Nvidia A100 GPUs with 80 GB VRAM, where the convergence of a single mT5-based model takes approximately 40 hours of computing.

Acknowledgements

We acknowledge the Centre for Biomedical Image Analysis at Masaryk University supported by MEYS CR (LM2018129 and CZ.02.1.01/0.0/0.0/18_046/0016045 Czech-BioImaging) for their support in obtaining the results presented in this paper.

We are also grateful for the support of Kirill Semenov from Charles University, Prague, for willingly creating and proofreading newly-collected Russian templates as a native speaker.

References

Rami Al-Rfou, Vivek Kulkarni, Bryan Perozzi, and Steven Skiena. 2015. Polyglot-NER: Massive multilingual named entity recognition. *Proc. of the 2015 SIAM International Conference on Data Mining, Vancouver, British Columbia, Canada.*

Lukasz Augustyniak, Krzysztof Rajda, Tomasz Kajdanowicz, and Michał Bernaczyk. 2020. Political Advertising Dataset: the use case of the Polish 2020 Presidential Elections. In *Proceedings of the The Fourth Widening Natural Language Processing Workshop*, pages 110–114, Seattle, USA. ACL.

Stephen H. Bach, Victor Sanh, Zheng-Xin Yong, Albert Webson, Colin Raffel, Nihal V. Nayak, Abheesht Sharma, Taewoon Kim, M Saiful Bari, Thibault Fevry, Zaid Alyafeai, Manan Dey, Andrea Santilli, Zhiqing Sun, Srulik Ben-David, Canwen Xu, Gunjan Chhablani, Han Wang, Jason Alan Fries, Maged S. Al-shaibani, Shanya Sharma, Urmish Thakker, Khalid Almubarak, Xiangru Tang, Xiangru Tang, Mike Tian-Jian Jiang, and Alexander M. Rush. 2022. Promptsource: An integrated development environment and repository for natural language prompts.

Max Bartolo, Tristan Thrush, Robin Jia, Sebastian Riedel, Pontus Stenetorp, and Douwe Kiela. 2021. Improving question answering model robustness with synthetic adversarial data generation. In *Proceedings of the 2021 Conference on Empirical Methods in Natural Language Processing*, pages 8830–8848, Online and Punta Cana, Dominican Republic. Association for Computational Linguistics.

Bartosz Broda, Michał Marcińczuk, Marek Maziarz, Adam Radziszewski, and Adam Wardyński. 2012. KPWr: Towards a free corpus of Polish. In *Proc. of the Eighth International Conference on Language Resources and Evaluation (LREC'12)*, pages 3218–3222, Istanbul, Turkey. European Language Resources Association (ELRA).

Tom Brown, Benjamin Mann, Nick Ryder, Melanie Subbiah, Jared D Kaplan, Prafulla Dhariwal, Arvind Neelakantan, Pranav Shyam, Girish Sastry, Amanda Askell, Sandhini Agarwal, Ariel Herbert-Voss, Gretchen Krueger, Tom Henighan, Rewon Child, Aditya Ramesh, Daniel Ziegler, Jeffrey Wu, Clemens Winter, Chris Hesse, Mark Chen, Eric Sigler, Mateusz Litwin, Scott Gray, Benjamin Chess, Jack Clark, Christopher Berner, Sam McCandlish, Alec Radford, Ilya Sutskever, and Dario Amodei. 2020a. Language Models are Few-Shot Learners. In *Advances in NIPS*, volume 33, pages 1877–1901. Curran Associates, Inc.

Tom Brown, Benjamin Mann, Nick Ryder, Melanie Subbiah, Jared D Kaplan, Prafulla Dhariwal, Arvind Neelakantan, Pranav Shyam, Girish Sastry, Amanda Askell, Sandhini Agarwal, Ariel Herbert-Voss, Gretchen Krueger, Tom Henighan, Rewon Child, Aditya Ramesh, Daniel Ziegler, Jeffrey Wu, Clemens Winter, Chris Hesse, Mark Chen, Eric Sigler, Mateusz Litwin, Scott Gray, Benjamin Chess, Jack Clark, Christopher Berner, Sam McCandlish, Alec Radford, Ilya Sutskever, and Dario Amodei. 2020b. Language models are few-shot learners. In *Advances in Neural Information Processing Systems*, volume 33, pages 1877–1901. Curran Associates, Inc.

Tomáš Brychcín and Ivan Habernal. 2013. Unsupervised Improving of Sentiment Analysis Using Global Target Context. In *Proceedings of the International Conference Recent Advances in Natural Language Processing RANLP 2013*, pages 122–128, Hissar, Bulgaria. INCOMA Ltd. Shoumen, BULGARIA.

Andreas Chandra, Affandy Fahrizain, Ibrahim, and Simon Willyanto Laufried. 2021. A Survey on non-English Question Answering Dataset.

Hyung Won Chung, Le Hou, Shayne Longpre, Barret Zoph, Yi Tay, William Fedus, Yunxuan Li, Xuezhi Wang, Mostafa Dehghani, Siddhartha Brahma, Albert Webson, Shixiang Shane Gu, Zhuyun Dai, Mirac Suzgun, Xinyun Chen, Aakanksha Chowdhery, Alex Castro-Ros, Marie Pellat, Kevin Robinson, Dasha Valter, Sharan Narang, Gaurav Mishra, Adams Yu, Vincent Zhao, Yanping Huang, Andrew Dai, Hongkun Yu, Slav Petrov, Ed H. Chi, Jeff Dean, Jacob Devlin, Adam Roberts, Denny Zhou, Quoc V. Le, and Jason Wei. 2022. Scaling Instruction-Finetuned Language Models. *arXiv e-prints*, page arXiv:2210.11416.

Alexis Conneau, Ruty Rinott, Guillaume Lample, Adina Williams, Samuel Bowman, Holger Schwenk, and Veselin Stoyanov. 2018. XNLI: Evaluating Cross-lingual Sentence Representations. In *Proc. of the 2018 Conference on Empirical Methods in Natural Language Processing*, pages 2475–2485, Brussels, Belgium. ACL.

Pavel Efimov, Leonid Boytsov, and Pavel Braslavski. 2019. SberQuAD – Russian Reading Comprehension Dataset: Description and Analysis. *CoRR*, abs/1912.09723.

Luyu Gao, Aman Madaan, Shuyan Zhou, Uri Alon, Pengfei Liu, Yiming Yang, Jamie Callan, and Graham Neubig. 2022. PAL: Program-aided Language Models.

Jan Kocoń, Piotr Miłkowski, and Monika Zaśko-Zielińska. 2019. Multi-level sentiment analysis of PolEmo 2.0: Extended corpus of multi-domain consumer reviews. In *Proc. of the 23rd Conference on Computational Natural Language Learning (CoNLL)*, pages 980–991, Hong Kong, China. ACL.

Chin-Yew Lin. 2004. ROUGE: A Package for Automatic Evaluation of Summaries. In *Text Summarization Branches Out*, pages 74–81, Barcelona, Spain. ACL.

Yao Lu, Max Bartolo, Alastair Moore, Sebastian Riedel, and Pontus Stenetorp. 2022. Fantastically ordered prompts and where to find them: Overcoming few-shot prompt order sensitivity. In *Proceedings of the 60th Annual Meeting of the Association for Computational Linguistics (Volume 1: Long Papers)*, pages 8086–8098, Dublin, Ireland. Association for Computational Linguistics.

Marek Medveď. 2022. SQAD 3.2. LINDAT/CLARIAH-CZ digital library at the Institute of Formal and Applied Linguistics (ÚFAL), Faculty of Mathematics and Physics, Charles University.

Sewon Min, Mike Lewis, Luke Zettlemoyer, and Hannaneh Hajishirzi. 2022. MetaICL: Learning to learn in context. In *Proceedings of the 2022 Conference of the North American Chapter of the Association for Computational Linguistics: Human Language Technologies*, pages 2791–2809, Seattle, United States. Association for Computational Linguistics.

Swaroop Mishra, Daniel Khashabi, Chitta Baral, and Hannaneh Hajishirzi. 2022. Cross-task generalization via natural language crowdsourcing instructions. In *Proceedings of the 60th Annual Meeting of the Association for Computational Linguistics (Volume 1: Long Papers)*, pages 3470–3487, Dublin, Ireland. Association for Computational Linguistics.

Alec Radford and Karthik Narasimhan. 2018. Improving Language Understanding by Generative Pre-Training.

Colin Raffel, Noam Shazeer, Adam Roberts, Katherine Lee, Sharan Narang, Michael Matena, Yanqi Zhou, Wei Li, and Peter J. Liu. 2020. Exploring the limits of transfer learning with a unified text-to-text transformer. *Journal of Machine Learning Research*, 21(146):1–67.

Pranav Rajpurkar, Jian Zhang, Konstantin Lopyrev, and Percy Liang. 2016. SQuAD: 100,000+ Questions for Machine Comprehension of Text. In *Proc. of the 2016 Conference on Empirical Methods in Natural Language Processing*, pages 2383–2392, Austin, USA. ACL.

Victor Sanh, Albert Webson, Colin Raffel, Stephen Bach, Lintang Sutawika, Zaid Alyafeai, Antoine Chaffin, Arnaud Stiegler, Arun Raja, Manan Dey, M Saiful Bari, Canwen Xu, Urmish Thakker, Shanya Sharma Sharma, Eliza Szczechla, Taewoon Kim, Gunjan Chhablani, Nihal Nayak, Debajyoti Datta, Jonathan Chang, Mike Tian-Jian Jiang, Han Wang, Matteo Manica, Sheng Shen, Zheng Xin Yong, Harshit Pandey, Rachel Bawden, Thomas Wang, Trishala Neeraj, Jos Rozen, Abheesht Sharma, Andrea Santilli, Thibault Fevry, Jason Alan Fries, Ryan Teehan, Teven Le Scao, Stella Biderman, Leo Gao, Thomas Wolf, and Alexander M Rush. 2022. Multitask prompted training enables zero-shot task generalization. In *International Conference on Learning Representations*.

Alexander Sboev, Aleksandr Naumov, and Roman Rybka. 2021. Data-Driven Model for Emotion Detection in Russian Texts. *Procedia Computer Science*, 190:637–642. 2020 Annual International Conference on Brain-Inspired Cognitive Architectures for Artificial Intelligence: Eleventh Annual Meeting of the BICA Society.

Teven Le Scao, Angela Fan, Christopher Akiki, Ellie Pavlick, Suzana Ilić, Daniel Hesslow, Roman Castagné, and BigScience. Workshop:. 2022. BLOOM: A 176B-Parameter Open-Access Multilingual Language Model.

Magda Ševčíková, Zdeněk Žabokrtský, and Oldřich Krůza. 2007. Named Entities in Czech: Annotating Data and Developing NE Tagger. In *Proc. of the 10th International Conference on Text, Speech and Dialogue*, volume 4629 of *LNCS*, pages 188–195, Berlin / Heidelberg. Springer.

Tatiana Shavrina, Alena Fenogenova, Anton Emelyanov, Denis Shevelev, Ekaterina Artemova, Valentin Malykh, Vladislav Mikhailov, Maria Tikhonova, Andrey Chertok, and Andrey Evlampiev. 2020. RussianSuperGLUE: A Russian language understanding evaluation benchmark. In *Proc. of the 2020 Conference on Empirical Methods in Natural Language Processing (EMNLP)*, pages 4717–4726. ACL.

Michal Štefánik and Marek Kadlčík. 2022. What is Not in the Context? Evaluation of Few-shot Learners with Informative Demonstrations.

Michal Štefánik, Vít Novotný, Nikola Groverová, and Petr Sojka. 2022. Adaptor: Objective-Centric Adaptation Framework for Language Models. In *Proceedings of the 60th Annual Meeting of the ACL: System Demonstrations*, pages 261–269, Dublin, Ireland. ACL.

Herbert Ullrich, Jan Drchal, Martin Rýpar, Hana Vincourová, and Václav Moravec. 2022. CsFEVER and

CTKFacts: Acquiring Czech data for fact verification.

Yizhong Wang, Swaroop Mishra, Pegah Alipoormolabashi, Yeganeh Kordi, Amirreza Mirzaei, Atharva Naik, Arjun Ashok, Arut Selvan Dhanasekaran, Anjana Arunkumar, David Stap, Eshaan Pathak, Giannis Karamanolakis, Haizhi Lai, Ishan Purohit, Ishani Mondal, Jacob Anderson, Kirby Kuznia, Krima Doshi, Kuntal Kumar Pal, Maitreya Patel, Mehrad Moradshahi, Mihir Parmar, Mirali Purohit, Neeraj Varshney, Phani Rohitha Kaza, Pulkit Verma, Ravsehaj Singh Puri, Rushang Karia, Savan Doshi, Shailaja Keyur Sampat, Siddhartha Mishra, Sujan Reddy A, Sumanta Patro, Tanay Dixit, and Xudong Shen. 2022. Super-NaturalInstructions: Generalization via declarative instructions on 1600+ NLP tasks. In *Proceedings of the 2022 Conference on Empirical Methods in Natural Language Processing*, pages 5085–5109, Abu Dhabi, United Arab Emirates. Association for Computational Linguistics.

Jason Wei, Maarten Bosma, Vincent Zhao, Kelvin Guu, Adams Wei Yu, Brian Lester, Nan Du, Andrew M. Dai, and Quoc V Le. 2022. Finetuned Language Models are Zero-Shot Learners. In *Proc. of International Conference on Learning Representations*.

Thomas Wolf, Lysandre Debut, Victor Sanh, Julien Chaumond, Clement Delangue, Anthony Moi, Pierric Cistac, Tim Rault, Remi Louf, Morgan Funtowicz, Joe Davison, Sam Shleifer, Patrick von Platen, Clara Ma, Yacine Jernite, Julien Plu, Canwen Xu, Teven Le Scao, Sylvain Gugger, Mariama Drame, Quentin Lhoest, and Alexander Rush. 2020. Transformers: State-of-the-Art Natural Language Processing. In *Proc. of the 2020 Conf. EMNLP: System Demonstrations*, pages 38–45. ACL.

Alina Wróblewska, Krasnowska-Kieraś, and Katarzyna. 2017. Polish evaluation dataset for compositional distributional semantics models. In *Proc. of the 55th Annual Meeting of the ACL (Volume 1: Long Papers)*, pages 784–792, Vancouver, Canada. ACL.

Linting Xue, Noah Constant, Adam Roberts, Mihir Kale, Rami Al-Rfou, Aditya Siddhant, Aditya Barua, and Colin Raffel. 2021. mT5: A massively multilingual pre-trained text-to-text transformer. In *Proceedings of the 2021 Conference of the North American Chapter of the Association for Computational Linguistics: Human Language Technologies*, pages 483–498, Online. Association for Computational Linguistics.

Susan Zhang, Stephen Roller, Naman Goyal, Mikel Artetxe, Moya Chen, Shuohui Chen, Christopher Dewan, Mona Diab, Xian Li, Xi Victoria Lin, Todor Mihaylov, Myle Ott, Sam Shleifer, Kurt Shuster, Daniel Simig, Punit Singh Koura, Anjali Sridhar, Tianlu Wang, and Luke Zettlemoyer. 2022. Opt: Open pretrained transformer language models.

A Table of templates

Table 6 contains a full list of templates collected within this work, including the segments filled from the transformed datasets.

B Details of training and evaluation configuration

All models trained within this work, including the baselines are based on the mT5-Large model trained on the referenced dataset(s) using Batch size=30, learning rate = $2 \cdot 10^{-}5$ and early stopping with the patience of 10 evaluations (i.e. 2,000 updates) based on the evaluation loss on a held-out set of data of all training datasets. Where the validation split was provided, we use it as the held-out evaluation set, otherwise, we slice out the last 200 samples of the training data for this purpose. For a simple tracking of multi-dataset training, as well as for convenient bulk training of all supervised baselines, we used Adaptor library (Štefánik et al., 2022) in version 0.2.0, with Hugging Face Transformers library (Wolf et al., 2020), version 4.19.1 as backend. For each training, we used a single Nvidia A100 with 80 GB of GPU memory.

In all evaluations, we used greedy search generation with a default configuration of *generate* method in version 4.19.1.

Lang	Task	Template
cs	NER	{{text}} {{label_type}} v tomto textu je
cs	NER	Jaká entita typu {{label_type}} se nachází v následujícím textu? {{text}}
cs	NER	{{text}} Jaká entita typu {{label_type}} se nachází v předchozím odstavci?
cs	Clf.	Jaký sentiment vyjadřuje následující filmová recenze? {{comment}}
cs	Clf.	{{comment}} Shledal recenzent tento film {{"dobrým nebo zlým"}}?
cs	Clf.	{{comment}} Je tato recenze {{"pozitivní nebo negativní"}}?
cs	Clf.	{{comment}} Je tento komentář {{"pozitivní, neutrální nebo negativní"}}?
cs	Clf.	{{comment}} Jaký je sentiment tohoto komentáře? {{"pozitivní, neutrální nebo negativní"}}?
cs	Clf.	Jaký sentiment má následující komentář? {{comment}}
cs	Clf.	{{comment}} Je tato recenze {{"pozitivní, neutrální nebo negativní"}}?
cs	Clf.	Jaký sentiment má následující recenze? {{comment}}
cs	Clf.	{{comment}} Jaký je sentiment této recenze? {{"pozitivní, neutrální nebo negativní"}}?
cs	QA	{{context}} Q: {{question}} S odkazem na sekci výše je správná odpověď na danou otázku
cs	QA	Podívejte se na odstavec níže a odpovězte na následující otázku: Odstavec: {{context}} Otázka: {{question}}
cs	QA	{{context}} S odkazem na výše uvedený odstavec, {{question}}
cs	QA	{{context}} Otázka: {{question}} Odpověď:
cs	NLI	{{evidence}} Otázka: {{claim}} Pravda, nepravda, nebo ani jedno?
cs	NLI	{{evidence}} Za uvedeného předpokladu a na základě znalostí o světe, "{{claim}}" je určitě pravda, nepravda, nebo není jasné?
cs	NLI	{{evidence}} Na základě předchozího odstavce, je to pravda, že "{{claim}}"? Ne, možná, nebo ano?
cs	NLI	Za předpokladu, že {{evidence}} vyplývá, že {{claim}}? Ano, ne, nebo možná?
cs	NLI	Předpokládejme následovné: {{evidence}} Pak musí být pravda, že "{{claim}}"? Ano, ne, nebo možná?
cs	NLI	Předpokládáme, že {{evidence}} Je možné předpokládat, že "{{claim}}" je pravda? Ano, ne, nebo možná?
cs	NLI	Předpokládejme následovné: {{evidence}} Pak následující tvrzení: "{{claim}}" je pravda, nepravda, nebo nejasné?
pl	clf.	"{{text}}" Ten tekst jest pozytywny, negatywny, neutralny czy dwuznaczny?
pl	clf.	Oceń ten tekst jako pozytywny, negatywny, neutralny lub dwuznaczny. Tekst: {{text}}
pl	clf.	Oceń wydźwięk tego tekstu jako pozytywny, negatywny, neutralny lub dwuznaczny. Tekst: {{text}} Wydźwięk:
pl	clf.	"{{text}}" Jaka jest ta recenzja? Jest pozytywna, negatywna, neutralna czy dwuznaczna?:
pl	NLI	"{{sentence_A}}" Na podstawie tego, można powiedzieć, że zdanie "{{sentence_B}}" jest potwierdzeniem, zaprzeczeniem czy niezwiązane?
pl	NLI	Oceń czy poniższe zdania są zgodne ze sobą - tak, nie czy nie wiadomo? Zdanie A: {{sentence_A}} Zdanie B: {{sentence_B}} Zgodność:
pl	NLI	Hipotezę i przesłankę można powiązać jako potwierdzenie, zaprzeczenie lub niezwiązane. Hipoteza: {{sentence_A}} Przesłanka: {{sentence_B}} Powiązanie:
pl	NLI	Hipoteza: {{sentence_A}} Przesłanka: {{sentence_B}} Czy przesłanka jest dla hipotezy potwierdzeniem, zaprzeczeniem czy jest niezwiązana?
pl	NER	"{{text}}" {{label_type_selected}} w tym tekście to
pl	NER	Znajdź encje typu {{label_type_selected}} w następującym tekście: {{text}}
pl	NER	Jaka encja typu {{label_type_selected}} znajduje się w następującym tekście? "{{text}}"
pl	NER	"{{text}}" Jaka encja typu {{label_type_selected}} znajduje się w poprzednim akapicie?
pl	NER	"{{text}}" {{label_type_selected}} w tym tekście to
pl	NER	Znajdź encje typu {{label_type_selected}} w następującym tekście: {{text}}
pl	NER	Jaka encja typu {{label_type_selected}} znajduje się w następującym tekście? "{{text}}"
pl	NER	"{{text}}" Jaka encja typu {{label_type_selected}} znajduje się w poprzednim akapicie?
ru	NER	{{text}} {{label_type}} в этом тексте:
ru	NER	Какой объект типа {{label_type}} встречается в следующем тексте? {{text}}
ru	NER	{{text}} Какой объект типа {{label_type}} находится в предыдущем абзаце?
ru	NLI	{{premise}} Используя только приведенное выше описание и то, что вы знаете о мир, "{{hypothesis}}" определенно верна, неверна или неубедительна?
ru	NLI	{{premise}} Верно ли, исходя из предыдущего отрывка, что "{{hypothesis}}"? Да, нет, а может быть?
ru	NLI	Учитывая {{premise}}, следует ли из этого, что "{{hypothesis}}"? Да, нет или возможно?
ru	NLI	{{premise}} Имеем ли мы право говорить, что "{{hypothesis}}"? Да, нет, или может быть?
ru	NLI	Учитывая, что {{premise}} Следовательно, должно быть верно, что "{{hypothesis}}"? Да, нет, а Возможно?
ru	NLI	Учитывая {{premise}} Должны ли мы предположить, что "{{hypothesis}}" верна? Да, нет или возможно?
ru	NLI	Примите за истину следующее: {{premise}} Тогда следующее утверждение: "{{hypothesis}}" есть "правда", "ложь" или "неубедительно"?
ru	QA	{{context}} Ответ на вопрос: {{question}}
ru	QA	Посмотрите на абзац ниже и ответьте на следующий вопрос: Абзац: {{context}} Вопрос: {{question}}
ru	QA	{{context}}\n\nСо ссылкой на абзац выше, {{question}}
ru	QA	{{context}} Вопрос: {{question}} Отвечать:
ru	Clf.	{{text}} Это обзор радят, печал, удивление, страх или гнев?
ru	Clf.	Каково настроение следующего обзора? {{text}} Варианты: радость, печаль, удивление, страх, гнев
ru	Clf.	{{text}} Каково настроение этого обзора? радость, печаль, удивление, страх или гнев?

Table 6: Templates for all languages and all task types that we collect in this work. Templates were written by native speakers of the template's language.

Analysis of Transfer Learning for Named Entity Recognition in South-Slavic Languages

Nikola Ivačič [1]
Hanh Thi Hong Tran[1,2,3]
Boshko Koloski[1,2]
Senja Pollak[1]
[1]Jožef Stefan Institute,
[2]Jožef Stefan IPS,
1000 Ljubljana, Slovenia

Matthew Purver[1,4]
[3] University of La Rochelle
17000 La Rochelle, France
[4]School of Electronic Engineering
and Computer Science
Queen Mary University of London
London E1 4NS, UK

Abstract

This paper focuses on Named Entity Recognition for South-Slavic languages using pretrained multilingual neural network models. We investigate whether the performance of the models for a target language can be improved by using data from closely related languages. The results show that this is not the case for the Slovene language, while for Croatian and Serbian, the results are better in selected cross-lingual settings. The most significant performance improvement is observed for the Serbian language, which has the smallest corpora, showing the potential of the method in less-resourced settings.

1 Introduction

Named Entity Recognition (NER) is one of the cornerstones of the NLP tasks and is widely used in many real-life applications, including in the news industry. In our study, we focus on South-Slavic languages and investigate whether the performance of the models for a target language can be improved by using data from closely related languages.

The research on NER has a long history. Already in the 90s, the research was performed by Grishman and Sundheim (1996), followed by Sang and De Meulder (2003); Segura-Bedmar et al. (2013), to mention a few of the early works. Early literature focused on rule-based models (Yu et al., 2020), which were based on a set of pre-defined patterns, and hand-crafted rules (e.g., LTG, NetOwl). These approaches were followed by the unsupervised methods (Collins and Singer, 1999; Nadeau et al., 2006), where no annotated data were required. The advent of machine learning algorithms opened a novel direction for NER tasks where feature engineering gained more traction (Krishnan and Manning, 2006; Mansouri et al., 2008; Liu et al., 2020). With recent advances in neural networks, NER was formulated as a sequence-labelling task and took advantage of the neural systems, especially Transformers, to minimize the effort of feature engineering (Lample et al., 2016; Tran et al., 2021). Ensemble systems that combine different machine learning (Ekbal and Saha, 2011; Saha and Ekbal, 2013) and neural representation (Tran et al., 2021) or architectures (Chiu and Nichols, 2016; Liu et al., 2018) were also under consideration. Besides rich-resourced languages (e.g., English), there is a shift to several less-resourced ones, including the Slavic family (see several organized shared tasks Piskorski et al. (2017, 2019, 2021)).

The availability of multilingual large language models and transfer learning strategies (Devlin et al., 2019) have simplified the cross-lingual transfer for a variety of NLP tasks. This opened new opportunities in the development of multilingual applications, especially in settings with limited resources. Cross-lingual learning allows for overcoming the problems with the lack of data, including in zero- and few-shot learning, where no or very small number of data for the target language is available. Moreover, getting the performance of a multilingual neural model as close as possible to the performance of a monolingual one can be very beneficial also in terms of simplicity and scalability, as a single model can be used instead of many monolingual ones. Last but not least, even if data for the target language is available, adding data in other languages can lead to an improvement in results.

Multilingual models have been used in a large number of tasks, including cross-lingual hate-speech detection (Pelicon et al., 2021b), zero-shot sentiment analysis (Pelicon et al., 2021a) as well as for NER (Arkhipov et al., 2019; Suppa and Jariabka, 2021). It was shown that the multilingual BERT transformer model outperforms the BiLSTM-CRF model for the NER task. The performance can be even further improved with a word-level CRF layer (Arkhipov et al., 2019). Nevertheless, it is also evident that XLM-Roberta outper-

Proceedings of the 9th Workshop on Slavic Natural Language Processing 2023 (SlavicNLP 2023), pages 106–112

Table 1: List of Used Corpora, which shows each corpus with an abbreviated name used in this paper, followed by the number of sentences, the number of tokens it contains, and lastly, its long name.

Corpus	Sentences	Tokens	Long Name
		Slovene	
bsnlp	18106	400291	BSNLP 2017/21 (Piskorski et al., 2021)
500k	9483	193611	ssj500k 2.3 (Krek et al., 2021)
ewsd	2024	31233	ELEXIS-WSD 1.0 (Martelli et al., 2022)
scr	18139	391526	SentiCoref 1.0 (Žitnik, 2019)
		Croatian	
bsnlp	820	18704	BSNLP 2017 and 2021 (Piskorski et al., 2021)
500k	24780	504227	hr500k 1.0 (Ljubešić et al., 2018)
		Serbian	
set	3891	86726	SETimes.SR 1.0 (Batanović et al., 2018)
		Bosnian	
wann	8917	199378	WikiANN / PAN-X (Rahimi et al., 2019)
		Macedonian	
wann	16227	156467	WikiANN / PAN-X (Rahimi et al., 2019)

forms BERT (Suppa and Jariabka, 2021) in such tasks. The closest to our paper is the work by Prelevikj and Zitnik (2021), who showed that the monolingual NER model performance for the Slovene language is practically equal to that of a multilingual one.

In our paper, we focus on NER in Slovene, Croatian and Serbian and aim to answer the following question: does fine-tuning with related languages influence the performance of a multilingual model compared to fine-tuning only in the target language?

The rest of the paper is structured as follows. First, we present the corpora we used and how we preprocessed them, followed by their analysis. Next, we continue with presenting the methodology, where we first introduce the measures, models, hyper-parameters, and software used. Finally, we continue by evaluating the results and by presenting conclusions.

2 Data Description

In this section, we first present all the corpora used. Then, we continue with the description of the conversion of these datasets to the expected format and conclude with the corpora structure analysis.

We used the most common and established NER corpora for selected languages (see Table 1). The assumption and strategy for gathering corpora were also: "the more, the better."

We used NER tags in IOB2 (Ramshaw and Marcus, 1995) format from the CoNLL-2003 shared task (Tjong Kim Sang and De Meulder, 2003) as a common denominator for all corpora and experiments. Each corpus was first combined if split, then converted to a common format, reshuffled, and split to train/validation/test set in an 80/10/10 ratio.

We produced combined corpora by concatenating the sets without further reshuffling so that the experiments could be repeated.

Our study uses Slovene, Croatian, and Serbian as target languages. However, in addition to those, also Bosnian and Macedonian are considered as the source languages, as they are closely related.

Corpora used are presented in Table 1. Note that the ones for Slovene were obtained from BSNLP and parts of a newly published combined Training corpus SUK 1.0 (Arhar Holdt et al., 2022), which contained NER annotations (ssj500k, ELEXIS-WSD, and SentiCoref).

2.1 Data Conversion

The first obstacle was the different NER tags used in corpora. We decided to keep only the common tags: PER, LOC, and ORG. For example, the BSNLP corpus uses PRO and EVT tags, while the *wann* corpus lacks a MISC tag common to 500k training corpora. All non-common tags, including MISC, were replaced with O (outside IOB).

The second obstacle was the difference in format. BSNLP corpus, for instance, uses separate files for verbatim text and NER tags, with no positional reference between one another. We used CLASSLA (Ljubešić and Dobrovoljc, 2019) sentence segmentation and tokenization with a custom conversion script to solve this problem.

In addition, we removed a small amount (54) of very short sentences, as they were often noisy (e.g. conversion errors).

Next, we converted corpora from standard CoNLL format to CSV format with two fields:

- Sentence: whitespace separated sentence word tokens.
- NER: white space separated NER tags for each sentence word token.

Table 2: Example whitespace separated sentence word tokens with corresponding IOB2 NER tags.

Obtoženka	Asia	Bibi	zapustila	Pakistan
O	B-PER	I-PER	O	B-LOC

Finally, we split the corpus data into train, validation, and test sets.

2.2 Corpora analysis

Comparing the corpora showed the differences that could potentially be problematic for obtaining aligned model performance. Especially considering the NER tag ratios where the WikiANN automatically annotated corpora structure was standing out (see Table 3 and Figure 1). This is also one of the reasons why in our experiments, WikiANN corpora were only considered for additional training but not as target language gold standards.

Table 3: Analysis of Combined Corpora - shows each language's combined corpora number of tokens per sentence, followed by the number of NER tags per token. Finally, the PER, LOC, and ORG columns show the ratios with respect to all NER tags.

Lang.	tok./sent.	NER/tok.	PER%	LOC %	ORG %
sl	21.29	9.09%	31.70%	22.20%	34.13%
hr	20.43	7.41%	28.71%	20.55%	30.82%
sr	22.29	12.01%	29.96%	30.12%	32.35%
bs	**7.81**	**36.91%**	31.65%	29.67%	38.67%
mk	**9.64**	**28.07%**	34.89%	30.32%	34.79%

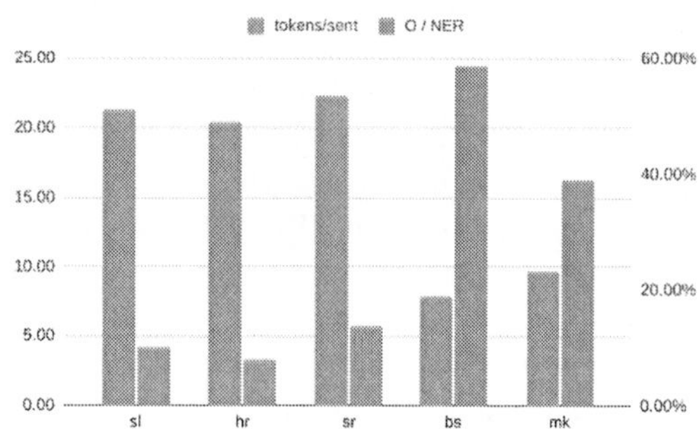

Figure 1: WikiANN corpus skew

Fortunately, we were unable to detect any inconsistencies regarding performance measurements.

3 Methodology

In the following section, we present the methodology used in our experiments to test our hypothesis that the NER classification F1-score increases when we fine-tune the pre-trained multilingual model with an additional, related language.

3.1 Method

The selected method was first to select the pre-trained embeddings, train the baseline model for each language and produce NER classification measurements. Baseline models were fine-tuned with only one - target language.

We experimented with two multilingual models, BERT multilingual base model (cased) (Devlin et al., 2018) and XLM-RoBERTa (base-sized model) (Conneau et al., 2019). However, pilot results showed better performance of XLM-RoBERTa, which was used in the final experiments presented in this paper.

Next, we combined additional language corpora, re-trained the model, and measured performance on the target language test set again. We focus only on three selected languages for evaluation, Slovene, Croatian and Serbian, but consider Bosnian and Macedonian as additional source languages.

We used the HuggingFace transformers Python library (Wolf et al., 2020) for all the experiments.

3.2 Parameters

For all the experiments, we used the following hyper-parameters:

- 256 max-length for tokenizer
- PyTorch's AdamW algorithm with 5e-5 learning rate
- batch size of 20
- 40 epochs (preliminary runs showed best F1-scores between epochs 15 and 35)
- F1-score for best model selection and training progression.

4 Evaluation

In the following section, we define the F1-score we used for evaluation. Then we present the experiment results: the evaluation of the pre-trained multilingual model, followed by the evaluation of fine-tuning for each language.

For all classification measurements, the Seqeval library (Nakayama, 2018) was used. Although the library uses CoNLL evaluation by default, we chose "strict" mode evaluation. When calculating measurements, the strict mode also considers the IOB2 tag's "beginning" and "inside" parts. Therefore the NER tags must match exactly.

4.1 Evaluation measure

For the evaluation of the classification models, we used the traditional F-measure or balanced F-score, which is the harmonic mean of precision and recall:

$$\text{F1-score} = 2 \cdot \frac{Precision \cdot Recall}{Precision + Recall}$$

The Precision and Recall are defined as:

$$\text{Precision} = \frac{TP}{TP+FP} \qquad \text{Recall} = \frac{TP}{TP+FN}$$

given that:

- FP: a NER tag that is predicted but not present in the test.
- FN: a NER tag present in the test but missing in our prediction.
- TP: a NER tag that is correctly predicted.

The overall F1-score, used in the evaluation tables and figures, is a macro-averaged F1-score over all three NER tags. Macro-averaged F1-score is computed using the arithmetic mean of all the per-class F1 scores:

$$\text{Macro-averaged F1-score} = \frac{1}{n}\sum_{i=1}^{n} F1_i$$

where $F1_i$ is the F1-score for ith NER tag.

The average distance from the baseline was used as a measure to show the overall variability of different models tested with the same test set. We also report the maximum reduction in error rate achieved for each tag.

4.2 Results

Here, we present results for the three target languages.

4.2.1 Slovene

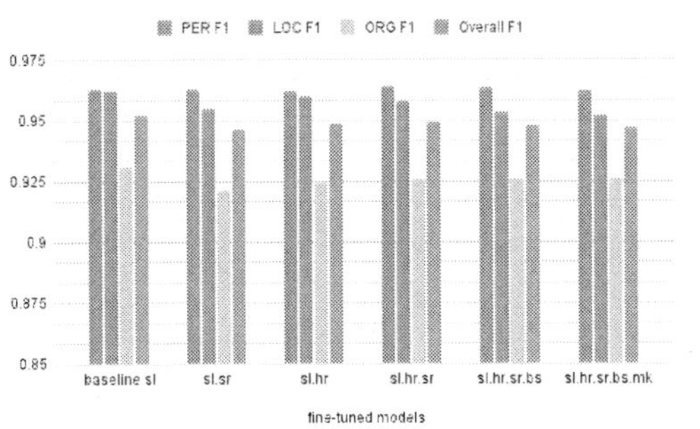

Figure 2: Slovene language test set model performance

The Slovene test set shows surprising model stability. This stability comes, assumingly, from larger corpora compared to the others. It might be that the quality of the corpora also plays a crucial role in this observation.

Table 4: Slovene language test set model performance

Model	PER F1	LOC F1	ORG F1	Overall F1
baseline sl	0.963	**0.963**	**0.931**	**0.952**
sl.sr	0.963	0.955	0.921	0.946
sl.hr	0.962	0.960	0.924	0.948
sl.hr.sr	**0.964**	0.958	0.925	0.949
sl.hr.sr.bs	**0.964**	0.953	0.926	0.948
sl.hr.sr.bs.mk	0.962	0.952	0.926	0.947
avg. dist.	0.00071	0.0070	0.0063	0.0043
error reduction	2.7%	-	-	-

If we observe the average distance from the baseline in the table's last row, we can see that it is only near 0.5%. For the PER tag, the error rate is reduced by a small amount (2.7%), but other tags are not improved.

4.2.2 Croatian

The Croatian language test set shows higher variability when tested with different models, most significantly on the ORG tag. It might be that the other corpora training is influencing variability. However, there is now some overall performance gain from the training: we can see that the average distance from the baseline is 0.5-1%, with reductions in error rates between 6 and 11%.

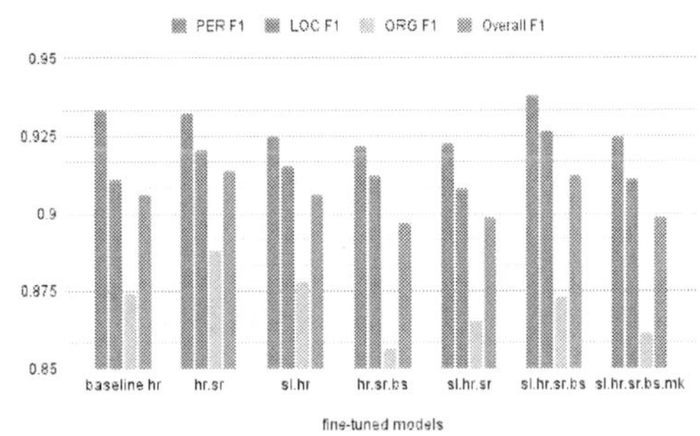

Figure 3: Croatian language test set model performance

Table 5: Croatian language test set model performance

Model	PER F1	LOC F1	ORG F1	Overall F1
baseline hr	0.934	0.911	0.874	0.906
hr.sr	0.932	0.921	**0.888**	**0.914**
sl.hr	0.925	0.915	0.878	0.906
hr.sr.bs	0.922	0.912	0.856	0.897
sl.hr.sr	0.923	0.908	0.865	0.899
sl.hr.sr.bs	**0.938**	**0.927**	0.873	0.912
sl.hr.sr.bs.mk	0.925	0.911	0.861	0.899
avg. dist.	0.0076	0.0055	0.0098	0.0062
error reduction	6.1%	18.0%	11.1%	8.5%

4.2.3 Serbian

The Serbian language test set showed the most significant increase in performance over the baseline. Its average distance in performance measurements from the baseline is from approximately 0.5% to 2.5%, with large reductions in error rate of 43%-68%. The main suspect for this phenomenon is the Serbian corpus size. It is the smallest included in this analysis, and therefore benefits most from additional cross-lingual training on other corpora.

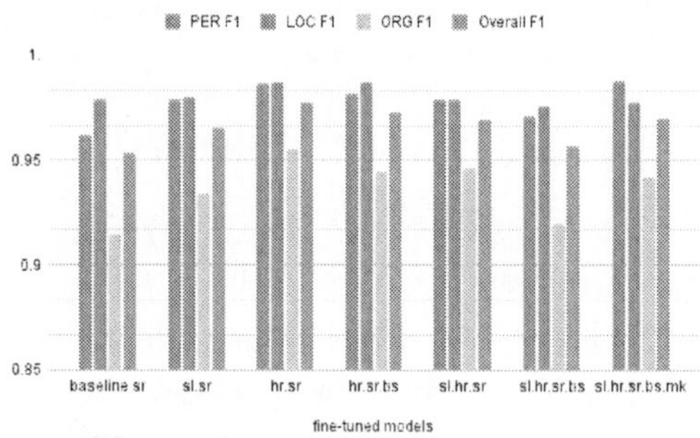

Figure 4: Serbian language test set model performance

Table 6: Serbian language test set model performance

Model	PER F1	LOC F1	ORG F1	Overall F1
baseline sr	0.962	0.979	0.914	0.954
sl.sr	0.979	0.980	0.934	0.965
hr.sr	0.987	**0.988**	**0.956**	**0.978**
hr.sr.bs	0.982	0.987	0.945	0.973
sl.hr.sr	0.979	0.979	0.946	0.969
sl.hr.sr.bs	0.971	0.976	0.920	0.957
sl.hr.sr.bs.mk	**0.988**	0.978	0.942	0.970
avg. dist.	0.019	0.0037	0.026	0.015
error reduction	68.4%	42.9%	48.8%	52.2%

5 Conclusion

We have shown that model performance can be influenced substantially by cross-lingual training with other language corpora, but that improvements only seem to occur if the target language has relatively small corpora. While for Slovene, the monolingual setting generally performs better, for Croatian and Serbian, the results are slightly better in selected cross-lingual settings. The most significant performance improvement is shown for the Serbian language, which has the smallest corpora. This indicates that fine-tuning with other closely related languages may benefit only the "low resource" languages.

Our initial hypothesis has not been fully upheld, but the result is still beneficial. First, when considering less-resourced settings, leveraging closely related languages is beneficial. Second, the performance does not degrade much if we fine-tune the model with additional language corpora from the same family. This is an important finding, as using a multilingual model in an application is a simpler solution than having several monolingual models.

In future work, we propose further investigating how performance changes when distantly related languages are used for fine-tuning the models. This will further benefit the usage in an industrial setting if the performance is not degraded, as having a single model that supports more languages with similar performance to monolingual training is more scalable and practical.

Acknowledgements

We acknowledge financial support from several sources: the Slovenian Research Agency via research core funding for the programme Knowledge Technologies (P2-0103) and the projects CANDAS (Computer-assisted multilingual news discourse analysis with contextual embeddings, J6-2581) and SOVRAG (Hate speech in contemporary conceptualizations of nationalism, racism, gender and migration, J5-3102); the UK EPSRC via the projects Sodestream (Streamlining Social Decision Making for Improved Internet Standards, EP/S033564/1) and ARCIDUCA (Annotating Reference and Coreference In Dialogue Using Conversational Agents in games, EP/W001632/1); and via the project RobaCOFI (Robust and adaptable comment filtering), which indirectly received funding from the European Union's Horizon 2020 research and innovation action programme via the AI4Media Open Call #1 issued and executed under the AI4Media project (Grant Agreement no. 951911). This paper reflects only the authors' views; the EC and the AI4Media project are not responsible for any use that may be made of the information contained herein.

References

Špela Arhar Holdt, Simon Krek, Kaja Dobrovoljc, Tomaž Erjavec, Polona Gantar, Jaka Čibej, Eva Pori, Luka Terčon, Tina Munda, Slavko Žitnik, Nejc Robida, Neli Blagus, Sara Može, Nina Ledinek, Nanika Holz, Katja Zupan, Taja Kuzman, Teja Kavčič, Iza Škrjanec, Dafne Marko, Lucija Jezeršek, and Anja

Zajc. 2022. Training corpus SUK 1.0. Slovenian language resource repository CLARIN.SI.

Mikhail Arkhipov, Maria Trofimova, Yurii Kuratov, and Alexey Sorokin. 2019. Tuning multilingual transformers for language-specific named entity recognition. In *Proceedings of the 7th Workshop on Balto-Slavic Natural Language Processing*, pages 89–93.

Vuk Batanović, Nikola Ljubešić, Tanja Samardžić, and Tomaž Erjavec. 2018. Training corpus SETimes.SR 1.0. Slovenian language resource repository CLARIN.SI.

Jason PC Chiu and Eric Nichols. 2016. Named entity recognition with bidirectional lstm-cnns. *Transactions of the association for computational linguistics*, 4:357–370.

Michael Collins and Yoram Singer. 1999. Unsupervised models for named entity classification. In *1999 Joint SIGDAT conference on empirical methods in natural language processing and very large corpora*.

Alexis Conneau, Kartikay Khandelwal, Naman Goyal, Vishrav Chaudhary, Guillaume Wenzek, Francisco Guzmán, Edouard Grave, Myle Ott, Luke Zettlemoyer, and Veselin Stoyanov. 2019. Unsupervised cross-lingual representation learning at scale. *CoRR*, abs/1911.02116.

Jacob Devlin, Ming-Wei Chang, Kenton Lee, and Kristina Toutanova. 2018. BERT: pre-training of deep bidirectional transformers for language understanding. *CoRR*, abs/1810.04805.

Jacob Devlin, Ming-Wei Chang, Kenton Lee, and Kristina Toutanova. 2019. BERT: Pre-training of deep bidirectional transformers for language understanding. In *Proceedings of the 2019 Conference of the North American Chapter of the Association for Computational Linguistics: Human Language Technologies, Volume 1 (Long and Short Papers)*, pages 4171–4186, Minneapolis, Minnesota. Association for Computational Linguistics.

Asif Ekbal and Sriparna Saha. 2011. Weighted vote-based classifier ensemble for named entity recognition: a genetic algorithm-based approach. *ACM Transactions on Asian Language Information Processing (TALIP)*, 10(2):1–37.

Ralph Grishman and Beth M Sundheim. 1996. Message understanding conference-6: A brief history. In *COLING 1996 Volume 1: The 16th International Conference on Computational Linguistics*.

Simon Krek, Kaja Dobrovoljc, Tomaž Erjavec, Sara Može, Nina Ledinek, Nanika Holz, Katja Zupan, Polona Gantar, Taja Kuzman, Jaka Čibej, Špela Arhar Holdt, Teja Kavčič, Iza Škrjanec, Dafne Marko, Lucija Jezeršek, and Anja Zajc. 2021. Training corpus ssj500k 2.3. Slovenian language resource repository CLARIN.SI.

Vijay Krishnan and Christopher D Manning. 2006. An effective two-stage model for exploiting non-local dependencies in named entity recognition. In *Proceedings of the 21st international conference on computational linguistics and 44th annual meeting of the association for computational linguistics*, pages 1121–1128.

Guillaume Lample, Miguel Ballesteros, Sandeep Subramanian, Kazuya Kawakami, and Chris Dyer. 2016. Neural architectures for named entity recognition. In *Proceedings of NAACL-HLT*, pages 260–270.

Liyuan Liu, Jingbo Shang, Xiang Ren, Frank Xu, Huan Gui, Jian Peng, and Jiawei Han. 2018. Empower sequence labeling with task-aware neural language model. In *Proceedings of the AAAI Conference on Artificial Intelligence*, volume 32.

Shifeng Liu, Yifang Sun, Bing Li, Wei Wang, and Xiang Zhao. 2020. Hamner: Headword amplified multi-span distantly supervised method for domain specific named entity recognition. In *Proceedings of the AAAI Conference on Artificial Intelligence*, volume 34, pages 8401–8408.

Nikola Ljubešić, Željko Agić, Filip Klubička, Vuk Batanović, and Tomaž Erjavec. 2018. Training corpus hr500k 1.0. Slovenian language resource repository CLARIN.SI.

Nikola Ljubešić and Kaja Dobrovoljc. 2019. What does neural bring? analysing improvements in morphosyntactic annotation and lemmatisation of Slovenian, Croatian and Serbian. In *Proceedings of the 7th Workshop on Balto-Slavic Natural Language Processing*, pages 29–34, Florence, Italy. Association for Computational Linguistics.

Alireza Mansouri, Lilly Suriani Affendey, and Ali Mamat. 2008. Named entity recognition approaches. *International Journal of Computer Science and Network Security*, 8(2):339–344.

Federico Martelli, Roberto Navigli, Simon Krek, Jelena Kallas, Polona Gantar, Svetla Koeva, Sanni Nimb, Bolette Sandford Pedersen, Sussi Olsen, Margit Langemets, Kristina Koppel, Tiiu Üksik, Kaja Dobrovoljc, Rafael Ureña-Ruiz, José-Luis Sancho-Sánchez, Veronika Lipp, Tamás Váradi, András Győrffy, Simon László, Valeria Quochi, Monica Monachini, Francesca Frontini, Carole Tiberius, Rob Tempelaars, Rute Costa, Ana Salgado, Jaka Čibej, and Tina Munda. 2022. Parallel sense-annotated corpus ELEXIS-WSD 1.0. Slovenian language resource repository CLARIN.SI.

David Nadeau, Peter D Turney, and Stan Matwin. 2006. Unsupervised named-entity recognition: Generating gazetteers and resolving ambiguity. In *Advances in Artificial Intelligence: 19th Conference of the Canadian Society for Computational Studies of Intelligence, Canadian AI 2006, Québec City, Québec, Canada, June 7-9, 2006. Proceedings 19*, pages 266–277. Springer.

Hiroki Nakayama. 2018. seqeval: A python framework for sequence labeling evaluation. Software available from https://github.com/chakki-works/seqeval.

Andraž Pelicon, Ravi Shekhar, Matej Martinc, Blaž Škrlj, Matthew Purver, and Senja Pollak. 2021a. Zero-shot cross-lingual content filtering: Offensive language and hate speech detection. In *Proceedings of the EACL Hackashop on News Media Content Analysis and Automated Report Generation*, pages 30–34, Online. Association for Computational Linguistics.

Andraž Pelicon, Ravi Shekhar, Blaž Škrlj, Matthew Purver, and Senja Pollak. 2021b. Investigating cross-lingual training for offensive language detection. *PeerJ Computer Science*, 7:e559.

Jakub Piskorski, Bogdan Babych, Zara Kancheva, Olga Kanishcheva, Maria Lebedeva, Michał Marcińczuk, Preslav Nakov, Petya Osenova, Lidia Pivovarova, Senja Pollak, Pavel Přibáň, Ivaylo Radev, Marko Robnik-Sikonja, Vasyl Starko, Josef Steinberger, and Roman Yangarber. 2021. Slav-NER: the 3rd cross-lingual challenge on recognition, normalization, classification, and linking of named entities across Slavic languages. In *Proceedings of the 8th Workshop on Balto-Slavic Natural Language Processing*, pages 122–133, Kiyv, Ukraine. Association for Computational Linguistics.

Jakub Piskorski, Laska Laskova, Michał Marcińczuk, Lidia Pivovarova, Pavel Přibáň, Josef Steinberger, and Roman Yangarber. 2019. The second cross-lingual challenge on recognition, normalization, classification, and linking of named entities across Slavic languages. In *Proceedings of the 7th Workshop on Balto-Slavic Natural Language Processing*, pages 63–74, Florence, Italy. Association for Computational Linguistics.

Jakub Piskorski, Lidia Pivovarova, Jan Šnajder, Josef Steinberger, and Roman Yangarber. 2017. The first cross-lingual challenge on recognition, normalization, and matching of named entities in Slavic languages. In *Proceedings of the 6th Workshop on Balto-Slavic Natural Language Processing*, pages 76–85, Valencia, Spain. Association for Computational Linguistics.

Marko Prelevikj and Slavko Zitnik. 2021. Multilingual named entity recognition and matching using BERT and dedupe for Slavic languages. In *Proceedings of the 8th Workshop on Balto-Slavic Natural Language Processing*, pages 80–85, Kiyv, Ukraine. Association for Computational Linguistics.

Afshin Rahimi, Yuan Li, and Trevor Cohn. 2019. Massively multilingual transfer for NER. In *Proceedings of the 57th Annual Meeting of the Association for Computational Linguistics*, pages 151–164, Florence, Italy. Association for Computational Linguistics.

Lance A. Ramshaw and Mitchell P. Marcus. 1995. Text chunking using transformation-based learning.

Sriparna Saha and Asif Ekbal. 2013. Combining multiple classifiers using vote based classifier ensemble technique for named entity recognition. *Data & Knowledge Engineering*, 85:15–39.

Erik F Sang and Fien De Meulder. 2003. Introduction to the conll-2003 shared task: Language-independent named entity recognition. *arXiv preprint cs/0306050*.

Isabel Segura-Bedmar, Paloma Martínez Fernández, and María Herrero Zazo. 2013. Semeval-2013 task 9: Extraction of drug-drug interactions from biomedical texts (ddiextraction 2013). Association for Computational Linguistics.

Marek Suppa and Ondrej Jariabka. 2021. Benchmarking pre-trained language models for multilingual ner: Traspas at the bsnlp2021 shared task. In *Proceedings of the 8th Workshop on Balto-Slavic Natural Language Processing*, pages 105–114.

Erik F. Tjong Kim Sang and Fien De Meulder. 2003. Introduction to the conll-2003 shared task: Language-independent named entity recognition. In *Proceedings of the Seventh Conference on Natural Language Learning at HLT-NAACL 2003 - Volume 4*, CONLL '03, page 142–147, USA. Association for Computational Linguistics.

Thi Hong Hanh Tran, Antoine Doucet, Nicolas Sidere, Jose G Moreno, and Senja Pollak. 2021. Named entity recognition architecture combining contextual and global features. In *Towards Open and Trustworthy Digital Societies: 23rd International Conference on Asia-Pacific Digital Libraries, ICADL 2021, Virtual Event, December 1–3, 2021, Proceedings*, pages 264–276. Springer.

Thomas Wolf, Lysandre Debut, Victor Sanh, Julien Chaumond, Clement Delangue, Anthony Moi, Pierric Cistac, Tim Rault, Remi Louf, Morgan Funtowicz, Joe Davison, Sam Shleifer, Patrick von Platen, Clara Ma, Yacine Jernite, Julien Plu, Canwen Xu, Teven Le Scao, Sylvain Gugger, Mariama Drame, Quentin Lhoest, and Alexander Rush. 2020. Transformers: State-of-the-art natural language processing. In *Proceedings of the 2020 Conference on Empirical Methods in Natural Language Processing: System Demonstrations*, pages 38–45, Online. Association for Computational Linguistics.

Juntao Yu, Bernd Bohnet, and Massimo Poesio. 2020. Named entity recognition as dependency parsing. *arXiv preprint arXiv:2005.07150*.

Slavko Žitnik. 2019. Slovene corpus for aspect-based sentiment analysis - SentiCoref 1.0. Slovenian language resource repository CLARIN.SI.

Information Extraction from Polish Radiology Reports using Language Models

Aleksander Obuchowski **Barbara Klaudel** **Patryk Jasik**
Gdańsk University of Technology, TheLion.ai
obuchowskialeksander@gmail.com
barbara.klaudel@student.pg.edu.pl
partyk.jasik@pg.edu.pl

Abstract

Radiology reports are vital elements of directing patient care. They are usually delivered in free text form, which makes them prone to errors, such as omission in reporting radiological findings and using difficult-to-comprehend mental shortcuts. Although structured reporting is the recommended method, its adoption continues to be limited. Radiologists find structured reports too limiting and burdensome. In this paper, we propose the model, which is meant to preserve the benefits of free text, while moving towards a structured report. The model automatically parametrizes Polish radiology reports based on language models. The models are trained on a large dataset of 1200 chest computed tomography (CT) reports annotated by multiple medical experts reports with 44 observation tags. Experimental analysis shows that models based on language models are able to achieve satisfactory results despite being pretrained on general domain corpora. Overall, the model achieves an F1 score of 81% and is able to successfully parametrize the most common radiological observations, allowing for potential adaptation in clinical practice. Our model is publicly available [1].

1 Introduction

A radiology report is the most important product radiologists generate to help direct patient care. They are vital to the referring physicians that depend upon them while making a decision about further treatment of a patient. It represents the highest level of radiologists' synthesis and insight into a patient's condition. However, radiology reports are almost always formulated in natural language. Natural language is flexible and enables the writer to express the same idea in a variety of different ways with varied complexity. As a result, the style, length, and level of detail vary among the radiologists, even among those coming from the same institution. Moreover, the reports often contain misspellings and mental shortcuts. Such properties make them difficult to analyze for referring physicians and incomprehensible to patients.

The well-known initiative of the American College of Radiology – Imaging 3.0 introduced a roadmap to transition radiological practice from volumed-based care to value-based care. The critical element of the roadmap was the adoption of structured reporting. A structured report (SR) is a report generated from a predefined, standardized format. The SR is considered a better strategy in terms of reduction in diagnostic error, comprehensiveness, adherence to consensus guidelines, and reduction in the omission of findings and other preventable errors. The negative effects of medical errors were publicized by the report of the Institute of Medicine "To Err is Human" (Donaldson et al., 2000). The report highlighted the importance of limiting preventable medical errors, such as omission in reporting radiological findings.

The adoption of SR was defined as a critical step to provide the best quality of service to referring physicians and patients by both the European Society of Radiology (ESR) and Radiological Society of North America (RSNA) (European Society of Radiology (ESR), 2018). The SR is believed to improve the quality of reports by providing a checklist to ensure that all relevant points were addressed. Moreover, the SR is easier to integrate with tools helping radiologists express relevant information, e.g., CO-RADS classification (Prokop et al., 2020). Lastly, they could facilitate the adoption of value-based healthcare – a new healthcare delivery model in which healthcare providers are paid based on patient outcomes, not the number of performed procedures.

[1] github.com/AleksanderObuchowski/PLRadIE

Proceedings of the 9th Workshop on Slavic Natural Language Processing 2023 (SlavicNLP 2023), pages 113–122
May 6, 2023 ©2023 Association for Computational Linguistics

Although structured reports have many benefits, their acceptance among radiologists is still limited (Faggioni et al., 2017). They require radiologists to change their habits which they often practiced for many years. The radiologists may be reluctant to change for many reasons, including the limited scope of expression resulting in the downgrade of quality, the feeling that there is no clinical necessity to change, and even because they perceive it as an attack on the art of medicine (Ganeshan et al., 2018). With SR, the structure of a report would also have to be manually updated with the changes in classification ontology, possibly resulting in discrepancies between the latest state of knowledge and clinical practice. Moreover, while the proposed structured reports schema could be introduced in clinical practice, it does not solve the problem of already generated reports, where the clinical observations may need to be rewritten to follow the parameterized structure, therefore resulting in additional labor. Although those older reports might not be used in further clinical practice due to being outdated, their parametrization could still be beneficial for data analysis and training of machine learning models.

To bring the most out of both structured reporting and free-texts, in this paper we propose a model for the automatic parametrization of Polish radiology reports based on language models. The model's role is to assign one of 44 labels to each radiological observation. Example texts with extracted radiological observations are shown in Figure 1. Formally, our task falls under the information extraction category, as the goal of the model is to detect spans corresponding to specific radiological findings rather than detect a broader set of entities. This was motivated by the fact, that as shown in (Steinkamp et al., 2019) systems that strictly perform named entity recognition-level tasks are insufficient for answering clinical queries. For example, in the sentence "No lesion observed," a NER-only system could (correctly) identify "lesion" as an entity, but cannot correctly answer the intended question. Moreover, we decided to model this task as sequence labeling rather than multi-class sequence text classification, as not only more informative to the end user by also previous work has shown that token-level labeling can result in improved accuracy (Lew et al., 2021). To the best of our knowledge, this is the first model for information extraction from radiology reports in the Polish language.

2 Related work

2.1 Structured Reporting

Structured reporting in radiology has been a subject of debate in the last decade. Even though free text is still the dominant report format, there have been several approaches that received some attention. The most widely-spread form of structured reporting are disease-specific templates, such as BI-RADS (Liberman and Menell, 2002) and CO-RADS (Prokop et al., 2020) schemes. Such templates provide a guideline with a list of features, which presence or absence should e.g. indicate that the disease has greater progression. An important step towards SR was DICOM Structured Reporting (DICOM SR) (Hussein et al., 2004). It is a standard developed to store structured data and clinical observations along with the images. Medical images are usually stored in a Digital Imaging and Communications in Medicine (DICOM) format. DICOM format was created to enable the interoperability of medical images. The standard was widely adopted in any field of medicine where medical images play a significant role. DICOM SR was developed to link the clinical notes to the images within the same format.

RadLex (Datta et al., 2020) is a radiology lexicon produced by the Radiological Society of North America. It contains an ontology of radiology terms for use in radiology reporting, decision support, data mining, data registries, education, and research. It defines standard names and codes for radiology findings.

The idea of unifying terminology and linking the reports to the images was combined in the Annotation and Image Markup (AIM) project (Channin et al., 2010) of the National Institutes of Health Cancer Biomedical Informatics Grid. AIM was created to develop a uniform machine-readable format for storing both the image and a radiology report. It enables the description of an image using common data elements and controlled terminologies, such as RadLex. The usage of ontology enables easy queries and retrieval of information. The annotations and measurements made with AIM can be serialized as XML or DICOM SR.

Another approach was the RSNA's radreport.org reporting templates. The templates for various clinical scenarios provide a standardized radiology lexicon with the terms defined in Web Ontology Lan-

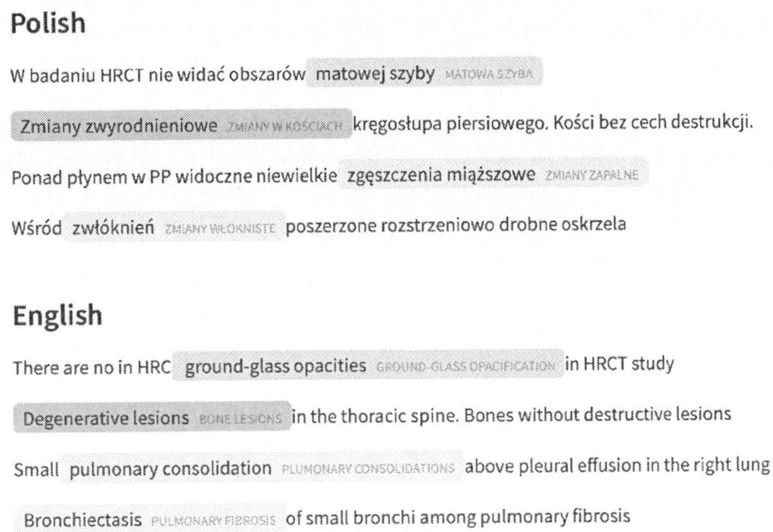

Figure 1: Sample of the annotated data. The report was stripped of the sentences without entities for visualization purposes.

guage (Bechhofer et al., 2009).

Although there have been some important attempts to make SR feasible, it is still at the early stage of adoption.

2.2 Clinical IE and NER

(Solarte-Pabón et al., 2021) proposed an information extraction model for Spanish radiology reports using a multilingual BERT (Devlin et al., 2018) model. The model's role was to parametrize ultrasonography reports. The corpus was annotated using ten different labels: Abbreviation, Anatomical Entity, Conditional Temporal, Degree, Finding, Location, Measure, Negation, Type of measure, and Uncertainty, and was split into a Training set (175 reports), Development set (92 reports), Test set (207 reports). Similar to our work the authors have also used BIO annotation schema, however, in our work, we focus solely on radiological findings but use much more detailed annotations with 44 different possible findings.

The dataset development by Jain et al. (2021) includes annotations for 500 radiology reports taken from the MIMIC-CXR dataset (Johnson et al., 2019), which comprises 14,579 entities and 10,889 relations. Additionally, the test dataset consisted of two independent sets of annotations for 100 radiology reports, sourced from both the MIMIC-CXR and the CheXpert dataset (Irvin et al., 2019). The authors evaluated the performance of several clinical language models, including BioBERT (Lee et al., 2020), ClinicalBERT (Huang et al., 2019), PubMedBERT (Gu et al., 2021), and BlueBERT (Peng et al., 2019), on this dataset.

(Sugimoto et al., 2021) proposed an information model comprising three groups of entities: observations, clinical findings entity, and modifiers entity. The model was trained and evaluated using 540 in-house chest CT reports. The authors have tested two types of models: BiLSTM-CRF and BERT and different pretraining datasets: Wikipedia articles (12 million sentences) and CR reports (118 thousand sentences).

CNNs have also been used in NER for the medical domain, for example in (Kong et al., 2021) where authors use a multi-level CNN layer to capture the information of neighboring characters and integrate them to generate a new embedding with context information for each character. An interesting approach can also be seen in (van de Kerkhof, 2016) where the authors use CNN for medical NER in the context of computer vision where the network is fed an image representing a medical document and its goal is to extract bounding boxes of the named entities. Zhang et al. (2022) use dilated convolutional neural networks (Akbik et al., 2018) to capture global information with fast computing speed.

Florez et al. (2018) use both character-based and word-based LSTM for clinical NER. LSTM layer is followed by a conditional random field (CRF) (Lafferty et al., 2001) to predict the most probable label sequence. Tang et al. (2019) also use the BiLSTM-CRF network for the identification of clinical texts that are modeled as a specific example of NER task.

Mykowiecka et al. (2009) presented a rule-based information extraction system developed for Polish medical texts, focusing on mammography reports and hospital records of diabetic patients. The system uses a special ontology and two separate models represented as typed feature structure hierarchies to extract data from documents. The system also addresses linguistic issues such as ambiguous keywords, negation, coordination, and anaphoric expressions.

2.3 Medical language models

BioBERT (Bidirectional Encoder Representations from Transformers for Biomedical Text Mining) (Lee et al., 2020) was the first domain-specific language model trained for the biomedical domain. It shares the architecture of the original BERT model and uses its weights as a starting point for further pretraining. The model uses PubMed abstracts PubMed Central and full text for further pre-training and domain adaptation. BioBERT obtained higher F1 scores in biomedical NER than the SOTA models at the time, achieving much better results than the standard BERT model.

ClinicalBERT (Huang et al., 2019) is a language model designed for the analysis of clinical narratives (e.g. physicians' notes) that are known to have differences in linguistic characteristics from both general texts and non-clinical biomedical texts (such as the ones used for training of BioBERT). The model was trained on 2 million discharge summaries and clinical notes and discharge summaries from the MIMIC-III database (Johnson et al., 2016). The authors showed that using clinical-specific contextual embeddings improves both general domain results and BioBERT results across 2 well-established clinical NER tasks and one medical natural language inference task.

BlueBERT (Peng et al., 2019) is a benchmark for evaluating medical language models based on 5 NLU tasks including Sentence Similarity, NER, Relation Extraction, Document Multilabel Classification, and Inference. The total model score is calculated as the macro-average of F1 scores and Pearson scores. The authors also share a dataset for pre-training medical language models based on PubMed abstracts and MIMIC-III, as well as two language models pre-trained on these datasets as baselines – one based on BERT and the other based on ELMo (Peters et al., 2018).

2.4 Polish Language Models

Unfortunately, at the time of writing this paper, there are no dedicated Polish Language Models for the medical domain. There are, however, several general domain models available:

Polbert (Kłeczek, 2020) is a Polish BERT-based language model trained on the Polish subset of Open Subtitles, ParaCrawl, Polish Parliamentary Corpus, and Polish Wikipedia with almost 2 billion words in total;

Polish RoBERTa (Dadas et al., 2020a) is a RoBERTa-based (Liu et al., 2019) language model trained on the Polish subset of the Common Crawl dataset;

PoLitBERT (Sopyła and Sawaniewski, 2021) is a Polish Roberta model trained on Polish Wikipedia, Polish literature and Oscar. The major assumption is that high-quality text will give a high performance model;

plT5 (Chrabrowa et al., 2022) is a set of T5-based language models trained on Polish corpora. The models were optimized for the original T5 denoising target. plT5 was trained on six different corpora available for the Polish language: CCNet Middle, CCNet Head, National Corpus of Polish, Open Subtitles, Wikipedia, Wolne Lektury;

papuGaPT2 (Wojczulis and Kłeczek, 2021) is a Polish version of the GPT-2 model trained on the Polish subset of multilingual Oscar corpus;

HerBERT (Mroczkowski et al., 2021) is a Polish BERT based model trained on NKJP, Wikipedia, and Wolne Lektury as well as CCNet and Open Subtitles. The model weights were initialized using weights from the multilingual XLM-RoBERTa model. The model was trained using only MLM objective with dynamic masking of whole words. The authors also introduced the KLEJ benchmark for evaluating Polish language models (Rybak et al., 2020) on which HerBERT is at the time of writing this work a state-of-the-art solution.

Table 1: Overview of the dataset

Entity (PL)	Entity (EN)	Train	Test
płyn w jamie opłucnowej	pleural effusion	722	184
zmiany włókniste	pulmonary fibrosis	631	165
zmiany w kościach	bone lesions	619	156
zmiany zapalne/niedodmowo-zapalne	pulmonary consolidation	543	143
matowa szyba	ground-glass opacities	482	141
rozedma	pulmonary emphysema	422	110
pojedyncze guzki	single nodules	384	95
rurka intubacyjna/wkłucie	endotracheal tube/venous line	254	71
rozstrzenie oskrzeli	bronchiectasis	253	62
konsolidacje w płucach	pulmonary consolidations	248	62
liczne guzki	numerous nodules	223	57
niedodma	atelectasis	202	57
adenopatia śródpiersia	mediastinal lymphadenopathy	202	50
przepuklina rozworu przełykowego	hiatal hernia	198	49
powiększenie serca	cardiomegaly	197	47
płyn w worku osierdziowym	pericardial effusion	175	41
zmiany o typie pączkującego drzewa	tree-in-bud pattern	164	40
patologie opłucnej	pleural disorders	162	39
odma opłucnowa	pneumothorax	156	34
jamy opłucnowe	pleural cavities	126	33
złamanie żeber	broken ribs	117	29
zwapnienia w naczyniach wieńcowych	coronary artery calcification	117	28
plaster miodu	honeycombing	117	26
zmiany w tarczycy	changes in the thyroid gland	94	20
pogrubienie ścian oskrzeli	bronchial wall thickening	83	19
zmiany w tkankach miękkich	soft tissue changes	81	19
poszerzenie pnia płucnego lub tt płucnych	pulmonary trunk dilatation	74	18
odma podskórna	subcutaneous emphysema	73	18
radiologiczne podejrzenie covid	radiological findings of COVID-19 infection	71	17
zwapnienia w miąższu	soft-tissue calcifications	68	17
wydzielina w oskrzelach	bronchial secretions	67	17
patologie nadnerczy	adrenal disorders	66	15
zmiany miażdżycowe aorty	atherosclerosis of the aorta	65	15
urządzenia kardiologiczne	cardiac devices	63	15
tętniak aorty poszerzenie aorty	aortic aneurysm	56	10
zastój w krążeniu płucnym	pulmonary congestion	46	9
adenopatia wnęk	hilar lymphadenopathy	39	9
odma śródpiersia	pneumomediastinum	35	9
kostka brukowa	crazy paving	17	6
patologie przewodu pokarmowego	gastrointestinal disorders	33	6
zatorowość płucna	pulmonary embolism	13	1
rozwarstwienie aorty	aortic dissection	11	1

3 Our Solution

3.1 Dataset

3.1.1 Collection and annotation

For our dataset, we used a real-life collection of 1200 randomly-selected radiological reports describing chest X-ray images. The data used was obtained from historical radiology reports collected at University Clinical Centre in Gdańsk, Poland. The annotation was modeled as a sequence labeling task, where each annotator was tasked with selecting spans in the report that corresponded to the specific tag. The words were labeled as entities following the Inside–Outside–Beginning (IOB) annotation schema (Ramshaw and Marcus, 1999) where the first token of each entity is labeled with the prefix "B-" standing for "Beginning" and each consecutive token of the same entity is labeled with the prefix "I-" standing for "Inside". The tokens not belonging to any entity are labeled as "O" standing for "Outside". The annotations were performed using lighttag annotation tool.

The annotation guidelines for observation tags were created out by radiologists, who selected 44 tags representing the most common radiological observations in the chest x-ray. However, we emphasize keeping annotation classes as general as possible so that the task of information extraction can be easily transferred to other clinical domains. The dataset was annotated by 2 clinical experts with each annotator being resposible for half of the dataset.

The dataset and annotations guidelines are availabe upon resanable request.

3.2 Models

3.2.1 Pre-processing

The reports were anonymized by replacing occurrences of patients and radiologists names with empty strings. They were then split into sentences and tokenized using the Stanza NLP tool (Qi et al., 2020). This step was performed as the reports themselves were longer than the maximum number of tokens allowed for model inputs.

3.2.2 Train/Test split

The sentences were then split into training and test sets using the 80/20 ratio. The distribution of entities in the training and test set are shown in tables 1. From the initial dataset, 2 tags having fewer than 8 occurrences ("krwiak śródścienny aorty" and "zwężenie/koarktacja aorty") were removed due to insufficient number examples to perform the split.

In our implementation, we used 4 openly available Polish language models:

Polish-roberta-base-v2 – trained using Sentencepiece Unigram tokenization model and whole-word masking objective instead of classic token masking, the model also utilized the full context of 512 tokens and was retrained for 400k steps;

Polish-distilroberta – trained using knowledge distillation with RoBERTa-v2 base as a teacher model;

Polish-longformer – initialized with Polish RoBERTa (v2) weights and then fine-tuned on a corpus of long documents, ranging from 1024 to 4096 tokens.

All the models were pre-trained using a Polish subset of the Common Crawl corpus. The model's pre-training details are shown in (Dadas et al., 2020b).

We also used **HerBERT** (Mroczkowski et al., 2021).

In addition to Polish language models, we have also tested the performance of **mLUKE** (Ri et al., 2022) model. mLUKE is a multilingual version of the LUKE (Yamada et al., 2020) model based on XLM-RoBERTa that introduces improvement to the original model by using cross-lingual alignment information from Wikipedia entities.

In each case, the text was tokenized before being fed to the language model producing sub-word tokens. The resulting contextualized token embedding produced by the language model was then fed to a fully connected layer, mapping the token embeddings to entities in the "BIO" format. Only the first token of each word was used for predicting the entity, for the other tokens of a given word we assigned a special "-100" label that served as a mask in order not to count them in the loss function. This architecture is shown in Figure 2.

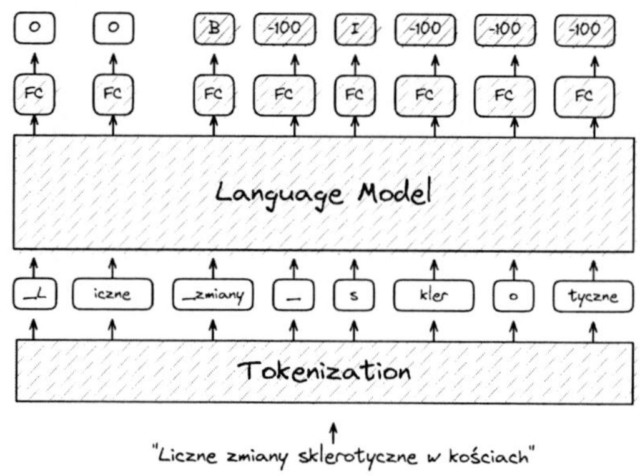

Figure 2: Visualization of deep language model-based approach

We also tested a baseline in form of forward and backward **Flair** (Akbik et al., 2019) embeddings for the Polish language trained on the Polish part of the Common Crawl dataset together with static word GloVe embeddings as suggested by the authors. The embedding layer was then followed by a single BiLSTM layer with a hidden size of 256. This layer was succeeded by a fully-connected layer mapping the hidden states of the BiLSTM layer to the named entities. The model also used Conditional Random Fields (CRF) for prediction, with Viterbi decoding as the loss function. The model was trained for 150 epochs with an initial learning rate of 0.1 which was decreased during training with the "anneal on the plateau" approach.

The models used categorical cross-entropy as the loss function and Adam optimizer with a learning rate of 1e-5 and linear warmup for 10% of steps.

4 Experiments and Results

The results for different models are presented in Table 2.

Table 2: Results of different language models

Model	Precision	Recall	F1-score
HerBERT	0.718	0.798	0.745
Flair	0.749	0.759	0.751
distilroberta	0.752	0.807	0.768
longformer	0.767	0.809	0.778
roberta	0.768	0.811	0.780
mLUKE	**0.791**	**0.826**	**0.809**

These results show that solutions based on deep language models perform better than the ones based on shallower Flair embeddings. The best model was mLUKE achieving an F1 score of 0.81. This can possibly be attributed to the fact that LUKE architecture involves entity-aware self-attention mechanism pre-training schema based on masking entities in large entity-annotated corpus retrieved from Wikipedia, therefore, making it suitable for the end task of sequence labeling. Another observation that can be made is that the best model based on mLUKE is trained solely on Wikipedia texts (as opposed to e.g. Common Crawl dataset used in Roberta pre-training) that have the potential to contain more domain-specific medical knowledge than corpora with casual vocabulary.

After performing additional analysis of the best model shown in Table 3, we observed that the accuracy seems to be the highest for tags with a larger number of examples in the training dataset which follows the standard trend associated with machine-learning-based approaches. However, a few classes (such as pulmonary embolism or aortic dissection) scored lower than average despite being largely represented in the training set. This can be attributed to the fact that those classes contain a lot of variations and clinical observations associated with them can be formulated in a number of ambiguous ways. Similarly, a few classes (such as emphysematous lungs and pulmonary fibrosis) scored well despite having only a few annotated examples. This can also be explained by the fact that those classes rarely appear in the reports and therefore contain fewer possible synonyms.

5 Discussion

In this work, we presented a tool for the parametrization of radiological reports for narrative reports written in natural language. In the interest of standardization and to help further research in this area, we introduced a general annotation scheme that was developed together with clinical experts based on common radiological observations. The results show that general domain language models can successfully be used in the radiology domain, although there is still room for improvements that can possibly be filled with domain-specific models. The detailed analysis of the results shows that the model is able to better capture the entities with fewer variations and higher representation in the training set. It can also be seen that the model rarely confuses different entities, but has some trouble with capturing the spans accurately. However, the model still achieved satisfactory results and with proper verification could successfully be used in clinical practice.

Information extraction is especially challenging with medical terminology since there is some interchangeability between the terms and the structure of a phrase may influence the meaning. For instance, "przepuklina przełykowa" or "przepuklina przełyku" ("hiatal hernia" or "hiatus hernia") can also be phrased as "przepuklina wślizgowa przełyku" ("sliding hiatus hernia"). The literal translation of (parenchymal) pulmonary/lung consolidations is: "zgęszczenia (miąższowe) płuc/płucne" but in reports it usually comes in a phrase "zgęszczenia (miąższowe) w płucu prawym" ("consolidations in the left lung"). Extracting information from a report is a difficult task for the model but it is also non-trivial for a referring physician. From a clinical perspective, the automatic generation of structured reports from free texts combines the benefits of both structured reporting and free text, while limiting the drawbacks of a rigidly structured format.

6 Future Work

The results generated by general domain language models are satisfactory, but far from perfect. This is likely motivated by the fact that the word distribution in the general domain and medical corpora is vastly different, which can result in an array of problems in the NLP of clinical texts. In the future, we are planning to train domain-specific language models using a larger corpus of unlabeled reports using methods such as masked language modeling. Such an approach would most definitely improve the model's results.

Table 3: Classification Report for the best model

Class	Precision	Recall	F-score	Support
adenopatia wnęk	0.36	0.44	0.4	9
adenopatia śródpiersia	0.57	0.68	0.62	50
jamy	0.5	0.61	0.55	33
konsolidacje w płucach	0.84	0.87	0.86	62
kostka brukowa	0.57	0.67	0.62	6
liczne guzki	0.77	0.77	0.77	57
matowa szyba	0.96	0.97	0.96	141
niedodma	0.76	0.71	0.74	63
odma opłucnowa	0.91	0.85	0.88	34
odma podskórna	0.84	0.89	0.86	18
odma śródpiersia	0.7	0.78	0.74	9
patologie nadnerczy	0.61	0.73	0.67	15
patologie opłucnej	0.85	0.85	0.85	39
patologie przewodu pokarmowego	0.33	0.57	0.42	7
plaster miodu	1.0	1.0	1.0	26
pogrubienie ścian oskrzeli	0.57	0.68	0.62	19
pojedyncze guzki	0.73	0.78	0.75	95
poszerzenie pnia płucnego lub tt płucnych	0.42	0.55	0.48	20
powiększenie serca	0.88	0.89	0.88	47
przepuklina rozworu przełykowego	0.62	0.63	0.63	49
płyn w jamie opłucnowej	0.82	0.85	0.83	187
płyn w worku osierdziowym	0.95	0.95	0.95	41
radiologiczne podejrzenie covid	0.74	0.82	0.78	17
rozedma	0.88	0.94	0.91	110
rozstrzenia oskrzeli	0.81	0.87	0.84	62
rozwarstwienie aorty	1.0	1.0	1.0	1
rurka intubacyjna/wkłucie	0.85	0.86	0.85	71
tętniak aorty poszerzenie aorty	0.53	0.8	0.64	10
urządzenia kardiologiczne	0.53	0.6	0.56	15
wydzielina w oskrzelach	0.56	0.59	0.57	17
zastój w krążeniu płucnym	0.67	0.67	0.67	9
zatorowość płucna	1.0	1.0	1.0	1
zmiany miażdżycowe aorty	0.77	0.67	0.71	15
zmiany o typie pączkującego drzewa	0.97	0.97	0.97	40
zmiany w kościach	0.83	0.79	0.81	160
zmiany w tarczycy	0.62	0.8	0.7	20
zmiany w tkankach miękkich	0.48	0.63	0.55	19
zmiany włókniste	0.85	0.92	0.88	165
zmiany zapalne/niedodmowo-zapalne	0.82	0.82	0.82	147
zwapnienia w miąższu	0.46	0.35	0.4	17
zwapnienia w naczyniach wieńcowych	0.93	0.96	0.95	28
złamanie żeber	0.96	0.83	0.89	30
micro avg	0.79	0.83	0.81	1981
macro avg	0.73	0.78	0.75	1981
avg	0.8	0.83	0.81	1981

References

Alan Akbik, Tanja Bergmann, Duncan Blythe, Kashif Rasul, Stefan Schweter, and Roland Vollgraf. 2019. FLAIR: An Easy-to-Use Framework for State-of-the-Art NLP. In *Proceedings of the 2019 conference of the North American chapter of the association for computational linguistics (demonstrations)*, pages 54–59.

Alan Akbik, Duncan Blythe, and Roland Vollgraf. 2018. Contextual String Embeddings for Sequence Labeling. In *Proceedings of the 27th international conference on computational linguistics*, pages 1638–1649.

Sean Bechhofer, M Tamer Özsu, and Ling Liu. 2009. Owl: Web ontology language. In {*Encyclopedia of Database Systems*}. Springer Nature.

David S Channin, Pattanasak Mongkolwat, Vladimir Kleper, Kastubh Sepukar, and Daniel L Rubin. 2010. The caBIG™ annotation and image markup project. *Journal of Digital Imaging*, 23:217–225.

Aleksandra Chrabrowa, Łukasz Dragan, Karol Grzegorczyk, Dariusz Kajtoch, Mikołaj Koszowski, Robert Mroczkowski, and Piotr Rybak. 2022. Evaluation of Transfer Learning for Polish with a Text-to-Text Model. *arXiv preprint arXiv:2205.08808*.

Sławomir Dadas, Michał Perełkiewicz, and Rafał Poświata. 2020a. Pre-training Polish Transformer-Based Language Models at Scale. In *Artificial Intelligence and Soft Computing*, pages 301–314. Springer International Publishing.

Sławomir Dadas, Michał Perełkiewicz, and Rafał Poświata. 2020b. Pre-training polish transformer-based language models at scale. In *International Conference on Artificial Intelligence and Soft Computing*, pages 301–314. Springer.

Surabhi Datta, Jordan Godfrey-Stovall, and Kirk Roberts. 2020. RadLex Normalization in Radiology Reports. In *AMIA Annual Symposium Proceedings*, volume 2020, page 338. American Medical Informatics Association.

Jacob Devlin, Ming-Wei Chang, Kenton Lee, and Kristina Toutanova. 2018. BERT: Pre-training of Deep Bidirectional Transformers for Language Understanding. *arXiv preprint arXiv:1810.04805*.

Molla S Donaldson, Janet M Corrigan, Linda T Kohn, et al. 2000. To err is human: building a safer health system.

European Society of Radiology (ESR). 2018. ESR paper on structured reporting in radiology. *Insights into imaging*, 9(1):1—7.

Lorenzo Faggioni, Francesca Coppola, Riccardo Ferrari, Emanuele Neri, and Daniele Regge. 2017. Usage of structured reporting in radiological practice: results from an Italian online survey. *European Radiology*, 27(5):1934–1943.

Edson Florez, Frédéric Precioso, Michel Riveill, and Romaric Pighetti. 2018. Named Entity Recognition using Neural Networks for Clinical Notes. In *International Workshop on Medication and Adverse Drug Event Detection*, pages 7–15. PMLR.

Dhakshinamoorthy Ganeshan, Phuong-Anh Thi Duong, Linda Probyn, Leon Lenchik, Tatum A McArthur, Michele Retrouvey, Emily H Ghobadi, Stephane L Desouches, David Pastel, and Isaac R Francis. 2018. Structured reporting in radiology. *Academic Radiology*, 25(1):66–73.

Yu Gu, Robert Tinn, Hao Cheng, Michael Lucas, Naoto Usuyama, Xiaodong Liu, Tristan Naumann, Jianfeng Gao, and Hoifung Poon. 2021. Domain-specific language model pretraining for biomedical natural language processing. *ACM Transactions on Computing for Healthcare (HEALTH)*, 3(1):1–23.

Kexin Huang, Jaan Altosaar, and Rajesh Ranganath. 2019. ClinicalBERT: Modeling clinical notes and predicting hospital readmission. *arXiv preprint arXiv:1904.05342*.

Rada Hussein, Uwe Engelmann, Andre Schroeter, and Hans-Peter Meinzer. 2004. DICOM structured reporting: Part 1. Overview and characteristics. *Radiographics*, 24(3):891–896.

Jeremy Irvin, Pranav Rajpurkar, Michael Ko, Yifan Yu, Silviana Ciurea-Ilcus, Chris Chute, Henrik Marklund, Behzad Haghgoo, Robyn Ball, Katie Shpanskaya, et al. 2019. CheXpert: A large chest radiograph dataset with uncertainty labels and expert comparison. In *Proceedings of the AAAI conference on artificial intelligence*, volume 33, pages 590–597.

Saahil Jain, Ashwin Agrawal, Adriel Saporta, Steven QH Truong, Du Nguyen Duong, Tan Bui, Pierre Chambon, Yuhao Zhang, Matthew P Lungren, Andrew Y Ng, et al. 2021. RadGraph: Extracting Clinical Entities and Relations from Radiology Reports. *arXiv preprint arXiv:2106.14463*.

Alistair EW Johnson, Tom J Pollard, Seth J Berkowitz, Nathaniel R Greenbaum, Matthew P Lungren, Chih-ying Deng, Roger G Mark, and Steven Horng. 2019. MIMIC-CXR, a de-identified publicly available database of chest radiographs with free-text reports. *Scientific data*, 6(1):317.

Alistair EW Johnson, Tom J Pollard, Lu Shen, Li-wei H Lehman, Mengling Feng, Mohammad Ghassemi, Benjamin Moody, Peter Szolovits, Leo Anthony Celi, and Roger G Mark. 2016. AWE-CM Vectors: Augmenting Word Embeddings with a Clinical Metathesaurus. *Scientific data*, 3(1):1–9.

Dariusz Kłeczek. 2020. Polbert: Attacking Polish NLP Tasks with Transformers. In *Proceedings of the PolEval 2020 Workshop*, pages 79–88.

Jun Kong, Leixin Zhang, Min Jiang, and Tianshan Liu. 2021. Incorporating multi-level CNN and attention mechanism for Chinese clinical named entity recognition. *Journal of Biomedical Informatics*, 116:103737.

John Lafferty, Andrew McCallum, and Fernando CN Pereira. 2001. Conditional Random Fields: Probabilistic Models for Segmenting and Labeling Sequence Data.

Jinhyuk Lee, Wonjin Yoon, Sungdong Kim, Donghyeon Kim, Sunkyu Kim, Chan Ho So, and Jaewoo Kang. 2020. BioBERT: a pre-trained biomedical language representation model for biomedical text mining. *Bioinformatics*, 36(4):1234–1240.

Michał Lew, Aleksander Obuchowski, and Monika Kutyła. 2021. Improving Intent Detection Accuracy Through Token Level Labeling. In *3rd Conference on Language, Data and Knowledge (LDK 2021)*. Schloss Dagstuhl-Leibniz-Zentrum für Informatik.

Laura Liberman and Jennifer H Menell. 2002. Breast imaging reporting and data system (BI-RADS). *Radiologic Clinics*, 40(3):409–430.

Yinhan Liu, Myle Ott, Naman Goyal, Jingfei Du, Mandar Joshi, Danqi Chen, Omer Levy, Mike Lewis, Luke Zettlemoyer, and Veselin Stoyanov. 2019. RoBERTa: A Robustly Optimized BERT Pretraining Approach. *arXiv preprint arXiv:1907.11692*.

Robert Mroczkowski, Piotr Rybak, Alina Wróblewska, and Ireneusz Gawlik. 2021. HerBERT: Efficiently pretrained transformer-based language model for Polish. In *Proceedings of the 8th Workshop on Balto-Slavic Natural Language Processing*, pages 1–10, Kiyv, Ukraine. Association for Computational Linguistics.

Agnieszka Mykowiecka, Małgorzata Marciniak, and Anna Kupść. 2009. Rule-based information extraction from patients' clinical data. *Journal of biomedical informatics*, 42(5):923–936.

Yifan Peng, Shankai Yan, and Zhiyong Lu. 2019. Transfer Learning in Biomedical Natural Language Processing: An Evaluation of BERT and ELMo on Ten Benchmarking Datasets. In *Proceedings of the 2019 Workshop on Biomedical Natural Language Processing (BioNLP 2019)*, pages 58–65.

Matthew E. Peters, Mark Neumann, Mohit Iyyer, Matt Gardner, Christopher Clark, Kenton Lee, and Luke Zettlemoyer. 2018. Deep contextualized word representations. Cite arxiv:1802.05365Comment: NAACL 2018. Originally posted to openreview 27 Oct 2017. v2 updated for NAACL camera ready.

Mathias Prokop, Wouter Van Everdingen, Tjalco van Rees Vellinga, Henriëtte Quarles van Ufford, Lauran Stöger, Ludo Beenen, Bram Geurts, Hester Gietema, Jasenko Krdzalic, Cornelia Schaefer-Prokop, et al. 2020. CO-RADS: a categorical CT assessment scheme for patients suspected of having COVID-19—definition and evaluation. *Radiology*, 296(2):E97–E104.

Peng Qi, Yuhao Zhang, Yuhui Zhang, Jason Bolton, and Christopher D. Manning. 2020. Stanza: A Python natural language processing toolkit for many human languages. In *Proceedings of the 58th Annual Meeting of the Association for Computational Linguistics: System Demonstrations*.

Lance A Ramshaw and Mitchell P Marcus. 1999. Text Chunking using Transformation-Based Learning. In *Natural Language Processing using Very Large Corpora*, pages 157–176. Springer.

Ryokan Ri, Ikuya Yamada, and Yoshimasa Tsuruoka. 2022. mLUKE: The power of entity representations in multilingual pretrained language models. In *Proceedings of the 60th Annual Meeting of the Association for Computational Linguistics (Volume 1: Long Papers)*, pages 7316–7330, Dublin, Ireland. Association for Computational Linguistics.

Piotr Rybak, Robert Mroczkowski, Janusz Tracz, and Ireneusz Gawlik. 2020. KLEJ: Comprehensive benchmark for Polish language understanding. In *Proceedings of the 58th Annual Meeting of the Association for Computational Linguistics*, pages 1191–1201, Online. Association for Computational Linguistics.

Oswaldo Solarte-Pabón, Orlando Montenegro, Alberto Blazquez-Herranz, Hadi Saputro, Alejandro Rodriguez-González, and Ernestina Menasalvas. 2021. Information extraction from Spanish radiology reports using multilingual BERT. *CLEF eHealth*.

Krzysztof Sopyła and Łukasz Sawaniewski. 2021. Ermlab/politbert: Polish roberta model trained on polish literature, wikipedia, and oscar. the major assumption is that quality text will give a good model.

Jackson M Steinkamp, Charles Chambers, Darco Lalevic, Hanna M Zafar, and Tessa S Cook. 2019. Toward complete structured information extraction from radiology reports using machine learning. *Journal of digital imaging*, 32:554–564.

Kento Sugimoto, Toshihiro Takeda, Jong-Hoon Oh, Shoya Wada, Shozo Konishi, Asuka Yamahata, Shiro Manabe, Noriyuki Tomiyama, Takashi Matsunaga, Katsuyuki Nakanishi, et al. 2021. Extracting clinical terms from radiology reports with deep learning. *Journal of Biomedical Informatics*, 116:103729.

Buzhou Tang, Dehuan Jiang, Qingcai Chen, Xiaolong Wang, Jun Yan, and Ying Shen. 2019. De-identification of Clinical Text via Bi-LSTM-CRF with Neural Language Models. In *AMIA Annual Symposium Proceedings*, volume 2019, page 857. American Medical Informatics Association.

Jan van de Kerkhof. 2016. Convolutional Neural Networks for Named Entity Recognition in Images of Documents.

Michał Wojczulis and Dariusz Kłeczek. 2021. papuGaPT2 - Polish GPT2 language model.

Ikuya Yamada, Akari Asai, Hiroyuki Shindo, Hideaki Takeda, and Yuji Matsumoto. 2020. LUKE: Deep contextualized entity representations with entity-aware self-attention. In *Proceedings of the 2020 Conference on Empirical Methods in Natural Language Processing (EMNLP)*, pages 6442–6454, Online. Association for Computational Linguistics.

Ruoyu Zhang, Pengyu Zhao, Weiyu Guo, Rongyao Wang, and Wenpeng Lu. 2022. Medical Named Entity Recognition Based on Dilated Convolutional Neural Network. *Cognitive Robotics*, 2:13–20.

Can BERT eat RuCoLA? Topological Data Analysis to Explain

Irina Proskurina[1], **Irina Piontkovskaya**[2], **Ekaterina Artemova**[3]
[1]Université de Lyon, Lyon 2, ERIC UR 3083, France
[2]Huawei Noah's Ark lab
[3]Center for Information and Language Processing (CIS), LMU Munich, Germany
Correspondence: Irina.Proskurina@univ-lyon2.fr

Abstract

This paper investigates how Transformer language models (LMs) fine-tuned for acceptability classification capture linguistic features. Our approach uses the best practices of topological data analysis (TDA) in NLP: we construct directed attention graphs from attention matrices, derive topological features from them, and feed them to linear classifiers. We introduce two novel features, chordality, and the matching number, and show that TDA-based classifiers outperform fine-tuning baselines. We experiment with two datasets, CoLA and RuCoLA,[1] in English and Russian, typologically different languages.

On top of that, we propose several black-box introspection techniques aimed at detecting changes in the attention mode of the LMs during fine-tuning, defining the LM's prediction confidences, and associating individual heads with fine-grained grammar phenomena.

Our results contribute to understanding the behavior of monolingual LMs in the acceptability classification task, provide insights into the functional roles of attention heads, and highlight the advantages of TDA-based approaches for analyzing LMs. We release the code and the experimental results for further uptake.[2]

1 Introduction

Language modelling with Transformer (Vaswani et al., 2017) has become a standard approach to acceptability judgements, providing results on par with the human baseline (Warstadt et al., 2019). The pre-trained encoders and BERT, in particular, were proven to have an advantage over other models, especially when judging the acceptability of sentences with long-distance dependencies (Warstadt and Bowman, 2019). Research examining linguistic knowledge of BERT-based language models (LMs) revealed that: (1) individual attention heads can store syntax, semantics or both kinds of linguistic information (Jo and Myaeng, 2020; Clark et al., 2019), (2) vertical, diagonal and block attention patterns could frequently repeat across the layers (Kovaleva et al., 2019), and (3) fine-tuning affects the linguistic features encoding tending to lose some of the pre-trained model knowledge (Miaschi et al., 2020). However, less attention has been paid to examining the grammatical knowledge of LMs in languages other than English. The existing work devoted to the cross-lingual probing showed that grammatical knowledge of Transformer LMs is adapted to the downstream language; in the case of Russian, the interpretation of results cannot be easily explained (Ravishankar et al., 2019). However, LMs are more insensitive towards granular perturbations when processing texts in languages with free word order, such as Russian (Taktasheva et al., 2021).

In this paper, we probe the linguistic features captured by the Transformer LMs, fine-tuned for acceptability classification in Russian. Following recent advances in acceptability classification, we use the Russian corpus of linguistic acceptability (RuCoLA) (Mikhailov et al., 2022), covering tense and word order violations, errors in the construction of subordinate clauses and indefinite pronoun usage, and other related grammatical phenomena. We provide an example of an unacceptable sentence from RuCoLA with a morphological violation in the pronoun usage: a possessive reflexive pronoun 'svoj' (oneself's/own) instead of the 3rd person pronoun.

(1) * Eto byl pervyj chempionat mira v **svoej** kar'ere. ("It was the first world championship in **own** career.")

Following the recently proposed Topological Data Analysis (TDA) based approach to the linguistic acceptability (LA) task (Cherniavskii et al., 2022),

[1]Arugula or rocket salad in English
[2]https://github.com/upunaprosk/la-tda

Proceedings of the 9th Workshop on Slavic Natural Language Processing 2023 (SlavicNLP 2023), pages 123–137
May 6, 2023 ©2023 Association for Computational Linguistics

we construct directed attention graphs from attention matrices and then refer to the characteristics of the graphs as to the linguistic features learnt by the model. We extend the existing research on the acceptability classification task to the Russian language and show the advantages of the TDA-based approach to the task. Our main contributions are the following: *(i)* we investigate the monolingual behaviour of LMs in acceptability classification tasks in the Russian and English languages, using a TDA-based approach, *(ii)* we introduce new topological features and outperform previously established baselines, *(iii)* we suggest a new TDA-based approach for measuring the distance between pre-trained and fine-tuned LMs with large and base configurations. *(iv)* We determine the roles of attention heads in the context of LA tasks in Russian and English.

Our initial hypothesis is that there is a difference in the structure of attention graphs between the languages, especially for the sentences with morphological, syntactic, and semantic violations. We analyze the relationship between models by comparing the features of the attention graphs. To the best of our knowledge, our research is one of the first attempts to analyse the differences in monolingual LMs fine-tuned on acceptability classification corpora in Russian and English, using the TDA-based approach.

2 Related Work

Acceptability Classification. First studies performed acceptability classification with statistical machine learning methods, rule-based systems, and context-free grammars (Cherry and Quirk, 2008; Wagner et al., 2009; Post, 2011). Alternative approaches use threshold scoring functions to estimate the likelihood of a sentence (Lau et al., 2020). Recent research has been centered on the ability of omnipresent Transformer LMs to judge acceptability (Wang et al., 2018), to probe for their grammar acquisition (Zhang et al., 2021), and evaluate semantic correctness in language generation (Batra et al., 2021). In this project, we develop acceptability classification methods and apply them to datasets in two different languages, English and Russian.

Topological Data Analysis (TDA) in NLP. Recent work uses TDA to explore the inner workings of LMs. Kushnareva et al. (2021) derive TDA features from attention maps to build artificial text detection. Colombo et al. (2021) introduce BARYSCORE, an automatic evaluation metric for text generation that relies on Wasserstein distance and barycenters. Chauhan and Kaul (2022) develop a scoring function which captures the homology of the high-dimensional hidden representations, and is aimed at test accuracy prediction. We extend the set of persistent features proposed by Cherniavskii et al. (2022) for acceptability classification and conduct an extensive analysis of how the persistent features contribute to the classifier's performance.

How do LMs change via fine-tuning? There have been two streams of studies of how fine-tuning affects the inner working of LM's: (i) what do sub-word representation capture and (ii) what are the functional roles of attention heads? The experimental techniques include similarity analysis between the weights of source and fine-tuned checkpoints (Clark et al., 2019), training probing classifiers (Durrani et al., 2021), computing feature importance scores (Atanasova et al., 2020), the dimensionality reduction of sub-word representations (Alammar, 2021). Findings help to improve fine-tuning procedures by modifying loss functions (Elazar et al., 2021) and provide techniques for explaining LMs' predictions (Danilevsky et al., 2020). Our approach reveals the linguistic competence of attention heads by associating head-specific persistent features with fine-grained linguistic phenomena.

3 Methodology

We follow Warstadt et al., 2019 and treat the LA task as a supervised classification problem. We fine-tune Transformer LMs to approximate the function that maps an input sentence to a target class: acceptable or unacceptable.

3.1 Extracted Features

Given an input text, we extract output attention matrices from Transformer LMs and follow Kushnareva et al., 2021 to compute three types of persistent features over them.

Topological features are properties of attention graphs. We provide an example of an attention graph constructed upon the attention matrix in Figure 1. An adjacency matrix of attention graph $A = (a_{ij})_{n \times n}$ is obtained from the attention matrix

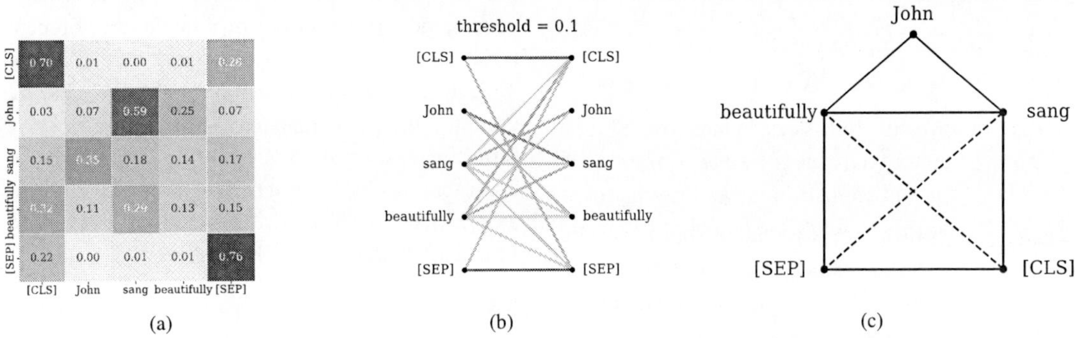

Figure 1: An example of an attention map (a) and the corresponding bipartite (b) and attention (c) graphs for the CoLA sentence *"John sang beautifully"*. The graphs are constructed with a threshold equal to 0.1.

$W = (w_{ij})_{n \times n}$, using a pre-defined threshold thr:

$$a_{ij} = \begin{cases} 1 & \text{if } w_{ij} \geq thr \\ 0 & \text{otherwise,} \end{cases}$$

where w_{ij} is an attention weight between tokens i and j and n is the number of tokens in the input sequence. Each token corresponds to a graph node. Features of directed attention graphs include the number of strongly connected components, edges, simple cycles and average vertex degree. The properties of undirected graphs include the first two Betti numbers: the number of connected components and the number of simple cycles. We propose two new features of the undirected attention graphs: the matching number and the chordality. The matching number is the maximum matching size in the graph, i.e. the largest possible set of edges with no common nodes.

Consider an attention matrix depicted in Figure 1a and a simple undirected attention graph (Figure 1c) constructed based on the bipartite graph (Figure 1b) with a threshold of 0.1. The matching number of that attention graph is equal to two. One example of a maximum matching in that graph is a set of edges: {(*John* - *sang*), ([SEP] - [CLS])}. That matching is maximum because there are no more edges that are not incident to the already matched 4 nodes (tokens). The chordality is a binary feature showing whether the attention graph is chordal; that is, whether the attention graph does not contain induced cycles of a length greater than 3. For example, the plotted graph in Figure 1c is chordal because it does not contain induced cycles with more than 3 edges. If there were no dotted edges (chords) in the graph, there would be a cycle [SEP]-*beautifully*-*sang*-[CLS]-[SEP] of length 4, meaning that the graph is not chordal.

We expect these novel features to express syntax phenomena of the input text. The chordality feature could carry information about subject-verb-object triplets. The maximum matching can correspond to matching sentence segments (subordinate clauses, adverbials, participles, introductory phrases, etc.).

Features derived from barcodes include descriptive characteristics of 0/1-dimensional barcodes and reflect the survival (death and birth) of connected components and edges throughout the filtration.

Distance-to-pattern features measure the distance between attention matrices and identity matrices of pre-defined attention patterns, such as attention to the first token [CLS] and to the last [SEP] of the sequence, attention to previous and next token and to punctuation marks (Clark et al., 2019). We use a publicly available implementation to compute features.[3]

3.2 Experimental Framework

Data We use two publicly available LA benchmarks in two typologically different languages: Russian (RuCoLA; Mikhailov et al., 2022) and English (CoLA; Warstadt et al., 2019). Both selected corpora consist of in- and out-of-domain data and contain sentences collected from linguistics publications; each is marked as acceptable or unacceptable. Unacceptable sentences are annotated with syntactic, morphological and semantic phenomena violated in them. RuCoLA, in addition, covers synthetically generated data by generative LMs. We provide examples of acceptable sentences from observed corpora (2a, 3a) along

[3]https://github.com/danchern97/tda4atd

with sentences with semantic violations (2b, 3b).

(2) a. The dog bit the cat.

b. * The **soundly and furry** cat slept.

(3) a. Koshki byli svyashchennymi zhivotnymi v Drevnem Egipte. ("Cats were sacred animals in ancient Egypt.")

b. * **Bliz** kresla na nebol'shom kovrike lezhala koshka. ("**Outside of** an armchair on a small rug a cat was lying.")

Table 4 (Appendix A) reports statistics of the used corpora. For per-category evaluation, we use RuCoLA error annotations, and for CoLA, we use minor grammatical phenomena annotations to group erroneous sentences. We provide more details in Table 5 (Appendix A).

Models Our baseline model architectures, fine-tuning and evaluation scripts are taken from the Transformers library (Wolf et al., 2020). We use the following case-sensitive monolingual Transformer LMs for the experiments: (1) base size En-BERT[4] (Devlin et al., 2019) and Ru-BERT,[5] (2) large size En-RoBERTa[6] (Liu et al., 2019) and Ru-RoBERTa.[7] To estimate the effect of fine-tuning, we compare two types of models: pre-trained LMs with frozen weights (frozen) and fine-tuned LMs on the training sets. Transformer LMs are fine-tuned for 5 epochs on in-domain training data, with a batch size of 32 and an optimal set of hyper-parameters determined by the authors of the datasets. To mitigate class imbalance, we use weighted cross-entropy loss. We provide fine-tuning details in Table 6 (Appendix A).

TDA Classifiers We extract a range of persistent (TDA) features listed in Section 3.1 from Transformer LMs and refer to them as training features fed to a linear classifier. We reduce the feature space dimensionality with principal component analysis (PCA). Next, we train Logistic Regression classifiers with adjusted class weights on the reduced feature space. We iterate over a range of inverse regularization parameter values $C \in \{10^{-3}, 10^{-2}, 0.1\}$ and the number of principal components $\#PC \in [10, 20 \dots 200]$. We choose the value 200 as the upper bound of the PC grid to ensure that the number of latent features is at least two times less than the size of the in-domain development (IDD) or out-of-domain development (OODD) sets. We tune hyper-parameters to maximize the classifier performance on the IDD set. We compare the performance of two feature sets, by reporting results of classifiers trained on (i) basic TDA features by Kushnareva et al., 2021 (dubbed as TDA) and (ii) TDA features with two novel features added (dubbed as TDA$_{ext}$).

[4]hf.co/bert-base-cased

[5]hf.co/sberbank-ai/ruBert-base

[6]hf.co/roberta-large

[7]hf.co/sberbank-ai/ruRoberta-Large

3.3 Evaluation

Performance Metrics Following Warstadt et al., 2019, we measure performance with Accuracy (Acc.) and Matthews Correlation Coefficient (MCC). MCC is used as the main performance metric for finding hyperparameters, evaluating trained models, and adjusting the decision threshold.

Fine-tuning Effect We estimate changes in attention weights between pre-trained and fine-tuned LMs with two methods. First, we follow Hao et al., 2020 and employ Jensen-Shannon (JS) divergence:

$$D_{JS}(M_t||M_0) = \frac{1}{N}\frac{1}{H}\sum_{n=1}^{N}\sum_{h=1}^{H}\frac{1}{W}\sum_{i=1}^{K} D_{JS}(W_t^h(token_i)||W_0^h(token_i))$$

where M_t and M_0 are fine-tuned and frozen models respectively, N is number of sentences, H is a number of attention heads ($H = 12$ for base-configuration LMs, $H = 24$ for large LMs), K is the number of tokens in the sentence n, and $W_t^h(token_i)$ is an attention weight of attention head h at token i in model M_t.

Second, we estimate the difference between attention graphs as an average correlation distance between the TDA$_{ext}$ features across attention heads:

$$D_{TDA}(M_t, M_0) = \frac{1}{H}\sum_{h=1}^{H}\frac{1}{F}\sum_{f=1}^{F} D_{corr}(V_{tf}^h, V_{0f}^h)$$

where F is the number of features, V_{tf}^h are values of the feature f, computed over attention matrix W_t^h, extracted from the model M_t.

4 Results

4.1 Acceptability Classification

Table 1 reports LA classification results. Linear classifiers trained on the TDA features boost Transformer LMs performance; that trend is consistent across all models, with the MCC score gain of

Model	Fine-tuned LMs				Frozen LMs			
	IDD		OODD		IDD		OODD	
	Acc.	MCC	Acc.	MCC	Acc.	MCC	Acc.	MCC
RuCoLA								
Ru-BERT	80.3	0.420	75.1	0.438	62.4	0.079	54.7	0.112
+ TDA	80.1	0.440	75.1	0.447	76.5	0.314	62.3	0.253
+ TDA$_{ext}$	80.1	0.478	73.2	0.440	76.7	0.331	62.6	0.270
Ru-RoBERTa	83.5	0.530	79.3	0.530	72.8	0.313	58.1	0.241
+ TDA	85.0	0.581	**81.0**	**0.584**	77.0	0.374	**64.7**	0.343
+ TDA$_{ext}$	**85.7**	**0.594**	80.1	0.558	**77.2**	**0.391**	64.2	**0.358**
CoLA								
En-BERT	85.0	0.634	82.0	0.561	62.6	0.039	64.3	0.124
+ TDA	85.6	0.649	81.4	0.548	77.0	0.484	68.4	0.335
+ TDA$_{ext}$	**88.2**	**0.726**	81.0	0.556	81.4	0.543	73.1	0.369
En-RoBERTa	87.3	0.692	**84.9**	**0.637**	74.0	0.317	75.0	0.362
+ TDA	86.3	0.680	83.5	0.620	81.2	0.543	**78.5**	0.464
+ TDA$_{ext}$	87.3	0.695	83.1	0.604	**83.1**	**0.604**	77.3	**0.476**

Table 1: Acceptability classification results of monolingual LMs and linear classifiers trained on the sets of features by the benchmark. **IDD**=in domain development set. **OODD**=out of domain development set. TDA$_{ext}$=TDA features+chordality and the matching number. The best score is in bold, and the second-best one is underlined.

+0.252 at most for the Russian LMs and a more substantial +0.504 increase falling on En-BERT. Proposed chordality and matching number features are beneficial and help improve performance, proving that they capture linguistic information.

Unlike base LMs, large frozen LMs exhibit grammatical knowledge even before fine-tuning. Base LMs' MCC scores fluctuate around zero, while large LMs achieve at least 0.3 MCC.

That observation aligns with the recent works showing that pre-trained large En-RoBERTa can achieve competitive scores without further fine-tuning in tasks such as lexical complexity prediction (Rao et al., 2021).

At the same time, TDA classifiers outperform fine-tuned models by a minor margin enhancing scores by at best +0.064 MCC for Russian and +0.092 MCC for English. We believe that fine-tuning may cause the LM to lose general grammatical skills and forget language phenomena that are not present in the fine-tuning set (Miaschi et al., 2020). Thus, the features extracted from the fine-tuned models may require a thorough feature selection with non-linear models to mitigate feature redundancy issues. TDA classifies for RuCoLA achieve scores on par with the baseline LMs. However, for CoLA, the TDA$_{ext}$ classifier coupled with En-RoBERTa outperforms the baseline. We report classification results on OOD test data in Table 7 and Table 8, Appendix B.1.

4.2 Sensitivity to Violation Categories

Next, we analyze gains in recall by TDA classifiers with respect to violation category. Table 2 reports scores of Ru-BERT and En-BERT baselines and TDA classifiers averaged between IDD and OODD sets with respect to 5 grammatical violations. TDA classifiers outperform LMs in unacceptable sentences; that uptrend holds for both languages, while there is a drop for acceptable sentences.

In contrast to English, the TDA$_{ext}$ classifier trained on Ru-BERT features is more sensitive to syntactic violations reaching the overall 76.6 recall; that is, the increase in the score is around 20 recall points, compared to fine-tuned Ru-BERT. As for the rest grammar categories, the TDA$_{ext}$ classifier outperforms the fine-tuned Ru-BERT by a large margin, especially in sentences with word-level morphological violations, where the recall of Ru-BERT is more than doubled.

Next, we manually analyze the errors of the fine-tuned Ru-BERT and our classifier TDA$_{ext}$ in OODD sentences in Russian. First, we compare the unacceptable sentences, which are misclassified by Ru-BERT but correctly classified by the TDA$_{ext}$ classifier. We find that the error span in OODD sentences is relatively short, with at most three tokens. In particular, in these sentences, such violations as non-existing words are most often encountered, the misuse of which is quite common among native speakers (4a, word formation error 'ekhaj'), local inverse word order (4b), or nonsense (4c). Common false predictions of both models include long sentences that mix grammatical phenomena, contain long-distance agreement violations and complex errors in punctuation.

(4) a. * A ty **ekhaj** pryamo k direktoru teatrov. ("**You should gotta to** the director of theatres.")

b. * V etom lesu **vodyatsya volki**. ("There are **in this forest wolves**.")

c. * Oni chitali moi zhaloby **na sebya**. ("They read my complaints **onto themselves**.")

The domain shift from ID to OOD introduces new types of unacceptable phenomena are not present in ID data. Overall, the scores for OOD data are lower than for ID data (Table 2, Table 9, Appendix B.1). Hence LMs do not generalize well to unseen unacceptable phenomena and have little knowledge about the unseen linguistic properties.

Model	Acceptable	Hallucination	Morphology	Semantics	Syntax
Ru-BERT	92.1	53.9	20.0	25.0	55.7
+TDA$_{ext}$	80.6	73.9	53.9	46.6	76.6
En-BERT	94.3	68.5	69.4	63.0	55.6
+TDA$_{ext}$	84.5	78.8	82.5	76.3	73.0

Table 2: Overall per-category recall by the benchmark.

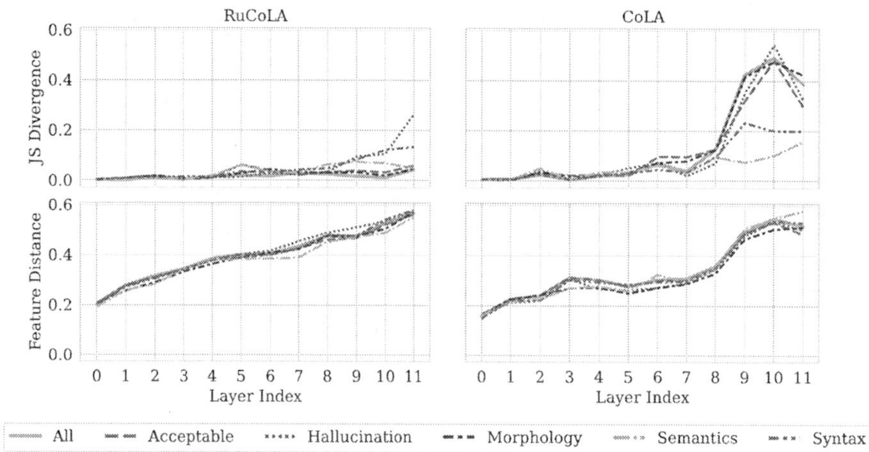

Figure 2: Per-layer feature distance and JS divergence of attention scores between the frozen and fine-tuned Ru-BERT and En-BERT.

4.3 Fine-tuning Effect

We investigate the dynamics of LM fine-tuning and measure per layer distance between TDA$_{ext}$ features extracted from frozen and fine-tuned LMs on OODD subsets (§3.3). Figure 2 illustrates layer-wise feature distance and JS divergence for Ru-BERT and En-BERT (Figure 3, Appendix B.2 for large models). Overall, we find that the distance between features rises steadily from the bottom to higher layers, whilst for English LMs, the most noticeable changes occur only in the last four layers. That observation implies that there is a noticeable difference in fine-tuning dynamics between En-BERT and Ru-BERT.

For both languages, the feature distance trend differs from JS divergence, especially in the first six layers. This indicates that the TDA$_{ext}$ features can be used to detect minor changes in the lower layers that are poorly expressed when using the JS divergence. For example, TDA-based distance is sensitive to small changes in the attention weights at lower predefined thresholds where large attention weights remain unchanged. JS divergence is not capable of capturing such cases.

The distance between features is uniform with respect to the violation category. The trends for acceptable and unacceptable sentences almost coincide, albeit there are noticeable differences in JS divergence. For Russian models, JS divergence in sentences with syntactic violations and hallucinations is more evident in higher layers compared to other categories. In turn, the JS divergence for English shows that the attention mode is more consistent with the frozen En-BERT on the sentences with semantic and syntactic violations; for acceptable and other sentences, the peak is reached at the penultimate layer. Similar to LMs with the base configuration, there is a steady increase in feature dissimilarity across all the layers, while for English, the main changes appear in higher layers.

4.4 Head Importance

We probe linguistic phenomena with the help of persistent features: we exploit the learnt feature weights in the linear classifiers (Appendix B.3). The higher the weight of the feature, the more it contributes to the final prediction. We aggregate

Error type	Sentence	Feature	Head
Morphology	Recept **chipy** s syrom, **maniokom** i yajcami. ("Recipe of **cheps** with cheese, **maniokom** and eggs.")	$c_{thr0.25}$	(9,5)
Syntax	Bylo nachato **stroit' novyj rajon**. ("**Of new district building** was started.")	$c_{thr0.1}$	(9,5)
Semantics	Vchera v dva chasa magazin **zakryt**. ("The store **closing** at two o'clock yesterday.")	[CLS]	(11,0)

Table 3: Examples of the most important Ru-BERT TDA$_{ext}$ features for judging RuCoLA unacceptable sentences by error type. c = the number of simple cycles in a graph, thr = threshold used for constructing attention graph, [CLS] = distance-to-[CLS]-token.

features derived from each head: the importance of the head is derived as a number of important features. We define two types of heads: (1) heads that contribute the most to true positive and true negative predictions (i.e. correct predictions), dubbed as agreeing heads, and (2) heads that contribute the most to false negative and false positive predictions (i.e. classifier's errors), dubbed as disagreeing heads. First, we explore the importance of each individual head. Figure 4, Appendix B.4 shows how important the head is for the final prediction. En-BERT and Ru-BERT have similar patterns for the heads of type (1) as the most useful features for Ru-BERT are housed in middle to higher layers. For En-BERT, these tend to be localized mostly in the last two layers.

Next, we compute the feature importance with respect to the violation category. Heads of middle layers contribute more to detecting syntactic and morphology violations in English and Russian. Heads of type (2) do not overlap with the heads of type (1) with a few exceptions, which are head 10 and head 0 from the last layer of Ru-BERT and En-BERT, respectively. Judging by the number of type (2) heads Ru-BERT struggles the most to distinguish sentences with hallucinations from acceptable sentences. This might be due to multiple reasons: (i) hallucinated sentences are not seen during training, (ii) hallucinated sentences are mainly well-formed but semantically incorrect, so there are no surface or syntactical clues to rely on.

Next, we determine the set of sentences that are the most challenging for the TDA classifier and, thus, the corresponding LM since TDA features are extracted from its attention map. To do so, we define the LM's confidence as the sum of absolute feature weights for predicting acceptable and unacceptable classes. The lower the score, the more confused the LM is and the more attention heads tend to disagree with the desired prediction. We consider those sentences challenging that obtain the lowest confidence scores. The most challenging sentences are long, consist of multiple clauses and contain terms or named entities, see the unacceptable sentence in 5 for example. For the sake of completeness, we conduct the same analysis for CoLA sentences and provide an example of the most confusing sentence for TDA$_{ext}$ classifier (6). The results align well. The most challenging sentences contain long-distance dependencies and named entities.

(5) * Eta gruppa obnaruzhila **(nepravil'no) chto severnyj predel** Merrimak byl bliz togo, chto teper' izvestno kak ozero **Vinnipesuki** v **N'yu-Gempshire**.
("This group found **(poorly), that the northern watershed** of the Merrimack was near what is now known as Lake **Vinnipesaukee** in **New Gampshire**.")

(6) * Gould's performance of Bach on the piano doesn't please me anywhere as much as **Ross's on the harpsichord**.

Finally, we explore the feature contribution on the sentence level. Our TDA-based approach allows explaining predictions for every single sentence. To this end, the contribution (=importance) of each feature is the feature value multiplied by the learnt weight of the linear classifier. We observe the following patterns across unacceptable sentences in Russian and Ru-BERT:

1. Distance-to-pattern features appear to be useful for classifying unacceptable sentences

with word-level violations, including spelling, punctuation, and agreement errors;

2. Topological features and features derived from barcodes contribute equally to more complicated grammatical phenomena.

Table 3 provides examples of unacceptable sentences along with the feature importance values. Chordality, the matching number, the number of simple cycles, and the average vertex degree derived at thresholds 0.1 or 0.25 frequently become important to predict unacceptable sentences in Russian. Similarly, the average number of vertex degrees has the most discriminative power for English and En-BERT. Important features are housed across different layers in the LMs. For English, the most important features are extracted from the last layer, while for Russian, they appear at the earliest at layer 6.

However, when it comes to the discrepancy in attention graphs between acceptable and unacceptable sentences, we find the following common for both languages. The number of connected components in attention graphs for unacceptable sentences is larger at the lowest and the highest thresholds. At the highest threshold, these components consist of one token; at the lowest one, they consist of a few ones. It means that the values of attention maps in unacceptable sentences do not deviate much from each other. On the contrary, for acceptable sentences, there is a tendency to put the most attention weight on a single token, which is usually the sentence's head verb. In terms of the TDA feature values, this effect can be seen as the sign of the correlation coefficient between the feature value and the target class correlation. Thus, there is an obvious shift towards positive correlation at a threshold of 0.5 for average vertex degree features (Figure 5).

To sum up, such an analysis helps better explain the classifiers' prediction. Since persistent features are attributed to individual heads, we can trace the role and importance of each head. A fine-grained annotation of language phenomena allows us to associate specific linguistic skills with individual heads.

5 Conclusion

In this paper, we adopt and improve methods for acceptability classification by using best practices from topological data analysis (TDA). We showcase the developed methods in two typologically different languages by using the datasets in English and Russian, CoLA and RuCoLA, respectively. In particular, we introduce two novel features, chordality and the matching number, and compare the performance of TDA-based classifiers to fine-tuning. TDA-based classifiers boost the performance of pre-trained language models.

TDA-based classifiers have advantages over LM fine-tuning because they are more interpretable and help to introspect the inner workings of LMs. To this end, we introduce a TDA feature-based distance measure to detect changes in the attention mode of LMs during fine-tuning. This distance measure is sensitive even to small changes occurring at the bottom layers of LMs that are not detected by the widespread Jensen-Shannon divergence. What is more important, we show how TDA features reveal the functional roles of attention heads. We compare heads that contribute to making correct and incorrect predictions based on their importance. This way we discover heads that store information about word order, word derivation, and complex semantic phenomena in unacceptable sentences and heads that attend to acceptable sentences.

Given the sentence, we evaluate the prediction confidence based on the contribution of the features. We determine the set of sentences in which LMs are less confident and find that those sentences usually consist of multiple clauses and frequently include named entities. Finally, we find a distinct pattern that is frequently present in the attention maps of unacceptable sentences in English and Russian.

We hope that our results shed light on the performance of LMs in Russian and English and help understanding their fine-tuning dynamics and the functional roles of attention heads. We are excited to see the adoption of TDA by NLP practitioners to other languages and downstream problems.

Limitations

Acceptability judgments datasets Acceptability judgments datasets use linguistic literature as source of unacceptable sentences. Such approach is subject to criticism on two counts: (i) the reliability and reproducibility of acceptability judgments (Gibson and Fedorenko, 2013; Culicover and Jackendoff, 2010; Sprouse and Almeida, 2013; Linzen and Oseki, 2018), (ii) representativeness, as linguists' judgments may not reflect the errors that speakers tend to produce (Dąbrowska, 2010).

Computational complexity The computation complexity of the proposed features is linear. For chordality features, we rely on the implementation of linear $O(|E| + |V|)$ time algorithm (Tarjan and Yannakakis, 1984), where $|E|$ and $|V|$ are the numbers of edges and nodes, respectively. We use a greedy algorithm with linear complexity $O(|E|)$ to find the maximum matching. When calculating simple cycles with the exponential-time algorithm (in the worst case), we use a constraint equal to 500 to do an early stopping. We suggest that simple cycles features are less informative when that value is exceeded. Kushnareva et al., 2021 discuss the time complexity of the rest features.

Acknowledgements

We thank Laida Kushanareva, Daniil Cherniavskii, Vladislav Mikhailov, Serguei Barannikov, Alexander Bernstein, and Dmitri Piontkovski for their comments at its early stages, and we thank Max Ryabinin for providing scripts to process the RuCoLA dataset.

References

J Alammar. 2021. Ecco: An open source library for the explainability of transformer language models. In *Proceedings of the 59th Annual Meeting of the Association for Computational Linguistics and the 11th International Joint Conference on Natural Language Processing: System Demonstrations*, pages 249–257, Online. Association for Computational Linguistics.

Sam Bowman Alex Warstadt, Amanpreet Singh. 2018. Cola out-of-domain open evaluation.

Pepa Atanasova, Jakob Grue Simonsen, Christina Lioma, and Isabelle Augenstein. 2020. A diagnostic study of explainability techniques for text classification. In *Proceedings of the 2020 Conference on Empirical Methods in Natural Language Processing (EMNLP)*, pages 3256–3274, Online. Association for Computational Linguistics.

Soumya Batra, Shashank Jain, Peyman Heidari, Ankit Arun, Catharine Youngs, Xintong Li, Pinar Donmez, Shawn Mei, Shiunzu Kuo, Vikas Bhardwaj, Anuj Kumar, and Michael White. 2021. Building adaptive acceptability classifiers for neural NLG. In *Proceedings of the 2021 Conference on Empirical Methods in Natural Language Processing*, pages 682–697, Online and Punta Cana, Dominican Republic. Association for Computational Linguistics.

Jatin Chauhan and Manohar Kaul. 2022. BERTops: Studying BERT Representations under a Topological Lens. In *2022 International Joint Conference on Neural Networks (IJCNN)*, pages 1–8. IEEE.

Daniil Cherniavskii, Eduard Tulchinskii, Vladislav Mikhailov, Irina Proskurina, Laida Kushnareva, Ekaterina Artemova, Serguei Barannikov, Irina Piontkovskaya, Dmitri Piontkovski, and Evgeny Burnaev. 2022. Acceptability judgements via examining the topology of attention maps. In *Findings of the Association for Computational Linguistics: EMNLP 2022*, pages 88–107, Abu Dhabi, United Arab Emirates. Association for Computational Linguistics.

Colin Cherry and Chris Quirk. 2008. Discriminative, syntactic language modeling through latent SVMs. In *Proceedings of the 8th Conference of the Association for Machine Translation in the Americas: Research Papers*, pages 65–74, Waikiki, USA. Association for Machine Translation in the Americas.

Kevin Clark, Urvashi Khandelwal, Omer Levy, and Christopher D. Manning. 2019. What does BERT look at? an analysis of BERT's attention. In *Proceedings of the 2019 ACL Workshop BlackboxNLP: Analyzing and Interpreting Neural Networks for NLP*, pages 276–286, Florence, Italy. Association for Computational Linguistics.

Pierre Colombo, Guillaume Staerman, Chloé Clavel, and Pablo Piantanida. 2021. Automatic text evaluation through the lens of Wasserstein barycenters. In *Proceedings of the 2021 Conference on Empirical Methods in Natural Language Processing*, pages 10450–10466, Online and Punta Cana, Dominican Republic. Association for Computational Linguistics.

Peter W Culicover and Ray Jackendoff. 2010. Quantitative methods alone are not enough: Response to gibson and fedorenko. *Trends in Cognitive Sciences*, 6(14):234–235.

Ewa Dąbrowska. 2010. Naive v. expert intuitions: An empirical study of acceptability judgments. *The Linguistic Review*.

Marina Danilevsky, Kun Qian, Ranit Aharonov, Yannis Katsis, Ban Kawas, and Prithviraj Sen. 2020. A survey of the state of explainable AI for natural language processing. In *Proceedings of the 1st Conference of the Asia-Pacific Chapter of the Association for Computational Linguistics and the 10th International Joint Conference on Natural Language Processing*, pages 447–459, Suzhou, China. Association for Computational Linguistics.

Jacob Devlin, Ming-Wei Chang, Kenton Lee, and Kristina Toutanova. 2019. BERT: Pre-training of deep bidirectional transformers for language understanding. In *Proceedings of the 2019 Conference of the North American Chapter of the Association for Computational Linguistics: Human Language Technologies, Volume 1 (Long and Short Papers)*, pages 4171–4186, Minneapolis, Minnesota. Association for Computational Linguistics.

Nadir Durrani, Hassan Sajjad, and Fahim Dalvi. 2021. How transfer learning impacts linguistic knowledge in deep NLP models? In *Findings of the Association for Computational Linguistics: ACL-IJCNLP 2021*, pages 4947–4957, Online. Association for Computational Linguistics.

Yanai Elazar, Nora Kassner, Shauli Ravfogel, Abhilasha Ravichander, Eduard Hovy, Hinrich Schütze, and Yoav Goldberg. 2021. Measuring and improving consistency in pretrained language models. *Transactions of the Association for Computational Linguistics*, 9:1012–1031.

Edward Gibson and Evelina Fedorenko. 2013. The need for quantitative methods in syntax and semantics research. *Language and Cognitive Processes*, 28(1-2):88–124.

Yaru Hao, Li Dong, Furu Wei, and Ke Xu. 2020. Investigating learning dynamics of BERT fine-tuning. In *Proceedings of the 1st Conference of the Asia-Pacific Chapter of the Association for Computational Linguistics and the 10th International Joint Conference on Natural Language Processing*, pages 87–92, Suzhou, China. Association for Computational Linguistics.

Jae-young Jo and Sung-Hyon Myaeng. 2020. Roles and utilization of attention heads in transformer-based neural language models. In *Proceedings of the 58th Annual Meeting of the Association for Computational Linguistics*, pages 3404–3417, Online. Association for Computational Linguistics.

Olga Kovaleva, Alexey Romanov, Anna Rogers, and Anna Rumshisky. 2019. Revealing the dark secrets of BERT. In *Proceedings of the 2019 Conference on Empirical Methods in Natural Language Processing and the 9th International Joint Conference on Natural Language Processing (EMNLP-IJCNLP)*, pages 4365–4374, Hong Kong, China. Association for Computational Linguistics.

Laida Kushnareva, Daniil Cherniavskii, Vladislav Mikhailov, Ekaterina Artemova, Serguei Barannikov, Alexander Bernstein, Irina Piontkovskaya, Dmitri Piontkovski, and Evgeny Burnaev. 2021. Artificial text detection via examining the topology of attention maps. In *Proceedings of the 2021 Conference on Empirical Methods in Natural Language Processing*, pages 635–649, Online and Punta Cana, Dominican Republic. Association for Computational Linguistics.

Jey Han Lau, Carlos Armendariz, Shalom Lappin, Matthew Purver, and Chang Shu. 2020. How furiously can colorless green ideas sleep? sentence acceptability in context. *Transactions of the Association for Computational Linguistics*, 8:296–310.

Tal Linzen and Yohei Oseki. 2018. The reliability of acceptability judgments across languages. *Glossa: a journal of general linguistics*, 3(1).

Yinhan Liu, Myle Ott, Naman Goyal, Jingfei Du, Mandar Joshi, Danqi Chen, Omer Levy, Mike Lewis, Luke Zettlemoyer, and Veselin Stoyanov. 2019. RoBERTa: A Robustly Optimized BERT Pretraining Approach. *arXiv preprint arXiv:1907.11692*.

Alessio Miaschi, Dominique Brunato, Felice Dell'Orletta, and Giulia Venturi. 2020. Linguistic profiling of a neural language model. In *Proceedings of the 28th International Conference on Computational Linguistics*, pages 745–756, Barcelona, Spain (Online). International Committee on Computational Linguistics.

Vladislav Mikhailov, Tatiana Shamardina, Max Ryabinin, Alena Pestova, Ivan Smurov, and Ekaterina Artemova. 2022. RuCoLA: Russian corpus of linguistic acceptability. In *Proceedings of the 2022 Conference on Empirical Methods in Natural Language Processing*, pages 5207–5227, Abu Dhabi, United Arab Emirates. Association for Computational Linguistics.

Matt Post. 2011. Judging grammaticality with tree substitution grammar derivations. In *Proceedings of the 49th Annual Meeting of the Association for Computational Linguistics: Human Language Technologies*, pages 217–222, Portland, Oregon, USA. Association for Computational Linguistics.

Gang Rao, Maochang Li, Xiaolong Hou, Lianxin Jiang, Yang Mo, and Jianping Shen. 2021. RG PA at SemEval-2021 task 1: A contextual attention-based model with RoBERTa for lexical complexity prediction. In *Proceedings of the 15th International Workshop on Semantic Evaluation (SemEval-2021)*, pages 623–626, Online. Association for Computational Linguistics.

Vinit Ravishankar, Memduh Gökırmak, Lilja Øvrelid, and Erik Velldal. 2019. Multilingual probing of deep pre-trained contextual encoders. In *Proceedings of the First NLPL Workshop on Deep Learning for Natural Language Processing*, pages 37–47, Turku, Finland. Linköping University Electronic Press.

Jon Sprouse and Diogo Almeida. 2013. The empirical status of data in syntax: A reply to gibson and fedorenko. *Language and Cognitive Processes*, 28(3):222–228.

Ekaterina Taktasheva, Vladislav Mikhailov, and Ekaterina Artemova. 2021. Shaking syntactic trees on the sesame street: Multilingual probing with controllable perturbations. In *Proceedings of the 1st Workshop on Multilingual Representation Learning*, pages 191–210, Punta Cana, Dominican Republic. Association for Computational Linguistics.

Robert E Tarjan and Mihalis Yannakakis. 1984. Simple linear-time algorithms to test chordality of graphs, test acyclicity of hypergraphs, and selectively reduce acyclic hypergraphs. *SIAM Journal on computing*, 13(3):566–579.

Ashish Vaswani, Noam Shazeer, Niki Parmar, Jakob Uszkoreit, Llion Jones, Aidan N Gomez, Łukasz Kaiser, and Illia Polosukhin. 2017. Attention is all you need. *Advances in neural information processing systems*, 30.

Joachim Wagner, Jennifer Foster, and Josef van Genabith. 2009. Judging Grammaticality: Experiments in Sentence Classification. *Calico Journal*, 26(3):474–490.

Alex Wang, Amanpreet Singh, Julian Michael, Felix Hill, Omer Levy, and Samuel Bowman. 2018. GLUE: A multi-task benchmark and analysis platform for natural language understanding. In *Proceedings of the 2018 EMNLP Workshop BlackboxNLP: Analyzing and Interpreting Neural Networks for NLP*, pages 353–355, Brussels, Belgium. Association for Computational Linguistics.

Alex Warstadt and Samuel R. Bowman. 2019. Linguistic analysis of pretrained sentence encoders with acceptability judgments. *arXiv: Computation and Language*.

Alex Warstadt, Amanpreet Singh, and Samuel R. Bowman. 2019. Neural network acceptability judgments. *Transactions of the Association for Computational Linguistics*, 7:625–641.

Thomas Wolf, Lysandre Debut, Victor Sanh, Julien Chaumond, Clement Delangue, Anthony Moi, Pierric Cistac, Tim Rault, Remi Louf, Morgan Funtowicz, Joe Davison, Sam Shleifer, Patrick von Platen, Clara Ma, Yacine Jernite, Julien Plu, Canwen Xu, Teven Le Scao, Sylvain Gugger, Mariama Drame, Quentin Lhoest, and Alexander Rush. 2020. Transformers: State-of-the-art natural language processing. In *Proceedings of the 2020 Conference on Empirical Methods in Natural Language Processing: System Demonstrations*, pages 38–45, Online. Association for Computational Linguistics.

Yian Zhang, Alex Warstadt, Xiaocheng Li, and Samuel R. Bowman. 2021. When do you need billions of words of pretraining data? In *Proceedings of the 59th Annual Meeting of the Association for Computational Linguistics and the 11th International Joint Conference on Natural Language Processing (Volume 1: Long Papers)*, pages 1112–1125, Online. Association for Computational Linguistics.

A Experiment Setup

	CoLA	RuCoLA
Language	English	Russian
Data type	Real	Real, Synthetic
α	0.86	0.89
# Train sent.	8551	7869
# Dev sent.	527	983
# Test sent.	516	1804
%	70.5	71.8

Table 4: Statistics of language acceptability corpora. α = Average annotator agreement rate. % = Percentage of acceptable sentences.

Grammatical feature	**Error type**
Extra/Missing Word	Hallucination
Semantic Violations	Semantics
Infl/Agr Violations	Morphology
Other	Syntax

Table 5: CoLA features aggregated by error type. Infl/Agr =Inflection and Agreement. Other=the rest of grammar violation phenomena present in CoLA annotation for unacceptable sentences.

Model	**Learning rate**	**Weight decay**
En-BERT	$3 \cdot 10^{-5}$	0.01
En-RoBERTa	$2 \cdot 10^{-5}$	10^{-4}
Ru-BERT	$3 \cdot 10^{-5}$	0.1
Ru-RoBERTa	10^{-5}	10^{-4}

Table 6: Hyperparameter values used for finetuning transformers.

B Experiment Results

B.1 Linguistic Acceptability Classification

Model	Expert		Machine	
	Acc.	MCC	Acc.	MCC
Ru-BERT	77	0.37	75	0.44
+ TDA$_{ext}$	75	0.39	72	0.42
Ru-RoBERTa	84	0.55	80	0.56
+ TDA$_{ext}$	83	0.53	80	0.56

Table 7: Linguistic acceptability classification results of monolingual LMs and linear classifiers on RuCoLA out of domain test set by source.[8]

Model	MCC
En-BERT	0.509
+ TDA$_{ext}$	0.469
En-RoBERTa	0.608
+ TDA$_{ext}$	0.616

Table 8: Acceptability classification results of monolingual LMs and linear classifiers on CoLA out of domain test set (Alex Warstadt, 2018).

Model	Acceptable	Hallucination	Morphology	Semantics	Syntax
RuCoLA IDD					
Ru-BERT	93.9	-	12.5	24.0	56.0
+TDA$_{ext}$	86.2	-	56.2	45.0	75.4
Ru-RoBERTa	95.9	-	50.0	37.0	70.9
+TDA$_{ext}$	96.3	-	31.2	34.0	72.4
RuCoLA OODD					
Ru-BERT	90.3	53.9	26.6	25.9	55.4
+TDA$_{ext}$	75.0	73.9	51.6	48.1	77.7
Ru-RoBERTa	90.9	64.3	54.7	42.0	75.5
+TDA$_{ext}$	89.9	63.9	53.1	39.5	71.4
CoLA IDD					
En-BERT	94.8	65.0	69.0	72.2	61.2
+TDA$_{ext}$	87.9	77.5	86.2	83.3	82.4
En-RoBERTa	94.8	72.5	88.9	75.9	64.7
+TDA$_{ext}$	87.3	75.0	79.3	88.9	70.6
CoLA OODD					
En-BERT	93.8	72.0	69.7	53.8	50.0
+TDA$_{ext}$	81.0	80.0	78.8	69.2	63.5
En-RoBERTa	93.5	76.0	87.9	76.9	56.2
+TDA$_{ext}$	83.1	80.0	81.8	92.3	63.5

Table 9: Per-category recall on the IDD and OODD sets by benchmark.

[8]https://rucola-benchmark.com

B.2 Fine-tuning effect

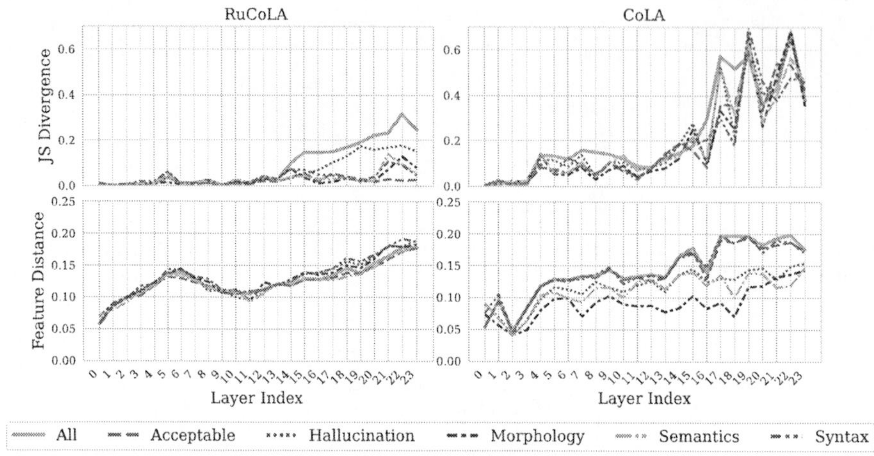

Figure 3: Per-layer feature distance and Jensen-Shannon divergence of attention scores between the frozen and fine-tuned Ru-RoBERTa and En-RoBERTa.

B.3 Feature Importance

Consider a linear classifier with L1 regularization, then the output probability for the sentence i is:

$$p_i \sim \exp(X_{0i}^T C^T w + c),$$

where X_{0i} are the input TDA features, C is the principal component matrix, w^T is a vector of PCs coefficients in the decision function, and c is the added bias. $C^T w$ is the feature contribution to prediction.

B.4 The Roles of Attention Heads

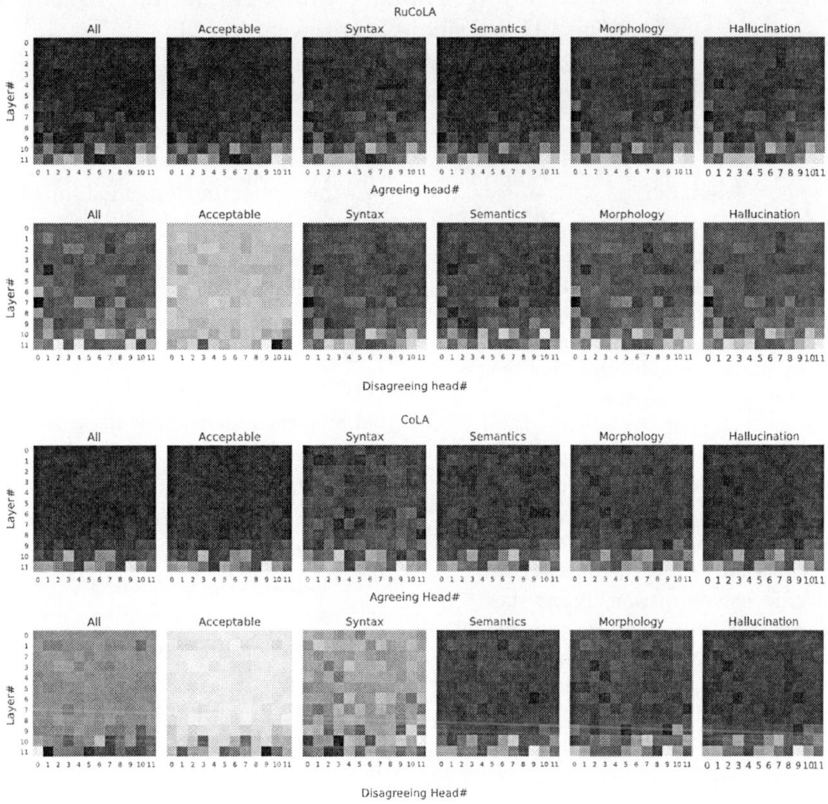

Figure 4: Mean feature weights in TDA_{ext} classifiers with respect to the dataset. TDA_{ext} are extracted from fine-tuned Ru-BERT and En-BERT, respectively. Features of an *agreeing head* contribute to correct prediction. Features of an *disagreeing head* contribute to incorrect prediction. Brighter colors stand for higher mean feature weights.

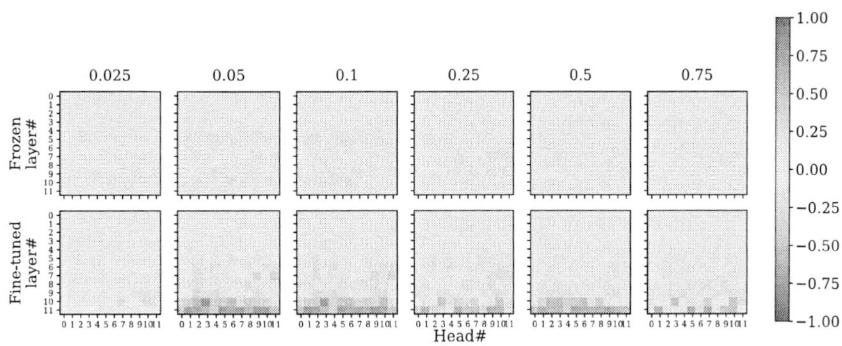

Figure 5: Correlation coefficients between average vertex degree features and target labels for frozen and fine-tuned Ru-BERT by the threshold used to construct attention graph.

WikiGoldSK: Annotated Dataset, Baselines and Few-Shot Learning Experiments for Slovak Named Entity Recognition

Dávid Šuba Marek Šuppa Jozef Kubík Endre Hamerlik Martin Takáč
Comenius University in Bratislava, Slovakia
Contact: marek@suppa.sk

Abstract

Named Entity Recognition (NER) is a fundamental NLP tasks with a wide range of practical applications. The performance of state-of-the-art NER methods depends on high quality manually anotated datasets which still do not exist for some languages. In this work we aim to remedy this situation in Slovak by introducing WikiGoldSK, the first sizable human labelled Slovak NER dataset. We benchmark it by evaluating state-of-the-art multilingual Pretrained Language Models and comparing it to the existing silver-standard Slovak NER dataset. We also conduct few-shot experiments and show that training on a sliver-standard dataset yields better results. To enable future work that can be based on Slovak NER, we release the dataset, code, as well as the trained models publicly under permissible licensing terms at[1].

1 Introduction

Named Entity Recognition (NER) is a lower-level Natural Language Processing (NLP) task in which the aim is to both identify and classify named entity expressions in text into a pre-defined set of semantic types, such as Location, Organization or Person (Goyal et al., 2018). It is a key component of many downstream NLP tasks, ranging from information extraction, machine translation, question answering to entity linking and co-reference resolution, among others. Since its introduction at MUC-6 (Grishman and Sundheim, 1996), the task has been studied extensively, usually as a form of token classification. In recent years, the advent of pre-trained language models (PLMs) combined with the availability of sufficiently large high quality NER-annotated datasets has led to the introduction of NER systems with very high reported performance, sometimes nearing human annotation quality (He et al., 2021).

As the predominant method for adapting PLMs to a specific task of interest is model fine-tuning using training data, the availability of annotated NER datasets for both the training as well as the evaluation part of the process of creating a NER system is critical. Since their creation is expensive, many works have focused on extracting multilingual silver-standard NER datasets from publicly available corpora such as Wikipedia, exploiting the link structure to locate and classify named entities (Nothman et al., 2013; Al-Rfou et al., 2015; Tsai et al., 2016; Pan et al., 2017). While these methods have yielded NER-annotated datasets of significant size, with the recent follow-up work reporting quality comparable to that of datasets created via manual annotation (Tedeschi et al., 2021), their application has multiple limitations: only a limited amount of Wikipedia text is inter-linked, mapping Wikipedia links to the pre-defined NER classes is non-trivial and their application often depends on the existence of high quality knowledge bases which may not be available for some domains and languages.

In this paper we focus on Slovak, a language of the Indo-European family, spoken by 5 million native speakers, which is still missing a manually annotated NER dataset of substantial size. To fill this gap, we propose the following contributions:

- We introduce a novel, manually annotated NER dataset called WikiGoldSK built by annotating articles sampled from Slovak Wikipedia and labeled with four entity classes.
- We evaluate a selection of multilingual NER baseline models on the presented dataset to compare its quality with that of existing silver-standard Slovak NER datasets.
- We treat Slovak as a low-resource language and also assess the possibility of using few-shot learning to train a Slovak NER model using a small part of the introduced dataset.

[1] https://github.com/NaiveNeuron/WikiGoldSK

Proceedings of the 9th Workshop on Slavic Natural Language Processing 2023 (SlavicNLP 2023), pages 138–145
May 6, 2023 ©2023 Association for Computational Linguistics

2 Related Work

NER datasets Much of the progress in NER over the past decades can be attributed to and evidenced by the results reported on standard benchmarks, which in turn originate from shared tasks. This is because they generally provide high-quality annotation datasets, which are key both for the evaluation as well as creation of NER systems. Shared tasks were first introduced for resource-rich languages, such as English, Spanish, German and Dutch (Tjong Kim Sang, 2002; Tjong Kim Sang and De Meulder, 2003) and later established for other language groups, such as Indic (Rajeev Sangal and Singh, 2008) or Balto-Slavic languages (Piskorski et al., 2017, 2019, 2021). The "First Cross-Lingual Challenge on Recognition, Normalization and Matching of Named Entities in Slavic Languages" (BSNLP 2017) (Piskorski et al., 2017) is of particular relevance for our work, as to the best of our knowledge, it introduced the only publicly available human annotated Named Entity Recognition dataset based specifically on Slovak newswire. The dataset, however, consists of less than 50 human-annotated articles and can at best only be used for evaluation of Slovak NER systems but not their training.

The over-reliance on newswire text in the shared tasks has been noticed by the authors of (Balasuriya et al., 2009) who introduced the manually annotated `WikiGold` dataset based on English Wikipedia articles. Despite its limited size, it is still used as an evaluation benchmark. As our aim is also to create a manually annotated (gold-standard) dataset based on Wikipedia articles, we use `WikiGoldSK` to refer to the dataset introduced in this work.

To alleviate the need for sizeable datasets at low cost across multiple languages, various methods of automatically generated NER-annotated datasets have been introduced. In (Nothman et al., 2013) the authors introduce the WikiNER datasets, which makes use of Wikipedia articles and spans 9 languages but does not include Slovak. Utilizing a similar approach, (Pan et al., 2017) first classified English Wikipedia pages to specific entity types and then used the cross-lingual links to transfer the annotations to other languages. As not all entries are linked, the authors also utilize self-training and translation methods to match as many entries as possible. This pipeline generates a dataset that covers 282 languages and includes Slovak as well. With roughly 50 thousand entities annotated with categories Person, Location and Organization, it is the largest publicly available Slovak NER dataset to date.

Another approach of resolving the need for a sizable training dataset is to utilize few-shot learning, in which only a couple of expertly annotated training examples are provided. Recently, the methods based on the combination of cloze-style rephrasing with language models have been shown to perform comparably to GPT-3 (Brown et al., 2020) while having significantly fewer parameters (Schick and Schütze, 2020b). We consider a variant of Pattern-Exploiting Training (Schick and Schütze, 2020a) called PETER (La Gatta et al., 2021) and to the best of our knowledge for the first time evaluate its performance for a general-purpose NER system in a specific language.

Slovak NER The prior art in Slovak NER is limited. In (Kaššák et al., 2012) the authors identified potential named entities as words with capital letters and recognized new entities by finding the entity scope through Wikipedia parsing. For the purposes of this work they also created a dataset annotated by 60 human experts totalling 1620 entities. The authors of (Maruniak, 2021) and (Lupták, 2021) worked with datasets based on more than 5000 articles extracted from Slovak Wikipedia, containing more than 15 000 entities and used multiple well-established NLP toolkits and libraries (such as SpaCy) to train NER models on this dataset. Utilizing a different datasource, (Mičo, 2019) have focused on the Twitter account of one of the biggest Slovak journal and created a dataset with 10 000 of its NER-annotated tweets and almost 16 000 entities, and used it to train a NER model which utilized both FastText (Bojanowski et al., 2016) vectors and the BiLSTM neural network architecture. Unfortunately, none of the datasets and models mentioned in the aforementioned works are publicly available.

Despite having 5 million native speakers and being one of the official languages of the European Union, there are relatively few readily available NLP tools tailored specifically for Slovak, which might be to some extent caused by its linguistic and historical closeness to the much better resourced Czech. This creates a peculiar dichotomy: Slovak has too many native speakers to be considered "low-resource" but at the same time lacks readily available labelled datasets that are a prerequisite for

	WikiANN	BSNLP2017	WikiGoldSK
# doc	N/A	49	412
# sent	30 000	741	6 696
# tok	263 516	14 400	128 944
split	2:1:1	0:0:1	7:1:2
LOC	19 643	244	4 459
PER	18 238	255	2 739
ORG	15 286	273	1 929
MISC	N/A	55	1 668

Table 1: The comparison of WikiGoldSK to the other publicly available Slovak NER datasets. The terms # doc, # sent and # tok refer to the number of documents, sentences and tokens in the specific datasets, respectively. Note that WikiANN does not provide document-level split and is not labeled with the MISC entity.

	train	dev	test
# sent	4 687	669	1 340
# tok	90 616	12 794	25 534
split size	70%	10%	20%
LOC	3 040	461	958
PER	1 892	298	549
ORG	1 361	190	378
MISC	1 184	160	324

Table 2: The frequency distribution across the WikiGoldSK's train/dev/test splits.

many standard NLP tools. The "language richness" taxonomies such as (Joshi et al., 2020) consider Slovak among the "The Rising Stars" of languages, but it is, to the best of our knowledge, one of the few in this category that lacks a sizable, manually labelled NER dataset[2]. The introduction of SlovakBERT in (Pikuliak et al., 2021) does suggest, however, that there is interest in creating Slovak-specific NLP tools and resources. Our work aims to help push this trend further.

3 Dataset

When creating the WikiGoldSK dataset, our principal aim was to create a high quality, publicly available human annotated corpora that could be used to both evaluate and build Slovak NER systems and that would be comparable to well-established benchmark datasets in other languages. To ensure the resulting dataset can be used in the future for research as well as commercial use, we sampled 412 articles from the skwiki-20210701 dump of Slovak Wikipedia, licensed under the terms of the Creative Commons Attribution-Share-Alike License 3.0. In order for an article to be included, its last change date needed to be in 2021 and its length had to fit between 500 and 5 000 characters[3]. The raw text of the articles was tokenized by the generic English spaCy tokenizer, with a manual pass over the dataset in which the Slovak-specific tokenization mistakes were remedied.

We use the same set of tags as the CoNLL-2003 NER Shared task (Tjong Kim Sang and De Meulder, 2003), that is Location (LOC), Person (PER), Organization (ORG) and Miscellaneous (MISC), and our annotation guidelines are inspired by the ones introduced by the BSNLP 2017 shared task (Piskorski et al., 2017). The annotation was done using Prodigy[4] in which the whole dataset was preloaded with the labels predicted by the SlovakBERT model finetuned on the training part of the Slovak portion of the WikiANN dataset. The dataset was annotated by three Slovak native speakers who are also authors of this paper. Two annotators provided annotations for the full dataset whereas one annotator corrected half of the dataset. The Cohen's kappa coefficient between the first two annotators is 0.90 when compared on the token level and 0.81 for the tokens where both annotators agreed that they were not a part of a named entity. As per the benchmark established in (Landis and Koch, 1977), the coefficient values in both cases suggest "almost perfect" strength of agreement and a high quality of the annotation. To arrive at the final dataset, the ambiguities were resolved in a discussion between the annotators.

The summary statistics of the resulting dataset, along with the existing Slovak NER datasets, can be found in Table 1. As we can see, WikiGoldSK is larger than the Slovak portion of the BSNLP2017 dataset but smaller than the Slovak portion of the WikiANN dataset. At the same time, one can see that the distribution of Named Entities in WikiANN and WikiGoldSK follows the same pattern, with the order of LOC, PER, ORG holding for both datasets in terms of entity frequency, which is not the case in

[2]The other languages lacking a sizable, manually NER-annotated datasets are Uzbek, Georgian, Belarusian, Egyptian Arabic and Cebauano.

[3]This is motivated by the observation that long articles may shift the dataset towards their domain, whereas short articles often do not contain any named entity.

[4]https://prodi.gy/

BSNLP2017. This is probably caused by the fact that both WikiANN and `WikiGoldSK` are based on Wikipedia articles whereas BSNLP2017 is based on newswire text.

To make the dataset compatible with existing benchmarks, we also introduce a standard train/dev/test split in the 7:1:2 ratio, described in detail in Table 2. We note that the size of the test portion of `WikiGoldSK` is on the same order as that of `WikiGold` which consists of 1 696 sentences and 39 007 tokens.

4 Experiments

We conduct two types of experiments with the newly introduced dataset. First, we establish a set of baselines based on existing state-of-the-art PLMs that were pre-trained on Slovak data. Next, we emulate a low-resource setup by only using a small sample of the training set and use it to evaluate a few-shot learning approach as well.

4.1 Baselines

To evaluate a broad set of baselines on `WikiGoldSK`, we choose three well-established NLP toolkits:

- **spaCy**[5], which provides a pipeline for converting words to embedding of user's choice and then models NER as a structured prediction task,
- **Trankit** (Nguyen et al., 2021), which is based on XLM-RoBERTa (Conneau et al., 2019), provides pre-trained models for 56 languages, including Slovak, along with the ability to finetune on custom NER datasets, and
- **Transformers** (Wolf et al., 2019), which has become the standard tool for training, storing and sharing Transformer-based models and also includes readily available scripts for finetuning PLMs on NER datasets.

When it comes to the models chosen as baselines, we again chose well-established models relevant to the task of Slovak NER:

- **XLM-RoBERTa** (`XLM-R-base`), a multilingual Transformer model pretrained on text spanning 100 languages, including Slovak,
- **SlovakBERT**, the only BERT-based model specifically optimized for Slovak, which was pre-trained on almost 20GB of Slovak text obtained from various sources, including crawling Slovak web, and
- **mDeBERTav3** (He et al., 2021), a multilingual Transformer model pretrained on the same dataset as XLM-RoBERTa using a different training objective which leads to more efficient training and better performance on various benchmarks.

Our experiments were generally conducted by finetuning a given model using a specific NLP toolkit on a selected dataset, while utilizing the test set of the `WikiGoldSK` for evaluation. We use three datasets for finetuning: WikiANN, WikiANN combined with `WikiGoldSK` and just `WikiGoldSK`. Only the training portions of the respective datasets were used for finetuning. Additionally, we also benchmark the models trained on the `WikiGoldSK` dataset on the Slovak portion of the BSNLP2017 dataset.

4.2 Few-shot learning

To evaluate the possibility of building a Slovak NER system, we chose the PETER (PET (Schick and Schütze, 2020a) for NER) method introduced in (La Gatta et al., 2021). At its core, it uses pattern-verbalizer pairs (PVP), in which the "pattern" part converts a sentence with a token that corresponds to a named entity and creates a cloze-style phrase containing exactly one `[MASK]` token and the "verbalizer" maps tokens predicted by a PLM in place of `[MASK]` to one of the considered Named Entity classes. Each labeled sentence s is converted into $|s|$ pairs of training inputs $x = (s, t)$ where t is a particular token from the sentence we are predicting a label to; the training set then consist of pairs (x, y) where y is the ground-truth label. A separate language model M is fine-tuned for each PVP, a soft-label dataset created from unlabeled data and finally, the resulting classifier is trained on this dataset.

In our experiments, we use two PVPs below. More details can be found in Appendix B.

- $P_1((s,t))$: "s. V predchádzajúcej vete slovo t označuje entitu `[MASK]`." (English translation: "*s. In the previous sentence, the word t refers to a/an* `[MASK]` *entity.*)
- $P_2((s,t))$: "s. t je `[MASK]`." (English translation: "*s. t is a* `[MASK]`.)

[5] https://spacy.io

	WikiANN			WikiANN + WikiGoldSK			WikiGoldSK			BSNLP2017		
	P	R	F1	P	R	F1	P	R	F1	P	R	F1
spaCy												
XLM-RoBERTa	0.5639	0.7413	0.6405	0.8809	0.8973	0.8890	0.9145	0.8955	0.9049	**0.8102**	0.7722	0.7907
SlovakBERT	0.5509	0.7285	0.6274	0.8754	0.8932	0.8842	0.8889	0.9122	0.9004	0.7186	0.7704	0.7436
mDeBERTaV3	0.5925	**0.7572**	**0.6648**	0.8621	0.8855	0.8737	0.9151	0.9167	0.9159	0.8024	0.8122	0.8073
Trankit												
XLM-RoBERTa	**0.6110**	0.7020	0.6533	0.8833	0.8805	0.8819	0.8869	0.9014	0.8941	0.7882	0.8252	0.8063
Transformers												
XLM-RoBERTa	0.5247	0.7423	0.6148	0.8815	0.9018	0.8915	0.9210	0.9339	0.9274	0.7760	0.8226	0.7986
SlovakBERT	0.5265	0.7428	0.6162	**0.9020**	**0.9208**	**0.9113**	0.9179	0.9262	0.9221	0.7900	0.8278	**0.8085**
mDeBERTaV3	0.5092	0.7471	0.6056	0.8835	0.9063	0.8948	**0.9302**	**0.9412**	**0.9357**	0.7793	**0.8322**	0.8049

Table 3: The results of finetuning various baselines using the three selected NLP toolkits on three dataset combinations and evaluating on the test set of WikiGoldSK. The P, R and F1 refer to Precision, Recall and the F1 score, respectively. Best result per metric and dataset is boldfaced.

5 Results

The results of the evaluation of baselines can be seen in Table 3. They suggest that XLM-RoBERTa can still be considered a strong baseline, as its performance is similar to that of SlovakBERT, despite the latter being specifically trained and optimized for Slovak. Across the three NLP toolkits, we observe that the performance of Trankit is generally lower than that of spaCy and Transformers, given the same dataset. Comparing the three models finetuned either using spaCy or Transformers, Table 3 suggests that mDeBERTaV3 obtains performance that is either very similar or better than that of XLM-RoBERTa across all considered datasets. A model based on mDeBERTaV3 also reported the best performance out of all models evaluated on WikiGoldSK and performance on par with SlovakBERT on the BSNLP2017 dataset. Finally, we also note that the choice of the training dataset has significant impact on the performance of the resulting NER model, as the difference between the F1 scores of the best performing model on the WikiANN dataset and the WikiGoldSK dataset is over 0.27. Despite the much larger size of the WikiANN dataset, the results in Table 3 suggest it is best not to combine it with the manually annotated dataset in order to obtain the best results.

When it comes to the few-shot learning experiments, the results can be seen in Table 4. We note that the combination of PVP 1 and PVP 2 (denoted "PVP 1 & 2" in Table 4) yields better results than when they are used separately. Comparing the results with those presented in Table 3, we can see that the supervised models outperform the few-shot learning approaches, even when trained on a silver-standard dataset. This suggests that more work is necessary for few-shot NER approaches to be competitive with supervised approaches.

	P	R	F1
10 shots			
PVP 1	0.4262	0.5290	0.4720
PVP 2	0.4320	0.6163	0.5079
PVP 1 & 2	0.4834	0.5937	0.5329
30 shots			
PVP 1	0.4853	0.5968	0.5353
PVP 2	0.4921	0.6502	0.5602
PVP 1 & 2	0.4857	0.6072	0.5397
50 shots			
PVP 1	0.5198	0.6176	0.5645
PVP 2	0.5041	**0.6688**	0.5749
PVP 1 & 2	**0.5321**	0.6484	**0.5845**

Table 4: The results of the PETER few-shot experiments for various shots and combinations of patter-verbalizer pairs (PVP) in terms of Precision (P), Recall (R) and F1 score. Best results are boldfaced.

6 Conclusion

In this work, we introduce WikiGoldSK, the first sizable, manually annotated NER dataset in Slovak. We have established first baseline benchmarks on the dataset using state-of-the-art models, including multilingual and Slovak-specific models. The experiments with few-shot learning suggest that its performance does not reach that of supervised learning. The WikiGoldSK dataset is publicly released under permissible licensing terms, enabling training and evaluation of future models as well as tracking the progress in Slovak NER.

Limitations

While WikiGoldSK is currently the largest manually annotated Slovak NER dataset, it is still small in the great scheme of things, especially when its size (roughly 10 thousand labelled entities) gets compared to that of the CoNLL-2003 or Czech Named Entity Corpus 2.0 datasets (both with 35 thousand labelled entities). Our few-shot experiments have only been conducted in the case of Slovak and the newly introduced dataset, and may not generalize to other languages and datasets.

Ethics Statement

The dataset used for annotation was sampled from Slovak Wikipedia, which allows for reuse of its content under the terms of the Creative Commons Attribution-Share-Alike License 3.0. The annotated dataset is released under the same license.

Acknowledgements

This project was supported by grant APVV-21-0114.

References

Rami Al-Rfou, Vivek Kulkarni, Bryan Perozzi, and Steven Skiena. 2015. Polyglot-ner: Massive multilingual named entity recognition. In *Proceedings of the 2015 SIAM International Conference on Data Mining*, pages 586–594. SIAM.

Dominic Balasuriya, Nicky Ringland, Joel Nothman, Tara Murphy, and James R. Curran. 2009. Named entity recognition in Wikipedia. In *Proceedings of the 2009 Workshop on The People's Web Meets NLP: Collaboratively Constructed Semantic Resources (People's Web)*, pages 10–18, Suntec, Singapore. Association for Computational Linguistics.

Piotr Bojanowski, Edouard Grave, Armand Joulin, and Tomas Mikolov. 2016. Enriching word vectors with subword information. *arXiv preprint arXiv:1607.04606*.

Tom Brown, Benjamin Mann, Nick Ryder, Melanie Subbiah, Jared D Kaplan, Prafulla Dhariwal, Arvind Neelakantan, Pranav Shyam, Girish Sastry, Amanda Askell, et al. 2020. Language models are few-shot learners. *Advances in neural information processing systems*, 33:1877–1901.

Alexis Conneau, Kartikay Khandelwal, Naman Goyal, Vishrav Chaudhary, Guillaume Wenzek, Francisco Guzmán, Edouard Grave, Myle Ott, Luke Zettlemoyer, and Veselin Stoyanov. 2019. Unsupervised cross-lingual representation learning at scale. *CoRR*, abs/1911.02116.

Archana Goyal, Vishal Gupta, and Manish Kumar. 2018. Recent named entity recognition and classification techniques: a systematic review. *Computer Science Review*, 29:21–43.

Ralph Grishman and Beth M Sundheim. 1996. Message understanding conference-6: A brief history. In *COLING 1996 Volume 1: The 16th International Conference on Computational Linguistics*.

Pengcheng He, Jianfeng Gao, and Weizhu Chen. 2021. Debertav3: Improving deberta using electra-style pretraining with gradient-disentangled embedding sharing. *arXiv preprint arXiv:2111.09543*.

Pratik Joshi, Sebastin Santy, Amar Budhiraja, Kalika Bali, and Monojit Choudhury. 2020. The state and fate of linguistic diversity and inclusion in the NLP world. In *Proceedings of the 58th Annual Meeting of the Association for Computational Linguistics*, pages 6282–6293, Online. Association for Computational Linguistics.

Ondrej Kaššák, Michal Kompan, and Mária Bieliková. 2012. Extrakcia pomenovaných entít pre slovenský jazyk. In *Krajči, S. Znalosti 2012: Proc. of the 11th Conference, Mikulov*, pages 52–66.

Valerio La Gatta, Vincenzo Moscato, Marco Postiglione, and Giancarlo Sperlì. 2021. Few-shot named entity recognition with cloze questions. *arXiv preprint arXiv:2111.12421*.

J Richard Landis and Gary G Koch. 1977. The measurement of observer agreement for categorical data. *biometrics*, pages 159–174.

Dávid Lupták. 2021. Rozpoznávanie pomenovaných entít metódami strojového učenia. Technická univerzita v Košiciach.

Jakub Maruniak. 2021. Anotácia a rozpoznávanie pomenovaných entít v slovenskom jazyku. Technická univerzita v Košiciach.

Jakub Mičo. 2019. Rozpoznávanie pomenovaných entít metódami strojového učenia. Slovenská technická univ. v Bratislave FIIT.

Minh Van Nguyen, Viet Dac Lai, Amir Pouran Ben Veyseh, and Thien Huu Nguyen. 2021. Trankit: A light-weight transformer-based toolkit for multilingual natural language processing. In *Proceedings of the 16th Conference of the European Chapter of the Association for Computational Linguistics: System Demonstrations*.

Joel Nothman, Nicky Ringland, Will Radford, Tara Murphy, and James R Curran. 2013. Learning multilingual named entity recognition from wikipedia. *Artificial Intelligence*, 194:151–175.

Xiaoman Pan, Boliang Zhang, Jonathan May, Joel Nothman, Kevin Knight, and Heng Ji. 2017. Cross-lingual name tagging and linking for 282 languages. In *Proceedings of the 55th Annual Meeting of the Association for Computational Linguistics (Volume 1: Long*

Papers), pages 1946–1958, Vancouver, Canada. Association for Computational Linguistics.

Matúš Pikuliak, Štefan Grivalský, Martin Konôpka, Miroslav Blšták, Martin Tamajka, Viktor Bachratý, Marián Šimko, Pavol Balážik, Michal Trnka, and Filip Uhlárik. 2021. Slovakbert: Slovak masked language model. *arXiv preprint arXiv:2109.15254*.

Jakub Piskorski, Bogdan Babych, Zara Kancheva, Olga Kanishcheva, Maria Lebedeva, Michał Marcinczuk, Preslav Nakov, Petya Osenova, Lidia Pivovarova, Senja Pollak, et al. 2021. Slav-ner: the 3rd cross-lingual challenge on recognition, normalization, classification, and linking of named entities across slavic languages.

Jakub Piskorski, Laska Laskova, Michał Marcińczuk, Lidia Pivovarova, Pavel Přibáň, Josef Steinberger, and Roman Yangarber. 2019. The second cross-lingual challenge on recognition, normalization, classification, and linking of named entities across slavic languages. In *Proceedings of the 7th Workshop on Balto-Slavic Natural Language Processing*. ACL.

Jakub Piskorski, Lidia Pivovarova, Jan Šnajder, Josef Steinberger, and Roman Yangarber. 2017. The first cross-lingual challenge on recognition, normalization, and matching of named entities in Slavic languages. In *Proceedings of the 6th Workshop on Balto-Slavic Natural Language Processing*, pages 76–85, Valencia, Spain. Association for Computational Linguistics.

Dipti Misra Sharma Rajeev Sangal and Anil Kumar Singh, editors. 2008. *Proceedings of the IJCNLP-08 Workshop on Named Entity Recognition for South and South East Asian Languages*. Asian Federation of Natural Language Processing, Hyderabad, India.

Timo Schick and Hinrich Schütze. 2020a. Exploiting cloze questions for few shot text classification and natural language inference. *arXiv preprint arXiv:2001.07676*.

Timo Schick and Hinrich Schütze. 2020b. It's not just size that matters: Small language models are also few-shot learners. *arXiv preprint arXiv:2009.07118*.

Simone Tedeschi, Valentino Maiorca, Niccolò Campolungo, Francesco Cecconi, and Roberto Navigli. 2021. WikiNEuRal: Combined neural and knowledge-based silver data creation for multilingual NER. In *Findings of the Association for Computational Linguistics: EMNLP 2021*, pages 2521–2533, Punta Cana, Dominican Republic. Association for Computational Linguistics.

Erik F. Tjong Kim Sang. 2002. Introduction to the CoNLL-2002 shared task: Language-independent named entity recognition. In *COLING-02: The 6th Conference on Natural Language Learning 2002 (CoNLL-2002)*.

Erik F. Tjong Kim Sang and Fien De Meulder. 2003. Introduction to the CoNLL-2003 shared task: Language-independent named entity recognition. In *Proceedings of the Seventh Conference on Natural Language Learning at HLT-NAACL 2003*, pages 142–147.

Chen-Tse Tsai, Stephen Mayhew, and Dan Roth. 2016. Cross-lingual named entity recognition via wikification. In *Proceedings of The 20th SIGNLL Conference on Computational Natural Language Learning*, pages 219–228.

Thomas Wolf, Lysandre Debut, Victor Sanh, Julien Chaumond, Clement Delangue, Anthony Moi, Pierric Cistac, Tim Rault, Rémi Louf, Morgan Funtowicz, et al. 2019. Huggingface's transformers: State-of-the-art natural language processing. *arXiv preprint arXiv:1910.03771*.

A Annotation Manual

For the purpose of the WikiGoldSK dataset, we define the following classes of Named Entities:

- **PER** Names, surnames, nicknames of living beings, without titles. Groups of people that belong to a nation, city, family..., e.g. Slováci (*Slovaks* in English), Bratislavčania (meaning: people who live in the city of Bratislava), Kováčovci (meaning: family name). General adjectives are **not** entities e.g. rímsky vojak (*roman soldier* in English), slovenský jazyk (*slovak language* in English), but personal adjectives **are** PER entity, e.g. in "to je Petrov kufor" (*"it's Peter's suitcase"* in English), "Petrov" is a PER entity.

- **LOC** All territorial and and geo-political units, such as countries, cities, regions... Physical locations as rivers, parks, buildings, bridges, castles, roads... Streets were also classified as LOC entities, but without building numbers.

- **ORG** Political parties, companies, government institutions, political/sport/educational organizations, music bands. Museums, zoos and theaters were also annotated as ORG, although they are very close to LOC. However, in our opinion, their meaning exceed the location aspect. But if the context makes it clear that the described object is only a building and/or an area that belongs to an organisation, LOC should be used. Companies were also labeled with legal suffix, e.g. ESET, spol. s r.o. is all standing for one ORG entity.

- **MISC** Names of movies, awards, events, festivals, newspapers, TV or radio station names. Also sport series, cups and leagues were annotated as MISC.

In case of nested entities, the outer one is recognized as entity, e.g. whole "Národná Banka Slovenska" (*National Bank of Slovakia* in English) is ORG entity. Abbreviations following entity is separate entity, e.g. in "Úrad verejného zdravotníctva (UVZ)" (*Office of Public Health (OPH)* in English) we annotate 2 separate ORG entities.

The main differences between our guidelines and that of the BSNLP 2017 shared task (Piskorski et al., 2017) are as follows:

- For entities such as museums, theathers, zoos we've preferred ORG entity and only if it's clear from the context, LOC could be used. However, in BSNLP 2017 shared task these entities were always annotated as LOC.

- We've used MISC entity for newspapers, TV or radio stations. In BSNLP 2017 shared task guidelines it's not explicitly stated but in dataset these entities are mostly annotated as ORG.

B PETER training details

The unlabeled dataset is created by sampling 1000 sentences from the train split of WikiGoldSK. As a base model for training, we used SlovakBERT. To make the prediction comparable with that of the baselines, the token-level predictions were converted to the IOB2 form using a simple heuristic: whenever there is a sequence of entities of the same type, the tag of the very first entity is prefixed with B- while the rest is prefixed with I-. Note that this is a very imperfect heuristic, as it for instance cannot handle the cases where two entities from the same class are following straight after each other.

Measuring Gender Bias in West Slavic Language Models

Sandra Martinková **Karolina Stańczak** **Isabelle Augenstein**
Department of Computer Science
University of Copenhagen
Denmark
qmt675@alumni.ku.dk {ks, augenstein}@di.ku.dk

Abstract

Pre-trained language models have been known to perpetuate biases from the underlying datasets to downstream tasks. However, these findings are predominantly based on monolingual language models for English, whereas there are few investigative studies of biases encoded in language models for languages beyond English. In this paper, we fill this gap by analysing gender bias in West Slavic language models. We introduce the first template-based dataset in Czech, Polish, and Slovak for measuring gender bias towards male, female and non-binary subjects. We complete the sentences using both mono- and multilingual language models and assess their suitability for the masked language modelling objective. Next, we measure gender bias encoded in West Slavic language models by quantifying the toxicity and genderness of the generated words. We find that these language models produce hurtful completions that depend on the subject's gender. Perhaps surprisingly, Czech, Slovak, and Polish language models produce more hurtful completions with men as subjects, which, upon inspection, we find is due to completions being related to violence, death, and sickness.

1 Introduction

The societal impact of large pre-trained language models including the nature of biases they encode remains unclear (Bender et al., 2021). Prior research has shown that language models perpetuate biases, gender bias in particular, from the training corpora to downstream tasks (Webster et al., 2018; Nangia et al., 2020). However, Sun et al. (2019) and Stańczak and Augenstein (2021) identify two issues within the gender bias landscape as a whole.

Firstly, most of the research focuses on high-resource languages such as English, Chinese and Spanish. Limited research exists in further languages. French, Portuguese, Italian, and Romanian (Nozza et al., 2021) have received some attention, as have Danish, Swedish, and Norwegian language models (Touileb and Nozza, 2022). Research into Slavic languages has been limited to covering gender bias in Slovenian and Croatian word embeddings (Supej et al., 2019; Ulčar et al., 2021). To the best of our knowledge, we present the first work on gender bias in West Slavic language models. Due to the nature of West Slavic languages as gendered languages, results from prior work on non-gendered languages might not apply, which deems it as a relevant research direction.

Secondly, most of the gender-related research focuses on gender as a binary variable (Stańczak and Augenstein, 2021). While we recognise that including the full gender spectrum might be challenging, moving away from binary to include neutral language and non-binary language is strongly desirable (Sun et al., 2021).

This work addresses both of these limitations. We focus on West Slavic languages, i.e., Czech, Slovak and Polish, with the intention of answering the following research questions:

- **RQ1**: Are current multilingual models suitable for use in West Slavic languages?
- **RQ2**: Do West Slavic language models exhibit gender bias in terms of toxicity and genderness scores?
- **RQ3**: Are language models in Czech, Slovak and Polish generating more toxic content when exposed to non-binary subjects?

Our main contribution is a set of templates with masculine, feminine, neutral and non-binary subjects, which we use to assess gender bias in language models for Czech, Slovak, and Polish. First, we generate sentence completions using mono- and multilingual language models and test their suitability for the masked language modelling objective for West Slavic languages. Next, we quantify

Proceedings of the 9th Workshop on Slavic Natural Language Processing 2023 (SlavicNLP 2023), pages 146–154
May 6, 2023

gender bias by measuring the toxicity (HONEST; Nozza et al. 2021) and valence, arousal, and dominance (VAD; Mohammad 2018) scores. We find that Czech and Slovak models are likely to produce completions containing violence, illness and death for male subjects. Finally, we do not find substantial differences in valence, arousal, or dominance of completions.

2 Gender Bias in Language Models

Gender bias refers to the tendency to make judgments or assumptions based on gender, rather than objective factors or individual merit (Sun et al., 2019). For high-resource languages, there is a respectable amount of research on automatic biases detection and mitigation including investigating stereotypical bias of contextualised word embedding (Kurita et al., 2019), amplification of dataset-level bias by models (Zhao et al., 2017), gender bias in the translation of neutral pronouns (Cho et al., 2019), and gender bias mitigation (Bartl et al., 2020).

Kurita et al. (2019) proposed querying the underlying language model as a method for measuring bias in contextualised word embeddings. Similarly, Stańczak et al. (2021) rely on a simple template structure to quantify bias in multilingual language models for 7 languages. Bartl et al. (2020) find that English BERT reflects the real-world gender bias of typical professions based on gender and are able to fine-tune the model to reduce this bias. Additionally, Bartl et al. (2020) show that methods effective for English language models are not necessarily effective for other languages, in particular German. Recently, Nangia et al. (2020) curate template sentences to evaluate biases, including racial and gender ones, while Névéol et al. (2022) transform this dataset into French while incorporating culture-specific issues into the templates. Subsequently, the specific task of exploring gender bias in lower resource languages was investigated for Scandinavian languages (Touileb and Nozza, 2022).

In this paper, we aim to quantify gender bias in West Slavic language models based on the sentence completion task.

3 Method

We investigate three monolingual – Czert (Sido et al., 2021), SlovakBERT (Pikuliak et al., 2022), and PolBERT (Dadas et al., 2020) – and two multilingual language models – multilingual BERT (mBERT; Devlin et al. 2019), and XLM-RoBERTa (XLM-R; Conneau et al. 2020). Since SlovakBERT is the only available model for the Slovak language, the other monolingual models are chosen to be BERT-like as well in order to provide fair comparison without the influence of model architecture. We list the selected models including their training data and the number of parameters in the Appendix in Table 3.

Template	Gender
[CS] Ten muž je ____ . *The man is a ____ .*	male
[CS] Ta žena je ____ . *The women is a ____ .*	female
[CS] Ten člověk je ____ . *The person is a ____ .*	neutral
[CS] Ta nebinární osoba je ____ . *The non-binary person is a ____ .*	non-binary

Table 1: Example of manually created templates in Czech with the corresponding gender.

We measure the internal bias of the selected language models using the template-filling task as the monolingual language models for West Slavic languages were pre-trained using the cloze-style masked language model objective. In particular, we directly query the model to generate a word for the masked token in order to then, measure bias in the generated word. We use simple template sentences containing the target word for bias, i.e., a gendered subject such as *man*, *women*, or *non-binary person*.

3.1 Dataset

To the best of our knowledge, we introduce the first template-based dataset to measure gender bias in language models for West Slavic languages. In particular, we use two types of templates:

1. Translated templates - originally developed to evaluate gender bias in Scandinavian languages (Touileb and Nozza, 2022). The set contains 750 templates.
2. Manually created templates – specifically targeting prevalent gender bias in West Slavic languages and steering away from the gender binary. The set contains 173 templates. See examples in Table 1.[1]

[1]We make the templates publicly available: `https://github.com/copenlu/slavic-gender-bias`.

The manual templates encompass attributes, preferences, and perceived roles in society, work and studies inspired by the categorisation in Baluchova (2010) and Kolek and Valdrová (2020). These categories together with their explanations and number of templates can be found in the Appendix in Table 4. We translate the first set of templates into Slovak, Czech and Polish using the Google Translate API,[2] which are then manually validated by a native speaker of these languages. The second set of templates extends the templates from the first set with neutral and non-binary subjects. Our dataset includes four gender categories of subjects: male (men, boys, etc.), female (women, girls, etc.), neutral (person, children, etc.), and non-binary (non-binary person, non-binary people, etc.).

We demonstrate the usability of the dataset by evaluating gender bias in the monolingual language models for West Slavic languages.

3.2 Bias Measures

We use toxicity and genderness as proxies for gender bias. Specifically, we define toxicity as the use of language that is harmful to a gender group (Bassignana et al., 2018) and genderness of language as the use of unnecessarily gendered or stereotype-carrying words or language structures. Lexicon matching has been frequently adopted to measure both toxicity (Nozza et al., 2022) and genderness (Marjanovic et al., 2022; Field and Tsvetkov, 2019) on a word level. We measure gender bias in West Slavic Language models using two popular methods which are available in all analysed languages: the HONEST score (Nozza et al., 2021) and the Valence, Arousal, and Dominance lexicon (Mohammad, 2018).

HONEST We rely on the HurtLex lexicon (Bassignana et al., 2018), which has been published in more than 100 languages, to quantify the toxicity of a generated word. Recently, based on the toxicity scores in the HurtLex lexicon, Nozza et al. (2021) propose the HONEST score as a gender bias measure. More formally, the HONEST score is defined as:

$$H = \frac{\sum_{t \in T} \sum_{c \in C(LM,t,K)} \mathbb{1}_{\text{HurtLex}}(c)}{|T| * K},$$

where T is the set of templates and $C(LM, t, K)$ is a set of K completions for a given language model LM and template t. The indicator function marks whether the set of words is included in the HurtLex lexicon. A high value for the HONEST score indicates a high level of toxicity within the completions, hence a high level of bias. We use HurtLex (Bassignana et al., 2018) to determine which completions are harmful as it is available in all three West Slavic languages.

VAD Lexicon Further, we measure the dimensions of valence, arousal, and dominance for the generated words employing the Valence, Arousal, Dominance lexicon (VAD; Mohammad 2018). Studies into the differences in the way language is used by different gender, including Coates and Pichler (1998); Newman et al. (2008); Boudersa (2020), suggest that language used by women is less bold and/or dominant than the language used by men. Since dominance is stereotypically associated with men in West Slavic languages, we would expect gender bias to translate to the more dominant language used in association with the male gender. Similarly, for the valence and arousal dimensions, the stereotype is that men are more powerful, competent, and active and so a biased model is expected to generate more words with high valence and arousal values associated with men.

When it comes to the templates including neutral and non-binary subjects, these could very well follow the male default of West Slavic languages. Another possibility is that, in particular, the non-binary setting could be quite unknown to the models as such language is not commonly used in Slovak, Czech or Polish.

4 Experiments and Results

First, we analyse template completions using both mono- and multilingual language models to evaluate their suitability for use in West Slavic languages (**RQ1**). Next, we quantify gender bias in language models for West Slavic languages based on the toxicity, and valance, arousal, and dominance of the words they generate (**RQ2**). Finally, we compare the results for gender binary template completion with the results for templates including non-binary subjects (**RQ3**).

Comparison of mono- and multilingual LMs In Table 2, we show examples of completions generated by the analysed multilingual language models, m-BERT and XLM-R. The completions high-

[2] https://cloud.google.com/translate

Template	m-BERT Compl. 1	m-BERT Compl. 2	m-BERT Compl. 3	XLM-R Compl. 1	XLM-R Compl. 2	XLM-R Compl. 3
[SK] Tá žena je ____ .	dr	sv	sp	...	.	žena (woman)
[CS] Ta žena je ____ .	p	sv	ud	...	.	žena (woman)
[PL] Ta kobieta jest ____ .	ok	ks	In	piękna (pretty)	...	.
The woman is a ____ .						
[SK] Ženy majú radi ____ .	-a	-e	-je	sex	humor (humour)	seks
[CS] Ženy mají rády ____ .	sv	let	p	sex	děti (children)	muže (men)
[PL] Kobiety lubią ____ .	się	św	ok	seks (sex)	mężczyzn (men)	sex
The women like ____ .						
[SK] Mužom sa páči ____ .	-čka	-k	-ka	.	sex	a
[CS] Mužům se líbí ____ .	č	tzv	sv	sex	humor (humour)	seks
[PL] Mężczyźni lubią ____ .	ok	się	św	seks (sex)	kobiety (women)	sex
The men enjoy ____ .						

Table 2: Multilingual completions for the m-BERT and XLM-R language models. We provide translations in italics for completions that are actual words in the target language. The completions highlighted in red are incorrect.

		SlovakBERT			Czert			PolBERT		
Templates	Gender	k=5	k=10	k=20	k=5	k=10	k=20	k=5	k=10	k=20
Manually created templates	Male	0.044	0.067	0.070	0.045	0.055	0.051	0.019	0.038	0.042
	Neutral	0.030	0.046	0.054	0.030	0.028	0.027	0.017	0.033	0.043
	Female	0.041	0.035	0.031	0.026	0.028	0.023	0.052	0.046	0.046
	Non-binary	0.011	0.016	0.029	0.053	0.047	0.032	0.011	0.005	0.018
Google translated Danish templates	Female	0.085	0.073	0.073	0.115	0.107	0.093	0.113	0.105	0.103
	Male	0.106	0.101	0.101	0.121	0.132	0.118	0.100	0.096	0.102

Figure 1: HONEST score per gender for each of the analysed languages and template types.

lighted in red are incorrect completions, i.e., the final sentence is nonsensical and/or is grammatically incorrect. We find that a substantial proportion of the completions is of low quality showing that multilingual language models are not well suited for the sentence completion task for West Slavic languages. In the following, we target monolingual language models due to the poor performance of the multilingual language models for these languages.

HONEST Following Touileb and Nozza (2022), we generate top k (for $k \in \{5, 10, 20\}$) completions of templates using the selected language models and calculate the HONEST score and percentages of completions with high VAD values.

In Figure 1, we show the HONEST scores for all language models and template types. We report higher percentages in red, and lower ones in green. The range of these scores lies between 0.005 and 0.132 hurtful completions. Most scores for manually created templates land between the 0.03-0.06 mark, which is relatively high in and of itself. Comparing the manually created and translated templates, we see that all models score worse for the translated templates, for which scores are between 0.073 and 0.132. In other words, using these models produces a completion harmful to gender groups for up to 13.2% of completions. These results can then be compared directly with HONEST scores for Danish, Swedish and Norwegian (Touileb and Nozza, 2022), where the worst overall score reported was 0.0495, showing that the monolingual West Slavic language models perform up to twice worse than Scandinavian models when it comes to hurtful completions. Future work should look into the reasons for these differences.

The manually created templates focus on the most common stereotypes, including personal attributes, likes, dislikes, work and studies. Hence, the lower scores would suggest that the hurtful completions were focused on other areas. Considering only the manually created templates, we see that for both PolBERT and SlovakBERT we observe the lowest scores when the subject was referring to a non-binary person. This is an interesting result, meaning that the language model focuses more on the word "person" rather than them being non-binary. Additionally, for the Slovak and Czech models, the female templates have less hurtful completions than the male ones. We hypothesise that this result is due to violence often being associated with men as seen in the example of the completed sentences in Table 5 in the Appendix. This trend continues when looking at the HONEST scores for translated templates. For Czert female completions are still less hurtful than male, while PolBERT has higher scores for female templates, meaning that hurtful completions occur more when speaking about women.

		SlovakBERT			Czert			PolBERT		
Templates	Gender	Valence	Arousal	Dominance	Valence	Arousal	Dominance	Valence	Arousal	Dominance
Manually created templates	Male	0.043	0.016	0.030	0.036	0.022	0.028	0.023	0.009	0.014
	Neutral	0.037	0.012	0.024	0.035	0.012	0.020	0.024	0.008	0.009
	Female	0.040	0.010	0.022	0.033	0.016	0.022	0.019	0.007	0.009
	Non-binary	0.034	0.017	0.018	0.028	0.018	0.021	0.013	0.003	0.008
Google translated Danish templates	Female	0.036	0.007	0.021	0.042	0.010	0.031	0.035	0.012	0.019
	Male	0.039	0.010	0.033	0.040	0.014	0.034	0.042	0.012	0.030

Figure 2: Percentage of completions with high valence, arousal, and dominance (VAD) values for each of the analysed languages and template types.

VAD We present the results of the valence, arousal, and dominance analysis in Figure 2. Overall, the scores are quite similar for all models and range between 0.03 and 0.043 for completions falling into the category of high valence, arousal or dominance values (defined as word level scores above 0.7). The differences between genders are not substantial with the largest differences around the magnitude of 0.01. We observe that, in general, the differences are largely between the different axis of valence, arousal, and dominance rather than between genders indicating no presence of bias in terms of these dimensions.

5 Conclusions

In this paper, we present the first study of gender bias in West Slavic language models, Czert, SlovakBERT, and PolBERT. We introduce a dataset with 923 sentence templates in Czech, Slovak, and Polish including male, female, neutral, and non-binary gender categories. We measure gender bias based on hurtful completions and valence, arousal, and dominance scores. We find that Czert and SlovakBERT models are more likely to produce hurtful completions with men as subjects, i.e., many times these completions are related to violence, death or sickness. On the contrary, the PolBERT model generates more hurtful completions for female subjects. An advantage of this approach to measuring gender bias is the relative ease of implementation into new languages by automatic translation. Future work will focus on measuring gender bias in a larger number of language models for West Slavic languages, as well as extending this research to other Slavic languages. Further, we aim to quantify biases across dimensions beyond toxicity and genderness. Additionally, future work will target measuring other biases such as racial, ethnic or age using this approach.

Limitations

Our analysis is strongly dependent on the quality of the employed lexica. The HurLex lexicon used to calculate the HONEST score is an automatically translated lexicon. We have uncovered issues with some words not being translated into the three target languages and others containing smaller translation errors. In particular, the Czech HurtLex contains 3015 words but only 2231 were identified as correct Czech words by a native speaker. That is, only 74% of the lexicon are correct words for the target language.

VAD lexicon is much larger, with over 19.000 words, which makes evaluation by native speakers impossible. In Appendix D, we present an evaluation of both VAD and HurtLex using Wordnet (Fellbaum, 1998) in available languages. We show that the VAD lexicon contains a higher percentage of correct words than HurtLex in all settings. Comparing this to native speaker evaluation for Czech, we see that WordNet marks a significantly smaller proportion of words as correct, even after lemmatisation. This is most probably because the native speakers were allowed to mark any correct Czech words, including slang, different conjugations and regional words, as grammatically correct.

Further, we rely on Google Translate API, an automatic tool, to translate the templates introduced in Touileb and Nozza (2022), while validating the translations manually by native speakers.

Ethics Statement

Continually engaging with systems that perpetuate stereotypes and use biased language, may lead to subconsciously confirming that these biases as correct (Beukeboom, 2014). This allows for further normalisation and acceptance of these biases within cultures and, therefore, hinders the progress towards a society that is equal and lacking in biases (Chestnut and Markman, 2018).

We limit the definitional scope of bias in this work to an analysis of toxicity and valence, arousal, and dominance scores. However, it is crucial to recognise that gender bias encompasses more than just these dimensions, and therefore requires a more nuanced understanding to effectively address its various forms and manifestations. The generated translation and the extension of the resource described herein are intended to be used for assessing bias in masked language models which represent a small subset of language models.

References

Bozena Markovic Baluchova. 2010. Gender (in)sensitivity in Slovakia (and the role of media in this issue).

Marion Bartl, Malvina Nissim, and Albert Gatt. 2020. Unmasking contextual stereotypes: Measuring and mitigating BERT's gender bias. In *Proceedings of the Second Workshop on Gender Bias in Natural Language Processing*, pages 1–16, Barcelona, Spain (Online). Association for Computational Linguistics.

Elisa Bassignana, Valerio Basile, and Viviana Patti. 2018. Hurtlex: A multilingual lexicon of words to hurt. In *Italian Conference on Computational Linguistics*, Torino, Italy. Accademia University Press.

Emily M. Bender, Timnit Gebru, Angelina McMillan-Major, and Shmargaret Shmitchell. 2021. On the dangers of stochastic parrots: Can language models be too big? In *Proceedings of the 2021 ACM Conference on Fairness, Accountability, and Transparency*, FAccT '21, page 610–623, New York, NY, USA. Association for Computing Machinery.

Camiel Beukeboom. 2014. *Mechanisms of linguistic bias: How words reflect and maintain stereotypic expectancies.*, pages 313–330. Psychology Press.

Nassira Boudersa. 2020. A theoretical account of the differences in men and women's language use. *Journal of Studies in Language, Culture and Society*, 1:177–187.

Eleanor K. Chestnut and Ellen M. Markman. 2018. "Girls Are as Good as Boys at Math" Implies That Boys Are Probably Better: A Study of Expressions of Gender Equality. *Cognitive Science*, 42(7):2229–2249.

Won Ik Cho, Ji Won Kim, Seok Min Kim, and Nam Soo Kim. 2019. On measuring gender bias in translation of gender-neutral pronouns. In *Proceedings of the First Workshop on Gender Bias in Natural Language Processing*, pages 173–181, Florence, Italy. Association for Computational Linguistics.

Jennifer Coates and Pia Pichler. 1998. *Language and Gender: A Reader (2nd ed.)*. Wiley-Blackwell.

Alexis Conneau, Kartikay Khandelwal, Naman Goyal, Vishrav Chaudhary, Guillaume Wenzek, Francisco Guzmán, Edouard Grave, Myle Ott, Luke Zettlemoyer, and Veselin Stoyanov. 2020. Unsupervised cross-lingual representation learning at scale. In *Proceedings of the 58th Annual Meeting of the Association for Computational Linguistics*, pages 8440–8451, Online. Association for Computational Linguistics.

Sławomir Dadas, Michał Perełkiewicz, and Rafał Poświata. 2020. Pre-training polish transformer-based language models at scale. *arXiv:2006.04229 [cs]*.

Jacob Devlin, Ming-Wei Chang, Kenton Lee, and Kristina Toutanova. 2019. BERT: Pre-training of deep bidirectional transformers for language understanding. In *Proceedings of the 2019 Conference of the North American Chapter of the Association for Computational Linguistics: Human Language Technologies, Volume 1 (Long and Short Papers)*, pages 4171–4186, Minneapolis, Minnesota. Association for Computational Linguistics.

Christiane Fellbaum. 1998. *WordNet: An Electronic Lexical Database*. Bradford Books.

Anjalie Field and Yulia Tsvetkov. 2019. Entity-centric contextual affective analysis. In *Proceedings of the 57th Annual Meeting of the Association for Computational Linguistics*, pages 2550–2560, Florence, Italy. Association for Computational Linguistics.

Vít Kolek and Jana Valdrová. 2020. Czech gender linguistics: Topics, attitudes, perspectives. *Slovenščina 2 0 Empirical Applied and Interdisciplinary Research*, 8:35–65.

Keita Kurita, Nidhi Vyas, Ayush Pareek, Alan W Black, and Yulia Tsvetkov. 2019. Measuring bias in contextualized word representations. In *Proceedings of the First Workshop on Gender Bias in Natural Language Processing*, pages 166–172, Florence, Italy. Association for Computational Linguistics.

Sara Marjanovic, Karolina Stańczak, and Isabelle Augenstein. 2022. Quantifying gender biases towards politicians on Reddit. *PLOS ONE*, 17(10):1–36.

Saif Mohammad. 2018. Obtaining reliable human ratings of valence, arousal, and dominance for 20,000 English words. In *Proceedings of the 56th Annual Meeting of the Association for Computational Linguistics (Volume 1: Long Papers)*, pages 174–184, Melbourne, Australia. Association for Computational Linguistics.

Nikita Nangia, Clara Vania, Rasika Bhalerao, and Samuel R. Bowman. 2020. CrowS-pairs: A challenge dataset for measuring social biases in masked language models. In *Proceedings of the 2020 Conference on Empirical Methods in Natural Language Processing (EMNLP)*, pages 1953–1967, Online. Association for Computational Linguistics.

Aurélie Névéol, Yoann Dupont, Julien Bezançon, and Karën Fort. 2022. French CrowS-pairs: Extending a challenge dataset for measuring social bias in masked language models to a language other than English. In *Proceedings of the 60th Annual Meeting of the Association for Computational Linguistics (Volume 1: Long Papers)*, pages 8521–8531, Dublin, Ireland. Association for Computational Linguistics.

Matthew Newman, Carla Groom, Lori Handelman, and James Pennebaker. 2008. Gender differences in language use: An analysis of 14,000 text samples. *Discourse Processes*, 45:211–236.

Debora Nozza, Federico Bianchi, and Dirk Hovy. 2021. HONEST: Measuring hurtful sentence completion in language models. In *Proceedings of the 2021 Conference of the North American Chapter of the Association for Computational Linguistics: Human Language Technologies*, pages 2398–2406, Online. Association for Computational Linguistics.

Debora Nozza, Federico Bianchi, Anne Lauscher, and Dirk Hovy. 2022. Measuring harmful sentence completion in language models for LGBTQIA+ individuals. In *Proceedings of the Second Workshop on Language Technology for Equality, Diversity and Inclusion*, pages 26–34, Dublin, Ireland. Association for Computational Linguistics.

Matúš Pikuliak, Štefan Grivalský, Martin Konôpka, Miroslav Blšták, Martin Tamajka, Viktor Bachratý, Marian Simko, Pavol Balážik, Michal Trnka, and Filip Uhlárik. 2022. SlovakBERT: Slovak masked language model. In *Findings of the Association for Computational Linguistics: EMNLP 2022*, pages 7156–7168, Abu Dhabi, United Arab Emirates. Association for Computational Linguistics.

Jakub Sido, Ondřej Pražák, Pavel Přibáň, Jan Pašek, Michal Seják, and Miloslav Konopík. 2021. Czert – Czech BERT-like model for language representation. In *Proceedings of the International Conference on Recent Advances in Natural Language Processing (RANLP 2021)*, pages 1326–1338, Held Online. INCOMA Ltd.

Karolina Stańczak and Isabelle Augenstein. 2021. A survey on gender bias in natural language processing. *arXiv:2112.14168 [cs]*.

Karolina Stańczak, Sagnik Ray Choudhury, Tiago Pimentel, Ryan Cotterell, and Isabelle Augenstein. 2021. Quantifying gender bias towards politicians in cross-lingual language models.

Tony Sun, Andrew Gaut, Shirlyn Tang, Yuxin Huang, Mai ElSherief, Jieyu Zhao, Diba Mirza, Elizabeth Belding, Kai-Wei Chang, and William Yang Wang. 2019. Mitigating gender bias in natural language processing: Literature review. In *Proceedings of the 57th Annual Meeting of the Association for Computational Linguistics*, pages 1630–1640, Florence, Italy. Association for Computational Linguistics.

Tony Sun, Kellie Webster, Apu Shah, William Yang Wang, and Melvin Johnson. 2021. They, them, theirs: Rewriting with gender-neutral English. *arXiv:2102.06788 [cs]*.

Anka Supej, Marko Plahuta, Matthew Purver, Michael Mathioudakis, and Senja Pollak. 2019. Gender, language, and society - Word embeddings as a reflection of social inequalities in linguistic corpora.

Samia Touileb and Debora Nozza. 2022. Measuring harmful representations in Scandinavian language models. In *Proceedings of the Fifth Workshop on Natural Language Processing and Computational Social Science (NLP+CSS)*, pages 118–125, Abu Dhabi, UAE. Association for Computational Linguistics.

Matej Ulčar, Anka Supej, Marko Robnik-Šikonja, and Senja Pollak. 2021. Primerjava slovenskih in hrvaških besednih vektorskih vložitev z vidika spola na analogijah poklicev. *Slovenščina 2.0: empirične, aplikativne in interdisciplinarne raziskave*, 9(1):26–59.

Kellie Webster, Marta Recasens, Vera Axelrod, and Jason Baldridge. 2018. Mind the GAP: A balanced corpus of gendered ambiguous pronouns. *Transactions of the Association for Computational Linguistics*, 6:605–617.

Jieyu Zhao, Tianlu Wang, Mark Yatskar, Vicente Ordonez, and Kai-Wei Chang. 2017. Men also like shopping: Reducing gender bias amplification using corpus-level constraints. In *Proceedings of the 2017 Conference on Empirical Methods in Natural Language Processing*, pages 2979–2989, Copenhagen, Denmark. Association for Computational Linguistics.

A List of Analysed Language Models

The analysed language models for West Slavic languages are listed below in Table 3.

B Manual Templates and Categories

Table 4 shows the categories of manually created templates, an example for each category and the number of templates per category. The gender of words denoted by "*_*" is changed to provide a comparison between genders.

C Example of Sentence Completion

In Table 5, we present examples of completed sentences.

D HurtLex and VAD Evaluation

In Table 6, we evaluate the two types of lexica using Wordnet (Fellbaum, 1998).

Model	Language	Architecture	Training data	# parameters
m-BERT	multi	BERT	largest Wikipedias (104 languages)	172M
XLM-RoBERTa	multi	RoBERTa	2.5TB of CommonCrawl data (100 languages)	270M
SlovakBERT	SK	BERT	Common crawl	125M
Czert	CS	BERT	Czech national corpus (28.2GB), Czech Wikipedia (0.9GB), Czech news crawl (7.8GB)	110M
PolBERT	PL	BERT	Polish subset of Open Subtitles, Polish subset of ParaCrawl, Polish Parliamentary Corpus, Polish Wikipedia - Feb 2020	110M

Table 3: List of the evaluated language models.

Number	Category	Example
85	attributes	The *woman* is very ___ .
35	work	The *manager* takes care of ___ .
31	perceived role	It is important for *people* to be ___ .
22	preferences	*Non-binary people* do not like ___ .

Table 4: Overview of the categories for the manual templates.

Template			Completions		
[CS] Moje dcera je __ .	učitelka	herečka	babička	matka	zpěvačka
My daughter is a __ .	*teacher*	*actress*	*grandmother*	*mother*	*singer*
[CS] Můj syn je __ .	hrdina	policista	gay	vrah	nemocný
My son is a __ .	*hero*	*police officer*	*gay*	*murderer*	*sick*
[SK] Ľudia si zaslúžia __.	žiť	rešpekt	dôstojnosť	budúcnosť	ochranu
People deserve __.	*life*	*respect*	*mother*	*future*	*protection*
[SK] Nebinárne osoby si zaslúžia __.	trest	väzenie	kritiku	smrť	liečbu
Non-binary persons deserve __.	*punishment*	*jail*	*criticism*	*death*	*cure*
[PL] Zmienili tę dziewczynę w __.	dziwkę	kobietę	gwiazdę	księżniczkę	mężczyznę
They changed the girl into a __.	*whore*	*woman*	*star*	*princess*	*man*
[PL] Zmienili tego chłopca w __.	bohatera	doktora	gwiazdę	policjanta	żołnierza
They changed the boy into a __.	*hero*	*doctor*	*star*	*police officer*	*soldier*

Table 5: Examples of templates with completions for Czech [CS], Polish [PL], and Slovak [SK] based on the selected models.

	Czech	Polish		Slovak	
	HurtLex	HurtLex	VAD	HurtLex	VAD
Total words	3046	3554	19971	2232	19971
WordNet words	-	1468	10887	644	8115
WordNet words (lemmatised)	-	1667	10723	801	9839
Manually checked	2231	-	-	-	-
% correct	73.24	41.31	54.51	28.85	40.63
% correct (lemmatised)	-	46.90	53.69	35.89	49.27

Table 6: Number of words validated by WordNet for each lexicon.

On Experiments of Detecting Persuasion Techniques in Polish and Russian Online News: Preliminary Study

Nikolaos Nikolaidis[1] Nicolas Stefanovitch[2] Jakub Piskorski[3]
[1]Athens University of Economics and Business, Athens, Greece nnikon@aueb.gr
[2]European Commission Joint Research Centre, Ispra, Italy nicolas.stefanovitch@ec.europa.eu
[3]Polish Academy of Sciences, Warsaw, Poland jpiskorski@gmail.com

Abstract

This paper reports on the results of preliminary experiments on the detection of persuasion techniques in online news in Polish and Russian, using a taxonomy of 23 persuasion techniques. The evaluation addresses different aspects, namely, the granularity of the persuasion technique category, i.e., coarse- (6 labels) versus fine-grained (23 labels), and the focus of the classification, i.e., at which level the labels are detected (subword, sentence, or paragraph). We compare the performance of mono- verus multi-lingual-trained state-of-the-art transformed-based models in this context.

1 Introduction

Nowadays, readers of online content are exposed more than ever to manipulation, disinformation and propaganda, which can potentially influence their opinion on relevant topics, such as, e.g., elections, health crises, migration crises, military conflicts, etc. Thus, the analysis of online media landscape is essestial in order to get a deeper insight on the presented narratives around certain topics across countries, to detect and identify manipulation attempts and to enchance users' media literacy. As a result, in the recent years, one could observe an ever-growing trend of research on automated methods supporting the detection of potentially deceptive and manipulative content, on narrative extraction, and on tools for comparative analysis of online media of different political orientations.

In this paper, we present the results of some preliminary experiments on the detection of persuasion techniques in online news in Polish and Russian. In order to perform our experiments, we exploit the datasets used in the *SemEval 2023 Shared Task 3: Detecting the Genre, the Framing, and the Persuasion Techniques in Online News in a Multilingual Setup* (Piskorski et al., 2023), whose one specific subtask focuses on the detection of persuasion techniques at paragraph level in nine languages, including, i.a., Polish and Russian, which, to the best of our knowledge, constitutes the first ever annotated resource for persuasion technique detection for these languages at intra-document level. While the aforementioned shared task revolves solely around paragraph-level detection and classification of persuasion techniques using a taxonomy of 23 techniques, in our work, we focus on the evaluation with different settings: (a) the granularity of the data after aggregating the results of the classifier: fine-grained (23 labels) versus coarse-grained (6 labels); and (b) the focus of the classification, i.e., at which level the labels are aggregated: subword, sentence, and paragraph level. The main drive behind the inclusion of these different dimensions in the evaluation is to gain a better understanding about the usability of automated persuasion technique detection for practical applications. The primary focus is to compare the performance of mono- versus multi-lingual-trained state-of-the-art transformed-based models in this context.

The rest of this paper is organized as follows. First, we report on related work in Section 2. Next, the persuasion technique detection task and the underlying taxonomy is introduced in Section 3. Subsequently, in Section 4 we report on the carried out experiments, including the description of the dataset, evaluation methodology, models explored, the results, and some rudimentary error analysis. We end up with the conclusions and future outlook in Section 5.

2 Related Work

The work on automated detection of persuasion techniques in text is related to work on propaganda detection. The work in the latter area initially focused on document-level analysis and predictions. For example, Rashkin et al. (2017) reports on prediction of four classes (*trusted*, *satire*, *hoax*, and *propaganda*) of documents, whereas

Proceedings of the 9th Workshop on Slavic Natural Language Processing 2023 (SlavicNLP 2023), pages 155–164
May 6, 2023 ©2023 Association for Computational Linguistics

Barrón-Cedeno et al. (2019) developed a corpus of documents tagged either as *propaganda* or *non-propaganda*) and further investigated writing style and readability level.

In parallel to the above, other research work focused on the detection of specific persuasion techniques in text. Habernal et al. (2017, 2018) presented a corpus with 1.3k arguments annotated with 5 fallacies that directly relate to propaganda techniques. A more fine-grained analysis was done by Da San Martino et al. (2019a), who developed a corpus of English news articles labelled with 18 propaganda techniques at span and sentence level, and proposed a deep learning-based solutions for this task. Improved models were proposed addressing the limitations of transformers by Chernyavskiy et al. (2021), whereas the topic of interpretable propaganda detection was addressed by Yu et al. (2021). Somewhat related is also the work on detection of use of propaganda techniques in memes (Dimitrov et al., 2021a), the relationship between propaganda and coordination (Hristakieva et al., 2022), and work studying COVID-19 related propaganda in social media (Nakov et al., 2021a,b). Bonial et al. (2022) reported on the creation of annotated text snippet dataset with logical fallacies for Covid-19 domain and evaluation or ML-based approaches using this corpus. Sourati et al. (2022) presents three-stage evaluation framework of detection, coarse-grained, and fine-grained classification of logical fallacies through adapting existing evaluation datasets, and evaluate various state-of-the-art models using this framework. Jin et al. (2022) proposed the task of logical fallacy detection and a new dataset of logical fallacies found in climate change claims. Noteworthy, all the persuasion techniques and logical fallacy taxonomies introduced in the aforementioned research works do, in principle, overlap to a very high degree, but are structured differently, and different naming conventions are used.

A comprehensive survey on computational propaganda detection is presented in (Da San Martino et al., 2020b).

Various shared tasks related to persuasion technique detection were organized in the recent years. For instance, *SemEval-2020 task 11 on Detection of Persuasion Techniques in News Articles* (Da San Martino et al., 2020a) focused on the detection of persuasion techniques (at text span level) in news articles. The *NLP4IF-2019 task on Fine-Grained Propaganda Detection* task proposed a similar-in-nature task with a taxonomy of 18 persuasion techniques. The *SemEval-2021 task 6 on Detection of Persuasion Techniques in Texts and Images* focused on the detection of propaganda techniques deployed in memes, and used a taxonomy of 22 techniques (Dimitrov et al., 2021b). Finally, WANLP'2022 (Alam et al., 2022) shared task centred around the detection of 20 propaganda techniques in Arabic tweets (Alam et al., 2022), while the *SemEval 2023 Shared Task 3: Detecting the Genre, the Framing, and the Persuasion Techniques in Online News in a Multi-lingual Setup* (Piskorski et al., 2023) has a subtask revolving around the detection of persuasion techniques at paragraph level in nine languages, including: English, French, Georgian, German, Greek, Italian, Polish, Russian, Spanish.

The work on persuasion detection for Polish and Russian is scarce, and focused mainly on the analysis of the use of persuasion techniques, not their detection. For instance (Stepaniuk K., 2021) studies the use of linguistic cues defined as Persuasive Linguistic Tricks (PLT) in social media (SM) marketing communication. (Andrusyak, 2019) studied the use of propaganda techniques in the Russian news in the context of the Russian military intervention in Ukraine in 2014, and also explored NLP-based models for their automated detection, however, this is done at document level, i.e., classification of articles into persuasive and non-persuasive ones, which is different from our work which is at the intra-document level. To our best knowledge, the resources used in the context of the SemEval 2023 Shared Task 3 (Piskorski et al., 2023) constitute the only resource for persuasion technique detection for Polish and Russian at text span level, on top of which we carry out our research reported in this paper.

3 Persuasion Technique Detection

Persuasion techniques are tools and strategies used by individuals to influence others' opinions or to motivate them to undertake or support some action or adopt new behaviour(s). In order to perform our set of experiments, we exploit the persuasion techniques taxonomy from the *SemEval 2023 Shared Task 3: Detecting the Genre, the Framing, and the Persuasion Techniques in Online News in a Multi-lingual Setup* (Piskorski et al., 2023), which is an extended version of the the taxonomy introduced in Da San Martino et al. (2019a,b). At the top level, there are 6 coarse-grained types of persuasion techniques:

- **Attack on reputation:** The argument does not address the topic, but rather targets the participant (personality, experience, deeds) in order to question and/or to undermine their credibility. The object of the argumentation can also refer to a group of individuals, an organization, an object, or an activity.
- **Justification:** The argument is made of two parts, a statement and an explanation or an appeal, where the latter is used to justify and/or to support the statement.
- **Simplification:** The argument excessively simplifies a problem, usually regarding the cause, the consequence or the existence of choices.
- **Distraction:** The argument takes focus away from the main topic or argument to distract the reader.
- **Call:** The text is not an argument, but an encouragement to act or to think in a particular way.
- **Manipulative wording:** the text is not an argument per se, but uses specific language, which contains words or phrases that are either non-neutral, confusing, exaggerating, loaded, etc., in order to impact the reader emotionally.

These six types are further subdivided into 23 fine-grained techniques. Figure 1 gives an overview of the two-tier taxonomy and a short definition of all fine-grained techniques.

The persuasion technique detection is a multi-class multi-label classification task. Some examples of persuasion techniques for Polish and Russian are provided in Figure 2.

4 Experiments

We explore the performance of state-of-the-art transformer-based models for the task at hand, on the two languages of interest, namely, Polish and Russian, and the effect of cross-lingual transfer learning using multi-lingual models. Specifically, we compared the performance of mono-lingual models with the current multi-lingual model XLM-RoBERTa (Conneau et al., 2020), we measured

ATTACK ON REPUTATION

Name Calling or Labelling: a form of argument in which loaded labels are directed at an individual, group, object or activity, typically in an insulting or demeaning way, but also using labels the target audience finds desirable.
Guilt by Association: attacking the opponent or an activity by associating it with a another group, activity or concept that has sharp negative connotations for the target audience.
Casting Doubt: questioning the character or personal attributes of someone or something in order to question their general credibility or quality.
Appeal to Hypocrisy: the target of the technique is attacked on its reputation by charging them with hypocrisy/inconsistency.
Questioning the Reputation: the target is attacked by making strong negative claims about it, focusing specially on undermining its character and moral stature rather than relying on an argument about the topic.

JUSTIFICATION

Flag Waiving: justifying an idea by exhaling the pride of a group or highlighting the benefits for that specific group.
Appeal to Authority: a weight is given to an argument, an idea or information by simply stating that a particular entity considered as an authority is the source of the information.
Appeal to Popularity: a weight is given to an argument or idea by justifying it on the basis that allegedly "everybody" (or the large majority) agrees with it or "nobody" disagrees with it.
Appeal to Values: a weight is given to an idea by linking it to values seen by the target audience as positive.
Appeal to Fear, Prejudice: promotes or rejects an idea through the repulsion or fear of the audience towards this idea.

DISTRACTION

Strawman: consists in making an impression of refuting an argument of the opponent's proposition, whereas the real subject of the argument was not addressed or refuted, but instead replaced with a false one.
Red Herring: consists in diverting the attention of the audience from the main topic being discussed, by introducing another topic, which is irrelevant.
Whataboutism: a technique that attempts to discredit an opponent's position by charging them with hypocrisy without directly disproving their argument.

SIMPLIFICATION

Causal Oversimplification: assuming a single cause or reason when there are actually multiple causes for an issue.
False Dilemma or No Choice: a logical fallacy that presents only two options or sides when there are many options or sides. In extreme, the author tells the audience exactly what actions to take, eliminating any other possible choices.
Consequential Oversimplification: is an assertion one is making of some "first" event/action leading to a domino-like chain of events that have some significant negative (positive) effects and consequences that appear to be ludicrous or unwarranted or with each step in the chain more and more improbable.

CALL

Slogans: a brief and striking phrase, often acting like emotional appeals, that may include labeling and stereotyping.
Conversation Killer: words or phrases that discourage critical thought and meaningful discussion about a given topic.
Appeal to Time: the argument is centred around the idea that time has come for a particular action.

MANIPULATIVE WORDING

Loaded Language: use of specific words and phrases with strong emotional implications (either positive or negative) to influence and convince the audience that an argument is valid.
Obfuscation, Intentional Vagueness, Confusion: use of words that are deliberately not clear, vague or ambiguous so that the audience may have its own interpretations.
Exaggeration or Minimisation: consists of either representing something in an excessive manner or making something seem less important or smaller than it really is.
Repetition: the speaker uses the same phrase repeatedly with the hopes that the repetition will lead to persuade the audience.

Figure 1: Persuasion techniques taxonomy. The six coarse-grained techniques are subdivided into 23 fine-grained ones.

Ci zaś, którzy nie pamiętają PRL, mogą sobie skojarzyć styl telewizji Jacka Kurskiego z Chinami albo innymi krajami Wschodu.
Guilt by Association [POLISH]

Już nigdy nie pozwolimy, by na polskiej ziemi stanęła noga rosyjskiego żołnierza – dmie w sztandar narodowej dumy premier.
Flag Waiving [POLISH]

Według najnowszych danych agencji badawczej Inquiry, aż 47 proc. respondentów w tej grupie deklaruje, że nie będzie się szczepić. Czy naprawdę w Polsce jesteśmy gotowi ryzykować życiem i zdrowiem naszych dzieci? Appeal to fear, prejudice [POLISH]

Jak słyszeliśmy dzisiaj prezydenta Niemiec, który mówi, że Nord Stream 2 to jest formuła reparacji czy spłaty długu za okropności, jakie zostały wyrządzone przez Niemcy Rosjanom w czasie drugiej wojny światowej, muszę powiedzieć, że nabiera to nowego znaczenia. Jeśli ten projekt tak miałby być traktowany, to Niemcy są gotowe do dyskusji o reparacjach dla Polski. Strawman [POLISH]

Była zastępczyni rzecznika praw obywatelskich w rozmowie z Interią stwierdziła, że „potrzebna jest partia, która w sposób pryncypialny podejdzie do kwestii walki z katastrofą klimatyczną i bezkompromisowo do praw zwierząt". - Bez weganizmu taka perspektywa nie będzie możliwa - oceniła. False Dilemma or No Choice [POLISH]

Taka jest prawda i koniec. Conversation killer [POLISH]

Aborcja to tylko zabieg medyczny Minimisation [POLISH]

Решение суда будет иметь пугающие последствия для всей Америки Casting doubt [RUSSIAN]

Решение суда будет иметь пугающие последствия для всей Америки Loaded language [RUSSIAN]

собрало беспрецедентно широкую поддержку Exaggeration or Minimisation [RUSSIAN]

Лавров сорвал маски и выдвинул требование Appeal to Hypocrisy [RUSSIAN]

Или вы говорите, что президент Зеленский герой, или вы пропутинская марионетка False dilemma [RUSSIAN]

Отмечается, что в первые дни спецоперации люди стремились поддержать Украину, однако сейчас фокус их внимания заострен на более актуальных проблемах Obfuscation [RUSSIAN]

Figure 2: Examples of text snippets in Polish and Russian with persuasion techniques. The text fragments highlighted in yellow are the actual text spans annotated.

	TRAIN			DEVELOPMENT			TEST
lang	#docs	#spans	A_{pt}	#docs	#spans	A_{pt}	#docs
PL	145	2839	19.6	49	985	20.1	47
RU	143	3399	23.8	48	739	15.4	72
FR	158	5595	35.4	53	1586	29.9	-
EN	446	7201	16.1	90	1801	20.0	-
DE	132	4501	34.1	45	1236	27.5	-
IT	227	6027	26.6	76	1934	25.4	-

Table 1: Dataset statistics: total number of documents (#docs), total number of text spans annotated (#spans), average number of persuasion techniques per document (A_{pt}).

the effect of training with extra annotations from different languages (English, French, German, and Italian).

4.1 Experiments Settings

For monolingual models we used HerBERT (Mroczkowski et al., 2021) and RuRoBERTa[1], for Polish and Russian respectively, and for multi-lingual data we used XLM-RoBERTa (Conneau et al., 2020). We used the *large* variants for all the models from *Huggingface*. Regarding hyper-parameters, from our previous experimentation with this task on a multi-lingual setting, we found the optimal settings to be $batch\ size = 12$, $lr = 3e-3$, $weight\ decay = 0.01$, and early stopping of with a patience of 750 steps. We used the aforementioned BERT variants in a multi-label token classification configuration where we added a sigmoid layer on the output of the last layer with binary-cross entropy as loss function. This way, for each token we get 23 predictions, one per label (then aggregated to 6 in the coarse-gained setting). Each token in this setting corresponds to a subword, emitted by the model's tokenizer. Using subword-level predictions, we further aggregated them in sentences and paragraphs in post-processing for additional evaluation.

4.2 Dataset

We exploit the dataset consisting of new articles with annotated persuasion techniques for Polish and Russian from the SemEval 2023 Shared Task 3 (Piskorski et al., 2023)[2]. This dataset contains span- and paragraph-level annotations of persuasion techniques, where the latter were simply derived from the span-level annotations. We also used the data for English, German, French and Italian from the same shared task to explore how exploitation of multi-lingual data boosts the performance for the target languages. The entire dataset is subdivided into *train*, *development* and *test* dataset. The overview of the high-level statistics of all three datasets[3] is provided in Table 1.

Detailed statistics on the coarse- and fine-grained persuasion techniques for Polish and Russian for

[1] `https://huggingface.co/sberbank-ai/ruRoberta-large/blob/main/README.md`

[2] `https://propaganda.math.unipd.it/semeval2023task3/index.html`

[3] The golden labels for the test dataset are currently not publicly available, however the shared task provides a web interface to carry out evaluations on this dataset

the *training* and *development* datasets are provided in Table 2. One can observe that these datasets are highly imbalanced. *Attack on Reputation* instances account for approx. 50% of the entire dataset for both languages, where *Name Calling-Labelling* (approx. 18-27% for Polish, 7-10% for Russian) and *Doubt* (approx. 11-12% for Polish, 18-22% for Russian) are the most prevalent fine-grained techniques. The second most populated coarse-grained class is *Manipulative Wording* (ca. 19-21% and 35-37% for Polish and Russian respectively), where *Loaded Language* is the most prominent fine-grained class (approx. 11-15% and 28-29% for Polish and Russian respectively). Finally, the third most populated coarse-grained class for Polish is *Justification* (approx. 15-22%), whereas it it significantly less populated for Russian (approx. 4-5% only).

4.3 Evaluation Methodology

For the purpose of evaluating different models we use $micro$ and $macro$, $recall$ and $precision$ and F_1 measures.

Additionally, we evaluate different settings: (a) the granularity of the data after aggregating the results of the classifier: fine-grained (23 labels), coarse-grained (6 labels); and (b) the focus of the classification, i.e., at which level the labels are aggregated: paragraph level (split at new lines), sentence level (using an ad-hoc language-aware sentence splitter) and natively at subword level.

4.4 Results

Tables 3 and 4 provide overall evaluation results for all models on fine- and coarse-grained classification task at different focus levels of evaluation, i.e., subword, sentence, and paragraph level, for Polish and Russian resp. All models were trained using *train* dataset and evaluated on the *development* dataset. The XLM-RoBERTa version trained on all multilingual data (6 languages) is referred to with XLM-RoBERTa$_{multi}$.

First, we can observe that including the other languages (XLM-RoBERTa$_{multi}$), yields the highest performance boost in almost all settings, especially in terms of macro scores, and that overall results for Russian are better than for Polish. Second, the performance in both micro and macro F_1 for Polish grows with the broader focus level of the evaluation, ranging for macro F_1 from .187 (.224) to .324 (.487) for fine-grained (coarse-grained) classification, and for Russian from .190 (.267) to .306 (.464). The mono-lingual HerBERT used for Polish performs worst in almost all settings, whereas the mono-lingual Russian ruRoBERTa-based model exhibits slightly better performance vis-a-vis XLM-RoBERTa and outperforms XLM-RoBERTa$_{multi}$ only in micro F_1 at the subword level. Since this is noticeable only at this level, we speculate that it is an effect of the difference in script (latin to cyrillic).

In order to get a deeper insight into the performance of the best performing classifier, namely, XLM-RoBERTa$_{multi}$ we provide in Table 7 precision, recall, and F_1 results per each persuasion technique evaluated at sentence level for both Polish and Russian. The classes obtaining best results (i.e., F_1 measure above .3) are highlighted in bold. One can observe some that the two models perform best in the same techniques. In both models, the best performing classes are *Name Calling-Labelling* .56 (.63), *Appeal to Fear-Prejudice* .47 (.46), and *Loaded Language* .46 (.46) for Polish (Russian). We also observe that the worst performing classes are also common. i.e., for both languages *Red Herring*, *Whataboutism*, *Obfuscation-Vagueness-Confusion* obtain zero scores. We hypotheisze the poor performance is most likely due to data scarcity, something observed for most languages of the dataset. We also compared the results of XLM-RoBERTa$_{multi}$ with the models trained without transfer learning from other languages on a per-class basis. We observed that transfer learning provides a noticeable boost on low-performing classes: the count of classes not predicted at all goes down from 9 to 3 for both Polish and Russian.

For the sake of completeness, in Table 6, we present the results of the models when trained on *train* with *development* as validation and evaluated on the *test* dataset only on sentence level using the fine-grained taxonomy. Due to the imbalanced nature of the data, and the high number of under-performing classes, we focus on the macro F_1 score. Here, we can clearly see that XLM-RoBERTa$_{multi}$ also provides a noticeable boost in both cases, while the micro scores remain at the same level as in the other cases. As before, we hypothesize that this effect is due to a boost in under-represented labels where the number of annotations in the target language is very low, but the contribution of annotations from other languages is sufficient to enable the detection of those labels.

We have carried an additional experiment to sim-

	Polish				Russian			
	TRAIN		DEV		TRAIN		DEV	
technique	#num	%	#num	%	#num	%	#num	%
Attack on Reputation	1620	57.06	484	49.14	1601	47.10	341	46.14
Name Calling-Labeling	764	26.91	177	17.97	331	9.74	56	7.58
Guilt by Association	111	3.91	37	3.76	32	0.94	12	1.62
Doubt	349	12.29	111	11.27	732	21.54	133	18.00
Appeal to Hypocrisy	192	6.76	91	9.24	125	3.68	19	2.57
Questioning the Reputation	204	7.19	68	6.90	381	11.21	121	16.37
Justification	413	14.55	218	22.13	185	5.44	36	4.87
Flag Waving	97	3.42	33	3.35	50	1.47	10	1.35
Appeal to Authority	43	1.51	50	5.08	10	0.29	2	0.27
Appeal to Values	111	3.91	60	6.09	54	1.59	9	1.22
Appeal to Popularity	31	1.09	28	2.84	8	0.24	2	0.27
Appeal to Fear-Prejudice	131	4.61	47	4.77	63	1.85	13	1.76
Simplification	49	1.73	22	2.23	147	4.32	31	4.19
Causal Oversimplification	12	0.42	5	0.51	40	1.18	6	0.81
Consequential Oversimplification	25	0.88	9	0.91	76	2.24	14	1.89
False Dilemma-No Choice	12	0.42	8	0.81	31	0.91	11	1.49
Distraction	40	1.41	14	1.42	30	0.88	16	2.17
Strawman	19	0.67	3	0.30	21	0.62	11	1.49
Red Herring	12	0.42	7	0.71	2	0.06	1	0.14
Whataboutism	9	0.32	4	0.41	7	0.21	4	0.54
Calls	115	4.05	58	5.89	211	6.21	39	5.28
Slogans	42	1.48	7	0.71	84	2.47	12	1.62
Conversation Killer	58	2.04	45	4.57	91	2.68	26	3.52
Appeal to Time	15	0.53	6	0.61	36	1.06	1	0.14
Manipulative Wording	602	21.20	189	19.19	1225	36.04	276	37.35
Loaded Language	422	14.86	112	11.37	971	28.57	216	29.23
Obfuscation-Vagueness-Confusion	37	1.30	11	1.12	20	0.59	10	1.35
Exaggeration-Minimisation	128	4.51	48	4.87	149	4.38	30	4.06
Repetition	15	0.53	18	1.83	85	2.50	20	2.71
all	2839		985		3399		739	

Table 2: Dataset statistics for the fine-grained persuasion techniques for *train* and *development* datasets.

	Fine-grained classification																	
	Subword						Sentence						Paragraph					
	micro			macro			micro			macro			micro			macro		
model	P	R	F_1	P	R	F_1	P	R	F_1	P	R	F_1	P	R	F_1	P	R	F_1
HerBERT	.236	.089	.129	.162	.056	.083	.331	.197	.247	.212	.110	.145	.423	.306	.355	.296	.170	.216
XLM-RoBERTa	.245	.096	.138	.176	.061	.091	.341	.204	.255	.227	.108	.146	.445	.336	.383	.289	.170	.214
XLM-RoBERTa$_{multi}$	.390	.154	**.221**	.331	.130	**.187**	.502	.254	**.337**	.382	.189	**.253**	.612	.338	**.435**	.473	.246	**.324**
	Coarse-grained classification																	
	Subword						Sentence						Paragraph					
	micro			macro			micro			macro			micro			macro		
model	P	R	F_1	P	R	F_1	P	R	F_1	P	R	F_1	P	R	F_1	P	R	F_1
HerBERT	.348	.132	.191	.186	.076	.108	.483	.281	.355	.258	.162	.199	.613	.430	.505	.354	.243	.288
XLM-RoBERTa	.362	.141	.203	.195	.081	.115	.500	.291	.368	.291	.166	.212	.640	.464	.538	.390	.260	.312
XLM-RoBERTa$_{multi}$	.519	.207	**.296**	.469	.164	**.244**	.675	.353	**.463**	.544	.261	**.353**	.808	.471	**.595**	.709	.371	**.487**

Table 3: Evaluation results for Polish for fine- and coarse-grained classification for models trained on *train* dataset and evaluated on the *development* dataset. Best results in terms of F_1 are highlighted in bold.

	Fine-grained classification																	
	Subword						Sentence						Paragraph					
	micro			macro			micro			macro			micro			macro		
model	P	R	F_1	P	R	F_1	P	R	F_1	P	R	F_1	P	R	F_1	P	R	F_1
RuRoBERTa	.241	.212	**.226**	.145	.075	.099	.309	.349	.327	.161	.139	.150	.360	.403	.381	.185	.169	.176
XLM-RoBERTa	.241	.095	.136	.217	.064	.099	.323	.150	.205	.220	.084	.122	.478	.221	.302	.295	.130	.181
XLM-RoBERTa$_{multi}$	.367	.161	.223	.314	.136	**.190**	.500	.269	**.350**	.363	.196	**.254**	.569	.329	**.417**	.416	.242	**.306**
	Coarse-grained classification																	
	Subword						Sentence						Paragraph					
	micro			macro			micro			macro			micro			macro		
model	P	R	F_1	P	R	F_1	P	R	F_1	P	R	F_1	P	R	F_1	P	R	F_1
RuRoBERTa	.362	.310	**.334**	.228	.156	.185	.460	.486	.473	.298	.282	.290	.516	.535	.525	.346	.318	.331
XLM-RoBERTa	.390	.152	.219	.471	.124	.196	.509	.243	.329	.540	.178	.268	.645	.325	.432	.654	.256	.368
XLM-RoBERTa$_{multi}$	.498	.221	.306	.458	.188	**.267**	.663	.374	**.478**	.541	.291	**.378**	.755	.470	**.580**	.630	.367	**.464**

Table 4: Evaluation results for Russian for fine- and coarse-grained classification for the models trained on *train* dataset and evaluated on the *development* dataset. Best results in terms of F_1 are highlighted in bold.

ulate a different scenario, in which it is assumed that the text fragments that contain persuasion techniques are already identified, and the remaining task is to classify those fragments with the corresponding fine-grained persuasion technique labels. As a matter of fact, we have trained XML-RoBERTa on all *training* data in six languages and evaluated on the task of classifying whether paragraphs and sentences are persuasive or not, and achieved F_1 scores of .823 and .669 respectively when evaluated on the *development* data. This indicates that a reliable binary persuasiveness classifier can be developed. Subsequently, we trained a linear multi-label SVM classifier with 3-5 character n-grams as features using solely the text spans labelled with fine-grained persuasion techniques in Polish/Russian and exploiting the respective *training* datasets and evaluated it on the *development* datasets. The evaluation results of this experiment are provided in Figure 4.4. We can observe that such linguistically-poor models achieve, not fully unexpected, reasonable results (F_1 score) for some classes, e.g., *Name Calling-Labeling* (.85), *Loaded Language* (.51), *Conversation Killer* (.49), *Slogans* (.49) and *Flag Waving* (.40) for Polish, and *Name Calling-Labeling* (.60), *Guilt by Association* (.54), *Doubt* (.46), *Appeal to Time* (.40), *Loaded Language* (.53) for Russian. These results indicate the discriminatory potential of lexical features, as one of the areas to explore in future.

	Polish			Russian		
technique	P	R	F_1	P	R	F_1
Name Calling-Labeling	.78	.44	**.56**	.79	.52	**.63**
Guilt by Association	.38	.19	.26	.23	.15	.18
Doubt	.49	.30	**.37**	.48	.28	**.35**
Appeal to Hypocrisy	.37	.20	.26	.44	.18	.25
Questioning the Reputation	.55	.08	.14	.60	.14	.22
Flag Waving	.25	.44	**.32**	.16	.28	.20
Appeal to Authority	.42	.15	.22	.46	.19	.27
Appeal to Values	.47	.15	.22	.52	.14	.22
Appeal to Popularity	.67	.13	.21	.47	.15	.23
Appeal to Fear-Prejudice	.49	.45	**.47**	.40	.53	**.46**
Causal Oversimplification	.20	.14	.16	.34	.26	.29
Conseq. Oversimplification	.23	.06	.09	.17	.06	.09
False Dilemma-No Choice	.49	.21	.29	.47	.21	.29
Straw Man	.16	.03	.05	.15	.04	.07
Red Herring	.00	.00	.00	.00	.00	.00
Whataboutism	.00	.00	.00	.00	.00	.00
Slogans	.63	.22	**.33**	.56	.33	**.41**
Conversation Killer	.44	.08	.14	.57	.15	.23
Appeal to Time	.69	.29	**.41**	.36	.26	**.30**
Loaded Language	.55	.39	**.46**	.56	.38	**.46**
Obfusc.-Vagueness-Confusion	.00	.00	.00	.00	.00	.00
Exaggeration-Minimisation	.39	.27	**.32**	.49	.17	.25
Repetition	.16	.13	.14	.17	.10	.13

Table 5: Evaluation results per class for Polish and Russian for fine-grained classification at sentence level using XLM-RoBERTa$_{multi}$ trained on the *train* dataset and evaluated on the *development* dataset. Results with F_1 score above .3 are shown in bold.

4.5 Error Analysis

We conducted some error analysis of the XLM-RoBERTa$_{multi}$ model, trained on the *train* dataset

model	P	R	micro F_1	macro F_1
		Russian		
ruRoBERTa	.271	.175	.212	.134
XLM-RoBERTa	341	.204	**.255**	.146
XLM-RoBERTa$_{multi}$	.379	.176	.240	**.211**
		Polish		
HerBERT	.343	.219	**.267**	.156
XLM-RoBERTa	.323	.150	.205	.122
XLM-RoBERTa$_{multi}$	.392	.199	.264	**.199**

Table 6: Evaluation results on the *test* dataset at sentence level for models trained and validated on *train* and *development* datasets respectively. The best F_1 scores are highlighted in bold.

	Polish			Russian		
technique	P	R	F_1	P	R	F_1
Name Calling-Labeling	.78	.95	**.85**	.56	.64	**.60**
Guilt by Association	.30	.24	.26	.62	.48	**.54**
Doubt	.28	.39	.33	.41	.52	**.46**
Appeal to Hypocrisy	.34	.43	.38	.18	.13	.15
Questioning the Reputation	.23	.21	.22	.25	.33	.28
Flag Waving	.39	.41	**.40**	.19	.12	.15
Appeal to Authority	.35	.18	.24	.00	.00	.00
Appeal to Values	.31	.33	.32	.28	.17	.21
Appeal to Popularity	.31	.17	.22	.33	.10	.15
Appeal to Fear-Prejudice	.32	.31	.31	.36	.21	.27
Causal Oversimplification	1.00	.12	.21	.00	.00	.00
Conseq. Oversimplification	.25	.03	.05	.17	.12	.14
False Dilemma-No Choice	.50	.10	.17	.44	.26	.33
Strawman	.25	.14	.18	.15	.06	.09
Red Herring	.50	.11	.17	.00	.00	.00
Whataboutism	.00	.00	.00	.00	.00	.00
Slogans	.68	.39	**.49**	.40	.25	.31
Conversation Killer	.50	.49	**.49**	.23	.20	.21
Appeal to Time	.33	.10	.15	.61	.30	**.40**
Loaded Language	.49	.54	**.51**	.49	.58	**.53**
Obfusc.-Vagueness-Confusion	.38	.13	.19	.00	.00	.00
Exaggeration-Minimisation	.24	.17	.20	.30	.25	.27
Repetition	.27	.13	.18	.24	.19	.21
micro average	.47	.49	.48	.40	.43	.41
macro average	.39	.26	.28	.27	.21	.23
weighted average	.45	.49	.46	.38	.43	.40

Table 7: Evaluation of text-span multi-label SVM classifier for Polish and Russian trained and evaluated using *training* and *development* dataset resp. The best performing classes in terms of F_1 score (above .40) are highlighted in bold.

and evaluated on the *development* one, and noticed that some of the False Positives (FP) seemed correct. To get a better understanding, we analyzed in detail a sample of 10 random FPs for Russian, results are reported Figure 3. As we can see from the results, Recall scores are lower than Precision which indicates that the challenge of the model is the number of False Negatives.

Interestingly, we can see that around half of the False Positives are actually correct detections of persuasion techniques, and 2 of the others are arguable and have at least the coarse-grained category correct. Our intuition is that an important part of the FPs could actually be correct, however we do not measure it here precisely as it would require an important annotation effort, and this is left for future work. This is to be expected in a task with an inherently significant amount of subjectivity such as persuasion technique detection.

We further noticed that, confusion in fine-grained labels seems to happen within the same coarse-grained category (e.g. *Appeal to Hypocrisy* is confused with *Questioning the reputation*, both under *Attack on Reputation* category). This is coherent with the fact that we observed in Tables 3 4, a strong increase on most micro scores when moving from fine to coarse-grained evaluation.

5 Conclusions and Future Work

In this paper we reported on some preliminary experiments on the detection of persuasion techniques in online news in Polish and Russian, using a taxonomy of 23 persuasion techniques, and considering different evaluations scenarios: fine- versus coarse-grained classification, the text-structure level at which the labels are detected (subword, sentence, or paragraph). The comparison of mono- and multi-lingual-trained state-of-the-art transformed-based models revealed the superiority of the latter in most evaluation settings, however, given the complexity of the task, there is significant space for improvement.

In our future research we envisage to: (a) enlarge the pool of transformer-based models for inclusion in the evaluation to get a more complete picture of the phenomena observed so far, (b) explore whether and how to exploit data augmentation (Feng et al., 2021) to boost the performance of the low-populated persuasion technique classes, and (c) investigate different pre-trained models for the task, like models fine-tuned on multi-lingual

Питались они в кафе[Casting Doubt]Not Correct: and not a technique
Но болгарское правительство удивило своих граждан [CASTING DOUBT] Correct

Единый подход воспитания и образования [APPEAL TO VALUES] Not Correct

В то же время, отмечает Селиванов, в ВСУ осознают, что значительная часть населения Украины не будет поддерживать страну [FLAG WAIVING] Almost Correct: Would have been correct without the negation, otherwise it is both Casting Doubt and Appeal to Popularity

развернутая США и их союзниками пропагандистская кампания о «российской агрессии» против Украины преследует провокационные цели, тем самым поощряя власти в Киеве к саботажу Минских соглашений [CASTING DOUBT] Correct

Есть Миша Кавелашвили, который всегда был верен принципам и был бойцом [APPEAL TO VALUES] Correct

Ранее прокуратура Санкт-Петербурга направила в суд иск о признании блокады Ленинграда геноцидом [LOADED LANGUAGE] Correct

На них денег в казне вечно не хватает [QUESTIONING REPUTATION] Correct

Схожим образом высказалась премьер Новой Зеландии Джасинда Ардерн [CASTING DOUBT] Not correct: and not a technique

сделать ставку на дальнейший развал России, то есть Российской Федерации [CAUSAL OVERSIMPLIFICATION] Almost Correct: it is rather an instance of False Dilemma

Figure 3: Analysis of 10 randomly sampled examples of False Positives in Russian.

QA (Artetxe et al., 2017) or NLI (Williams et al., 2018) corpora to investigate their performance on thought coherent classes (like *Simplification* or *Distraction* families).

Limitations

The results reported in this paper are to a certain degree limited since the range of state-of-the-art mono- and multilingual models explored is by far not complete. Therefore, the main findings of the paper should be considered as of preliminary nature. We envisage to carry out more comprehensive explorations both in terms of models, architectures and languages in future. It is also important to emphasize that the underlying dataset used for the sake of carrying out the experiments exhibits some data scarcity problems, which might have led to some partially poor results, and which constitutes another aspect to be addressed in future research.

References

Firoj Alam, Hamdy Mubarak, Wajdi Zaghouani, Giovanni Da San Martino, and Preslav Nakov. 2022. Overview of the WANLP 2022 shared task on propaganda detection in Arabic. In *Proceedings of the Seventh Arabic Natural Language Processing Workshop*, Abu Dhabi, UAE.

Bohdan Andrusyak. 2019. Principle-Guided Propaganda Analysis - Case Study on Russian Military Intervention in Ukraine. `https://diglib.tugraz.at/download.php?id=6144a2c5719c6&location=browse`.

Mikel Artetxe, Gorka Labaka, and Eneko Agirre. 2017. Learning bilingual word embeddings with (almost) no bilingual data. In *Proceedings of the 55th Annual Meeting of the Association for Computational Linguistics (Volume 1: Long Papers)*, pages 451–462, Vancouver, Canada. Association for Computational Linguistics.

Alberto Barrón-Cedeno, Israa Jaradat, Giovanni Da San Martino, and Preslav Nakov. 2019. Proppy: Organizing the news based on their propagandistic content. *Information Processing & Management*, 56(5).

Claire Bonial, Austin Blodgett, Taylor Hudson, Stephanie M. Lukin, Jeffrey Micher, Douglas Summers-Stay, Peter Sutor, and Clare Voss. 2022. The search for agreement on logical fallacy annotation of an infodemic. In *Proceedings of the Thirteenth Language Resources and Evaluation Conference*, pages 4430–4438, Marseille, France. European Language Resources Association.

Anton Chernyavskiy, Dmitry Ilvovsky, and Preslav Nakov. 2021. Transformers: "The end of history" for NLP? In *Proceedings of the European Conference on Machine Learning and Principles and Practice of Knowledge Discovery in Databases*, ECML-PKDD'21.

Alexis Conneau, Kartikay Khandelwal, Naman Goyal, Vishrav Chaudhary, Guillaume Wenzek, Francisco Guzmán, Edouard Grave, Myle Ott, Luke Zettlemoyer, and Veselin Stoyanov. 2020. Unsupervised cross-lingual representation learning at scale. In *Proceedings of the 58th Annual Meeting of the Association for Computational Linguistics*, pages 8440–8451, Online. Association for Computational Linguistics.

Giovanni Da San Martino, Alberto Barrón-Cedeño, Henning Wachsmuth, Rostislav Petrov, and Preslav Nakov. 2020a. SemEval-2020 task 11: Detection of propaganda techniques in news articles. In *Proceedings of the International Workshop on Semantic Evaluation*, SemEval '20, Barcelona, Spain.

Giovanni Da San Martino, Stefano Cresci, Alberto Barrón-Cedeño, Seunghak Yu, Roberto Di Pietro, and Preslav Nakov. 2020b. A survey on computational propaganda detection. In *IJCAI*.

Giovanni Da San Martino, Seunghak Yu, Alberto Barrón-Cedeño, Rostislav Petrov, and Preslav Nakov. 2019a. Fine-grained analysis of propaganda in news articles. In *EMNLP*.

Giovanni Da San Martino, Seunghak Yu, Alberto Barron-Cedeno, Rostislav Petrov, and Preslav Nakov. 2019b. Fine-grained analysis of propaganda in news articles. In *EMNLP*.

Dimitar Dimitrov, Bishr Bin Ali, Shaden Shaar, Firoj Alam, Fabrizio Silvestri, Hamed Firooz, Preslav Nakov, and Giovanni Da San Martino. 2021a. Detecting propaganda techniques in memes. In *Proceedings of the Joint Conference of the 59th Annual Meeting of the Association for Computational Linguistics and the 11th International Joint Conference on Natural Language Processing*, ACL-IJCNLP '21, pages 6603–6617.

Dimiter Dimitrov, Bishr Bin Ali, Shaden Shaar, Firoj Alam, Fabrizio Silvestri, Hamed Firooz, Preslav Nakov, and Giovanni Da San Martino. 2021b. Task 6 at SemEval-2021: Detection of persuasion techniques in texts and images. In *Proceedings of the 15th International Workshop on Semantic Evaluation*, SemEval '21, Bangkok, Thailand.

Steven Y. Feng, Varun Gangal, Jason Wei, Sarath Chandar, Soroush Vosoughi, Teruko Mitamura, and Eduard Hovy. 2021. A survey of data augmentation approaches for NLP. In *Findings of the Association for Computational Linguistics: ACL-IJCNLP 2021*, pages 968–988, Online. Association for Computational Linguistics.

Ivan Habernal, Raffael Hannemann, Christian Pollak, Christopher Klamm, Patrick Pauli, and Iryna Gurevych. 2017. Argotario: Computational argumentation meets serious games. In *EMNLP*.

Ivan Habernal, Patrick Pauli, and Iryna Gurevych. 2018. Adapting serious game for fallacious argumentation to German: Pitfalls, insights, and best practices. In *LREC*.

Kristina Hristakieva, Stefano Cresci, Giovanni Da San Martino, Mauro Conti, and Preslav Nakov. 2022. The spread of propaganda by coordinated communities on social media. In *Proceedings of the 14th ACM Web Science Conference*, WebSci '22, pages 191–201, Barcelona, Spain.

Zhijing Jin, Abhinav Lalwani, Tejas Vaidhya, Xiaoyu Shen, Yiwen Ding, Zhiheng Lyu, Mrinmaya Sachan, Rada Mihalcea, and Bernhard Schoelkopf. 2022. Logical fallacy detection. In *Findings of the Association for Computational Linguistics: EMNLP 2022*, pages 7180–7198, Abu Dhabi, United Arab Emirates. Association for Computational Linguistics.

Robert Mroczkowski, Piotr Rybak, Alina Wróblewska, and Ireneusz Gawlik. 2021. HerBERT: Efficiently pretrained transformer-based language model for Polish. In *Proceedings of the 8th Workshop on Balto-Slavic Natural Language Processing*, pages 1–10, Kiyv, Ukraine. Association for Computational Linguistics.

Preslav Nakov, Firoj Alam, Shaden Shaar, Giovanni Da San Martino, and Yifan Zhang. 2021a. COVID-19 in Bulgarian social media: Factuality, harmfulness, propaganda, and framing. In *Proceedings of the International Conference on Recent Advances in Natural Language Processing*, RANLP '21.

Preslav Nakov, Firoj Alam, Shaden Shaar, Giovanni Da San Martino, and Yifan Zhang. 2021b. A second pandemic? Analysis of fake news about COVID-19 vaccines in Qatar. In *Proceedings of the International Conference on Recent Advances in Natural Language Processing*, RANLP '21.

Jakub Piskorski, Nicolas Stefanovitch, Giovanni Da San Martino, and Preslav Nakov. 2023. Semeval-2023 task 3: Detecting the category, the framing, and the persuasion techniques in online news in a multi-lingual setup. In *Proceedings of the 17th International Workshop on Semantic Evaluation*, SemEval 2023, Toronto, Canada.

Hannah Rashkin, Eunsol Choi, Jin Yea Jang, Svitlana Volkova, and Yejin Choi. 2017. Truth of varying shades: Analyzing language in fake news and political fact-checking. In *EMNLP*.

Zhivar Sourati, Vishnu Priya Prasanna Venkatesh, Darshan Deshpande, Himanshu Rawlani, Filip Ilievski, Hông-Ân Sandlin, and Alain Mermoud. 2022. Robust and explainable identification of logical fallacies in natural language arguments.

Jarosz K. Stepaniuk K. 2021. Persuasive linguistic tricks in social media marketing communication-The memetic approach. *PLoS One*, 16(7).

Adina Williams, Nikita Nangia, and Samuel Bowman. 2018. A broad-coverage challenge corpus for sentence understanding through inference. In *Proceedings of the 2018 Conference of the North American Chapter of the Association for Computational Linguistics: Human Language Technologies, Volume 1 (Long Papers)*, pages 1112–1122. Association for Computational Linguistics.

Seunghak Yu, Giovanni Da San Martino, Mitra Mohtarami, James Glass, and Preslav Nakov. 2021. Interpretable propaganda detection in news articles. In *Proceedings of the International Conference on Recent Advances in Natural Language Processing*, RANLP '21, pages 1597–1605.

Exploring the Use of Foundation Models for Named Entity Recognition and Lemmatization Tasks in Slavic Languages

Gabriela Pałka and **Artur Nowakowski***
Faculty of Mathematics and Computer Science, Adam Mickiewicz University, Poznań, Poland
{gabriela.palka,artur.nowakowski}@amu.edu.pl

Abstract

This paper describes Adam Mickiewicz University's (AMU) solution for the 4th Shared Task on SlavNER. The task involves the identification, categorization, and lemmatization of named entities in Slavic languages. Our approach involved exploring the use of foundation models for these tasks. In particular, we used models based on the popular BERT and T5 model architectures. Additionally, we used external datasets to further improve the quality of our models. Our solution obtained promising results, achieving high metrics scores in both tasks. We describe our approach and the results of our experiments in detail, showing that the method is effective for NER and lemmatization in Slavic languages. Additionally, our models for lemmatization will be available at: https://huggingface.co/amu-cai.

1 Introduction

Named entity recognition and lemmatization are important tasks in natural language processing. Fine-tuning pre-trained neural language models has become a popular approach to achieve the best results in these tasks. However, the performance of this method can vary across languages and language families. In this paper, we investigate the performance of fine-tuned, language-specific neural language models in named entity recognition and lemmatization in a set of Slavic languages and compare them with multilingual solutions.

We describe Adam Mickiewicz University's (AMU) solution for the 4th Shared Task on SlavNER, which is a part of The 9th Workshop on Slavic Natural Language Processing (Slavic NLP 2023). Our solution is based on foundation models (Bommasani et al., 2021). In particular, we used models based on the popular BERT and T5 model architectures. To increase the effectiveness of our approach, we conducted experiments with different versions of monolingual and multilingual models, investigating the potential benefits of each model variant for specific tasks. The data provided by the organizers and external resources used for named entity recognition and lemmatization were processed and prepared as described in section 2. Specific details regarding the approach are further discussed in section 3.

In order to evaluate the effectiveness of our method, we performed several experiments on the previous Shared Task edition test set. This particular set was chosen because it is a well-known benchmark for named entity recognition and lemmatization in Slavic languages. The results of our experiments are described in section 4.

2 Data

This section provides a brief description of the datasets used in our solution. In addition to the data released by the organizers, we also used external datasets for named entity recognition and lemmatization. All training and validation samples containing named entities were converted to a CoNLL-2003 dataset format (Tjong Kim Sang and De Meulder, 2003).

2.1 Shared Task Dataset

The 4th Shared Task on SlavNER focuses on recognition, lemmatization, and cross-lingual linking of named entities in Polish, Czech and Russian languages. The training and validation data provided by the organizers come from the previous editions of the Shared Task and consist of news articles related to a single entity or event such as Asia Bibi, Brexit, Ryanair, Nord Stream, COVID-19 pandemic and USA 2020 Elections. The documents contain annotations of the following named entities: person (PER), location (LOC), organization (ORG), event (EVT) and product (PRO) (Piskorski et al., 2021).

*Artur Nowakowski is a scholarship recipient of the Adam Mickiewicz University Foundation for the 2022/2023 academic year.

Proceedings of the 9th Workshop on Slavic Natural Language Processing 2023 (SlavicNLP 2023), pages 165–171
May 6, 2023 ©2023 Association for Computational Linguistics

To obtain NER training and validation samples in the CoNLL-2003 format, we processed the data using the code provided by the Tilde team (Vīksna and Skadina, 2021)[1].

2.2 External NER Datasets

One way to improve the performance of NER models is to use external NER datasets to increase the volume of the training data. These datasets contain pre-labeled documents that have been annotated with named entities, and can be used to fine-tune existing models. This technique allows the model to learn from the additional data, which can provide a more comprehensive understanding of the context and complexities of the named entities.

2.2.1 Collection3

The *Collection3* dataset (Mozharova and Loukachevitch, 2016) is based on *Persons-1000*, a publicly available Russian document collection consisting of 1,000 news articles. Currently, the dataset contains 26,000 annotated named entities (11,000 persons, 7,000 locations and 8,000 organizations).

2.2.2 MultiNERD

The *MultiNERD* dataset (Tedeschi and Navigli, 2022) covers 10 languages, including Polish and Russian, and contains annotations of multiple NER categories, from which we extracted categories present in the Shared Task. The labels were obtained by processing the Wikipedia and Wikinews articles. In addition, the sentences were tagged automatically, in a way that can also be adapted to the Czech language.

2.2.3 Polyglot-NER

A *Polyglot-NER* dataset (Al-Rfou et al., 2015) covers 40 languages, including Polish, Czech and Russian. The annotations were automatically generated from Wikipedia and Freebase. The obtained entity categories are: person, location and organization.

2.2.4 WikiNEuRal

The *WikiNEuRal* dataset (Tedeschi et al., 2021) consists of named entities in the following categories: person, location, organization and miscellaneous. Wikipedia was used as the source for the labels, which were automatically obtained using a combination of knowledge-based approaches and neural models. The datasets cover 9 languages, including Polish and Russian.

[1] https://github.com/tilde-nlp/BSNLP_2021

2.3 External Lemmatization Datasets

Lemmatization, the process of reducing a word or phrase to its base form, is an essential component, especially for tasks such as information retrieval and text mining. External lemmatization datasets can improve the quality of lemmatization models by providing additional training samples that contain more inflectional variants of phrases. Such data consists of inflected words, collocations or phrases with corresponding lemmatized forms.

2.3.1 SEJF

SEJF (Czerepowicka and Savary, 2018) is a linguistic resource consisting of a grammatical lexicon of Polish multi-word expressions. It contains two modules: an intensional module, which consists of 4,700 multiword lemmas assigned to 100 inflection graphs, and an extensional module, which contains 88,000 automatically generated inflected forms annotated with grammatical tags.

2.3.2 SEJFEK

SEJFEK (Savary et al., 2012) refers to a lexical and grammatical resource related to Polish economic terms. It contains a grammatical lexicon module with over 11,000 terminological multi-word units and a fully lexicalized shallow grammar with over 146,000 inflected forms, which was produced by an automatic conversion of the lexicon.

2.3.3 PolEval 2019: Task 2

PolEval 2019: Task 2 (Marcińczuk and Bernaś, 2019) is a part of a workshop focusing on natural language processing in the Polish language. The main goal of this task was to lemmatize proper names and multi-word phrases. The train set consists of over 24,000 annotated and lemmatized phrases. The validation set and the test set contain 200 and 1,997 phrases, respectively.

2.3.4 Machine Translation of External Datasets

Due to the lack of external Czech and Russian datasets dedicated to lemmatization tasks, we decided to use OPUS-MT (Tiedemann and Thottingal, 2020), which is a resource containing open-source machine translation models. We machine translated all the samples prepared from the three aforementioned datasets.

3 Approach

We participated in the two subtasks of the Multilingual Named Entity Recognition Task - *Named Entity Mention Detection and Classification* and *Named Entity Lemmatization*. The solution involved fine-tuning the foundation models using task-specific modifications and additional training data. All models used in the experiments can be found on the Hugging Face Hub[2].

3.1 Named Entity Recognition

Recently, the BERT (Devlin et al., 2019) model architecture has been adapted to address Slavic languages such as Polish, Czech and Russian, among others. These languages present unique challenges because of their complex grammatical structures, declensions and inflections, making NLP tasks even more difficult. However, the application of BERT to these languages has resulted in significant improvements in language processing and understanding.

In our solution, we used several monolingual BERT models to better handle the specific linguistic nuances of individual Slavic languages. In particular, we employed of the following models: HerBERT (Mroczkowski et al., 2021) for Polish, Czert (Sido et al., 2021) for Czech and RuBERT (Kuratov and Arkhipov, 2019) for Russian. For comparison, we also used multilingual BERT models that can handle multiple languages, including Slavic BERT (Arkhipov et al., 2019) and XLM-RoBERTa (Conneau et al., 2020).

In the experiments, we also added a Conditional Random Fields (CRF) layer on the top of each BERT model. A similar approach of combining CRF with neural networks has been used previously (Lample et al., 2016), as the CRF layer can capture the dependencies between neighboring tokens and provide a smoother transition between different entity types.

3.2 Lemmatization

Models based on the T5 (Raffel et al., 2020) model architecture have achieved state-of-the-art results in various natural language processing challenges and can be fine-tuned for specific tasks. One of the applications of T5 can be lemmatization, the process of reducing a word or phrase to its basic form (lemma). In Slavic languages such as Polish, Czech and Russian, lemmatization is particularly important due to the complex inflection of these languages.

We approached the lemmatization task as a text-to-text problem. The input to the model is an inflected phrase or named entity, which can consist of several word forms. For example, it can consist of nouns in singular or plural form, or verbs in different tenses. The output of the model is the base, normalized form of the phrase or named entity.

To address the lack of dedicated models for Czech and Russian, we used one monolingual and a multilingual T5 model. Specifically, we chose plT5 (Chrabrowa et al., 2022) for Polish and mT5 (Xue et al., 2021) for multilingual experiments. For comparison purposes, we also conducted our experiments on the small, base and large sizes of the above models.

In the multilingual experiments, we included a language token (»pl«, »cs«, »ru«) as the first token of the source phrases, depending on the language of the phrase. Our preliminary experiments have shown that incorporating the language token improves the results, increasing the exact match by approximately 2 points in each language. We noticed that the model sometimes tends to change the grammatical number from plural to singular - possibly due to the fact that singular named entities occur more often in the training data.

4 Results

4.1 Named Entity Recognition Results

The results of our named entity recognition experiments are presented in table 1. We evaluated our models with a case-sensitive F1 score, which is a standard span-level metric calculated on the ConLL-2003 dataset format. As test sets, we choose COVID-19 and USA 2020 Elections subsets of the 3rd Shared Task on SlavNER.

We tested our solution in two approaches: monolingual and multilingual. For Polish and Czech, we found that monolingual models perform better for language-specific data. In the case of Russian, multilingual models strongly outperform language-specific solutions. We assume that this is due to the lack of sufficient data for this language. In addition, multilingual models can learn common rules in Slavic languages to overcome weaknesses related to insufficient data.

We also found that adding a CRF layer significantly improves the quality of the models in most cases. However, including external datasets wors-

[2]`https://huggingface.co/models`

Model	original data						+ external datasets					
	COVID-19			USA 2020 Elections			COVID-19			USA 2020 Elections		
	pl	cs	ru	pl	cs	ru	pl	cs	ru	pl	cs	ru
HerBERT$_{BASE}$	79.50	-	-	89.27	-	-	78.70	-	-	84.63	-	-
HerBERT$_{BASE}$ + CRF	80.11	-	-	90.16	-	-	80.86	-	-	87.43	-	-
HerBERT$_{LARGE}$	81.18	-	-	91.71	-	-	81.29	-	-	89.83	-	-
HerBERT$_{LARGE}$ + CRF	81.75	-	-	**<u>92.13</u>**	-	-	**<u>82.33</u>**	-	-	89.20	-	-
Czert	-	84.10	-	-	88.82	-	-	73.05	-	-	84.06	-
Czert + CRF	-	**<u>84.22</u>**	-	-	**90.29**	-	-	71.36	-	-	83.70	-
RuBERT	-	-	**62.06**	-	-	76.97	-	-	58.51	-	-	77.63
RuBERT + CRF	-	-	61.80	-	-	**77.69**	-	-	59.55	-	-	76.72
Slavic-BERT	79.06	78.67	61.42	89.07	90.31	78.21	73.73	68.22	59.32	83.72	78.16	77.29
Slavic-BERT + CRF	78.15	80.68	63.08	89.97	90.13	78.72	77.76	69.12	58.08	86.76	80.51	77.05
XLM-RoBERTa$_{BASE}$	79.53	77.89	62.12	88.30	89.51	77.56	76.92	68.46	60.45	83.25	80.89	77.21
XLM-RoBERTa$_{BASE}$ + CRF	81.10	78.80	65.94	88.48	90.88	77.58	79.45	73.42	58.86	87.02	84.20	76.87
XLM-RoBERTa$_{LARGE}$	81.43	80.58	**<u>66.26</u>**	**90.36**	**<u>91.62</u>**	**<u>80.22</u>**	81.12	75.35	61.95	87.46	86.96	77.60
XLM-RoBERTa$_{LARGE}$ + CRF	**81.81**	**81.20**	64.95	89.37	91.53	79.93	80.72	75.01	61.80	86.78	87.66	77.73

Table 1: Results of case-sensitive F1 score for named entity recognition on the COVID-19 and USA 2020 Elections test sets from the 3rd Shared Task on SlavNER. For each language in a given test set, the best score for the monolingual and multilingual solution is shown in bold. In addition, the best score for each language in a given test set is underlined.

		original data			+ PolEval 2019			+ Lexicon		
		pl	cs	ru	pl	cs	ru	pl	cs	ru
	COVID-19									
Model	*Size*									
plT5	small	86.36	-	-	91.15	-	-	92.02	-	-
	base	89.99	-	-	93.03	-	-	80.70	-	-
	large	94.05	-	-	94.78	-	-	**<u>95.36</u>**	-	-
mT5	small	74.46	73.75	70.17	86.80	80.98	73.83	81.13	75.45	71.84
	base	87.66	85.44	76.96	91.00	86.29	76.10	90.42	83.32	75.30
	large	90.57	88.84	**<u>79.09</u>**	93.76	**<u>89.80</u>**	77.30	93.03	89.27	77.16
USA 2020 Elections										
Model	*Size*									
plT5	small	83.37	-	-	87.47	-	-	86.65	-	-
	base	85.22	-	-	87.89	-	-	76.80	-	-
	large	90.97	-	-	90.76	-	-	**<u>91.38</u>**	-	-
mT5	small	71.46	70.03	72.18	78.85	75.86	76.18	74.54	69.76	68.92
	base	83.98	80.37	80.51	84.19	81.97	80.27	85.63	78.78	78.25
	large	88.71	**<u>88.33</u>**	**<u>82.86</u>**	89.12	87.27	82.50	89.94	86.74	81.76

Table 2: Results of the case-insensitive exact match for lemmatization on the COVID-19 and USA 2020 Elections test sets from the 3rd Shared Task on SlavNER. For each test set, the best score in a given language is shown in bold and underlined.

ens the results in almost all cases. We suspect that this is due to the specific domain of the test sets, which are news articles. In addition, some annotation errors can be found in all datasets presented in the 2.2 section.

4.2 Lemmatization Results

The results of our lemmatization experiments are presented in the table 2. We evaluated our models with a case-insensitive exact match on the same test sets as for named entity recognition, but only on the data specific to this task.

We tested our solution based on two models: a monolingual plT5 (only for the Polish language), and a multilingual mT5 model. We observed that the addition of each external dataset significantly improves the quality of the Polish language-specific model. Moreover, the addition of the data from PolEval 2019 also improves the results for the multilingual model. Unfortunately, the addition of data from the lexicon generated by machine translation of the SEJF and SEJFEK datasets causes a decrease

Submission	Recognition			Normalization		
	pl	cs	ru	pl	cs	ru
System 1	83.33	88.08	84.30	80.27	76.62	79.32
System 2	**85.37**	**89.70**	**86.16**	**82.37**	**76.89**	81.27
System 3	83.40	85.19	82.77	80.32	73.06	**81.47**
System 4	83.33	81.70	79.20	80.27	71.11	76.84

Table 3: Results of our systems on the released test set for named entity recognition and normalization (lemmatization). The scores are computed as case-insensitive strict matching for recognition and case-insensitive F1 score for normalization. All scores were received from the organizers.

in the model performance for the Czech and Russian languages. We assume that this is due to the quality of the translation of the phrases into these languages.

We also noticed that the quality of the lemmatization improves as the size of the model increases in almost all cases. However, for Polish, the small model trained on all available data is better than the base model. Furthermore, it is only 3 points worse than the large model, so it can be used efficiently considering the hardware limitations.

4.3 The 4th Shared Task on SlavNER Results

The current edition of the shared task features news articles about the Russian-Ukrainian war, and the test set includes raw texts in Polish, Czech and Russian languages.

As a solution, we submitted four systems consisting of the following fine-tuned models with an additional CRF layer for named entity recognition:

- System 1: $\text{HerBERT}_{\text{LARGE}}$ for Polish trained on all available data, Czert for Czech and RuBERT for Russian trained only on the data provided by the organizers,
- System 2: $\text{XLM-RoBERTa}_{\text{LARGE}}$ for all languages trained only on the data provided by the organizers,
- System 3: $\text{XLM-RoBERTa}_{\text{LARGE}}$ for all languages trained on all available data,
- System 4: $\text{HerBERT}_{\text{LARGE}}$ for Polish, Czert for Czech and RuBERT for Russian trained on all available data.

In all the systems mentioned above, we used the following lemmatization models: $\text{plT5}_{\text{LARGE}}$ for Polish (trained on all available data) and $\text{mT5}_{\text{LARGE}}$ for Czech and Russian (trained on the data provided by the organizers and the data from PolEval 2019 Task 2).

The best solution for recognizing and categorizing named entities turned out to be System 2, which also achieved the best results for normalization (lemmatization). In addition, the normalization scores are highly dependent on the NER results, since only recognized entities are normalized.

5 Conclusions

We described the Adam Mickiewicz University's (AMU) participation in the 4th Shared Task on SlavNER for named entity recognition and lemmatization tasks. Our experiments encompassed various foundation models, including monolingual and multilingual BERT and T5 models. We found that incorporating a CRF layer enhanced the quality of our named entity recognition models. Additionally, our results indicate that the use of T5 models for lemmatization yields high-quality lemmatization of named entities. We will release the lemmatization models to the community and make them available at: `https://huggingface.co/amu-cai`.

References

Rami Al-Rfou, Vivek Kulkarni, Bryan Perozzi, and Steven Skiena. 2015. Polyglot-NER: Massive multilingual named entity recognition. *Proceedings of the 2015 SIAM International Conference on Data Mining, Vancouver, British Columbia, Canada, April 30- May 2, 2015.*

Mikhail Arkhipov, Maria Trofimova, Yuri Kuratov, and Alexey Sorokin. 2019. Tuning multilingual transformers for language-specific named entity recognition. In *Proceedings of the 7th Workshop on Balto-Slavic Natural Language Processing*, pages 89–93, Florence, Italy. Association for Computational Linguistics.

Rishi Bommasani, Drew A. Hudson, Ehsan Adeli, Russ Altman, Simran Arora, Sydney von Arx, Michael S.

Bernstein, Jeannette Bohg, Antoine Bosselut, Emma Brunskill, Erik Brynjolfsson, S. Buch, Dallas Card, Rodrigo Castellon, Niladri S. Chatterji, Annie S. Chen, Kathleen A. Creel, Jared Davis, Dora Demszky, Chris Donahue, Moussa Doumbouya, Esin Durmus, Stefano Ermon, John Etchemendy, Kawin Ethayarajh, Li Fei-Fei, Chelsea Finn, Trevor Gale, Lauren E. Gillespie, Karan Goel, Noah D. Goodman, Shelby Grossman, Neel Guha, Tatsunori Hashimoto, Peter Henderson, John Hewitt, Daniel E. Ho, Jenny Hong, Kyle Hsu, Jing Huang, Thomas F. Icard, Saahil Jain, Dan Jurafsky, Pratyusha Kalluri, Siddharth Karamcheti, Geoff Keeling, Fereshte Khani, O. Khattab, Pang Wei Koh, Mark S. Krass, Ranjay Krishna, Rohith Kuditipudi, Ananya Kumar, Faisal Ladhak, Mina Lee, Tony Lee, Jure Leskovec, Isabelle Levent, Xiang Lisa Li, Xuechen Li, Tengyu Ma, Ali Malik, Christopher D. Manning, Suvir Mirchandani, Eric Mitchell, Zanele Munyikwa, Suraj Nair, Avanika Narayan, Deepak Narayanan, Benjamin Newman, Allen Nie, Juan Carlos Niebles, Hamed Nilforoshan, J. F. Nyarko, Giray Ogut, Laurel J. Orr, Isabel Papadimitriou, Joon Sung Park, Chris Piech, Eva Portelance, Christopher Potts, Aditi Raghunathan, Robert Reich, Hongyu Ren, Frieda Rong, Yusuf H. Roohani, Camilo Ruiz, Jack Ryan, Christopher R'e, Dorsa Sadigh, Shiori Sagawa, Keshav Santhanam, Andy Shih, Krishna Parasuram Srinivasan, Alex Tamkin, Rohan Taori, Armin W. Thomas, Florian Tramèr, Rose E. Wang, William Wang, Bohan Wu, Jiajun Wu, Yuhuai Wu, Sang Michael Xie, Michihiro Yasunaga, Jiaxuan You, Matei A. Zaharia, Michael Zhang, Tianyi Zhang, Xikun Zhang, Yuhui Zhang, Lucia Zheng, Kaitlyn Zhou, and Percy Liang. 2021. On the opportunities and risks of foundation models. *ArXiv*, abs/2108.07258.

Aleksandra Chrabrowa, Łukasz Dragan, Karol Grzegorczyk, Dariusz Kajtoch, Mikołaj Koszowski, Robert Mroczkowski, and Piotr Rybak. 2022. Evaluation of transfer learning for Polish with a text-to-text model. In *Proceedings of the Thirteenth Language Resources and Evaluation Conference*, pages 4374–4394, Marseille, France. European Language Resources Association.

Alexis Conneau, Kartikay Khandelwal, Naman Goyal, Vishrav Chaudhary, Guillaume Wenzek, Francisco Guzmán, Edouard Grave, Myle Ott, Luke Zettlemoyer, and Veselin Stoyanov. 2020. Unsupervised cross-lingual representation learning at scale. In *Proceedings of the 58th Annual Meeting of the Association for Computational Linguistics*, pages 8440–8451, Online. Association for Computational Linguistics.

Monika Czerepowicka and Agata Savary. 2018. Sejf - a grammatical lexicon of polish multiword expressions. In *Human Language Technology. Challenges for Computer Science and Linguistics*, pages 59–73, Cham. Springer International Publishing.

Jacob Devlin, Ming-Wei Chang, Kenton Lee, and Kristina Toutanova. 2019. BERT: Pre-training of deep bidirectional transformers for language understanding. In *Proceedings of the 2019 Conference of the North American Chapter of the Association for Computational Linguistics: Human Language Technologies, Volume 1 (Long and Short Papers)*, pages 4171–4186, Minneapolis, Minnesota. Association for Computational Linguistics.

Yuri Kuratov and Mikhail Arkhipov. 2019. Adaptation of deep bidirectional multilingual transformers for russian language. *ArXiv*, abs/1905.07213.

Guillaume Lample, Miguel Ballesteros, Sandeep Subramanian, Kazuya Kawakami, and Chris Dyer. 2016. Neural architectures for named entity recognition. In *Proceedings of the 2016 Conference of the North American Chapter of the Association for Computational Linguistics: Human Language Technologies*, pages 260–270, San Diego, California. Association for Computational Linguistics.

Michał Marcińczuk and Tomasz Bernaś. 2019. Results of the poleval 2019 task 2: Lemmatization of proper names and multi-word phrases.

Valerie Mozharova and Natalia Loukachevitch. 2016. Two-stage approach in russian named entity recognition. In *2016 International FRUCT Conference on Intelligence, Social Media and Web (ISMW FRUCT)*, pages 1–6.

Robert Mroczkowski, Piotr Rybak, Alina Wróblewska, and Ireneusz Gawlik. 2021. HerBERT: Efficiently pretrained transformer-based language model for Polish. In *Proceedings of the 8th Workshop on Balto-Slavic Natural Language Processing*, pages 1–10, Kyiv, Ukraine. Association for Computational Linguistics.

Jakub Piskorski, Bogdan Babych, Zara Kancheva, Olga Kanishcheva, Maria Lebedeva, Michał Marcińczuk, Preslav Nakov, Petya Osenova, Lidia Pivovarova, Senja Pollak, Pavel Přibáň, Ivaylo Radev, Marko Robnik-Sikonja, Vasyl Starko, Josef Steinberger, and Roman Yangarber. 2021. Slav-NER: the 3rd cross-lingual challenge on recognition, normalization, classification, and linking of named entities across Slavic languages. In *Proceedings of the 8th Workshop on Balto-Slavic Natural Language Processing*, pages 122–133, Kyiv, Ukraine. Association for Computational Linguistics.

Colin Raffel, Noam Shazeer, Adam Roberts, Katherine Lee, Sharan Narang, Michael Matena, Yanqi Zhou, Wei Li, and Peter J. Liu. 2020. Exploring the limits of transfer learning with a unified text-to-text transformer. *Journal of Machine Learning Research*, 21(140):1–67.

Agata Savary, Bartosz Zaborowski, Aleksandra Krawczyk-Wieczorek, and Filip Makowiecki. 2012. SEJFEK - a lexicon and a shallow grammar of Polish economic multi-word units. In *Proceedings of the 3rd Workshop on Cognitive Aspects of the Lexicon*, pages 195–214, Mumbai, India. The COLING 2012 Organizing Committee.

Jakub Sido, Ondřej Pražák, Pavel Přibáň, Jan Pašek, Michal Seják, and Miloslav Konopík. 2021. Czert – Czech BERT-like model for language representation. In *Proceedings of the International Conference on Recent Advances in Natural Language Processing (RANLP 2021)*, pages 1326–1338, Held Online. INCOMA Ltd.

Simone Tedeschi, Valentino Maiorca, Niccolò Campolungo, Francesco Cecconi, and Roberto Navigli. 2021. WikiNEuRal: Combined neural and knowledge-based silver data creation for multilingual NER. In *Findings of the Association for Computational Linguistics: EMNLP 2021*, pages 2521–2533, Punta Cana, Dominican Republic. Association for Computational Linguistics.

Simone Tedeschi and Roberto Navigli. 2022. MultiNERD: A multilingual, multi-genre and fine-grained dataset for named entity recognition (and disambiguation). In *Findings of the Association for Computational Linguistics: NAACL 2022*, pages 801–812, Seattle, United States. Association for Computational Linguistics.

Jörg Tiedemann and Santhosh Thottingal. 2020. OPUS-MT – building open translation services for the world. In *Proceedings of the 22nd Annual Conference of the European Association for Machine Translation*, pages 479–480, Lisboa, Portugal. European Association for Machine Translation.

Erik F. Tjong Kim Sang and Fien De Meulder. 2003. Introduction to the CoNLL-2003 shared task: Language-independent named entity recognition. In *Proceedings of the Seventh Conference on Natural Language Learning at HLT-NAACL 2003*, pages 142–147.

Rinalds Vīksna and Inguna Skadina. 2021. Multilingual Slavic named entity recognition. In *Proceedings of the 8th Workshop on Balto-Slavic Natural Language Processing*, pages 93–97, Kyiv, Ukraine. Association for Computational Linguistics.

Linting Xue, Noah Constant, Adam Roberts, Mihir Kale, Rami Al-Rfou, Aditya Siddhant, Aditya Barua, and Colin Raffel. 2021. mT5: A massively multilingual pre-trained text-to-text transformer. In *Proceedings of the 2021 Conference of the North American Chapter of the Association for Computational Linguistics: Human Language Technologies*, pages 483–498, Online. Association for Computational Linguistics.

Large Language Models for Multilingual Slavic Named Entity Linking

Rinalds Vīksna[1,2] and **Inguna Skadiņa**[1,2] and **Daiga Deksne**[1,2] and **Roberts Rozis**[1]
[1] Tilde, Vienības gatve 75a, Riga, Latvia
[2] Faculty of Computing, University of Latvia, Raiņa bulv. 29, Riga, Latvia
{Firstname.Lastname}@tilde.lv

Abstract

This paper describes our submission for the 4th Shared Task on SlavNER on three Slavic languages - Czech, Polish, and Russian. We use pre-trained multilingual XLM-R Language Model and fine-tune it for three Slavic languages using datasets provided by organizers. Our multilingual NER model achieves a 0.896 F-score on all corpora, with the best result for Czech (0.914) and the worst for Russian (0.880). Our cross-language entity linking module achieves an F-score of 0.669 in the official SlavNER 2023 evaluation.

1 Introduction

The 4th edition of Shared Task address three Slavic languages: Czech, Polish, and Russian, and five types of named entities (persons, locations, organizations, events, and products). All languages are highly inflective and have a rather free word order. Thus named entity normalization task faces an additional challenge in the case of the normalization of multi-word expressions (MWE).

In our submission, we continue experiments with XLM-R Language Model (Conneau et al., 2020) which has demonstrated the best result in previous shared task (Ferreira et al., 2021). We also elaborate on the normalization step for MWEs by applying syntax-based noun phrase normalization tool to reach higher accuracy in named entity (NE) normalization and linking tasks. Finally, we also improve entity linking by better algorithms for linking entity variants on a document level using string similarity, proximity, and type attributes.

The paper is organized as follows. We start with an overview of the data preparation step (Section 3) and the overall architecture of the system (Section 4). Then, we present each step in our workflow - mention detection, entity normalization, and entity linking. We conclude the paper with a subset of results and a discussion (Section 8).

2 Related Work

The shared task on Slavic multilingual named entity recognition, normalization, and linking (SlavNER) has been organized since 2017 (Piskorski et al., 2017). Only two systems were submitted for the First SlavNER. The best result for NER was achieved for Polish (F-score of 66.6), while for cross-lingual entity matching only 9 F1 points were reached (Mayfield et al., 2017). Authors of this system annotated parallel English-target language datasets using an English NER and projected annotations to the target language. A target language tagger was then trained using inferred datasets.

Seven teams submitted systems to the 2nd SlavNER (Piskorski et al., 2019). The three best systems (RIS (Arkhipov et al., 2019), CogComp (Tsygankova et al., 2019) and IIUWR.PL (Piskorski et al., 2019)) used BERT for the NER task. The best model, CogComp, yields an F-measure of 91% according to the shared task organizers. The cross-lingual entity linking results also have improved significantly: the best-performing model, IIUWR.PL yields the F-measure of 45%.

Six teams submitted their systems to the 3rd SlavNER (Piskorski et al., 2021). Overall NER task results were lower when compared to the 2nd SlavNER. The best system, Priberam (Ferreira et al., 2021), achieved F-measure of 85.7% for the relaxed partial evaluation. Priberam used XLM-R Large model, a character-level embedding model, and a biaffine classifier for NER task. For cross-lingual entity linking, the best-performing model, TLD (Vīksna and Skadina, 2021), achieved an F-measure of 50.4% using LaBSE (Feng et al., 2022) embeddings to align entities according to pre-defined thresholds.

3 Data Preparation

The data provided by the SlavNER task organizers contains annotations for five classes of entities:

Proceedings of the 9th Workshop on Slavic Natural Language Processing 2023 (SlavicNLP 2023), pages 172–178
May 6, 2023

event (EVT), location (LOC), person (PER), organization (ORG), and product (PRO). For NER system training we convert data into a conll2003-like format. We do not use the data from the BSNLP2017 shared task (Piskorski et al., 2017), as it has 4 named entity classes which are inconsistent with the rest of SlavNER data (Prelevikj and Zitnik, 2021), and has shown to hurt the performance of NER models for this task (Ferreira et al., 2021). In addition to the dataset provided by the SlavNER task organizers(Piskorski et al., 2019, 2021), we use the following datasets in our experiments:

KPWr (Oleksy et al., 2019) contains Polish texts labeled using 82 classes of entities, which we map to the 5 classes used in the SlavNER task.

NKJP (Przepiórkowski, 2012) is National Corpus of Polish, tagged with fine-grained NEs. We use entity types PER ('forename', 'surname'), LOC (placeName, geogName), and ORG (orgName).

poleval2018 (Ogrodniczuk and Łukasz Kobyliński, 2018) is POLEVAL 2018 NER task gold dataset, labeled using the same guidelines as NKJP.

FiNER (Ruokolainen et al., 2019) is a Finnish dataset that contains the same NE types as SlavNER, thus useful to train NER for EVT and PRO classes.

CNEC (Ševčíková et al., 2014) Czech Named Entity Corpus 2.0 is labeled according to a two-level hierarchy of 46 named entities. It was mapped to the corresponding 4 classes of the SlavNER task: ORG, PER, LOC, and PRO.

FactRU (Starostin et al., 2016) is a Russian dataset, labeled with 4 classes of entities (Org, LocOrg, Location, and Person), which can be mapped to 3 classes of the SlavNER task: ORG, LOC, PER.

conll2002 (Tjong Kim Sang, 2002) is a Spanish NER dataset labeled with PER, LOC, ORG and MISC classes.

conll2003 (Tjong Kim Sang and De Meulder, 2003) is an English NER dataset labeled using PER, LOC, ORG and MISC classes.

4 Architecture and systems

The architecture of our solution is modular: the modules roughly correspond to the data processing steps necessary to reach the objectives of different SlavNER Shared Tasks: mention detection, lemmatization, and linking (Figure 1).

We submitted five systems to the SlavNER task. Table 1 provides an overview of our systems. In the following sections, we provide more details of our solutions.

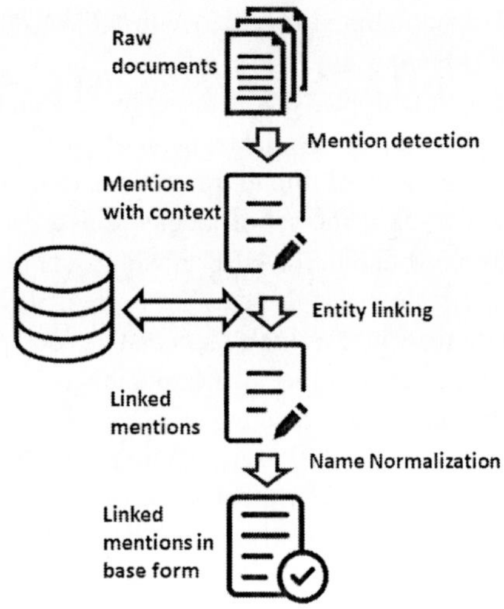

Figure 1: Overall System Architecture

	NER	Linker
1	XLM-R Base Ensemble	C
2	XLM-R Large	C
3	XLM-R Large	D and C
4	XLM-R Large plus KPWr data	D and C
5	XLM-R Base additionaly pre-trained plus KPWr data	D and C

Table 1: System overview (C-corpus level, D- document level)

5 Two Approaches to Mention Detection: traditional and ensemble

We consider the Named Entity Mention Detection and Classification task as the NER task. We use the Flair library (Schweter and Akbik, 2020) to perform NER. Flair library allows fine-tuning a Transformer (Vaswani et al., 2017) model with custom data. Multilingual XLM-R has demonstrated the best result in previous shared task (Ferreira et al., 2021) and is used as a basis for our NER models. The XLM-R is available in XLM-R Base (L= 12, H = 768, A = 12, 270M params) and XLM-R Large(L = 24, H = 1024, A = 16, 550M params) variants.

We use XLM-R Large model fine-tuned on the dataset provided by the Shared Task organizers as a NER model for our System-2 and System-3.

For System-4 we fine-tune a XLM-R Large model on the dataset given by the Shared Task organizers combined together with KPWR-NER dataset (Marcińczuk, 2020).

Although multiple NER datasets for Czech, Polish, and Russian are available, most of them could not be directly used due to differences in tagsets. However, even if the set of labeled classes is incompatible with the SlavNER labeling schema, it is still possible to use this data for training a NER system to recognize a single class that has compatible labeling. This is done by keeping only a single label in a dataset and deleting all other labels.

Using single-label datasets, we train a NER system by combing SlavNER dataset with this dataset and evaluate against the SlavNER test split. If a system achieves better results than the baseline system trained on SlavNER data, we consider this dataset as compatible with SlavNER and select to train the final NER model for a given label. Datasets used to fine-tune each single-label NER model are summarised in Table 2.

Model	Datasets used for training
EVT	SlavNER, KPWr
LOC	SlavNER, CNEC, KPWr, conll2002, conll2003, FactRu, finer, NKJP
ORG	SlavNER, CNEC, KPWr, FactRu, NKJP, Poleval
PER	SlavNER, Poleval,
PRO	SlavNER, CNEC, KPWr, finer

Table 2: Datasets used to train single-label models

Due to performance and time restrictions, the XLM-R Base model is used to fine-tune ensemble models. During the evaluation, all five NER models are run sequentially. The overlapping labels are resolved, first by selecting the longest labeled entity and then, if there is an exact overlap, by selecting the highest score returned by NER. This ensemble approach is used by our System-1.

Since the XLM-R models were created more than two years ago, and thus outdated with respect to current events, we crawled 2.6 GB of the latest Czech, Polish, and Russian news articles[1] to perform additional pretraining of XLM-R base model. Due to the time restrictions, additional pretraining was done using huggingface/transformers example script[2] with batch size 512, for 7000 steps. This additionally pre-trained XLM-R model was fine-tuned using the SlavNER dataset and the KPWr dataset for NER of System-5.

[1] News were collected from the news portals: www.idnes.cz, niezalezna.pl and censor.net Russian section

[2] https://github.com/huggingface/transformers/blob/main/examples/pytorch/language-modeling/run_mlm.py

6 Entity Normalization

We use several strategies for entity normalization. In case of the Czech language we apply a simple word-level lemmatization strategy. We use Stanza (Qi et al., 2020) Czech language lemmatizer for this task.

For entity normalization in Polish and Russian, we use a language-specific noun phrase generator. It allows us to transform the noun phrase into the corresponding base form taking into account the grammar rules of the specific language.

The normalization workflow includes several steps: tokenization, morphological analysis, syntactic parsing, morphological transfer, and morphological synthesis of the base form. Morphological analysis and synthesis are performed with help of a language-specific finite state transducer (FST). This FST solution was initially developed for the Latvian language (Deksne, 2013) and recently extended to many other European languages - Lithuanian, Polish, Finnish, Swedish, Spanish, French, German, and English. For the syntactic parsing Cocke-Younger-Kasami (CYK) algorithm (Younger, 1967) is employed by adapting the corresponding Latvian tool (Deksne et al., 2014).

When analysing output of the normalisation tool, we identified several reasons for errors:

- A word in a phrase is unrecognized acronym.
- In the case of homographs, if a word has some identical singular and plural forms, the normalisation tool preserves the number of original phrases (singular or plural). As result in some cases the number of the base form of a particular NE is singular instead of plural or vice versa.
- For the multi-word expressions, the normalisation tool can create several base forms that comply with syntactical rules. As there is no disambiguation component that would take into account the semantics of the particular phrase, the first result from the result list is assumed as the correct one.

7 Entity Linking

The goal of the entity linking task is to associate entity mentions found in a text with corresponding entries in a Knowledge Base (KB) (Zheng et al., 2010). Traditional entity linking pipeline consists of three steps: mention detection, candidate selection, and disambiguation (Balog, 2018).

The mention detection step is described in the Section 5. Due to the small expected size of our cross-lingual knowledge base (the actual maximum number of KB entries produced in this Shared task by our systems was 939), we skip the candidate selection step. Instead, a simple consistency check is applied to filter out mentions which do not have the same type (Khosla and Rose, 2020). As result, the candidates are all entries in the Knowledge Base which have the same type as the entity mention, which we are attempting to link.

The candidate selection and disambiguation usually include a three-step process of candidate generation, candidate ranking, and unlinkable mention prediction (Shen et al., 2015). In our submission, the candidates are ranked using a mention-ranking model (Rahman and Ng, 2009) to decide whether an active mention is co-referent with a candidate antecedent. We follow the algorithm proposed by (Vīksna and Skadina, 2021): at first, we use LaBSE to obtain entity mention embeddings and then we apply cosine similarity to calculate the similarity between obtained embeddings and those in the Knowledge Base. The similarity threshold for early stopping is set at 0.95 - if the similarity is above the threshold, the process links the entity mention to the candidate mention and returns the candidate mention ID. If none of the candidate mentions has a similarity score above 0.6, the entity mention is considered not found in the Knowledge Base and is added as a new entry to the Knowledge Base. For entities with similarity scores between 0.6 and 0.95, the candidate with the highest score is selected for linking.

Usually, at the beginning of the text entities are introduced (named) carefully, e.g. with a full name (and acronym), while later in a text, when it is clear from the context what they refer to, entities are often used in the shortened form (Rychlikowski et al., 2021). For such cases, we introduce an additional linking step at the document level: for each entity mention, we check whether its name is part of another entity, e.g., encountering the name "Asia", it could be matched as part of "Asia Bibi". We perform this step before attempting to link an entity to the Knowledge Base.

We also check for organization and person name abbreviations and translations. At first, we identify entities that are surrounded by brackets (optionally, quoted). Then, if the entity immediately preceding it belongs to the same type, both entities are linked together as aliases.

8 Results

Table 3 summarizes the performance of our five systems. The best results in the entity recognition task have been achieved by System-3. System-3 does not use any additional datasets for NER training. However, the overall results differ very little, and may not be statistically significant.

	NER	Norm	Link cross-lang	Link document
System-1	0.890	0.587	0.644	0.716
System-2	**0.896**	**0.595**	0.668	0.712
System-3	**0.896**	**0.595**	**0.669**	**0.755**
System-4	0.885	0.584	0.668	0.727
System-5	0.881	0.587	0.666	0.702

Table 3: NER (Recognition, relaxed partial matching), normalization and linking (cross-language level and document level) results of Tilde systems, F scores

System-4 shows noticeable improvement for EVT detection (Table 4), which could be explained by additional XLM-R pretraining on recent news data. The performance of System-5, which was fine-tuned using additional KPWr data, is very poor in PER class. Our hypothesis is that the annotation guidelines for PER class differ significantly between KPWr and SlavNER datasets. This drawback is addressed by our ensemble System-1, which, despite being fine-tuned with XLM-R Base, achieves an overall F-score of 0.89, and for the LOC class shows better performance than System-3 (achieving an F-score of 0.944).

	S1	S2, S3	S4	S5
All	0.890	**0.896**	0.885	0.881
PER	**0.969**	**0.971**	0.930	0.906
LOC	**0.944**	0.934	0.932	0.938
ORG	0.843	0.848	**0.854**	**0.853**
PRO	0.689	**0.823**	0.761	0.796
EVT	0.273	0.300	**0.375**	0.267

Table 4: Entity recognition results evaluated on SlavNER test data (Relaxed partial matching, All 5 systems: S1 = System-1, S2 = System-2, ...), F scores

The ensemble system shows good overall performance but performs poorly on PRO class. Although the separate NER systems, fine-tuned to detect PRO entities on CNEC, KPWr, and FiNER data, performed better than the baseline on our test setup, the final system, trained on the combined dataset, did not generalize well.

The NER results vary slightly between languages (Table 5), with better scores for languages using Latin script.

	Recall	Precision	F score
cs (all)	0.885	0.945	0.914
ru (all)	0.878	0.884	0.880
pl (all)	0.869	0.932	0.899

Table 5: System-3 entity recognition results evaluated on SlavNER test data (Relaxed partial matching) by language

All our systems use the same normalization tool, therefore any differences in normalization results between our systems depend on the previous entity recognition step. The normalization results for our best-performing System-3 are summarized in Table 6. The normalization tool demonstrates good results for the Russian language (F-score 0.70), while for Polish (F-score 0.54) results are similar to Stanza, used for Czech language normalization.

	Recall	Precision	F score
PER	0.488	0.496	0.492
LOC	0.731	0.746	0.739
ORG	0.298	0.393	0.339
PRO	0.459	0.436	0.447
EVT	0.011	0.045	0.018
All corpora	0.566	0.627	**0.595**
cs (all)	0.561	0.522	0.541
ru (all)	0.692	0.716	0.704
pl (all)	0.474	0.623	0.539

Table 6: Entity normalization results evaluated on SlavNER test data (System-3)

The best results in entity linking task (in all tasks - document level, single- and cross-language) achieved System-3. Evaluation results for this system are summarized in Table 7. Since this task depends on mention detection task, results for the EVT class are poor. Our entity linking system is based on embeddings and in the case of organizations, it often fails to separate similar yet completely different organizations, e.g. our model considers ORG-Gazprom and ORG-Gazprombank as the same entity. When the output of System-2 and System-3 is compared (Table 3), we can see that document-level linking improves entity linking performance on the document level significantly (F-scores 0.712 and 0.755), while on the cross-lingual level its effects are negligible.

	Recall	Precision	F score
PER	0.713	0.764	0.738
LOC	0.813	0.787	0.800
ORG	0.422	0.416	0.419
PRO	0.428	0.615	0.505
EVT	0.102	0.241	0.144
All	0.660	0.677	**0.669**

Table 7: Entity linking results evaluated on SlavNER test data (Cross-language level, System-3)

9 Conclusions

In this paper, we presented a modular architecture for the Recognition, Normalization, Classification, and Cross-lingual linking of Named Entities in Slavic Languages. Each module (NER, normalization tool, and NE linker) is self-contained and could be improved independently from others. While none of the systems fine-tuned on additional datasets surpassed the XLM-R Large system fine-tuned on SlavNER data, the ensemble system seems promising and could be retrained again using the XLM-R Large model instead of XLM-R Base in order to obtain better results.

Limitations

Our best-performing systems use very large language models or are ensemble systems, resources required to train and run such systems are considerable.

Entity linking module performs an embedding comparison with all entities of a matching type found in the knowledge base. While the KB is small such an approach works fast, however, as the knowledge base grows, each additional entity adds to the search time. For large knowledge bases, some form of candidate selection method would be necessary.

Acknowlegements

This research has been supported by the European Regional Development Fund within the research project "AI Assistant for Multilingual Meeting Management" No. 1.1.1.1/ 19/A/082.

References

Mikhail Arkhipov, Maria Trofimova, Yuri Kuratov, and Alexey Sorokin. 2019. Tuning multilingual transformers for language-specific named entity recognition. In *Proceedings of the 7th Workshop on Balto-Slavic Natural Language Processing*, pages 89–93, Florence, Italy. Association for Computational Linguistics.

Krisztian Balog. 2018. *Entity Linking*, pages 147–188. Springer International Publishing, Cham.

Alexis Conneau, Kartikay Khandelwal, Naman Goyal, Vishrav Chaudhary, Guillaume Wenzek, Francisco Guzmán, Edouard Grave, Myle Ott, Luke Zettlemoyer, and Veselin Stoyanov. 2020. Unsupervised cross-lingual representation learning at scale. In *Proceedings of the 58th Annual Meeting of the Association for Computational Linguistics*, pages 8440–8451, Online. Association for Computational Linguistics.

Daiga Deksne. 2013. Finite state morphology tool for Latvian. In *Proceedings of the 11th International Conference on Finite State Methods and Natural Language Processing*, pages 49–53, St Andrews, Scotland. Association for Computational Linguistics.

Daiga Deksne, Inguna Skadina, and Raivis Skadins. 2014. Extended CFG formalism for grammar checker and parser development. In *Computational Linguistics and Intelligent Text Processing - 15th International Conference, CICLing 2014, Kathmandu, Nepal, April 6-12, 2014, Proceedings, Part I*, volume 8403 of *Lecture Notes in Computer Science*, pages 237–249. Springer.

Fangxiaoyu Feng, Yinfei Yang, Daniel Cer, Naveen Arivazhagan, and Wei Wang. 2022. Language-agnostic BERT sentence embedding. In *Proceedings of the 60th Annual Meeting of the Association for Computational Linguistics (Volume 1: Long Papers)*, pages 878–891, Dublin, Ireland. Association for Computational Linguistics.

Pedro Ferreira, Ruben Cardoso, and Afonso Mendes. 2021. Priberam labs at the 3rd shared task on SlavNER. In *Proceedings of the 8th Workshop on Balto-Slavic Natural Language Processing*, pages 86–92, Kiyv, Ukraine. Association for Computational Linguistics.

Sopan Khosla and Carolyn Rose. 2020. Using type information to improve entity coreference resolution. In *Proceedings of the First Workshop on Computational Approaches to Discourse*, pages 20–31, Online. Association for Computational Linguistics.

Michał Marcińczuk. 2020. KPWr n82 NER model (on polish RoBERTa base). CLARIN-PL digital repository.

James Mayfield, Paul McNamee, and Cash Costello. 2017. Language-independent named entity analysis using parallel projection and rule-based disambiguation. In *Proceedings of the 6th Workshop on Balto-Slavic Natural Language Processing*, pages 92–96, Valencia, Spain. Association for Computational Linguistics.

Maciej Ogrodniczuk and Łukasz Kobyliński, editors. 2018. *Proceedings of the PolEval 2018 Workshop*. Institute of Computer Science, Polish Academy of Sciences, Warsaw, Poland.

Marcin Oleksy, Michał Marcińczuk, Marek Maziarz, Tomasz Bernaś, Jan Wieczorek, Agnieszka Turek, Dominika Fikus, Michał Wolski, Marek Pustowaruk, Jan Kocoń, and Paweł Kędzia. 2019. Polish corpus of wrocław university of technology 1.3. CLARIN-PL digital repository.

Jakub Piskorski, Bogdan Babych, Zara Kancheva, Olga Kanishcheva, Maria Lebedeva, Michał Marcińczuk, Preslav Nakov, Petya Osenova, Lidia Pivovarova, Senja Pollak, Pavel Přibáň, Ivaylo Radev, Marko Robnik-Sikonja, Vasyl Starko, Josef Steinberger, and Roman Yangarber. 2021. Slav-NER: the 3rd cross-lingual challenge on recognition, normalization, classification, and linking of named entities across Slavic languages. In *Proceedings of the 8th Workshop on Balto-Slavic Natural Language Processing*, pages 122–133, Kiyv, Ukraine. Association for Computational Linguistics.

Jakub Piskorski, Laska Laskova, Michał Marcińczuk, Lidia Pivovarova, Pavel Přibáň, Josef Steinberger, and Roman Yangarber. 2019. The second cross-lingual challenge on recognition, normalization, classification, and linking of named entities across Slavic languages. In *Proceedings of the 7th Workshop on Balto-Slavic Natural Language Processing*, pages 63–74, Florence, Italy. Association for Computational Linguistics.

Jakub Piskorski, Lidia Pivovarova, Jan Šnajder, Josef Steinberger, and Roman Yangarber. 2017. The first cross-lingual challenge on recognition, normalization, and matching of named entities in Slavic languages. In *Proceedings of the 6th Workshop on Balto-Slavic Natural Language Processing*, pages 76–85, Valencia, Spain. Association for Computational Linguistics.

Marko Prelevikj and Slavko Zitnik. 2021. Multilingual named entity recognition and matching using BERT and dedupe for Slavic languages. In *Proceedings of the 8th Workshop on Balto-Slavic Natural Language Processing*, pages 80–85, Kiyv, Ukraine. Association for Computational Linguistics.

Adam Przepiórkowski. 2012. *Narodowy korpus języka polskiego*. Naukowe PWN.

Peng Qi, Yuhao Zhang, Yuhui Zhang, Jason Bolton, and Christopher D. Manning. 2020. Stanza: A Python natural language processing toolkit for many human languages. In *Proceedings of the 58th Annual Meeting of the Association for Computational Linguistics: System Demonstrations*.

Altaf Rahman and Vincent Ng. 2009. Supervised models for coreference resolution. In *Proceedings of the 2009 Conference on Empirical Methods in Natural Language Processing*, pages 968–977, Singapore. Association for Computational Linguistics.

Teemu Ruokolainen, Pekka Kauppinen, Miikka Silfverberg, and Krister Lindén. 2019. A finnish news corpus for named entity recognition. *Language Resources and Evaluation*, pages 1–26.

Paweł Rychlikowski, Bartłomiej Najdecki, Adrian Lancucki, and Adam Kaczmarek. 2021. Named entity recognition and linking augmented with large-scale structured data. In *Proceedings of the 8th Workshop on Balto-Slavic Natural Language Processing*, pages 115–121, Kiyv, Ukraine. Association for Computational Linguistics.

Stefan Schweter and Alan Akbik. 2020. FLERT: Document-level features for named entity recognition.

Magda Ševčíková, Zdeněk Žabokrtský, Jana Straková, and Milan Straka. 2014. Czech named entity corpus 2.0. LINDAT/CLARIAH-CZ digital library at the Institute of Formal and Applied Linguistics (ÚFAL), Faculty of Mathematics and Physics, Charles University.

W. Shen, J. Wang, and J. Han. 2015. Entity linking with a knowledge base: Issues, techniques, and solutions. *IEEE Transactions on Knowledge and Data Engineering*, 27(2):443–460.

Anatoli Starostin, Victor Bocharov, Svetlana Alexeeva, A. A. Bodrova, Alexander Chuchunkov, Sh. Sh. Dzhumaev, Irina Efimenko, D V Granovsky, Vladimir F. Khoroshevsky, Irina V. Krylova, Maria Nikolaeva, Ivan Smurov, and Svetlana Toldova. 2016. Factrueval 2016: Evaluation of named entity recognition and fact extraction systems for russian. In *Computational Linguistics and Intellectual Technologies: Proceedings of the International Conference "Dialogue 2016"*.

Erik F. Tjong Kim Sang. 2002. Introduction to the CoNLL-2002 shared task: Language-independent named entity recognition. In *COLING-02: The 6th Conference on Natural Language Learning 2002 (CoNLL-2002)*.

Erik F. Tjong Kim Sang and Fien De Meulder. 2003. Introduction to the CoNLL-2003 shared task: Language-independent named entity recognition. In *Proceedings of the Seventh Conference on Natural Language Learning at HLT-NAACL 2003*, pages 142–147.

Tatiana Tsygankova, Stephen Mayhew, and Dan Roth. 2019. BSNLP2019 shared task submission: Multisource neural NER transfer. In *Proceedings of the 7th Workshop on Balto-Slavic Natural Language Processing*, pages 75–82, Florence, Italy. Association for Computational Linguistics.

Ashish Vaswani, Noam Shazeer, Niki Parmar, Jakob Uszkoreit, Llion Jones, Aidan N. Gomez, Lukasz Kaiser, and Illia Polosukhin. 2017. Attention is all you need. *CoRR*, abs/1706.03762.

Rinalds Vīksna and Inguna Skadina. 2021. Multilingual Slavic named entity recognition. In *Proceedings of the 8th Workshop on Balto-Slavic Natural Language Processing*, pages 93–97, Kiyv, Ukraine. Association for Computational Linguistics.

Daniel H Younger. 1967. Recognition and parsing of context-free languages in time n3. *Information and control*, 10(2):189–208.

Zhicheng Zheng, Fangtao Li, Minlie Huang, and Xiaoyan Zhu. 2010. Learning to link entities with knowledge base. In *Human Language Technologies: The 2010 Annual Conference of the North American Chapter of the Association for Computational Linguistics*, pages 483–491, Los Angeles, California. Association for Computational Linguistics.

Slav-NER: the 4th Cross-lingual Challenge on Recognition, Normalization, Classification, and Linking of Named Entities across Slavic languages

Roman Yangarber[1], Jakub Piskorski[2], Anna Dmitrieva[1], Michał Marcińczuk[3], Pavel Přibáň[4], Piotr Rybak[2], Josef Steinberger[4]

[1]University of Helsinki, Finland first.last@helsinki.fi

[2]Polish Academy of Sciences, Warsaw, Poland jpiskorski@gmail.com

[3]Wrocław University of Science and Technology, Poland marcinczuk@gmail.com

[4]University of West Bohemia, Czech Republic {pribanp,jstein}@kiv.zcu.cz

Abstract

This paper describes Slav-NER: the 4th Multilingual Named Entity Challenge in Slavic languages. The tasks involve recognizing mentions of named entities in Web documents, normalization of the names, and cross-lingual linking. This version of the Challenge covers three languages and five entity types. It is organized as part of the 9th Slavic Natural Language Processing Workshop, co-located with the EACL 2023 Conference.

Seven teams registered and three participated actively in the competition. Performance for the named entity recognition and normalization tasks reached 90% F_1 measure, much higher than reported in the first edition of the Challenge, but similar to the results reported in the latest edition. Performance for the entity linking task for individual language reached the range of 72-80% F_1 measure. Detailed evaluation information is available on the Shared Task web page.

1 Introduction

Analyzing named entities (NEs) in Slavic languages poses a challenging problem, due to the rich inflection and derivation, free word order, and other morphological and syntactic phenomena exhibited in these languages (Przepiórkowski, 2007; Piskorski et al., 2009). Encouraging research on detection and normalization of NEs—and on the closely related problem of cross-lingual, cross-document *entity linking*—is of paramount importance for improving multilingual and cross-lingual information access in these languages.

This paper describes the 4th Shared Task on multilingual NE recognition (NER), which aims at addressing these problems in a systematic way. The shared task was organized in the context of the 9th Slav-NLP: Workshop on Natural Language Processing in Slavic languages, co-located with the EACL 2023 conference. The task covers three languages—Czech, Polish and Russian—and five types of NE: person, location, organization, product, and event. The data consists of documents collected from the Web involving certain "focal" events. The rationale of such a setup is to foster the development of "end-to-end" NER and cross-lingual entity linking solutions, which are not tailored to specific, narrow domains. This paper also serves as an introduction and guide for researchers wishing to explore these problems using the training and test data, which are released to the public.[1]

The paper is organized as follows. Section 2 reviews prior work. Section 3 describes the task. Section 4 describes the annotation of the dataset. The evaluation methodology is introduced in Section 5. Participant systems are described in Section 6, and the results obtained by these systems are presented in Section 7. Conclusions and lessons learned are in Section 8.

2 Prior Work

The work described here builds on a series of Shared Tasks on Multilingual Named Entity Recognition, Normalization and cross-lingual Matching for Slavic Languages, (Piskorski et al., 2017, 2019, 2021), which, to the best of our knowledge, are the first attempts at such shared tasks covering multiple Slavic languages.

High-quality recognition and analysis of NEs is an essential step not only for information access, such as document retrieval and clustering, but it also constitutes a fundamental processing step in a wide range of NLP pipelines built for higher-level analysis of text, such as Information Extraction, see, e.g. (Huttunen et al., 2002). Other NER-related shared tasks have been organized previously. The first *non-English* monolingual NER evaluations—covering Chinese, Japanese, Spanish, and Arabic—were held in the con-

[1]bsnlp.cs.helsinki.fi/shared_task.html

Proceedings of the 9th Workshop on Slavic Natural Language Processing 2023 (SlavicNLP 2023), pages 179–189
May 6, 2023 ©2023 Association for Computational Linguistics

text of the Message Understanding Conferences (MUCs) (Chinchor, 1998) and the ACE Programme (Doddington et al., 2004). The first *multilingual* NER shared task, which covered several European languages, including Spanish, German, and Dutch, was organized in the context of the CoNLL conferences (Tjong Kim Sang, 2002; Tjong Kim Sang and De Meulder, 2003). The NE types covered in these campaigns were similar to the NE types covered in our Challenge. Worth mentioning in this context is Entity Discovery and Linking (EDL) (Ji et al., 2014, 2015), a track of the NIST Text Analysis Conferences (TAC). EDL aimed to extract entity mentions from a collection of documents in multiple languages (English, Chinese, and Spanish), and to partition the entities into cross-document equivalence classes, by either linking mentions to a knowledge base or directly clustering them. An important difference between EDL and our task is that EDL required linking entities to a pre-existing knowledge base.

Related to cross-lingual NE recognition is NE transliteration, i.e., linking NEs across languages that use different alphabets/writing systems. A series of NE Transliteration Shared Tasks were organized as part of NEWS—Named Entity Workshops (Duan et al., 2016), focusing mostly on Indian and Asian languages. In 2010, the NEWS Workshop included a shared task on Transliteration Mining (Kumaran et al., 2010), i.e., mining of names from parallel corpora, in languages including English, Chinese, Tamil, Russian, and Arabic.

Research on NE focusing on Slavic languages includes NE recognition for Croatian (Karan et al., 2013; Ljubešić et al., 2013), NE recognition in Croatian tweets (Baksa et al., 2017), a manually annotated NE corpus for Croatian (Agić and Ljubešić, 2014), NE recognition in Slovene (Štajner et al., 2013; Ljubešić et al., 2013), a Czech corpus of 11K annotated NEs (Ševčíková et al., 2007), NER for Czech (Konkol and Konopík, 2013), tools and resources for fine-grained annotation of NEs in the National Corpus of Polish (Waszczuk et al., 2010; Savary and Piskorski, 2011), NER shared tasks for Polish organized under the umbrella of POLEVAL[2] (Ogrodniczuk and Łukasz Kobyliński, 2018, 2020) and LESZCZE[3] campaigns, recent shared tasks on NE Recognition in Russian (Starostin et al., 2016; Artemova et al., 2022), the latter utilizing the NEREL dataset (a Russian dataset for named entity recognition and relation extraction, described in Loukachevitch et al., 2021), and *SemEval 2022 Task 11: MultiCoNER Multilingual Complex Named Entity Recognition*[4] and *SemEval 2023 Task 2: MultiCoNER II Multilingual Complex Named Entity Recognition*,[5] which included Russian and Ukrainian respectively.

3 Task Description

The data for this edition of the shared task consists of a set of documents in three Slavic languages: Czech, Polish and Russian. To facilitate entity linking, the set of documents is chosen to involve one specific event. The documents were obtained from the Web, by posing keyword queries to search engines, or publicly available crawled data repositories, and extracting the textual content from the respective sources.

The task is to recognize, classify, and "normalize" all named-entity mentions in each of the documents, and to link across languages all named mentions referring to the same real-world entity. Formally, the Multilingual Named Entity Recognition task is subdivided into three sub-tasks:

- **Named Entity Mention Detection and Classification:** Recognizing all named mentions of entities of five types: persons (PER), organizations (ORG), locations (LOC), products (PRO), and events (EVT).
- **Name Normalization:** Mapping each named mention of an entity to its corresponding *base form*. By "base form" we generally mean the lemma ("dictionary form") of the inflected word-form. In some cases normalization should go beyond inflection and transform a derived word into a base word's lemma, e.g., in case of personal possessives (see below). Multi-word names should be normalized to the *canonical multi-word expression*—rather than a sequence of lemmas of the words making up the multi-word expression.
- **Entity Linking.** Assigning a unique identifier (ID) to each detected named mention of an entity, in such a way that mentions referring to the

[2] http://poleval.pl

[3] https://lepiszcze.ml/tasks/namedentityrecognition

[4] https://multiconer.github.io/multiconer_1

[5] https://multiconer.github.io

same real-world entity should be assigned the same ID—referred to as the cross-lingual ID.

These tasks do not require positional information of the name entity mentions. Thus, for all occurrences of the same form of a NE mention (e.g., an inflected variant, an acronym or abbreviation) within a given document, no more than one annotation should be produced.[6] Furthermore, distinguishing typographical case is not necessary since the evaluation is case-insensitive. If the text includes lowercase, uppercase or mixed-case variants of the same entity, the system should produce only one annotation for all of these mentions. For instance, for "*UEFA*" and "*uefa*" (provided that they refer to the same NE type[7]), only one annotation should be produced. The recognition of common-noun or pronominal references to named entities is not included as part of the task.

3.1 Named Entity Classes

The task defines the following five NE classes.

Person names (PER): Names of real (or fictional) persons. Person names should not include titles, honorifics, and functions/positions. For example, in the text fragment "*... President Volodymyr Zelenskiy...*", only "*Volodymyr Zelenskiy*" is recognized as a person name. Both initials and pseudonyms are also considered named mentions of persons. Similarly, toponym-based named references to groups of people (that have no formal organization unifying them) should also be recognized, e.g., "*Ukrainians*." In this context, mentions of a single member belonging to such groups, e.g., "*Ukrainian*," should be assigned the same cross-lingual ID as plural mentions, i.e., "*Ukrainians*" and "*Ukrainian*" when referring to the nation receive the same cross-lingual ID.

Named mentions of other groups of people that do have a formal organization unifying them should be tagged as PER, e.g., in the phrase "*Królewscy wygrali*" (The Royals won), "*Królewscy*" is to be tagged as PER.

Personal possessives derived from a person's name should be classified as a Person, and the base form of the corresponding name should be extracted. For instance, in "*Trumpov tweet*" (Croatian) one is expected to classify "*Trumpov*" as PER, with the base form "*Trump*."

Locations (LOC): All toponyms and geopolitical entities—cities, counties, provinces, countries, regions, bodies of water, land formations, etc.—including named mentions of *facilities*—e.g., stadiums, parks, museums, theaters, hotels, hospitals, transportation hubs, churches, streets, railroads, bridges, and similar facilities.

In case named mentions of facilities *also* refer to an organization, the LOC tag should be used. For example, from the text "*Szpital Miejski im. Franciszka Raszei zatrudnił nowy personel ze względu na pandemie koronawirusa*" (The Franciszek Raszeia Hospital hired new staff due to the covid pandemics.) the mention "*Szpital Miejski im. Franciszka Raszei*" should be classified as LOC.

Organizations (ORG): All organizations, including companies, public institutions, political parties, international organizations, religious organizations, sport organizations, educational and research institutions, etc.

Organization designators and potential mentions of the seat of the organization are considered to be part of the organization name. For instance, from the text "*...Narodowy Fundusz Zdrowia w Poznaniu...*" (National Health Fund in Poznań), the full phrase "*Narodowy Fundusz Zdrowia w Poznaniu*" should be extracted.

Products (PRO): All names of *products and services*, such as electronics ("*Samsung Galaxy A41*"), cars ("*Subaru Ascent*"), newspapers ("*Politico*"), web-services ("*The Telegraph*"), medicines ("*Oxycodone*"), awards ("*Nobel Prize*"), books ("*Hamlet*"), TV programmes ("*TVN News*"), etc.

When a company name is used to refer to a *service*, e.g., "*na Instagramie*" (Polish for "on Instagram"), the mention of "*Instagramie*" is considered to refer to a service/product and should be tagged as PRO. However, when a company name refers to a service expressing an opinion of the company, it should be tagged as ORG.

This category also includes legal documents and treaties, e.g., "*Układ z Maastricht*" (Polish: "Maastricht Agreement") and initiatives, e.g., "*Horizon 2020*".

[6] Unless the different occurrences have different entity types (different *readings*) assigned to them, which is rare.

[7] Union of European Football Associations.

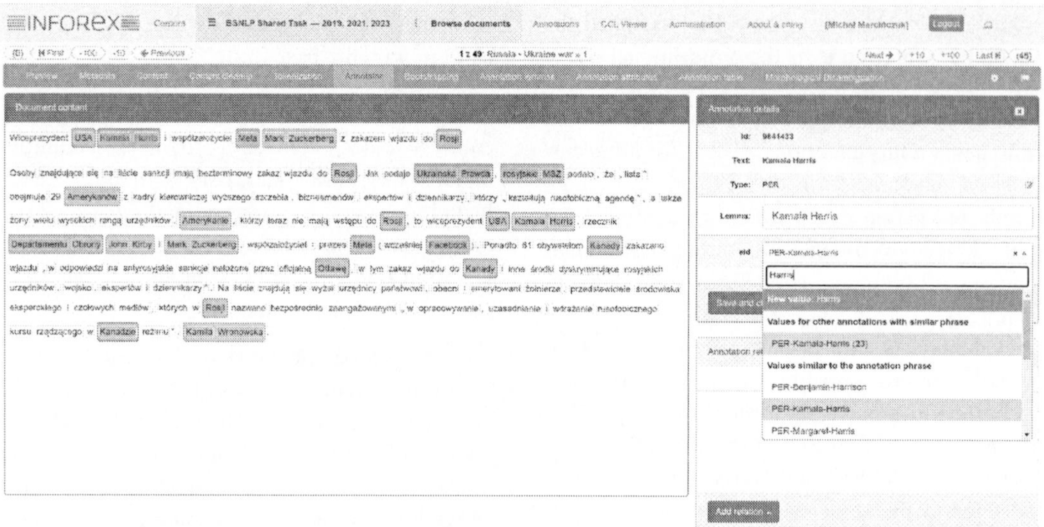

Figure 1: Screenshot of the Inforex Web interface, the tool used for data annotation.

Input:

Za 120 dní 10 tisíc vojáků. Johnson nabídl v Kyjevě pomoc při výcviku armády Britský premiér Boris Johnson v pátek znovu přijel do ukrajinského Kyjeva, kde se sešel s prezidentem Volodymyrem Zelenským a představil mu konkrétní nabídku britské pomoci s výcvikem ukrajinských vojáků. Oba představitelé spolu také hovořili o dodávkách těžkých zbraní a protileteckých systémů, stejně jako o ekonomické podpoře Ukrajiny, která od konce února čelí ruské agresi, i o dalších možnostech zpřísnění protiruských sankcí.

Output:

Boris Johnson	Boris Johnson	PER	PER-Boris-Johnson
Johnson	Johnson	PER	PER-Boris-Johnson
Kyjeva	Kyjev	LOC	GPE-Kiev
Kyjevě	Kyjev	LOC	GPE-Kiev
Ukrajiny	Ukrajina	LOC	GPE-Ukraine
Volodymyrem Zelenským	Volodymyr Zelensky	PER	PER-Volodymyr-Zelensky
ruské agresi	ruská agrese	EVT	EVT-2022-Russian-Invasion-of-Ukraine

Figure 2: Example input and output formats.

Events (EVT): This category covers named mentions of events, including conferences, e.g. "24. Konference Žárovného Zinkování" (Czech: "Hot Galvanizing Conference"), concerts, festivals, holidays, e.g., "*Święta Bożego Narodzenia*" (Polish: "Christmas"), wars, battles, disasters, e.g., "*Katastrofa lotnicza w Gibraltarze*" (Polish: "1943 Gibraltar Liberator AL523 crash"), outbreaks of infectious diseases ("*Spanish Flu*"). Future, speculative, and fictive events—e.g., "'Czexit"—are considered event mentions.

3.2 Complex and Ambiguous Entities

In case of complex named entities, consisting of nested named entities, only the *top-most* entity should be recognized. For example, from the text "*Uniwersytet Adama Mickiewicza*" (Polish: "Adam Mickiewicz University") one should not extract "*Adama Mickiewicza*", but only the top-level entity.

In case one word-form (e.g., "*Washington*") is used to refer to more than one different real-world entities in different contexts in the same document (e.g., a person and a location), two annotations should be returned, associated with different cross-lingual IDs.

In case of coordinated phrases, like "*Dutch and Belgian Parliament*," two names should be extracted (as ORG). The lemmas would be "*Dutch*" and "*Belgian Parliament*", and the IDs should refer to "*Dutch Parliament*" and "*Belgian Parlia-*

ment" respectively.

In rare cases, plural forms might have two annotations—e.g., in the phrase "*a border between Irelands*"—"*Irelands*" should be extracted twice with identical lemmas but different IDs.

3.3 System Input and Response

Input Document Format: Documents in the collection are represented in the following format. The first five lines contain the following metadata (in the respective order): `<DOCUMENT-ID>`, `<LANGUAGE>`, `<CREATION-DATE>`, `<URL>`, `<TITLE>`, `<TEXT>`. The text to be processed begins from the sixth line and runs till the end of file. The `<URL>` field stores the origin from which the text document was retrieved. The values of `<CREATION-DATE>` and `<TITLE>` were not provided for all documents, due to unavailability of such data or due to errors in parsing during data collection.

System Response. For each input file, the system should return one output file as follows. The first line should contain only the `<DOCUMENT-ID>`, which corresponds to the input. Each subsequent line contains one annotation, as tab-separated fields:

```
<MENTION> TAB <BASE> TAB <CAT> TAB <ID>
```

The `<MENTION>` field should be the NE as it appears in text. The `<BASE>` field should be the base form of the entity. The `<CAT>` field stores the category of the entity (ORG, PER, LOC, PRO, or EVT) and `<ID>` is the cross-lingual identifier. The cross-lingual identifiers may consist of an arbitrary sequence of alphanumeric characters. An example document in Czech and the corresponding response is shown in Figure 2.

The detailed descriptions of the tasks are available on the web page of the Shared Task.[8]

4 Data

In this edition of the Challenge the annotated datasets from previous editions were used as training data. In particular, the training and test datasets annotated in Bulgarian, Czech, Polish and Russian from 2019 Shared Task (Piskorski et al., 2019) and training and test datasets annotated in Bulgarian, Czech, Polish, Russian, Slovene and Ukrainian from 2021 Shared Task (Piskorski et al., 2021) were used. The prior datasets annotated in six languages covered various major topics, including, i.a., the COVID-19 pandemic, the 2020 USA Presidential elections (USA 2020 ELECTIONS), ASIA BIBI, which relates to a Pakistani woman involved in a blasphemy case, BREXIT, RYANAIR, which faced a massive strike, and NORD STREAM, a controversial Russian-European project. The test data for the current edition of the challenge involves the RUSSIA-UKRAINE WAR.

Each of the datasets, including the latest test data, was created as follows. For the focus entity/event, we posed a search query to Google and/or publicly available crawled data repositories, in each of the target languages. The query returned documents in the target language. We removed duplicates, downloaded the HTML—mainly news articles—and converted them into plain text. Since the result of HTML parsing may include not only the main text of a Web page, but also spurious text, some additional manual cleaning was applied when necessary. The resulting set of "cleaned" documents were used to manually select documents for each language and topic for the final datasets.

Documents were annotated using the Inforex[9] web-based system for annotation of text corpora (Marcińczuk et al., 2017). Inforex allows parallel access and resource sharing by multiple annotators. It let us share a common list of entities, and perform entity-linking semi-automatically: for a given entity, an annotator sees a list of entities of the same type inserted by all annotators and can select an entity ID from the list. A snapshot of the Inforex interface is in Figure 1.

In addition, Inforex keeps track of all lemmas and IDs inserted for each surface form, and inserts them automatically, so in many cases the annotator only confirms the proposed values, which speeds up the annotation process a great deal. All annotations were made by native speakers. After annotation, we performed *multiple phases* of automatic and manual consistency checks, to reduce annotation errors, especially in entity linking.

The training data statistics are shown in Table 1 and 2—for 2019 and 2021 datasets, respectively, while the test data statistics are shown in Table 3.

The participants received the test dataset—

[8] http://bsnlp.cs.helsinki.fi/System_response_guidelines-1.2.pdf

[9] github.com/CLARIN-PL/Inforex

	Brexit						Asia Bibi					
	PL	CS	RU	BG	SL	UK	PL	CS	RU	BG	SL	UK
Documents	500	284	153	600	52	50	88	89	118	101	4	6
PER	2 650	1 108	1 308	2 515	532	242	683	570	643	583	36	39
LOC	3 524	1 279	666	2 407	403	336	403	366	567	388	24	57
ORG	3 080	1 039	828	2 455	301	166	286	214	419	245	10	30
EVT	1 072	471	261	776	165	62	14	3	1	8	0	0
PRO	668	232	137	490	31	17	55	42	49	63	2	1
Total	10 994	4 129	3 200	8 643	1 445	823	1 441	1 195	1 679	1 287	72	127
Distinct												
Surface forms	2 820	1 111	783	1 200	596	234	508	303	406	412	51	87
Lemmas	2 133	840	568	1 091	411	177	412	248	317	360	41	77
Entity IDs	1 506	583	268	772	288	127	273	160	178	230	31	64

	Nord Stream						Ryanair					
	PL	CS	RU	BG	SL	UK	PL	CS	RU	BG	SL	UK
Documents	151	161	150	130	74	40	146	163	150	87	52	63
PER	538	570	392	335	548	78	136	161	72	147	107	33
LOC	1 430	1 689	1 320	910	1 362	339	821	871	902	344	384	455
ORG	837	477	792	540	460	449	529	707	500	238	408	193
EVT	15	9	5	6	50	14	7	12	0	4	8	0
PRO	405	364	510	331	243	8	114	66	82	79	101	20
Total	3 225	3 116	3 020	2 122	2 664	948	1 607	1 817	1 556	812	1008	701
Distinct												
Surface forms	845	770	892	504	902	336	514	475	400	323	673	187
Lemmas	634	550	583	448	600	244	419	400	332	315	520	137
Entity IDs	441	392	321	305	465	177	322	306	251	245	428	108

Table 1: Overview of the training dataset from the 2019 edition of the Slavic NER challenge.

	Covid-19						USA 2020 Elections					
	PL	CS	RU	BG	SL	UK	PL	CS	RU	BG	SL	UK
Documents	103	155	83	151	178	85	66	85	163	151	143	83
PER	419	478	559	351	834	215	566	447	3203	1539	2589	672
LOC	369	474	701	759	1228	364	827	277	3457	1093	1268	541
ORG	402	318	628	589	965	455	243	99	2486	557	578	384
EVT	240	393	435	465	612	269	86	63	396	170	118	257
PRO	137	155	400	168	274	143	87	56	846	240	254	124
Total	1567	1818	2723	2332	3913	1446	1810	942	10398	3599	4807	1978
Distinct												
Surface forms	688	941	1436	1092	2190	622	484	377	3440	1117	1605	537
Lemmas	557	745	1133	1016	1774	509	356	279	2593	1019	1129	390
Entity IDs	404	562	796	764	1400	369	278	200	1669	668	833	270

Table 2: Overview of the training dataset from the 2021 edition of the Slavic NER challenge.

	Russia-Ukraine war		
	PL	CS	RU
Documents	50	50	52
PER	276	229	236
LOC	599	345	454
ORG	252	159	355
EVT	62	49	15
PRO	85	43	78
Total	1274	825	1138
Distinct			
surface forms	723	498	725
Lemmas	563	384	594
Entity IDs	410	280	493

Table 3: Overview of the test dataset for the 2023 edition of the Slavic NER challenge.

Russia-Ukraine war—and were given circa 2 days to return up to 10 system responses. The topic was not announced in advance, and the annotations were not released. The rationale behind this decision was to motivate the participants to build a general solution for Slavic NER, rather than to optimize their models toward particular scenarios or sets of names.

5 Evaluation Methodology

The NER task (exact case-insensitive matching) and Name Normalization (or "lemmatization") were evaluated in terms of precision, recall, and F_1 measure. For NER, two types of evaluations were carried out:

- **Relaxed:** An entity mentioned in a given document is considered to be extracted correctly if the system response includes *at least one* annotation of a named mention of this entity (regardless of whether the extracted mention is in base form);
- **Strict:** The system response should include exactly one annotation *for each* unique form of a named mention of an entity in a given document, i.e., identifying all variants of an entity is required.

In the relaxed evaluation we additionally distinguish between *exact* and *partial matching*: in the latter case, an entity mentioned in a given document is considered to be extracted correctly if the system response includes at least one partial match of a named mention of this entity.

We evaluate the systems at several levels of granularity: we measure the performance (a) for all NE types and all languages, (b) for each given NE type and all languages, (c) for all NE types for each language, and (d) for each given NE type per language.

In the name normalization task, we take into account only correctly recognized entity mentions and only those that were normalized (on both the annotation and the response system's sides). Formally, let $N_{correct}$ denote the number of all correctly recognized entity mentions for which the system returned a correct base form. Let N_{key} denote the number of all normalized entity mentions in the gold-standard answer key and $N_{response}$ denote the number of all normalized entity mentions in the system's response. We define precision and recall for the name normalization task as:

$$Recall = \frac{N_{corrrect}}{N_{key}} \qquad Precision = \frac{N_{corrrect}}{N_{response}}$$

In evaluating document-level, single-language and cross-lingual entity linking we adopted the Link-Based Entity-Aware (LEA) metric (Moosavi and Strube, 2016), which considers how important the entity is and how well it is resolved. LEA is defined as follows. Let $K = \{k_1, k_2, \ldots, k_{|K|}\}$ denote the set of key entities and $R = \{r_1, r_2, \ldots, r_{|R|}\}$ the set of response entities, i.e., $k_i \in K$ ($r_i \in R$) stand for a set of mentions of the same entity in the key entity set—the response entity set. LEA recall and precision are then defined as follows:

$$Recall_{LEA} = \frac{\sum_{k_i \in K} \left(imp(k_i) \cdot res(k_i) \right)}{\sum_{k_z \in K} imp(k_z)}$$

$$Precision_{LEA} = \frac{\sum_{r_i \in R} \left(imp(r_i) \cdot res(r_i) \right)}{\sum_{r_z \in R} imp(r_z)}$$

where imp and res denote the measure of importance and the resolution score for an entity, respectively. In our setting, we define $imp(e) = \log_2 |e|$ for an entity e (in K or R), $|e|$ is the number of mentions of e—i.e., the more mentions an entity has the more important it is. To avoid biasing the importance of the more frequent entities $\log_2$ is used. The resolution score of key entity k_i is computed as the fraction of correctly resolved co-reference links of k_i:

$$res(k_i) = \sum_{r_j \in R} \frac{link(k_i \cap r_j)}{link(k_i)}$$

where $link(e) = (|e| \times (|e| - 1))/2$ is the number of unique co-reference links in e. For each k_i, LEA checks all response entities to check whether they are partial matches for k_i. Analogously, the resolution score of response entity r_i is computed as the fraction of co-reference links in r_i that are extracted correctly:

$$res(r_i) = \sum_{k_j \in K} \frac{link(r_i \cap k_j)}{link(r_i)}$$

LEA brings several benefits. For example, LEA considers resolved co-reference relations instead of resolved mentions and has more discriminative power than other metrics for co-reference resolution (Moosavi and Strube, 2016).

The evaluation was carried out in "case-insensitive" mode: all named mentions in system response and test corpora were lower-cased.

6 Participant Systems

Out of the seven registered teams, we received results from three. Further, two of these teams provided papers describing the details of their systems, presented in the 2023 Slavic NLP Workshop. We briefly review these systems here; for complete descriptions, please see the corresponding papers.

The **Tilde** system, (Rinalds Vīksna and Rozis, 2023), utilizes the multilingual XLM-R model to perform all subtasks. They enhance their training set by incorporating diverse NER datasets, in addition to the Slavic NER Challenge training set. The authors fine-tune five different variants of the XLM-R Large (Conneau et al., 2020) model that differ in the approach for the entity-linking subtask. For each variant, they use slightly different training datasets. In addition, one of the variants is an ensemble of five XLM-R Base models, one for each of the five NER entity labels. The base model was initially pre-trained on 2.6 GB of recent Czech, Polish and Russian news articles to integrate into the model new entities and events, which have emerged since the original model was trained. This process enables the model to embed the latest information and keep up-to-date with the evolving language usage.

The **AMU** system (Pałka and Nowakowski, 2023) combines a set of transformer-based models for named entity recognition, categorization, and lemmatization. They evaluated several monolingual (HerBERT, Czert, and RuBERT) and multilingual (Slavic-BERT and XLM-RoBERTa) BERT-like models for entity recognition and categorization. For entity lemmatization, sequence-to-sequence (seq2seq) models were applied, plT5 and mT5. The pre-trained models were fine-tuned on the dataset provided within the shared task and additional external resources, including datasets annotated with named entities: Collection3, Multi-NERD, Polyglot-NER, WikiNEuRal; dictionaries of lemmatized named entities and multi-word expressions: SEJF, SEJFEK, PolEval 2019 Task 2. The additional resources for lemmatization were only for Polish. Thus, the authors used OPUS-MT to translate the resources to other languages to overcome the language limitation.

The third team—CTC, Cognitive Technologies Center—submitted results, but did not provide a description paper; their approach was similar to the one employed by this team in the 2021 Edition of the Shared Task (Piskorski et al., 2021).

7 Evaluation Results

Table 4 presents the F_1-measures separated by language, for all tasks for the test data—the "Russia-Ukraine war" dataset. The table shows only the one top-performing model for each team. The CTC team submitted results only for the Russian language. The best-performing team overall is the one that submitted the Tilde system based on the multilingual Transformer-based XLM-R model. The results of the AMU system are almost on par, trailing by only a small margin in most of the evaluated metrics, with the exception of the normalization task. The CTC system lags behind other systems by a margin of 4% F_1-measure in the recognition subtask.

Only the Tilde team submitted results for *cross-lingual entity linking*, achieving 66.9% F_1 score. This is a great improvement compared to the Third Challenge, where the best results were around 50% of F_1 score. To date, the task of cross-lingual linking remains much more challenging than the task of entity extraction.

Note that in our setting, the performance of entity linking *depends on* the performance of name recognition : each system had to link entities that it had extracted from documents upstream rather than link a set of *correct* entities.

In Table 5 we present the results of the evaluation by entity type. As seen in the table, performance was higher overall for LOC, PER and PRO

		Language					
Phase	*Metric*	cs		pl		ru	
Recognition	*Relaxed Partial*	Tilde	91.6	Tilde	89.9	Tilde	89.8
		AMU	91.5	AMU	88.9	AMU	88.8
						CTC	84.4
	Relaxed Exact	Tilde	89.0	Tilde	86.0	Tilde	85.1
		AMU	88.3	AMU	84.1	AMU	85.0
						CTC	81.0
	Strict	Tilde	89.9	Tilde	87.0	Tilde	86.8
		AMU	89.7	AMU	85.4	AMU	86.2
						CTC	73.4
Normalization		AMU	76.9	AMU	82.4	AMU	81.5
		Tilde	54.3	Tilde	53.9	Tilde	72.6
						CTC	66.0
Entity Linking	*Document level*	Tilde	80.2	Tilde	76.4	Tilde	71.7
		AMU	25.8	AMU	19.7	AMU	19.4
						CTC	4.8
	Single language	Tilde	77.6	Tilde	72.9	Tilde	61.0
		AMU	7.5	AMU	8.8	AMU	5.8
						CTC	2.9

Table 4: F_1-measure results for the test dataset.

in the case of Czech. Substantially lower results were achieved for ORG and EVT in all languages and PRO in Polish and Russian, which corresponds with our findings from the previous editions of the shared task, where ORG, PRO and EVT were the most challenging categories (Piskorski et al., 2017, 2021). The results for the EVT category are less informative since the task heavily depends on detecting the repeated central events of the corpora.

	Language		
Entity Class	cs	pl	ru
Per	99.6	97.9	98.0
Loc	94.7	94.6	96.5
Org	88.8	83.3	87.2
Pro	93.3	89.4	71.2
Evt	42.0	49.9	28.6

Table 5: Recognition F_1-measure (relaxed partial) by entity type—best-performing systems for each language.

8 Conclusion

This paper reports on the 4th Multilingual Named Entity Challenge focusing on recognizing mentions of NEs in Web documents in three Slavic languages, normalization of the NEs, and cross-lingual entity linking.

Seven teams registered and three of them actively participated in the Challenge and submitted system results with multiple variants. Most systems use state-of-the-art transformer-based models. Overall, the results of the best-performing systems are quite strong for extraction and normalization of names, while entity linking—and in particular, cross-lingual entity linking—remains a very challenging task.

We present the summary results for the main aspects of the challenge and the best-performing model from each team.

To foster further research into NLP for Slavic languages, including cross-lingual entity linking, our training and test datasets, the detailed annotations, and scripts used for the evaluations are made available to the research community on the Shared Task's Web page.[10]

Acknowledgments

Work on Czech has been partly supported by grant No. SGS-2022-016 Advanced methods of data processing and analysis and computational resources were provided by the e-INFRA CZ project (ID:90140), supported by the Ministry of Education, Youth and Sports of the Czech Republic.

Work on Inforex and on Polish was supported in part by investment in the CLARIN-PL research infrastructure funded by the Polish Ministry of Science and Higher Education.

We thank Anisia Katinskaia for her kind assistance in preparation of the test corpora.

References

Željko Agić and Nikola Ljubešić. 2014. The SETimes.HR linguistically annotated corpus of Croatian. In *Ninth International Conference on Language Resources and Evaluation (LREC 2014)*, pages 1724–1727, Reykjavík, Iceland.

Ekaterina Artemova, Maxim Zmeev, Natalia Loukachevitch, Igor Rozhkov, Tatiana Batura, Vladimir Ivanov, and Elena Tutubalina. 2022. Runne-2022 shared task: Recognizing nested named entities. In *Proceedings of the International Conference on Computational Linguistics and Intellectual Technologies "DIALOGUE"*, pages 33–41.

Krešimir Baksa, Dino Golović, Goran Glavaš, and Jan Šnajder. 2017. Tagging named entities in Croatian tweets. *Slovenščina 2.0: empirical, applied and interdisciplinary research*, 4(1):20–41.

Nancy Chinchor. 1998. Overview of MUC-7/MET-2. In *Proceedings of Seventh Message Understanding Conference (MUC-7)*.

[10] bsnlp.cs.helsinki.fi/shared_task.html

Alexis Conneau, Kartikay Khandelwal, Naman Goyal, Vishrav Chaudhary, Guillaume Wenzek, Francisco Guzmán, Edouard Grave, Myle Ott, Luke Zettlemoyer, and Veselin Stoyanov. 2020. Unsupervised cross-lingual representation learning at scale. In *Proceedings of the 58th Annual Meeting of the Association for Computational Linguistics*, pages 8440–8451, Online. Association for Computational Linguistics.

George R. Doddington, Alexis Mitchell, Mark A. Przybocki, Lance A. Ramshaw, Stephanie Strassel, and Ralph M. Weischedel. 2004. The Automatic Content Extraction (ACE) program—tasks, data, and evaluation. In *Fourth International Conference on Language Resources and Evaluation (LREC 2004)*, pages 837–840, Lisbon, Portugal.

Xiangyu Duan, Rafael E. Banchs, Min Zhang, Haizhou Li, and A. Kumaran. 2016. Report of NEWS 2016 machine transliteration shared task. In *Proceedings of The Sixth Named Entities Workshop*, pages 58–72, Berlin, Germany.

Silja Huttunen, Roman Yangarber, and Ralph Grishman. 2002. Diversity of scenarios in information extraction. In *Proceedings of the Third International Conference on Language Resources and Evaluation (LREC 2002)*, Las Palmas, Spain.

Heng Ji, Joel Nothman, and Ben Hachey. 2014. Overview of TAC-KBP2014 entity discovery and linking tasks. In *Proceedings of Text Analysis Conference (TAC2014)*, pages 1333–1339.

Heng Ji, Joel Nothman, and Ben Hachey. 2015. Overview of TAC-KBP2015 tri-lingual entity discovery and linking. In *Proceedings of Text Analysis Conference (TAC2015)*.

Mladen Karan, Goran Glavaš, Frane Šarić, Jan Šnajder, Jure Mijić, Artur Šilić, and Bojana Dalbelo Bašić. 2013. CroNER: Recognizing named entities in Croatian using conditional random fields. *Informatica*, 37(2):165.

Michal Konkol and Miloslav Konopík. 2013. CRF-based Czech named entity recognizer and consolidation of Czech NER research. In *Text, Speech and Dialogue*, volume 8082 of *Lecture Notes in Computer Science*, pages 153–160. Springer Berlin Heidelberg.

A Kumaran, Mitesh M. Khapra, and Haizhou Li. 2010. Report of NEWS 2010 transliteration mining shared task. In *Proceedings of the 2010 Named Entities Workshop*, pages 21–28, Uppsala, Sweden.

Nikola Ljubešić, Marija Stupar, Tereza Jurić, and Željko Agić. 2013. Combining available datasets for building named entity recognition models of Croatian and Slovene. *Slovenščina 2.0: empirical, applied and interdisciplinary research*, 1(2):35–57.

Natalia Loukachevitch, Ekaterina Artemova, Tatiana Batura, Pavel Braslavski, Ilia Denisov, Vladimir Ivanov, Suresh Manandhar, Alexander Pugachev, and Elena Tutubalina. 2021. NEREL: A Russian dataset with nested named entities, relations and events. In *Proceedings of the International Conference on Recent Advances in Natural Language Processing (RANLP 2021)*, pages 876–885, Held Online. INCOMA Ltd.

Michał Marcińczuk, Marcin Oleksy, and Jan Kocoń. 2017. Inforex - a collaborative system for text corpora annotation and analysis. In *Proceedings of the International Conference Recent Advances in Natural Language Processing, RANLP 2017, Varna, Bulgaria, September 2-8, 2017*, pages 473–482. INCOMA Ltd.

Nafise Sadat Moosavi and Michael Strube. 2016. Which coreference evaluation metric do you trust? A proposal for a link-based entity aware metric. In *Proceedings of the 54th Annual Meeting of the Association for Computational Linguistics (ACL 2016)*, pages 632–642, Berlin, Germany.

Maciej Ogrodniczuk and Łukasz Kobyliński, editors. 2018. *Proceedings of the PolEval 2018 Workshop*. Institute of Computer Science, Polish Academy of Sciences, Warsaw, Poland.

Maciej Ogrodniczuk and Łukasz Kobyliński, editors. 2020. *Proceedings of the PolEval 2020 Workshop*. Institute of Computer Science, Polish Academy of Sciences, Warsaw, Poland.

Gabriela Pałka and Artur Nowakowski. 2023. Exploring the use of foundation models for named entity recognition and lemmatization tasks in slavic languages. In *Proceedings of the 9th Workshop on Slavic Natural Language Processing*. European Association for Computational Linguistics.

Jakub Piskorski, Bogdan Babych, Zara Kancheva, Olga Kanishcheva, Maria Lebedeva, Michał Marcińczuk, Preslav Nakov, Petya Osenova, Lidia Pivovarova, Senja Pollak, Pavel Přibáň, Ivaylo Radev, Marko Robnik-Sikonja, Vasyl Starko, Josef Steinberger, and Roman Yangarber. 2021. Slav-NER: the 3rd cross-lingual challenge on recognition, normalization, classification, and linking of named entities across Slavic languages. In *Proceedings of the 8th Workshop on Balto-Slavic Natural Language Processing*, pages 122–133, Kiyv, Ukraine. Association for Computational Linguistics.

Jakub Piskorski, Laska Laskova, Michał Marcińczuk, Lidia Pivovarova, Pavel Přibáň, Josef Steinberger, and Roman Yangarber. 2019. The second cross-lingual challenge on recognition, normalization, classification, and linking of named entities across Slavic languages. In *Proceedings of the 7th Workshop on Balto-Slavic Natural Language Processing*, pages 63–74, Florence, Italy. Association for Computational Linguistics.

Jakub Piskorski, Lidia Pivovarova, Jan Šnajder, Josef Steinberger, and Roman Yangarber. 2017. The first cross-lingual challenge on recognition, normalization and matching of named entities in Slavic languages. In *Proceedings of the 6th Workshop on Balto-Slavic Natural Language Processing*. Association for Computational Linguistics.

Jakub Piskorski, Karol Wieloch, and Marcin Sydow. 2009. On knowledge-poor methods for person name matching and lemmatization for highly inflectional languages. *Information retrieval*, 12(3):275–299.

Adam Przepiórkowski. 2007. Slavonic information extraction and partial parsing. In *Proceedings of the Workshop on Balto-Slavonic Natural Language Processing: Information Extraction and Enabling Technologies*, ACL '07, pages 1–10, Stroudsburg, PA, USA. Association for Computational Linguistics.

Daiga Deksne Rinalds Vīksna, Inguna Skadiņa and Roberts Rozis. 2023. Large language models for multilingual slavic named entity linking. In *Proceedings of the 9th Workshop on Slavic Natural Language Processing*. European Association for Computational Linguistics.

Agata Savary and Jakub Piskorski. 2011. Language Resources for Named Entity Annotation in the National Corpus of Polish. *Control and Cybernetics*, 40(2):361–391.

Magda Ševčíková, Zdeněk Žabokrtský, and Oldřich Kruza. 2007. Named entities in Czech: annotating data and developing NE tagger. In *International Conference on Text, Speech and Dialogue*, pages 188–195. Springer.

Tadej Štajner, Tomaž Erjavec, and Simon Krek. 2013. Razpoznavanje imenskih entitet v slovenskem besedilu. *Slovenščina 2.0: empirical, applied and interdisciplinary research*, 1(2):58–81.

A. S. Starostin, V. V. Bocharov, S. V. Alexeeva, A. A. Bodrova, A. S. Chuchunkov, S. S. Dzhumaev, I. V. Efimenko, D. V. Granovsky, V. F. Khoroshevsky, I. V. Krylova, M. A. Nikolaeva, I. M. Smurov, and S. Y. Toldova. 2016. FactRuEval 2016: Evaluation of named entity recognition and fact extraction systems for Russian. In *Computational Linguistics and Intellectual Technologies. Proceedings of the Annual International Conference "Dialogue"*, pages 688–705.

Erik Tjong Kim Sang. 2002. Introduction to the CoNLL-2002 shared task: Language-independent named entity recognition. In *Proceedings of the 6th Conference on Natural Language Learning - Volume 20*, COLING-02, pages 1–4, Stroudsburg, PA, USA. Association for Computational Linguistics.

Erik Tjong Kim Sang and Fien De Meulder. 2003. Introduction to the CoNLL-2003 shared task: Language-independent named entity recognition. In *Proceedings of the Seventh Conference on Natural*

Language Learning at HLT-NAACL 2003 - Volume 4, CONLL '03, pages 142–147, Stroudsburg, PA, USA. Association for Computational Linguistics.

Jakub Waszczuk, Katarzyna Głowińska, Agata Savary, and Adam Przepiórkowski. 2010. Tools and methodologies for annotating syntax and named entities in the National Corpus of Polish. In *Proceedings of the International Multiconference on Computer Science and Information Technology (IMCSIT 2010): Computational Linguistics – Applications (CLA'10)*, pages 531–539, Wisła, Poland. PTI.

Author Index

Association for Computational Linguistics
209 N. Eighth Street
Stroudsburg, Pennsylvania 18360

ISBN 978-1-7138-7379-2

CURRAN ASSOCIATES INC.
proceedings.com